Tears & Tiers

The Life and Times of Joseph "Mad Dog" Sullivan, the only man to escape Attica Prison
The True Story of A Legend

By
Gail W. Sullivan

Tears & Tiers

First Edition

OCT 17 2006

Tears & Tiers   The life and times of Joseph "Mad dog" Sullivan the only man to escape Attica prison…The true story of a legend

ISBN 0-9772656-0-9

Gail W. Sullivan, M.Ed.

For the men in my life….Joe, Ramsey, Kelly, Harry.
In loving memory of Mom

Tears and Tiers will make you cringe, cry, and laugh while you take a vicarious ride along one man's journey of reckless abandonment.

My fascination with the story and the central character Joseph "Mad Dog" Sullivan is similar to most white male suburbanites; deep inside we all long to have just a moment of the brutal toughness he exudes. The cold dead stare, the solid physique chiseled from years of "box" work outs, the ability to stand up to confrontation regardless of the consequences. Yes, indeed most of us wish for just a moment we could "wack" that one person who at one point in our life really deserved it. Of course the difference is even if we could muster the might and nerve to unleash a full force deadly rage, we would shit our pants at the thought of paying the price for such impulsive deeds. So a man who killed not for passion or revenge but as a choice of vocation, is an intriguing story, and the story told reveals a life that while hard to imagine at first, evolves to one of parallels with those in the "civilized" world.

The prison culture that forms such hardened souls, or breaks weaker ones; has its own code of conduct and justice system, it's a place where brute force and violence are the most effective tools of communication, and yet the knowledge of human nature becomes the key ingredient to long term survival. The racial hatreds of society magnified to the tenth power, and tamed over the first non-segregated football game in 1968 at Attica. The escape in 1971, the bloody streets of New York from 1976 thru 1981. It's all there, in detail that takes the reader along for the ride and occasionally invites us in for a closer look at the mind of the man.

I witnessed the final trial of Joseph "Mad Dog" Sullivan in 1982 in Riverhead, NY. He was in the press and in person a man devoid of most human emotions. He had cold dark eyes of a killer, a deep unrepentant voice, which complimented the rugged rock hard physique. You could see the triceps the papers wrote about, the product of thousands of daily push ups, pressing the seams of his Glen Plaid suit.

For twenty years I recounted the stories to friends on occasion, when the topic of discussion was crime genre in print or film. Then by chance or maybe not, I got to meet him and read the biography his wife Gail wrote.

It was then I learned that in the darkest of earth's places, in the darkest of earth's souls, there is the human factor that cannot be extinguished, that possesses compassion, and insight, and in the twilight of the day, tears.

Thomas Roach
Long Island, NY

Preface

When I was a little girl I wanted to marry someone who could take care of me. I thought it would be nice to have a husband who was strong kind and wonderful--we all have our dreams and that was one of mine. I never thought I would have married someone who murdered people, did robberies, or escaped from prison. I wanted some kind of normal marriage like you see in the movies. Maybe not *that* conventional because I am not that way at heart, but I wanted to have someone home with me to share my days and nights and to have a family with. I had no clue as to what my future would bring. Growing up someone had said to me that I did like those "bad boy" types. Not that I consciously sought it out, but perhaps I did, always being around ex-cons my dad and mom often hired as attendants in the family ambulance service business.

I wanted a big wedding, to have those things that young girls and later young ladies wanted. I had no idea that I would meet a man like my husband, fall in love with him, and have to live my life the way I have been doing for the past twenty plus years.

We had one of those stormy courtships. Things were fine when we were alone together but, when Joe "had" to go somewhere and be with his "friends", we had fights that I thought we would never get over. But we stuck with it; maybe because we both were scared of what our lives would be like without each other. I had found that strong man I was looking for and Joe found someone who understood him for what he really wanted to be, someone more like his dad than what he turned out to be.

Joe certainly had qualities of his dad but he learned other things while being in prison so many years, things that kept him upon a bad and dangerous path.

In our own way, we have managed to keep whatever we had going. I feel that we have something special; as most couples must feel with the loved one they have chosen. In retrospect, at our age, we do have that. It took a lot of years, a lot of learning to get to the point where we are today, but we got here, together.

I honestly don't know how I survived it all. It might be because I don't dwell on the past. I don't want to live in the past. I live my life to the fullest I can each day, forgetting bad times as best I can. Sometimes that is very hard to do. But I always knew that Joe was different, that he moved to the beat of his own drum. I knew he had to do what he felt he had to do, and that is why I fell in love with him. I didn't know about the life Joe led when he wasn't home with me until he came home one night and threw out a perfectly good suit that he had just bought. I looked at him and all of a sudden everything clicked into place.

Why I stayed with him then, I can't recall now, except that we were going to have a baby, we were married, and he was my life. It would have been easier to just tell him to leave the house and never come back. But, even then, I knew he wasn't like that-- he would always come back. I never really discussed his "other" life with him when he was out here with me. I live best when I live in denial and that was mostly how I lived during that time. I didn't let Joe get away with not doing the basic things that I thought a husband had to do, but I did turn my back on what he was doing independently. I really didn't want to deal with the truth because that is often the hardest thing to deal with. So I went about my business, Joe went about his, and when he was home he went about mine.

Drinking and drugs weren't done in my family. However, Joe's family was good at the drinking and Joe was good with the drugs. We dabbled together for a while but it wasn't something that I really wanted to do in my life, especially since we had a son and wanted another one. Joe needed to sew his oats so he went to the clubs and I stayed home. He wanted a new car so he got a Corvette. He wanted someone who wouldn't "nag" him, so he found a girlfriend. I made all those excuses for him whenever people asked me why he did this or that, I would say, "He was away for a long time in prison, maybe twenty years before we got together, so he is trying to catch up to life!" At the time I was too naive to think that he would cheat on me. Sure he did cocaine, robbed and killed people but I was sure he would never cheat on me-- boy did I learn a lot! We both did for that matter. I told Joe, "if you cheat on a wife do it with loads of women not just one because then it becomes an affair and you can get a fatal attraction." And that's just what he got or should I say we *both* got, for what happened to him also happened to me.

I always made excuses for Joe and still do in some ways. I remember when Ramsey (our son) and our niece who lived upstairs at our house wanted to play in our house. They would ask "Dad" or "Uncle Joe" if he was in a good mood or a bad mood. Then they would know if they could come in and play in Ramsey's room or not. I had trained my family that Joe was a very moody man but when he was "on" he was wonderful. When he wasn't, everyone was really afraid of him-- but not me. I knew that he would never hurt any of us. He was the only adult male figure around and while my sister, mother, and other family and friends were afraid of Joe, they loved him at the same time. We use to help my mother take care of my Aunt and Uncle and my cousins, he didn't even mind when Cousin Harry moved in with us. We loved it when he was on. We took people in when they needed a place, even my ex-husband who was his friend in the joint. That is the kind of guy he is.

Joe would talk to my mom for hours while I was at work. He would yell at my sister for mistreating her kids, and she would be shaking in her pants trying to please him. He was always there when someone needed something. Once a friend of mine couldn't pay her rent; Joe was there giving her money and didn't want it back. He is liked by most people, feared by others, but is always respected. When Joe walks into a place anywhere, people know he is there; his presence is felt and heard without a sound. Not many people I know have that quality and, to be honest, that is another thing I love about him. It's amazing to see people look at him, wonder about him, and even learn from him. That is what our sons see in him and in turn try to emulate.

If nothing else, I got a great education from my life with Joe. More than one wants, but that makes me who I am and I know that I'm OK and that my life could be worse. Of course it could be better too-- I just need Joe home and a million in the bank! But all kidding aside, I have a good life. When someone would kid Joe about the homos in prison he would reply that that was not for him, that he would have to look at himself in the mirror and see his reflection. I too can look into that mirror and say that life is great. Joe just made it more interesting than most. In some ways I can say that it suited my personality. I really never wanted a boring life-- I just got a bit more than I anticipated. But as my mother said, "You made your bed now you have to lie in it." And I have with Joe.

I am still with him and have no real regrets except that he isn't home and won't be. A smaller bid would have been nice but that wasn't in the cards. We will just have to grow old together the way we are now; one day at a time with him there in prison and me at home. We have come to terms with a lot of things and that is one of them. We help each other grow. We bounce things off each other. We **communicate** and that is undoubtedly the biggest reason, outside of our love for each other, that has kept us together and strong.

Joe wasn't like most prisoners: making me visit every week, asking where I was when he called and couldn't get me, and he never really asked for much. I try to visit and be with him as much as possible after once moving to Las Vegas for five years to attend school there only able to come back to see Joe several times a year. After I graduated college, and Ramsey graduated High School, I moved back to New York to be near Joe. I missed him not seeing him so much. He seemed to understand that and feel the same way, and that made me love him even more. Things like that have kept my love alive for him.

As time has gone by we have grown to understand each other better. Better though, I still don't really understand why Joe ended up like he did for he is an intelligent man. When Joe wrote to the Syracuse Newspaper to thank the people for acquitting him on a bank robbery charge, the editor of the paper called his lawyer asking him if he had written the letter for Joe. He couldn't believe that Joe had the level of intelligence and education evident in the letter.

It is the complexity of it all that makes it simple at times. We can look around a visiting room observing couples and we can say: we were like that... we did that... or he did that or I did that. We are still together because we took the time to understand each other and our relationship. We have been through so much over the years that those experiences help us work things out better. Even our sons know that we have a more "quality" life than a "quantity" life. Joe is a captive audience and they know they can go to him for anything. I love to hear them talk and watch them interact on visits.

You have to think outside of the box to understand the life that I lead. Most people don't quite understand and to be honest it doesn't bother me a bit either way. Once people realize who my husband is, they kind of look at me funny. I find it kind of amusing as we all have our own skeletons in the closet. Joe is a unique guy and that is why I love him, even with the load of obstacles in our way. Even though Joe isn't home with us he is with us all the time. I am more fortunate than most single mothers as I am married to a man whom, though he doesn't live at home, still plays an active role and important part in the lives of his family. Joe has taught his sons how to think like a man as his father taught him: manners, common decency, respect and pride in oneself. I'm sure that people assume that Joe couldn't possibly possess such qualities, being who he is and having done what he has done. But it doesn't matter what people think, and that is what this is all about.

My husband escaped from Attica prison in April of 1971 and has been the only prisoner ever to do so. That event was soon thereafter overshadowed by the tragic Attica riot that took place from September 9th through the 13th that same year. There is little doubt in my mind that if Joe was still there when the riot occurred that he would have been right in the middle of it and would have been one of the forty-three killed in the riot. Indeed part of my husband's motivation to escape was the desire not to get caught up in such an occurrence as he rightly thought something like that wasn't far off.

I felt the only way to properly tell Joe's story was by writing it as if Joe was telling it himself. Indeed I have gone to great pains to tell it just as he and others have told it to me and supplied me with facts and information needed to put it together. In this quest I have not only had the benefit of twenty plus years of marital conversation and many thousands of letters from Joe, but have spoken to friends, family, lawyers, cops, prosecutors, ex-prisoners, current prisoners, and even a judge or two.

Nothing in life is all good or all bad and my husband's life is no exception to that. The story isn't always pretty but I believe it's an important and interesting story that should be told. Just as importantly no one has been, or will be hurt in its telling. This is a step into the life of the man I married, the man that I love with all of my heart, the man that gave me two fine sons that we both are very proud of, the man who law enforcement speculates might have murdered as many as thirty people.

***

--G.W.S.
Winter 2004

v

A PRODUCT OF THE STATE

PART I
1952–1971

"A Brief Family History"

My given name is Joseph George Sullivan. (My confirmation name is John) named such in March 1939 in Rockaway Beach, (Irish-Town) Queens. Third generation Irish-American, and second eldest of six children. Four boys and two girls. I was named such in honor of my father's brother "Joe", who died four years before my birth at the young age of twenty-two. Uncle Joe was literally the shining star of the staunch Irish-Catholic Sullivan family from Belle Harbor, New York. Uncle Joe was doted on by his mother and father and worshipped by his five brothers and two sisters who he led the way for and was very defensive of, at a time when there was still a good deal of W.A.S.P. prejudice against Irish Catholics. Signs such as "Irish Need Not Apply," and "Irish Keep off the grass," were still a common sight. None adored Uncle Joe more than my Dad, nor was more devastated upon his untimely death. The exception of course being his mom, Julia McLoughlin Sullivan and my grandfather "Big Tim Sullivan", who all said died of a broken-heart within a year of Joe's passing. Big Tim, as all called him, had been the N.Y.C. handball champion while serving as Captain on the Police Force for over twenty years. Uncle Joe was a strapping six foot two, drop dead handsome left-tackle for the "Fighting Irish" of Notre Dame at South Bend, Indiana. He planned to go into the Monastery upon graduation in his senior year of 1935, and had just been voted co-captain at the start of the '35 season, his final year under head coach Elmer Layden, one of the Heralded "Four Horsemen" of the Knute Rockne era. When suddenly, in the bone chilling cold of a South Bend, Indiana winter, Joe contracted pneumonia and died a very few short days later. Some of the family say his death was due to a head injury in that era of Leather-Helmet Football. Uncle Joe's greatest battles on the gridiron were against Army and Navy as two of his younger brothers, Frank and Eddie, played for Navy and Army in Joe's third year at Notre Dame.

As a wide-eyed eight year old in my grandmothers' house in Belle Harbor, N.Y., I heard all the loving stories and thought I was in a museum dedicated to his memory. His presence was everywhere... in the pictures, medals and trophies for football, Javelin, and the shot-putt. And of course in the news clippings, which I read with a young boy's awe. Though my most sacred moments came whenever I snuck down into the basement, silently undoing the huge brass clamps on a steamer trunk, which held all my Uncle Joe's football paraphernalia. Before which, I'd sit for hours on the damp basement floor holding and fingering the muddy high-topped cleats, blood stained jersey, and battered leather helmet in my trembling hands. All the while listening for footsteps on the cellar stairs, for it was Taboo --an unspoken agreement that the trunk was never to be opened, or those Holy Relics ever touched again. But something I had been doing every week since the age of eight, hearing the Notre Dame fight song in my fertile mind and heart, and visualizing myself, one day running out onto that same field in the shadow of the Golden Dome to finish where Uncle Joe had left off. Those were my most memorable moments as a child. I remember when Dad and Mom, and my brothers and sisters would all get into the Green Hornet, a beat up old Hudson and take a fifteen mile ride for our Ritual Sunday Dinner at Grandma's house. I think Grandma favored me just a bit, being her first grandson and named after Uncle Joe to boot. One particular Sunday, without saying a word, she handed me a book written about four athletes titled "All-Stars of Christ" by a priest from South Bend, Indiana, to the shock of all my Aunts and Uncles. They never spoke about Joe around her.

The book went far beyond his athletic prowess, and spoke of his gentle decency as a God fearing man. But it was the authors opening statement I have carried in my heart. "The Irish are running out onto the field (1935 vs. Army in Yankee Stadium) but a glum silence has come over the crowd, for No. 79, Big Joe Sullivan is not there."

Well, I have failed miserably, and disgraced this tragic legacy of my youth long ago by falling into that same murky pit of self-pity and despair that destroyed that too proud generation of Sullivan's before me. And for which I shall not seek redemption through my son's. They shall not be burdened by the ghosts of the past, no matter how impure. Nor the terrible sins of their father - for the chain must be broken. What follows, is not the man I planned to be, but an agonizingly slow chronological metamorphosis of an aberration I've somehow allowed myself to become. The Good, Bad and downright Ugly. I think the two most influential people in my life, were the uncle I never knew and my father, whom I needed to believe I did know. Although my Dad died when I was only thirteen, it was to him I whispered in the darkness of my cell where God does not live. For strength and support in face of the physical and moral degradation that could easily become the daily fare of a young prisoner who contemplates the luxury of self-pity or weakness in any form. He did not always answer me. But I always felt his presence. And though I know he frowned upon the actions that led me to be incarcerated, he never deserted me. So I tried to carry myself as a gentleman and respond to intimidation and immorality in the manner I instinctively felt he would expect of me. He was bigger than life in that young boys eye, even in death. And forty years later he has not diminished one iota. I just had the true essence of his values ass backwards all these years.

***

"When you're the anvil, you must bear.
When you're the hammer, strike!"

- Anon

***

Attica – 9 April 1971

As I lay in the coal pile before trying to escape and scale the high gray wall of Attica Prison, focusing clearly upon the menacing turreted tower above me, my entire senseless life seemed to race through my mind as I contemplated whether the faceless watchdog inside was to be my executioner. I had looked at many walls before, but this one seemed to have no top. I wondered how many years these mechanical men--this particular bird--had been perched in his nest up there, just waiting for a chance to kill someone. Anyone!

Did they really have those new AR-15's up there? I understood that even if they hit you in an arm or leg the shock impact alone could shatter your nervous system and kill you. I derived some comfort telling myself that these guys probably had very little practice and were lousy shots, but deep inside I knew that all these "country boys" could knock the sweat off a gnat's ass at seeing distance.

My throat was dry and the pains in my stomach nearly doubled me over. I turned my eyes to the storehouse platform seventy yards away and stared at the man standing there, almost rigid with a street-sweeper type of broom clenched in my hands. Mike, my friend (the poor bastard), was more anxious and frightened for me than I was for myself. I knew this from the conversation we had the day before, as we paced back and forth on the gravel-packed driveway just outside the entrance to the storehouse and garage. He was so sincere in his attempt to discourage me, continually bringing up all the bad points concerning the escape that it was beginning to unnerve me. I knew he was right, but I couldn't allow myself to listen to it. "Shut up for Christ's sake. Shut Up! Don't you think by now I should know what the chances are?"

He fell silent and then seconds later muttered, "I know, Sully, but, God Damn, there's got to be *something* better than this shit, " he whispered fiercely, shaking his head. "This shit's *impossible!*"

The solemn seriousness on his face and his choking words moved me deeply and I couldn't help but throw my arm around his neck and hug him, laughing and trying to swallow the tears I felt welling within me.

These hard, supposedly insensitive men are all I have known in the last seventeen years of my life, with the exception of about five short-lived months as a free man. To this day, I have never found an inmate who was insensitive. On the contrary, beneath their sullen-like facade they are very emotional men, oversensitive to the point that they cannot allow themselves to be deceived by the falseness and inhumane treacheries and inconsistencies of the outside "civilized world." And I would not trade the loyalty I have known with these men for the life of any "Sunday good-guy," for we are all the same people, for better or for worse, seven days a week.

"Listen, Mike," I said, smiling foolishly, and he standing there looking stupid. "I know this whole thing is shit. I gag on the smell of it myself." We both laughed. "I also know that in any other place, under any other conditions or circumstances, it would be impossible. But this is Attica! Remember that. This is Attica, the modern-day Devil's Island, one of the few escape-proof bastions left in the United States, right?" I smiled.

"Well yeah! But what does th--"

"It has everything to do with it, Mike. You were right when you said there's got to be a better way. There is. But nobody's ever found it! How long has this fucking joint been standing here?"

"I don't know--thirty--forty years, I guess."

"Yeah, something like that. And how many guys you heard of that tried this joint? I mean *really* tried!! Not some Joker scratching on steel bars with a nail clipper!"

"To be honest, I ain't heard of none." He raised his hands in mock defeat, still grinning like a moron.

"Neither have I, and neither has Willie, and he's been here seventeen years!"

"You mean Sutton?"

"Yeah. I used to rap with him almost every day, in the afternoon when I worked in the laundry---"

"What'd you rap about, I mean--"

"Everything, Mike. The guy's a really beautiful person, from the old school, know what I mean?"

"Yeah, but would he really open up and talk personally with you?"

"I know where you're coming from and I was a little awed at first, but he's just a man like you and me, understand? There was no holier than thou attitude or phony airs. It was just casual at the beginning. When he sensed he could trust me, we spoke about a lot of things. I should say he spoke and I listened," we both laughed, "and believe me, listening to Willie talk is like getting History first hand. He took me back to the 20's and 30's: the prohibition with Waxey Gordon, Dutch Schultz, and all that. I really felt like the guy was my father, the way he schooled me against the use of unnecessary violence. Damn, when I ran down the crime I was convicted of to him, he only looked at me condescendingly and shook his head sadly. It actually hurt him to think that I could have been so uncompassionate."

"Are you serious, Sully?" Mike asked in jest, but really disbelieving.

"I'm dead serious, Mike. Of course, when he was young, he was a wild son of a bitch, but back then, so was everyone. They were thieves and stick-up men, but all they wanted was a dude's money, not his fucking life!!"

"Yeah," he sighed, "but dig, if Sutton was as smart as they all say, how come he ain't never got out of here? He ain't never even tried. Why not, he had a million fucking years!" he snorted.

"Yeah, Mike." I mimicked him heatedly. "He had a million fucking years. He also had a guard to watch him eat, shit and breathe, twenty-four hours a day for the first six years he was here. And even till the day he left, he couldn't take ten fucking steps in any direction without some moron doing his duty, in guarding a 63-year-old man from escaping. They made him work in the laundry for seventeen years, which in itself, is no more than a big cell. You're locked in and out on every movement."

"Shit, Sully, you'd think when a man got that old, they'd ease up on him. Especially after they put that tube in his chest. They got to be some cold-blooded cock suckers, huh?"

"Listen, Mike, this whole joint is a bullshit myth, built on seventeen years of one poor bastard's misery and heartache; a man who was unfortunate enough to become the wrong kind of legend in an extremely unpopular profession. The means may have appeared to be subtle, but they were all callously designed to break one man, to strip him of the small shreds of dignity he so consciously struggled to preserve. They couldn't do it, Mike, and though his body has wilted with age, that glint of fierce pride and boyish devilishness has never left his eyes."

"Listen, Sully, I can understand how you feel about the guy, but how do you figure any of this is going to help you over that wall?" He nodded his head toward the awesome wall, which I no longer cared to look at. I would see enough of it tomorrow.

"I didn't say anything was going to help me, I've just been trying to show you how this administration, from top to bottom, has become, over the period of seventeen years; it's own greatest fan and believer in the myth that they, themselves have built for us. This is why I believe it can be done. I may be a fool in many ways, but I harbor no suicidal tendencies whatsoever."

"I'm beginning to wonder, you nut!" he smiled.

"Another thing, Mike, these people are great believers of the pattern-process that most criminals follow throughout their lives, which I agree is true to a great degree. But who doesn't live by a certain type of schedule? Who sets a clearer and more vivid pattern of movement and habits that these people? They're like Goddamned robots. You've watched them with me. Lenny too! You could set your watch according to how many times they scratch their ass!"

"Yeah," Mike laughed unconvincingly, "but just suppose that tomorrow their assholes aren't itchy, and don't need no scratching. Then what?" he asked smugly.

"Then my ass will be getting scratched, you dirty bastard!" I smiled. "Listen, all I need to get over is 12, maybe 15 seconds at most, and when a truck comes through that back gate these cops in them towers are so elated over any interruption, that they follow its path like some dirty old men going after some young filly till she's out of sight, but only till the next one comes along. This is the chance I've got to take. I've got to try. If I don't, then I belong here. You know what I mean, Hoss? I don't ever want to be just another head in the herd, a piece of meat to go on a 'count' a dozen times a day! To tell the truth, I don't even know what I'm escaping to, where I will go, or what I will do. But I do know what I'm escaping from. We are living in a graveyard of eunuchs. We are looked upon as one would look upon a dung heap, but in reality even less, because these farmers can find means of utilizing a good dung heap. Do you wonder why I feel this place can be had? Well it's just for this very reason. Since these people stand in awe of this well renowned fortress, and cannot conceive the thought of a possible escape were they themselves in this position, ego-wise it is only natural that they have come to believe that everyone possesses their same lack of courage. Especially *common* criminals such as ourselves. But enough of that crap. Is everything ready?"

"Yeah, Johnny brought over those other lengths of foot-length pipe this morning."

"Were they all threaded on both ends? Did you check all of them? How many are in the bag?"

"Of course I checked them all! There are 32 lengths with all the couplings attached, along with other pipes and elbows for the hook. Why so much depth in the hook, Joe? It's too clumsy to handle."

"I know it's clumsy, but the top of the wall isn't flat. It's rounded off and designed to throw off a hook like this one if any weight is applied to it. With this, the gripping prongs are long enough, so even when my whole weight is on the pipe and it slides, it will still grip the wall."

"Right, but how about the scraping sounds? He's bound to hear them."

"I got quite a bit of tape from the hospital, I'll wrap some strips of sheet around it first before I tape it. How much do you think will make contact with the wall, Mike?" I asked.

"Shit, I don't know!" he laughed. "I'm no authority on these types of actions, Joe. How much do you think?"

"I'm not sure either, Hoss. The last time I went over a wall was in Jersey, and we used a ladder for that! This will be the first time I have to resort to such a primitive means to deliver myself. Or should I say, abscond from within a restricted premise."

"Stop, for Christ's sake. I'm trying to be patient with this lunacy. Now, how much do you think should be taped? Be serious, Joe, huh?" He was serious.

"I'm sorry, Mike. But really, how can I be sure how much makes contact? It all depends on how much the hook slides. I hope it doesn't slide too much because neither the elbows nor the couplings could take the pressure at such an angle, even if I'm climbing fluidly without jerking on it. I figure I'll wrap and tape both top and bottom six feet and the rest shouldn't hit at all naturally."

"How much money you got altogether?"

"About seventy bucks, counting the twenty you got yesterday."

"It ain't much to go on, Joe. I wish we could have got more."

"It's enough to go on if I make it. If I don't, it wouldn't matter how much I had, would it?"

"No, I guess not. I hope Lenny can get that pipe off the wall once you're over. You need time," Mike said worriedly.

"If there's any way he can get it, he will, don't worry. But I told him I don't want him making a move unless there's no reaction at all. He should be able to tell within three or four seconds after I'm over. He must move within that time or forget it. If he does get it down, he knows what to do with it."

"All right, let's suppose he gets it down. You still won't have much time. If they don't find you missing before we go back to the cells for lunch, you've got two hours at best. You can't even drive a fucking car and you're in the middle of the country. What then?"

"First of all, genius, if I walk around that parking lot I'm going to have a lot more than two hours. Willie Sutton told me that some time back, maybe six to eight years, the count came up short. Everybody was kept locked in and the search began. About nine or ten hours later, they found this 'nut' inside a garbage can in the back of the hospital. The guy wasn't even trying to escape. He was a bug."

"So--"

"What do you mean, so? Don't get so shitty all the time! Here's a guy missing for almost ten hours and no alert was put out at all! Why? Because these people are so sure it can't be done. If they waited ten hours and still didn't cover half this institution in their search, how much longer would they have waited? There's no telling, but I'd probably have enough time to *walk* clear out of New York State."

"You better get clear out of the state, because if you're caught anywhere in the immediate vicinity around here, there ain't no giving up Joe. They'll whack you out for sure."

"I know. I'm well aware of how they think, Mike. There's the stick. [At that time, convicts in marching formation moved and stopped at the sound of nightstick rapped on the ground or concrete wall.] It's time for chow and if there ain't no trucks to unload, I'll catch you, Lenny and Mack out back this afternoon. I want to go over this completely one more time, Okay? Let them come out after two o'clock, a few minutes apart. Oh well, let's go eat, my friend."

"If I can." He smiled, curling up his lip in mock-like disgust.

"I've yet to see the day you couldn't eat, you buzzard!"

"Fuck you, Sully."

***

9 April 1971, 9:05 A.M.

The sweat burned and stung my eyes as I worked on the pipes furiously but methodically, screwing the short lengths together and tightening them as much as the strength in my hands would allow. Then padding and taping, easing its long length out from under the railroad track, whose construction offered me temporary asylum from my enemy above.

The sweat turned cold on my chest and back now that I had finished my main task. Kneeling on both knees, I extended my left hand, gripping the pipe tightly as far up as I could without losing any leverage.

I gripped the base with my right pushing down, pulling slowly but steadily with my left. It was heavy and bent to some degree in the middle, but it would be all right, I hoped.

I lay back against the coal pile, daring to close my eyes for a few precious seconds. The giant steel gate took almost ten seconds to slide back completely before any vehicle could move through. It was electronically controlled.

I opened my eyes again quickly, remembering where I was. Looking at my watch, it was only 9:13. Only 13 minutes I've been lying here? I feel like I was born here! Why am I doing this? What is the sense in it? How many times have you waited like this before? You don't have to do this. What are you trying to prove? To whom? It's not too late to turn back. They'll understand? Why should I care if they understand? They wouldn't, anyway. Damn, I feel so tired, so alone... so ... so sleepy...

***

1952 - 13 years old

"Joseph, come in the house, you have to get dressed. Your father just died."

"W-What, Aunt Ceil?" I asked, numb with disbelief, not really understanding nor wanting to believe that I had understood just what this cold-blooded bitch of an aunt was so casually saying to me. After all, I was all of thirteen years old and should have been able to accept such things, right?

I approached the screen door, which she was standing behind. God, I hated to look into that terrible face with its cold, beady eyes and thin bloodless lips. I knew, even at that young age, that she hated men, hated me. It was something I could feel, even in her slightest glance. I was seething now. I felt terribly hurt and empty because she was saying something I knew was bad, but couldn't really grasp the meaning of.

"W-What did you say, Aunt Ceil?" I asked shakily, tears I can still taste running into my mouth. I asked her very nicely, very politely, barely in control hoping I had misunderstood her. "I said," she replied in that imperious tone, "your father is dead, an..."

"OOOhhh, you Bitch, you dirty Bitch!" Out came the keening wail of the wounded animal within me, slamming the basketball against the screened portion of the door she peered through almost breaking her nose. And I was still wailing uncontrollably on the grass when my father's brother John, came into the back yard.

" What did you tell him Ceil?" he asked softly, barely controlling his anger. "I- told him his father was dead, that's all!" She snapped indignantly, yet staring aghast at my venom filled face.

"That's *all* you said. Just like *that*?"

"Why ---yes--yes, I--"

"Go upstairs now!" Uncle John growled, and she scurried away like some indignant rodent.

"Come on inside, Joe." Uncle John said in that firm but gentle way he had. "I'm sorry about this, I wanted to talk to you first, but..."

"Is it true what she said, Uncle John?" I sobbed, still hoping it was all a mistake.

"Yes, Joe, your dad, my brother, passed away early this morning and I miss him very, very much, just as I know you will..."

I knew he meant well, but what was there to be understood? I was young, selfish, and above all, felt terribly cheated by some cruel hoax. My father was my hero--young, handsome, strong. He was Superman. How could Superman die?! Never knowing or caring that there were others who felt this loss as much as I. (My father, at the time of his death, was a decorated, 1st grade Detective in Brooklyn 79th precinct. He was a sixteen-year veteran, and just 36 years old. But my mother never received a pension in spite of being left with six kids, because he was a few years short of eligibility, despite the fact that his ulcer problems were job related. So much for, "We look out for ours.")

My beautiful mother, who I had always felt was strong in so many ways (and she was), sought her own escape and eventual destruction by turning to alcohol. The only weakness she had (I know this now) was her love for my father. She did not want to live without him.

***

1952 - "You Killed Him"

Shortly after the funeral, Uncle John and Aunt Ceil took me to live with them to ease my mother's burden, since I was one of six children. But Uncle John saw that Aunt Ceil did not know how to treat or handle a boy, having raised two girls with an iron fist in her domineering, man-hating manner.

Mary, the older daughter, went into a convent a few years later. And Claire, the "Tom-boy," attended an all-girls Catholic high school, was forbidden to accept even the most innocent of dates, and was not even allowed to go to the movies on a Saturday afternoon.

The real conflict began when after school she would not allow me the freedom or free time to play stick-ball, punch-ball, or engage in the activities boys do once they run home from school and change their clothes -- to the raggedy play-clothes acceptable for street games. She demanded I look prim and proper, like Little Lord Fauntleroy, and that I accompany her and the girls everywhere, shopping and all the tea and crumpet parties! I was bursting with indignation inside. And besides trying to put an "internal skirt" on me, she was a religious freak to the point of it being a mental illness. I understood why Uncle John would come off the train from work in the evenings and stop in the corner bar and drink beer with the guys, whom he had nothing in common with, and didn't arrive home till in the evenings when everyone, particularly Aunt Ceil, were all asleep. He had to be a saint to live in that house! Where not only Aunt Ceil, but also his own daughters whom Ceil had turned against him, were cold and indifferent in his presence. But he just went his way quietly.

My final act of rebellion came when "The Bitch," as I came to think of her, chirped "chapel time" each evening in her pseudo-sweet voice, a call I had come to dread and even have nightmares about. Aunt Ceil had converted a spare room upstairs into a little chapel of sorts; with statues of all the saints and religious artifacts hanging from all the walls but one, which was reserved solely for a huge cross I could have nailed a midget on. The floor was bare and highly polished wood planking. It was on that floor the four of us would kneel, babbling in prayer while fingering our rosary beads, from six till nine o'clock every night after our homework was done. We needed to beg for forgiveness for all of our real and imagined sins we had committed during the course of the day. After months of kneeling in excruciating pain, praying and mumbling incoherently to two chunks of wood on a wall, rebellion began to set in. One night, Aunt Ceil noticed I wasn't grimacing in deserved agony as I usually did.

"Stand up and pull your pants down, Joseph!" She stood and demanded it in self-righteous anger, while both girls turned their heads to glare at me with some knee-jerk inbred hatred.

"Uh...what's w-wrong?" I retorted angrily.

"You're cheating the Lord, Joseph!" The Bitch hissed.

"Without pain you cannot feel the cleansing of your soul!"

"Aww, Aunt Ceil..." I whined.

"Pull your pants down, Joseph!" She demanded, stepping towards me in a threatening manner.

"Okay! Okay!!" I said wickedly, lowering my pants that exposed the strips of bath towels I had wrapped around my bruised and swollen knees.

"Cheater! Cheater! Cheater!!!" The three hate-filled faces chanted in a chorus, a wailing ritual they must have admonished each other with for years.

And it was at that very moment I realized they were all crazy in some way I couldn't quite understand. But I did understand I'd had enough, and began to walk from the room when Aunt Ceil's bloody scream froze me in both fear and anger.

"Where do you think you're going? Come back here this instant and kneel down!"

"N-No, I a-ain't kneeling no more. It hurts." I quivered.

"What did you say? What did you say, Joseph?!"

All the months of emotion exploded inside me. "I said, fuck you, Aunt Ceil! Fuck you!! Fuck you!!!" I screamed as cousin Claire, a big girl and as demented as her mother, hopped to her feet and started after me, upon which I took flight. Flying down the stairs and into the living room where I was trapped. I immediately grasped an iron poker from the fireplace and turned to meet my demonic attacker.

"C'mon, you bitch, and I'll split your head open! C'mon!" I screamed. "All of you!"

"Claire, don't go near him!" The Bitch called from where she and Mary stood, looking over the stairway banister. "Move away from him, can't you see he's mentally disturbed?" Those venomous words: which for some reason caused me to laugh and cry simultaneously, after they had withdrawn to the safety of their godless chapel.

When Uncle John came home I told him everything that had happened. The monsters were upstairs sleeping peacefully as if nothing unusual had taken place.

"I'm sorry, Joe." Uncle John shook his head sadly, hugging me close to him. "I had hoped your living here would somehow work out. I should have known better. But I think, for everybody's sake, it would be best if you moved back home with your mother."

"I understand, Uncle John." He was a great guy, but had no control in his own home, and had long ago lost his will and energy to try.

My first impression upon moving home was that I had ascended from hell into heaven. But I soon found that our fatherless home had become a purgatory, somewhere between heaven and hell. My mother had fallen into that well of alcohol that inspires self-pity and defeat. When she should have been strong and kept our ship afloat, if only in memory of her husband, which our presence should have represented to her. Instead, like Aunt Ceil, she had become another nightmare - at least for me, being the oldest of four sons and two daughters, at thirteen years of age.

The first night home I was awakened from my sleep at about ten o'clock. "W-what's wrong, Mom?" I thought I was dreaming.

"Put your clothes on and come downstairs," she hiccupped drunkenly.

When I went down into the semi-darkened living room, Mom was pouring a glass of beer from a quart bottle of "Piels" and staring at the TV screen that emitted no sound. I stood before her with confused, quiet obedience.

"I-I want you to go around to the Willow," she spoke in a slurred voice. She was speaking of the "Willow Bar and Grill" around the corner on Atlantic Ave. "They have some money. Your father's friends have taken up a collection for us. Bring it back."

"M-money? W-who should I ask, Mom?"

"Any--anyone! Ask anyone!" she snapped.

"Please, Mom. We don't need it. Don't t-take it from them." Somehow, even then, I knew it was a humiliating thing, especially for my mother.

"Don't you question me!" she screamed. "Just do as I tell you. Now go on!"

"All right, Mom." I sniffled, slinking out into the dark night, shivering from the cold, as I ran around the corner.

There was nobody on the street and only a few cars moved along Atlantic Avenue as I stood on my toes to peer into the bar. There were only about ten or twelve regular customers. Two of the men were friends of my father and were playing shuffleboard. I was so embarrassed to go inside, and stood outside the window practicing how to ask for what I was supposed to get. When I finally got up my nerve and slunk into this adults' domain, everything went quiet, as I walked, head down, to the short end of the bar. The identical spot I was to kill a man twelve years later.

"Hey, you're one of the Sullivan kids, ain't you?" the bartender, Phil Rubin asked.

"Y-yes, sir," I replied. "M-my mother told me to c-come here... She said you h-had something for her." I was relieved to get the words out.

"Huh? I don't know wh-- Oh, yeah! The beer container on the other end of the bar. Ain't much kid? Some of the guys been dipping into it for the jukebox and phone calls," he laughed.

And that was the first time I ever entertained the thought of killing another human being. Are these my father's friends? I thought, fighting back the tears as I stepped on the rung of the bar stool to reach the quart cardboard beer container the collection was taken upon. It said "Sullivan Kids" on it.

"Hey Kid!" One of the drunks grabbed my arm, almost causing me to spill the container. "Where's your mother? Ain't seen her for a while. Tell her to come on around and have a few drinks with us!" He said with a suggestive wink I did not fail to get the meaning of. I went cold, just staring at him, beginning to cry and not really knowing why. I ran out of the bar.

"Twenty-four dollars?" Mom exclaimed drunkenly. "You take anything out of here?" she slurred as I stood before her looking at the little stacks of quarters, dimes, nickels, and even pennies she had counted out.

"T-take out? N-no, Mom, I wouldn't."

"Kneel down, Joe," she ordered me. All I could think of was Aunt Ceil.

"Please, no more of that!" I whimpered.

"Kneel down!" she shouted, reaching for an old 8x10 photo of my dad, which she held in her lap facing me as she slouched back on the couch. I knelt down with my head lowered, beginning to cry in confusion.

"Tell him you didn't mean it!" Mom hiccuped again.

"M-mean w-what, Mom?" I begged pitifully.

"Please, Joseph!" She always used my given name when she was angry or annoyed. "You know he was sick before he went into the hospital. If you had been a good son, he would have lived! **You** killed him with your selfishness, Joseph! Now pray and ask him for his forgiveness. Don't look away, dammit! Look at his face, you bastard!"

"P-please, Mom, I didn't h-hurt him. I d-didn't k-kill him," I cried uncontrollably.

"Look up at him!" She screamed, clenching her fingers cruelly in my hair and jerking my head up to look at the picture of the face I had worshipped. "Say It!" She screamed again, slapping me back and forth across the face as I cried out in unison to the blows.

"I'm sorry! Forgive me, Dad! I-I'm sorry," I choked brokenly, and repeated till Mom fell back against the couch with an exhausted breath and finally fell asleep in a drunken stupor. This was a scene that would be repeated night after night for months, till I finally began to believe her monstrous accusations.

During the day she was all right, just short-tempered and mean, and never once mentioned the nightly episodes. Did she remember them?

This went on until one day she asked me, "Honey, get me a bottle of beer from the refrigerator?"

I knew she was getting an early start and I couldn't take any more. I decided to run away from home, though not with out a sense of guilt at leaving my brothers and sisters behind. I later learned that she never accused or abused them in the manner she did me, but made their lives hell in numerous other ways.

Running away from home in those days brought the serious charge of being a truant. I was eventually sent to the New York State Training school for Boys, a reform school for Juvenile delinquents in Warwick, New York. I was a very bitter and naive young boy, one who would learn the harsh realities of life slowly, but ever so surely! I'd learn that the world was a lonely place and people were not always nice. I learned that I had to act like a man, and fight like a man, before I had mentally or physically become a man. That, or become a human punching bag for every emotionally disturbed kid--worse off than myself--who came down the pike.

Thankfully, at that stage of my life I had a good Rabbi, trainer and corner man in a huge, loving and emphatically black woman named Mrs. Ransom--who was not only the "House Mother" but also the "High Sheriff" of B-2 Cottage in Warwick. And **nobody** fucked with her!!

***

Warwick – 1953, N.Y.S. Training School for Boys

I was on the "lawn mowing gang" most of the time I was in Warwick, when I wasn't again running away. I was really out of my environment and felt like a Cheerio in a bowl of Rice Krispies being in "cottage B-2," where ninety percent of the kids were black, as were the cottage "parents" Mr. and Mrs. Ransom.

Mrs. Ransom looked like a big African queen, close to six foot tall and pushing two hundred pounds; and none of it was loose, it all belonged there. She was an awesome sight when she was angry, but I remember her with fondness because if it wasn't for her I would have had those wild ghetto-trained kids kicking my ass 24-7--twenty-four hours a day, seven days a week! These kids didn't need a reason to punch you out. It seemed whenever they felt bored and wanted to get their shit off, they would pass up fifty dudes to get to the local punching bag, me! I guess besides my being white, they instinctively sensed, "here was 'cracker' all soft and creamy on the inside, an easy mark and victim." I can laugh when I look back on it now, but I don't think I smiled five times the whole time I was there. On one particularly bad day I came back from mowing grass with two black eyes and a busted lower lip. While trying to sneak past Mrs. Ransom into the house, she grabbed me by the arm and pulled me into the kitchen and spun me around to face her.

"Look at me, boy." she whispered. I was too ashamed to lift my chin off my chest. "Look at me, boy!" She yelled, shaking me by both shoulders until I thought my neck would pop. I looked up and felt more ashamed to see the tears running down her cheeks.

"Whatcha gonna do boy? This shit got to stop," she said with unfelt gruffness.

"I--I don't know," I muttered feeling sorry for myself.

"Are you afraid to fight?" she asked. "Are you a pussy boy?"

"No!" I muttered defensively.

"Well, then you gonna learn to fight, boy. I know it was that Scott boy that whipped upon your ass again! You gonna go in that dorm and whip up on him, and if you don't... you don't never talk wit me again, you hear me boy?"

She yeasted me up, rubbing my shoulders like she was my "cornerman" in a championship fight.

"You want a stick or sumpin'?"

"No-no ma'am." I was scared to death, but more of her fury than of Scott. "Well, get on out there!" She ordered with a raised arm, finger pointed majestically, sending her frightened knight into battle.

As I walked out of the kitchen, my eyes darting about wildly for escape, I noticed the doors were already locked for the night. As I walked down the corridor toward the dormitory I could see the guys there (there were 52 boys in the dorm) getting ready for bed and lights out. I'll go in the bathroom here and pretend I'm taking a crap. She couldn't blame me for that, I got bad cramps in my stomach and have to go anyway! Besides... I can fight with Scott in the morning. Yeah, that's what I'll do. I was sitting on the bowl for about twenty minutes and was almost asleep when I heard a heavy knock on the door. I felt I was going to shit all over myself because if it was one of the guys, he'd just walk in.

"Who is it?" I croaked weakly.

"Are you in there Joseph?" she growled. "Joseph?"

I shuddered, "I'm c-coming Mrs. Ransom." I squeaked, pulling my pants up, I had no need to wipe my ass.

"Now, don't you mind cause I'm coming in!"

And with that, the door bust open, and in flew my tormentor, the

Scott kid looking more scared than me. He wasn't cool at all, and seeing him like this, he somehow didn't look as big or as mean to me anymore. Mrs. Ransom stepped inside smiling, and standing with her back against the door, exclaimed, "All Right! Fight you little Bastards! And Ah wants to see a good one!" she barked. We both flew at each other on command, and while we were punching the shit out of each other, I felt good.

I felt proud, and even when both of us were so lumped up and exhausted, she pushed us on screaming, "Ya'll ain't finished yet, don't hang on to each other you little sissies! I don't like that wrastling shit! Fight!"

Mr. Ransom was banging on the door with his cane. "Mary! You let them boys on out of here, that's enough!" he commanded. "You hear me Mary?" "Mind you business Pa, and get on away from here!" she growled through the door at him. "All right, but enough is enough Mary," he said quietly and went away.

Shit we were all through anyway. I was lying under the sink and he was lying half in the pisser, both of us warily watching each other, gasping and licking our wounds. Each of us was hoping the other didn't want any more action. Mrs. Ransom could have screamed, "Fight!" for the rest of the night, but neither of us was about to move. She left the bathroom and a few minutes later came back with our pajamas, towels, soap, etc.

"Alright boys," said she ever so gently, "you both take a nice warm shower and when you're finished, come to my apartment, okay?"

"Yes Ma'am," I said.

"Me too!" said Scott.

"Me too what?" she scowled darkly.

"Oh shit!" I thought.

"Me too! Yes Ma'am!" he ventured quickly.

Mrs. Ransom laughed thunderously and left us to shower. We showered cautiously still eying each other warily.

After a few minutes, Scotty muttered, "Damn that crazy bitch would have let us kill each other if we didn't stop huh?"

"Yeah man!" I agreed happily with a growing sense of pride and accomplishment, feeling more a co-conspirator with him.

"What's she want us to come to her apartment for? She gonna fuck with us some more? Man, my fucking back's killing me," he groaned.

Afterward, Mrs. Ransom greeted us with two big bowls of ice cream and told us to get our asses into bed and if we felt like fighting again, to come and see her.

The next morning, when I woke up every bone in my body was hurting but I felt like a different person. I felt puffed up with pride and felt like fighting again, just to see if that rumble in the shit house was really me! When I walked into the kitchen after chow, Mrs. Ransom winked knowingly at me and I grinned at her from ear to ear, silently thanking and loving her for what she did. About a week later, she asked if I would like to go fishing with her out on the lake. I gratefully accepted. She made sandwiches and a big thermos of lemonade. It was a beautiful sunny day with a light cool breeze blowing across the lake. Mrs. Ransom carried on like a young girl every time she thought something was biting, "Oh-Oh! I-I can feel it, it--its a monster!" and then, "Sheeit, the son of a bitch jumped off a my hook again!"

Needless to say, neither one of us caught any fish that day. But it didn't matter. The lemonade was cold and the sandwiches were delicious and we both had a great time. As I was rowing back to shore, she told me to pull the oars in and rest a while.

"You're hands hurting boy?" She asked catching me licking the blisters on my palms.

"Naw--they're all right." I answered bravely as she laughed happily and leaned toward me messing up my hair fondly.

"You gonna be alright boy, you gonna be alright. Don't you feel better now that you fought that boy? Don't you feel better to be able to hold your head up high?"

"Yes Ma'am." I whispered, feeling contented as she scratched lightly behind my ear. I wished I could stay out in this boat for the rest of my life but I knew this wasn't possible. I basked under, and drew forth, every small gesture of affection I could manage until she laughed knowingly and pushed my head away chuckling. "I'm gonna spoil you boy!" she said wistfully. She then sat up to her full height and pointed to shore, commanding me with a smile. "Row!" and I rowed, blisters and all, never feeling a thing.

Everything was going fine for a while. I seemed to be fighting every other day now, still coming back to the cottage with black eyes and busted lips but I was beginning to give out more than I got; until things got so bad, I could only get about one fight a week. I learned that most dudes don't want a real fight. They pick their shots and shy away from anyone they feel might put something on their ass. These are the same cats that will "Jap" you three steps away from the "man". They figure if they don't knock you out, or break your jaw, the man will break it up before you get a chance to retaliate. The dudes who can really thump, and don't mind bringing their lunch with them, don't resort to these different types of punk-like tactics since they possess the heart for a prolonged affair and can take as much as they give. The few times I've been offered into a shithouse or in the back of a tier in a cellblock, I knew instinctively that this dude was a man and he sure enough *wanted* to fight. But there is not too much of this because, after a while, like in anything else in life, a certain closeness develops; a certain respect for those others who share the same principles you yourself live by as a man. I have found that everyone respects a MAN, black or white.

When I was transferred from Mrs. Ransom's cottage a few months later, for fighting, I just started running away again, only to be brought back and tried by the inmate "Kangaroo Court" made up of the cottages top notch little sadists. When a guy ran away, the whole cottage would lose credits, etc., thus reducing their chance for their monthly visit home. I was never acquitted, always convicted, and the penalty never changing; a kangaroo court ass whipping!! I finally made it to New York City on my seventh try. A friend of mine (who turned out to be a bona-fide stool-pigeon) and I took off one night, running through woods and swamps for about five miles. I had to half carry this prick most of the way, and at one point had to pull him out of what appeared to be quick-sand because he was waist deep in shit on first contact.

"Sssulleee!!" He squealed like a pig and started crying even before he could have possibly known what had happened. I spun around and my first reaction was to laugh cause it was dark and all I could see was his body from the waist up sticking out of the ground. "I-I th-think I'm in-in quicksand," he squeaked pitifully.

I remember waiting a few minutes, expecting him to disappear like in the movies. Plop! All of a sudden like. "Please, Sully, h-h-h-help me!"

I was about ten yards away from him and I suddenly became very conscious of the ground I was standing on but, damn, I had to try and help him. "All right, take it easy Tommy," I rasped, getting down on all fours, inching my way toward him, stretching one arm out in front of the other, pressing easily as I went until my hand hit some type of shit that didn't want to stay still beneath it.

"C-c-come on S-S-Sully, P-Pull me out, huh?"

"Yeah, yeah, take it easy, will ya!" I was becoming shaky now, cause it was moving almost to his chest now.

"T-take it easy? I-I f-feel it moving, do--s-s-omething, PLEASE!" What can I do I thought desperately, searching the woods around me with my eyes for a stick, a branch of some sort. There was none.

"Sully!!" He screamed frantically, his hand reaching out in desperation. He was at least seven yards away. I sure wasn't going to step into that shit. "Use y-your belt." He was whimpering now. Damn, why didn't I think of that! Quickly I pulled off my shirt and pants and tied them all together tightly along with my canvas-type belt that we are issued.

"All right, Tommy, I'm going to throw it, don't pull on it, I'll do the pulling, O.K.? 'Cause the pants might rip!"

"Y-yeah, oh-oh ss-sure r-right--I-I know," he stuttered. "Hurry up, huh?"

I lay on my stomach with my right arm down at my side, behind me. My left extended, palm down on the ground for balance, I whipped it suddenly over my head. Too short!! But, just a little.

"Shit, Sully, damn!! Hurry up, th-throw it again, huh?"

"Take it easy Tommy. Stop moving so much," I said. It was almost to his armpits. I threw it again.

"I--got--it---I got it, Sully!"

"Don't pull you fucking dope, just hang onto it!!"

"All right Sully," he choked.

I never thought I would ever get him out but after about an hour of pulling, he was completely free, gasping and choking and puking his guts out.

We eventually slid into our mud-caked clothes and continued on our way. After that, every hundred yards we walked, I had to listen to his whining about going back but was dissuaded each time when I told him I would kick his ass. We finally came out of the woods on the edge of some small town. I figured it was about three in the morning.

"You sure you know how to jump the wires?" I asked as we approached some car parked on a dark street.

"Yeah, I told you I used to do it every day. There's nothing to it."

"All right, which one we gonna take?"

"Let's get that one!" It was a forty-nine ford; he was under the hood only a matter of seconds and was finished. I was very impressed. What a genius, I thought.

"Don't slam the hood or they'll hear it in the house." He eased it down until it was closed but not locked. We slammed it shut a few blocks away.

We got to New York City with no trouble and four hours later we were caught. Since we were outside the car when we were caught, he wasted no time putting the finger on me. He said I *forced* him to run away, *I* jumped the wires and *I* drove the car. His mother, father, aunts and uncles all swore to it. Their good word and about twenty five hundred got him out but not before I broke the rat-bastard's nose and got a few teeth. The Judas Bastard!!!

I got three years in Elmira Reformatory for not having someone who would pay twenty five hundred for me. I had just turned sixteen three days before. I didn't know how to drive a car then. I was in jail for over 25 years before I got my license at the age of 38.

***
Attica 1971, 9:15 A.M.

My heart jumped and my eyes flew open as I heard the distant motor of what sounded like a truck. It was, but it was coming out from the garage and around in the direction of the school. Mike was still poised on the platform watching the rear gate intently. Lenny was sitting just outside the back door of the powerhouse, casually smoking a cigarette, but I knew he was watching me from the corner of his eye with anxiety, waiting for my move. The blue denim shirt and dungarees I had changed into were soaked with sweat and clung coldly under my arms. I smiled when my eyes fell to the tin badge on my chest. Charlie had really outdone himself when he worked these into shape. The one on what appeared to be an officer's hat was even better, almost to perfection. Not bad for tin cans! I told him not to kill himself working on them because if I had to come in range for a close inspection, I'd be a dead ass anyway.

"Listen Sully, I don't know what you're doing and I don't want to know. It's better that way, understand? If something goes wrong, I want to be above any suspicion. I like our friendship too much for that."

"I understand, Charlie. But be cool, huh!" I said in mock terror, putting my hand over my heart.

"Don't worry, Sully," he grinned. "I hope you get those creep bastards. God, I hope you get them."

"Me too, Charlie."

***
9:16 A.M.

I can't look up at that tower once I get out there next to the wall because I'll swear he's looking at me or about to turn around, even if he isn't. I'd use it as an excuse for myself. You've got to rely on their habits. Why shouldn't they watch the trucks today? Why should they act differently? Damn, if the wall wasn't so high--just a little shorter, just a few feet shorter. My fucking eyes feel like they're on fire. I--I'll just close my eyes and rest for a few more seconds.

***
Coxsackie - 1955

"Abuse is the weapon of cowards. Those who apply it know this fact, as well as those who have to accept it."

After three months in Elmira Reception Center, where I was labeled #13316, I was sent to Coxsackie Reformatory (Bop City - #10192) to do my time, zip three! This fucking place destroyed any sense of feeling I had in me for quite some time to come. It was a racist institution because it was kept that way by a sick administration. Their philosophy was that as long as they can keep blacks and whites at each other's throats, stabbing, fighting and fucking one another like animals; they knew we would never have the time to wonder *why* certain things were as they were or who our real enemies were.

The yard itself was a sick kind of joke. It was divided into sections: Black, White and Puerto Rican, and each in turn divided their own into three categories (in different manners). The whites had the "Gees" (or "good boys," as they were called), "Half-asses" and "Creeps." The Gees were supposedly the elite of the white fighting force, though probably almost half either knew someone from the street or paid five or ten cartons of cigarettes for the distinguished honor of standing with the Gees. There were really only a handful of dudes who could really thump (fight). The rest were phonies and were getting a free ride through the joint on their reputation.

Well anyway, these guys had the larger portion of real estate (the wall) in the yard with maybe a dozen guys "owning" and "running" a portion of about five to ten yards apiece. These were white lines on the walls themselves and on the ground about ten yards from the wall, sectioning off each individual's property (or "pads," as they were called). Anywhere from five to twenty guys "stood" in these "pads" and it was their duty to go "up on" (fight) any dude who crossed that line unless he had permission from the "pad owner" to do so.

At one time it was Gees' policy that anyone who wanted to stand with them had to go up on a "shine" (black) to prove his courage. And most of them did, usually by japing the dude when he wasn't looking. This policy was abandoned when some guy found that the guards were too slow in getting there.

The Gees were allowed to talk to Half-ass guys (who, in reality, were tougher dudes than the good boys), but not for too long. And they were not permitted to speak to a so-called Creep at all. That was immediate expulsion!

The Half-ass guys had the same set-up as the Gees but didn't have the illustrious history to go with it. The Creeps had no wall to lean against and no place to sit. They stood in the middle of the yard, which was no bigger than a football field. When they got bored standing still, all they could do was keep walking in circles, even in the winter when all the snow was pushed out in the middle of the yard. It really hurt me to look at them on the really bitter cold days; no wall to protect them from the cutting winds or galoshes to protect their feet when the snow piles they stood in began to thaw. We didn't have to go through this because we shoveled all our snow out on them. In reality, we treated ourselves with more disrespect as human beings than the cops did, but it was a result of what they and their fathers created for years.

The infamous Captain Follette (Peg-leg Follette) was "God" in this joint while I was there. He later became warden of Green Haven. The prick died about two years ago; sixteen years too late as far as my life and that of many others are concerned.

Follette's idea of punishment for minor infractions was to take your eyeglasses, glass eye, crutches, beds, etc., for three or four months, or thirty days bread and water with one meal every third day. For serious offenses like a bad fistfight, you were automatically beaten up with clubs from the place the fight took place to the "box" up in "A-3." There, surrounded by eight or ten officers, you were made to strip (if you were still conscious), get down on all fours and bark, meow or moo, according to what type of animal Capt. Follette desired to hear. When they all tired of this, everyone that was in the box would be told to get up on their doors and watch another of their "Gees" slide by. They didn't want you to simply crawl on your hands and knees, you were beaten until you got on your belly and pulled yourself along the floor with your hands and forearms while they continued to beat you across your back and legs. If you didn't scream, "I'm a punk, a faggot and a motherfucker" for everyone to hear, they'd feel cheated and indignant. This is the point where many kids, 16 or 17 years old, could get their heads split open, crying not from the pain but from the unbelievable humiliation. I was in the box on a number of occasions when this took place, and cried like a baby every time I was forced to watch it. If you didn't watch, you were forced to join them out there.

The kids that were really hurt seriously were sent to Mattawan State Mental Hospital. This was Mattawan in the fifties, where they were killing a dozen guys a year or more! Their excuse: you either cracked up or had a terrible fall.

The same low-life captains, lieutenants and sergeants of fifteen years ago are now the diplomatic wardens of our prison system today. Out of that one sadistic crew at Coxsackie, three are wardens today: Captain Follette, Captain LaVallee and Sergeant Fritz. I would bet that they are proud and their families are proud of how they "worked" their way to the top. My God, how they worked!

Around March 1958, many of the guys who had been in Coxsackie for two years or more were shipped out because the administration (Capt. Follette) felt we were a bad example for the "new jacks," together with the fact that we owned "pads" in the yard. About two hundred guys were shipped out to different places: Auburn, Green Haven, Attica, etc.

***

Napanoch - 1958

Six other guys and myself were sent to Napanoch, a joint for "retard" criminals (they used to say for slower men). Most of them had "one day to life" sentences for bullshit beefs, but these cats were really insane. They had all kinds of bugs there--you name it! They told us when we got there that they were changing the place into a regular reformatory and that we just happened to be the first shipment of "regular" guys to come. A lot of these sick bastards were "asshole bandits" and just loved young kids.

My friend Hurley (a black dude) knocked one out cold and we weren't in the joint an hour yet! We quickly forgot our Coxsackie prejudices and agreed that we would stick together in this joint at least until others came and the joint got normal. Because, frankly, 90 percent of these guys, white and black, weren't playing with a full deck.

I was assigned to a machine shop and wasn't there a half-hour when this dude slid up on me (obviously these guys thought we were "green" and came right off the streets) with the works: candy bars, magazines, etc. Usually if a cat accepted, well, that was it--get ready to wear a skirt.

I was really smoking mad and just smiled when he gave it to me. I even thanked him. I was not only going to take his shit and eat it, too, I planned to take his fucking life! I probably could have got to this dude with my hands, but I wanted to kill him. He was a happy cocksucker, just grinning and winking at me.

I could see all those other vultures in the shop just waiting to see where I was. This dude slid over to me and whispered, "Dig, Baby, you want to come out back and help me shovel the platform?"

"Yeah, all right," I said innocently. "You go on out, I got to put my galoshes and stuff, okay?"

"Sure, Baby," his confidence and anxiety mounting. "I'll get the shovels."

As soon as the door shut behind him, I went to my locker and put on my jacket. There were pieces of pipe laying all over the shop all solid steel and different sizes. I grabbed one about a foot long and stuck it in my belt beneath my jacket. I had never hit anyone with a weapon like this before and I really didn't give it too much thought because it was no more than his hand called for. I walked out of the shop into the Carpenter Shop, pausing momentarily to look out the window. He was at the far end of the platform shoveling off the heavy drifts that began to pile up. Still facing the window, I took my jacket off and brought it in front of me, sliding the pipe out and into the jacket. I tucked it under my left arm and stepped out the door onto the platform. He made it easy for me because he had on some kind of cloth earmuffs and never heard me walk up on him until I spoke.

"Hey!" I called in a normal tone. When he spun his head, he still never got the chance for it to register who or what hit him. I drove the pipe down on his head with terrible hatred and his whole face seemed to burst open before my very eyes. His body hit the snowdrift with a soft thud and he didn't move. In a matter of seconds it seemed that the whole platform was red. I threw the pipe into a snow bank alongside the building and walked back inside. He was still in the hospital when I went home about five months later. I was nineteen years old.

***

1958 - 19 Years Old

This was indeed a strange world to me. People smiled at you only with the outer surface of their beings, expecting me to do the same to "get along" in the world. "Inside" I had learned what was expected of me and what to expect. Out in the world, things were moving too fast for me. Go to work! Get that dollar! Get that dollar, that's all that counts in this life!! "FUCK THAT DOLLAR!!" is what I felt after blowing three jobs in a period of eight days. All three were factory jobs and besides the fact that I couldn't stand being inside, the bastards wanted my fucking soul for fifty dollars a week sweeping floors, folding boxes, etc.

On this one job, I had to clean the bathroom at the end of the day and I felt so embarrassed that I would lock myself in the maintenance room until I knew all the young girls had left. Only then would I slide out of the room with my mops, pail, and toilet brush, etc. I was doing all right though. I felt proud that I was working four days already. A record! I was cleaning the shit bowls with the toilet brush when the foreman came in. A small, weasel-type of man who had been exerting his authority on me since I started but somehow I managed a smile on each occasion figuring he'd see I wasn't a wise guy and lighten up on me.

What I didn't know until some time later was that this guy knew I had done "time" and he didn't feel I had a right to work amongst good normal people. I guess he took it upon himself to play St. George and slay the dragon. "What are you doing, Sullivan?" he asked his foreman's voice, standing over me while I was on one knee. This rotten fucking creep! What am I doing? Why am I taking this crap for fifty dollars a week? Fuck the pay! Why am I taking it all? I smiled inwardly, having reached my decision. Fuck it; let me see just how this guy would push me even if I did try to be nice.

"I'm cleaning the toilet bowls, Mr. Carlton," I said nicely.

"I can see that," he snapped.

"How the hell do you ever expect to get them clean with that thing?" He pointed to the toilet brush in my hand.

"They don't look bad and besides, I'm doing the best I can on them." I could see his sick fucking mind working and- yep! He went over to the cabinet where the steel wool and Lava soap were kept.

"Now, mister, we'll get them like they should be, just rub a little of this on and use a little elbow grease, kid!" He extended the stuff toward me and I felt like I was going to faint from the burning anger and humiliation. My head was pounding and every muscle in my body was coiled, but I was still smiling.

"I never did it that way before, Mr. Carlton, show me how its done!" I whispered viciously with all the venom and contempt I felt for him.

"W--what--," he stuttered. "Who do you think you're talking to?" At the same time, he was looking over his shoulder to see if the door was still in the same place. I jumped between him and the door.

"What's *wrong* with you?" he quivered, his eyes getting as big as saucers. I threw the steel wool at his feet.

"You're what's wrong with me, tough guy, now get in the shit bowl!!!" I screamed.

"G-Get in w-what, h-how?" he whimpered.

"Get in there just like you wanted me to get in there." I said.

"N-No, I-I won't do it--I--"

BANG! I caught him right on the point of his chin and he went down like a shot! The second he hit the floor; he was scurrying on his hands and knees for the shit bowls.

"W-which --o-one?" He gasped looking at me, horrified. I remembered seeing a wedding band on his finger and asked him, "What would your wife think of this, mister?" This ripped him apart and great wracking sobs tore loose from deep inside him. With all this, my anger subsided and I truly felt a deep pity for him and disgust with myself for allowing him to bring me to such a level because his shame was also my own. I walked over to him. I wanted him to get up and hit me. At least it would justify my action a little bit! He just sat there, quietly, his body convulsing as if in great physical pain.

"I'm sorry, Mr. Carlton," I offered pitifully.

"Th-that's a-all right," he managed to get out wheezingly.

"Y-You were right!" he said. I understood that he felt he deserved this. But, he didn't. Yes, he tried to humiliate me but the difference was that I could have walked away from him, even quit as I had planned to do in any event, but I didn't give him a chance to walk a way with his dignity.

"No, I wasn't right, Mr. Carlton," I said more to myself than to him. "I would like my four days pay in the morning if it's all right?" I couldn't even look at him.

"Yes, of course." He said it quietly, not in fear but in the voice of the person he really was. Not the voice of the petty tyrant foreman or of the job he had become, but that of a basically good man. I knew this but at nineteen, I didn't want to believe there were good people. Maybe this way of thinking made me sleep easier at night. I don't know.

About three days after this incident, I got a phone call from a boyhood friend of mine named Blackie. My mother and sister implored me not to meet him since they felt he had a great deal of influence over me in my younger years (he did). I just brushed it aside saying something like I was nineteen years old now and that he didn't do my thinking for me. So I thought! I met him that night in a bar after not seeing him for about five years. He was only two years older than myself but already looked like he was in his early thirties. I had a beer with him and eventually he gave me the pitch. He had just come out of Bellevue after a thirty day drying up period from alcohol. I found out later that he was using drugs. Since they don't usually mix, I figured he had been kicking a habit and he still looked strung out at the time. He went on to tell me that he was facing two charges for "sale" of heroin.

"What did you want to see me for, Blackie?" I asked suspiciously but still the sucker.

"Damn, Sully we've been friends since we were kids, you're the only friend I've got!! When you were up there in Coxsackie, I wrote ya. Didn't you get my letters? I even tried to get in, but they wouldn't let me. Did ya think I forgot about you?" He asked, looking hurt that I would even think such a thing!

"I never got no letters Blackie. I never heard nothing about you trying to visit!"

"You know how they are, Sully," he said. He knew all my weak spots.

"Yeah, I guess so," I said, starting to go on the defensive, feeling I owed him a great debt.

"What did you want from me, Blackie?"

"I didn't want nothing, Sully, I just wanted you to come with me," he said.

"Go with you where? What for?" I thought of my mother and sister and how hurt they could feel if they could see what I was allowing him to do.

"Puerto Rico, out West, anywhere. I'll get a lot of time if I stay in New York. You got to go with me Sully, I don't want to go by myself."

This was the first time I had ever seen the weak side of him and I felt uncomfortable seeing him in this position.

"I ain't got no money, clothes, nothing! How are we going to travel anywhere?" I finished. He laughed at this and waved it aside.

"Don't worry," he laughed. "I got the bread and you're the same size as me, you can wear my clothes." I was really impressed. Little did I know the suit on his back was the only one he owned and that it was stolen.

"When did you want to leave, Blackie?" I asked anxiously with visions of Texas, ranches, and rodeos dancing in my head.

"Tomorrow morning, come over to my house and we'll leave from there, O.K.?"

I left without telling my mother, sister or my girl, all of whom I loved dearly. I didn't want to leave but I left! Who was I trying to hurt? Them or myself? Was I trying to hurt them because they did love me or because I was afraid to love them? There was no money. There was no fancy suits. He told me he had put all the stuff in the lockers in the bus station and that everything was stolen. I knew this was bullshit but I still went with him. I was the one that was really running away, from myself! We hitch-hiked from New York to California to Las Vegas and on to Cheyenne, Wyoming where we were finally stopped. I hurt many people along the way and it is a virtual nightmare to remember, no less describe.

***
Cheyenne, Wyoming - 1958

We were picked up in Cheyenne because Blackie was almost a double for some guy wanted for bank jobs in Canada. When the F.B.I. and sheriff's men converged on us, we were sitting in the Greyhound Bus station. It was about twenty degrees below in November 1958, during one of the worst blizzards ever to hit Wyoming. Even the cattle froze to death standing up straight. When they snatched hold of me, I was sitting on a bench with a Smith and Wesson .38, a hammer, and a bread knife; all in a small airline bag. We were taken to the Cheyenne County Jail and after they found out that Blackie wasn't the notorious bank robber they were looking for, they sent out for information on us.

We were put in different bullpens. I was put in a pen that I thought was on the second floor since they brought me up a flight from where we were finger printed. Blackie remained downstairs. A single guard walked me down a corridor to my cell, we went through one door (unlocked) then another about ten yards further away. As I stepped through this door, directly ahead of me about fifteen yards was a big picture window without bars on it, but it was so dark out I couldn't see a thing. The cell was to my left as soon as I stepped through this door.

"We'll be taking you out again in about a half hour for questioning, you eat yet?" he asked me locking the cell door.

"No, sir." I replied.

"All right, I'll try to get something, I can't promise it though!"

"Thank you officer" I said and meant it. He left closing the door, the outer one too. As soon as I heard it close, I jumped on the bars like a monkey trying to see out the window and still couldn't see a thing. Right below the windowsill was a steam radiator that jutted out from the wall. It was actually level with the windowsill and the bottom of the sill was about six feet from the ground. Shit, with a running start I could grab hold of that radiator, tuck my head on my chest and go through the window; sailor style with my hands at my sides. I gotta get a good pull on that radiator though to get completely through it. I'd sure hate to get hung up half way through. This has to be the second floor I thought, so when I get clear of the window, I'll have enough time to straighten my body up and land on my feet. With all that snow out there, I can't hurt myself.

All during the brief interrogation, my mind was on that window. When they started to slap me around, my mind was still on the window. I just got out only a month ago, and wasn't ready for more time. In New

York you could get a pound (five years) for a gun charge. God knows what they give out here. Good, same thing! One guard, no handcuffs. This dude's pretty young, good shape too, no big belly which is usually the trademark of New York City cops and detectives. He probably can move. I'll have to get a good jump! I walked down the narrow corridor with the guard right on my ass. He went through the first door and approached the second. As I reached for the doorknob, I took a deep breath and started pulling it open slowly, then in one quick motion stepping inside on the run, slamming the door and eyeing the radiator as I burst toward the window, it felt good. I had gotten off quickly and had built up good speed for so short distance. I hit the top of the radiator, grabbing with both hands propelling my body into what I had thought was regular window glass, it was not. It was plate glass, the type used on cars. That was my first surprise! When my head hit the window, I was knocked half-unconscious by the impact. I felt a great burning sensation as the sides of the window cut into my arms that were down against my sides but I went completely through. My second dismaying surprise was to find out that I was not on the second floor, but the first, and the bottom of the windowsill was at ground level. And there wasn't even snow on the ground, because it was the front of the building and had just been shoveled. I must have slid along on the concrete on my face quite some ways because it took the skin off my forehead, nose and chin almost to the bone (which took almost two years to heal up). Between the impact of that plate glass and riding that cement on my mug, I felt someone had hit me in the face with a flamethrower. I couldn't see with all the blood in my eyes, and I really wasn't conscious but somehow managed to get to my feet and tried to run. What I was actually doing was staggering around in circles on the main street. If it hadn't been for the snow, which made the traffic crawl, I'd have really run into something. I heard the horns blaring and saw the lights, but didn't know what they were doing.

Then I was being tackled and felt the handcuffs being snapped on my wrists before I passed out. I woke up in the hospital about two hours later with my head wrapped like a mummy. I got stitches in my arms, hearing doctors and nurses whispering, "poor kid, must have cracked up" or, "he's definitely insane." After talking to a few psychiatrists and narrowly missing being sent to the funny farm, about four sheriff's men took me back to the County Jail. They didn't have four guards with me for security, they were there to make sure I didn't try to kill myself again. They really believed this and I wasn't about to say differently. They put me back in the same cell. The only thing that appeared wrong with the window was that it had what looked to be a large, perfectly round bullet hole in it. The rest of the glass wasn't even cracked. How I ever went clearly through it I'll never know. At 9:30 that morning, I went before the judge. The vagrancy charge was dismissed and when he sentenced me for carrying a concealed weapon and gave me 22 days, I almost fainted. For 22 days I almost killed myself! You were allowed to have guns out there; the only offense was if you concealed them. The Feds took Blackie back to New York after the third day.

I didn't want to leave that warm jail, but they threw me out into the sub-zero Wyoming weather with seven cents in my pocket, an old army field jacket five sizes too big, a big cowboy hat two sizes too big and a pair of high top work shoes size 11 (I wear size 9)! My whole face was one big scab, still oozing with pus. I must have been a fucked up mess (there were no mirrors in the bull-pen), because when I stopped a few people to ask for a hand out, they cringed away from me in horror. Even the blood bank refused my blood. I just couldn't get a dollar anywhere. I was just on the verge of throwing a garbage can through a window. I seemed to have two choices; go back to that warm jail or freeze to death. I was only outside for about fifteen minutes and it was that frigid! I was really contemplating that garbage can when I happened to see a guy across the street pointing a finger at me! Join Now!! The sign read, and I was ready to join **anything**! The Army, Navy and Marines got a big kick out of me but said they weren't accepting hospital cases. The Marine recruiter said I looked like I just crawled back from a war zone and that I should go home for R&R. I wasn't about to leave the comfort of that recruiting office on my own free will so I went out and sat on the top step of the steel staircase leading down to the street. I was sitting there beginning to think really evil thoughts when some captain in the Army walked in. He was half way up when he suddenly stopped still in his tracks. After a few minutes of staring at me in wonderment, he burst out laughing and couldn't stop. I really had enough this time.

"What's so funny, mister?" I shouted at him. The laugh disappeared and he came up the steps slowly looking in my eyes until they were level with my own.

"What's wrong, kid?" He asked, and the *way* he asked made all the tiredness from my eyes disappear and the coldness in my brows vanish.

"N-nothing," I muttered weakly.

"Were you trying to join up?" he asked.

"Yeah," I said pitifully "but they wouldn't take me."

He smiled at me and said, "You're really messed up kid. Do you think maybe you scared them?"

"Yeah, I guess so," smiling myself now.

"How old are you?" he asked.

"Nineteen."

"Ever been in trouble?"

"No!" I said instinctively but too quickly.

"Was it anything serious?" he questioned firmly.

"J-just a stolen car, but I was a youthful offender and they said it doesn't count!"

"Everything counts kid, everything!!" he was almost whispering now. "Why do you want to join?"

I just shrugged my shoulders. I was going to lie but I couldn't.

"Cold out there, huh?" He smiled again, and I knew everything was going to be all right. He was the kind of guy I knew couldn't walk away from a person knowing the position he was leaving you in.

"Yeah" I grinned.

"Well, come on, let's go inside and see what we can do."

This guy was really something and he really went out of his way to take care of my needs. He let me take the test two times before I passed. He bought my bus ticket for Denver, Colorado, where I would take three days of physicals, etc. He also gave me meal tickets and a personal letter to some guy in the Mayflower Hotel in Denver. When he was putting me on the bus, I was really choked up and didn't even know how to thank him because I didn't feel I could, properly.

"I really appreciate this, mister!" I said stumbling up the steps of the bus.

"Forget it, kid. I'm glad I could help, you take care of yourself." he called after me. I waved back at him without looking because I knew I would cry.

I passed my physicals and three days later was sent to Fort Carson, Colorado. During the course of calisthenics, I was unable to raise my right arm above my shoulder without a great deal of pain. I was sent to the infirmary. After x-rays, I was informed I had a broken shoulder, which I could only have gotten diving through the window of that jail. Damn!!! It was real sore so I thought it was maybe a bad bruise. I never dreamed it could be busted. I blew about four weeks of basic training. When I was back in the groove again, I had to recycle all over, but not in Fort Carson. I was sent to Fort Hood, Texas. In a matter of three weeks, I grew weary and bored with all the pompous, militaristic bullshit!! But more, I just wanted to see my girl who I left without so much as good-bye.

***
Governors Island, Stockade - 1959

This Army shit was almost as bad as being in jail. It took me three days by bus to reach New York City. Two more days before I was caught and put in the stockade on Governors Island. Immediately upon arrival, it became a challenge. The prisoners in the stockade were used like flunkies for all the First Army Brass (officers) on the Island by washing their cars, windows, mowing their lawns and whatever else their "Little Women" could find for you to do. I was going out of the stockade on these different details for about a week when I had a run in with one of my MP guards. We had been doing some meaningless task outside one of the general's houses. This guy spotted a cigarette butt lying on the lawn. Obviously, it was bothering him very much because he singled me out of about twenty guys.

"Hey, Sullivan, come over here!" he was sitting on a stonewall that marked the boundaries of the properties.

"Yeah, what's happening?" I asked approaching him.

He pointed indifferently to the cigarette lying only a few feet from where he sat.

"Get that butt and strip it. It looks bad," he said with the same indifference.

I knew he couldn't possibly care about any feelings that I might have or he wouldn't act this way so what's the sense of arguing pettily with him. I simply ignored his order.

"WHAT?" he truly appeared stunned that any mortal man might dare defy him. After all, wasn't he a military policeman?

"Are you disobeying an order, Sullivan?" He rose to his full gigantic stature of five and a half feet, with his boots responsible for half of the 140 pounds he was carrying.

"No."

"Then pick up that butt like I ordered," he pointed again.

"My back hurts, sir," I said sarcastically. "I can't bend over. I want to but I just couldn't. It would be too painful," I smiled nastily.

He jumped up in front of me like he was going to rough me up, then had second thoughts and said huffily, "This is the last time you're coming out on a detail, Sullivan! From now on you don't come out of the stockade!! I'll see to that," he roared looking very satisfied with the way he handled the situation. I wanted to tell him what an inconsequential moron he really was but didn't want to push my luck. Well, anyway, I got a good look at the whole island and pretty well mapped my plan for escape. It was early December and the river was ice cold already. If I could get out of the stockade some night and make it down to the dock, I could make it! There were always one of the Governor's Island ferries at the pier, which were not in use, and I could cut loose one of the life preservers. Brooklyn looked to be only two or three hundred yards away and though I was a pretty good swimmer, I knew these waters had three or four different currents. Looking from the dock to my left was Manhattan and South Street where the Staten Island Ferry went out; to the extreme left was the Statue of Liberty.

The stockade itself was a circular bastion dubbed Castle Williams. The walls were giant granite blocks, solid and about four feet thick. The bars were as thick as the barrel of a baseball bat. The walls couldn't have been gotten through with anything short of a jackhammer. It could be gotten over though, but this would be a wasted effort, because of lack of time. I spoke to a few friends of mine who had been in a couple months and who knew the routine much better than I. They told me that the only one they knew who got outside the Castle during the dark hours was the guy who worked in the kitchen. Every morning about 4:30, he wheeled the slop barrels across the compound. When he reached the heavy steeled-barred gate, an MP would come out of the shack just outside the gate and let him through. I watched for about eight consecutive mornings. It was always the same, give or take about five minutes. There were two MPs in the shack, not one. Through another friend, I got a job in the kitchen about three days later. I got pretty tight with the Sergeant there who was my friend's connection for booze, etc. I wanted that job in the potato room and only one guy could be assigned to it. It was a nasty fucking job; cleaning out all those filthy slop pails and mountainous heaps of rotten potato peels, but it was my only sure way out. This guy that had the job was a "known rat" and I didn't want to offer him money, booze or cigarettes for the job because I'd only raise suspicion. The creep looked like he was in perfect health and not about to get sick anytime soon. My friend had a good idea, which I turned down because the outcome would have been the loss of all our jobs. I had no scruples about what my friend figured to do, because the guy was a real piece of shit anyway. He'd rat on his mother for a pack of butts. My friend, Sammy, said this guy cleaned all the potato cans in the potato room once a week, and to really get them clean, he had to use a steam hose. The room was so small that in a matter of minutes it was impossible to see three feet in front of you. Sammy figured he could ease in there and pipe him (hit him in the head with a pipe), leaving the job open for me. When I told him no, he really felt hurt because he really liked the plan.

"Shit, why not? It will work. He'll never see me!!" he wailed. I couldn't help but laugh. Sammy really got indignant.

"I know it will work," I laughed, "but when they can't find the guy that piped him, they'll just get rid of all of us. We're not indispensable, you know. They could get twenty-five guys in ten minutes and teach them all our jobs in five. You know what I mean?"

"You think they'd go that far, Sully, just because one guy gets his head cracked?"

"I know they would," I said.

"So, how are you going to get the job?" "I don't know--just wait and hope the prick dies. Maybe the steam in there will kill him, who knows?"

Unbelievably, three days later the guy was transferred out. I didn't care enough to ask where; all I knew was that he was GONE!! I had no trouble getting the job but I didn't envy the guy a bit. Those garbage cans were so rotten I puked twice the first day. When I had to hose those cans, I'd step outside the room, fill my lungs and dash back inside, hosing them down as quickly as possible. I'd have to repeat this process about twenty times and by the time I'd finished, I was ready for bed. I thought of getting off the Island by getting in the trunk of one of the officer's cars. But once the alert was out, which would be immediately, I couldn't possibly make it. ALL cars would be searched by the MPs who had a station right on the dock, which was the only way off the Island. I had to go in the water. It was the only way. No sense waiting any longer.

It was December and as I walked across the dark quiet compound early that morning, I felt the cold bite right to my bones. The icy winds coming in off the ocean could really get bad at times. Funny, though, I had not thought about the coming winter until that day. I thought about two Spanish guys who took off from a work detail sometime in August and tried to swim across. I got the story from Sammy.

"No shit, Sully," he was saying with disbelief. "These two guys were three quarters of the way across, towards Manhattan, when they ran out of gas. That wasn't bad enough for them. You know what the stupid bastards did, Sully? Can you guess what?" Sammy implored me to answer, his hands out in front of him, palms up and his eyes closed dramatically. Sammy was a real "winner."

"No," I couldn't help laughing, "what did they do?"

Sammy opened his eyes and curled his lips in exasperation, as if what they did personally affronted him. I just waited. "They turned around and tried to come back. MY God! Three quarters of the way across and they're trying to come---SHIT! And they were only a few hundred yards away when they drowned." He just looked at me shaking his head in wonderment.

"They could have made it easily if they had not turned back, huh, Sammy?"

"Yeah, Sully, easily!!!" he said quietly looking me right in the eye.

"You trying to tell me something, Sammy?" I asked, moved by his deep emotion in his eyes, knowing the concern he felt.

"Yeah," he tried to laugh it off, "I just told you."

I was still seeing Sammy's eyes when I opened up the potato room and quickly stripped my clothes off, wondering just how cold the weather would be and if I could take it. It took me two weeks, but I got to the point where I could stand my shower ice cold, forcing myself to stand under it, without moving. After about five minutes, I would be completely numb, but still able to flex my muscles.

Taking the two pounds of margarine I had stashed in the potato peeler, I began to rub my body down from my neck to the soles of my feet. After rubbing most of it in really good, I just spread the rest on for good luck. It wasn't so bad while standing naked but when I put my clothes back on, my skin crawled in disgust. I felt like a big pussy sore that had just been heavily salved and wrapped in gauze. I reached under the potato machine and pulled out a butcher knife. I had taken it the night before from the cabinet. It wouldn't be missed 'til the butchers came to work about 8 o'clock. Ready! I thought opening up the door slightly and staring across the dark gloomy compound. I could see into both the Sergeant and MP's office and the MPs' shack outside the gate. Everything seemed normal, nothing to make me feel they suspected anything. I opened the door completely and laughed silently at my own nervousness. "Fuck them!!" I said loudly and rolled out of the potato room, moving slowly but noisily across the 40 yards I had to cover to reach the gate. Each one of the four cans of slop weighed about 300 pounds so I really had to dig in to move them. The MP came out of the shack when he heard the noise, big key poised in his hand to open the gate. He was a big country-boy type, about the same age as myself with fat healthy red cheeks, and a big 45. on his hip. Shit! He wasn't even going to see me much less get a chance to shoot me!! I was supposed to park the hand truck against the wall just outside the gate and come right back in. They really hawked me with their hands resting on the flaps of their holsters. I never could understand that; by the time they unsnapped the flap over their gun and got it out, it was too late to do anything. Just like a guy getting his first piece of ass, trying to get his gun out through his fly before he came in his anxiety of the prey before him. In both cases, it would make sense to be prepared before the perilous trials of life arrive.

The gate swung open and I rolled through, veering at once to the left, almost pinning the young MP to the wall. He was very alert and extremely quick, jumping and rolling away on the ground. I was off and running. The dry docks were on the other side of the Island, almost three quarters of a mile away. I shot across the airport (used by the brass - only helicopters and light crafts could land here), cutting down on my speed, in case I might need it later. As I approached the lighted area around the PX, I stopped running but kept walking at a fast pace. I heard sirens or whistles being blown. I felt naked and very vulnerable as I walked the lighted area between the commissary (PX) and the dock. My chest was burning and my eyes straining, expecting to hear screeching tires or HALT!! Only about twenty more yards!! I'm gonna make it, I'm gonna make it!! Only ten more yards!! I walked out of the glowing light into the darkness surrounding the docks. Only then did I look back, holding my breath so as not to hear my heart pounding as I listened. Smiling, I knew that the hardest part was yet to come. If I got caught or even shot in the water, it wouldn't be so bad. At least I had the chance to try.

I walked silently across the dock. There were lights on in the wheelhouse of the ferry. I jumped up grasping the wooden railing, pulling myself over and aboard. Lying quietly, I listened. There was no movement and the only noise was the eerie, soft washing sounds of the water lapping against the boat and the great horns of the tugboats somewhere in the harbor. The sounds, the fresh salty air, it was all so peaceful, so relaxing. I wanted to lie on the deck awhile but was brought back to reality by the harsh, bark-like orders from above; up along the sea wall that encircled the island. I crept silently across the deck, pulling the knife from my belt. I cut loose the life preservers, which were tied to the railings. Hooking the preserver in my right arm, I stepped over the railing hesitating momentarily, looking down into the gray, brooding depths, and then springing as far out from the ferry as possible in an arching dive, which sliced the water's icy surface.

Everything stopped!! My heart, my mind!! The sudden shock almost made me lose consciousness. I wanted to get right out, right then! No cold shower was ever like this. I finally surfaced and tried to get my head together. I knew Brooklyn was only a short distance away on my right. But now, submerged in this excruciating water, it was hard to believe there was any such place as Brooklyn out in the darkness. I looked up at the sea hunters spread about fifty yards apart along the top of the wall, but facing inward toward the island, not ever dreaming that I could be in this water. I changed the preserver to my left arm and tried to crawl with my right. It was impossible! The strong current kept sucking me to the left and I was moving away fast. In desperation, I tried to lie on top of the preserver so that I would have both arms free but in doing so, I fell off to the side. My preserver shot away from me and in a matter of seconds was beyond my reach. I was mad and cursing myself for a damn fool but with my anger came a new determination. Turning in the direction of what I believed to be Brooklyn, I put my face in the water and began stroking deep and strong. I felt the heavy weight of my combat boots as I pumped my feet steadily and rhythmically. I knew that as long as I could keep moving, the freezing water would not get to me.

After what must have been at least fifteen minutes, I could feel my strength slowly ebbing from my body. As I continued swimming one slow stroke at a time, I knew that I was drifting at a fast pace and was absolutely unable to prevent it. I no longer had the strength to fight the tide. My shoulders began to knot up. Every muscle in my body was on fire! It's these God damned boots!! They feel like two anvils tied to my feet. If I could only get them off!! It's too late for that now so don't think about them, just kick them once in awhile to keep your legs up. Damn, I feel like I'm getting numb. Are you sure you're just tired? Is the water freezing you up slowly? MORE, Joe! More man!! Damn, I almost fell asleep. Is that possible? Take it easy, just one stroke at a time! Thump! Thump! Thump! What's that? What's going on? Thump! Thump!! THU--, My God! My heart jumped and froze in my chest. Thump!! Thump!! Thump!! All the lights, looks like a   f-err---, It was a ferry!!! Whether it was Staten Island or the Governor's Island, I didn't know. It didn't really matter which one it was. I knew I couldn't possibly swim out of its path. I was too tired and it was coming too fast for that. "Joe! do something, anything!!" my mind screamed. THUMP! THUMP! THUMP!!! Go under water now!! Go deep!! No, wait! let it get a little closer. BOOM! BOOM!! BOOM!! NOW!! NOW!! NOW!! Throwing my head back, I pulled in all the air possible then flipped forward diving, threading, pumping my legs furiously. umph! umph! umph! My legs, the propellers will probably cut them off. Do ferries have propellers? Umph! umph! -- I got to go up! ump! ump! I can't take it no longer, I-I-- need air! I started coming up, UMP! UMP! Putting my hands up over my head, thinking I could help protect my head. You're gonna die, Joe!! You're gonna di--

splash! It's gone-- It's g-gone! I thought stupidly, being rolled about in the wake of choppy waves left behind by the ferry. I expected to hear a Coast Guard boat, figuring someone must have seen me and called the Coast Guard station. This thought only spurred me on to greater efforts. I had to get out of the water fast. I thought of what Sammy told me about those two Spanish boys. No, Sammy, I won't turn back. I've come too far and I'm not thinking about the distance I already covered either!! How long have I been in the water now, an hour, five hours? I just couldn't imagine. I couldn't kick my feet at all anymore and I could barely move my arms. Just when I was seriously beginning to doubt that I had a chance and thinking how nice it would be to just stop this struggling, somebody turned a light on. I could see! It was hazy, a dock no more than sixty feet away! Strength! Where did it come from? I felt like a lion!! The great exhilaration I felt surged through my body. I MADE IT! I wanted to just leap from the water fifty feet away, right onto the dock! I wanted to stand up straight with both fists clenched in the air in victory and scream across to my cold defeated foe left behind. Look! Look! Over here you son-of-a-bitches!! "Yeah," I would have laughed across at them. "Look at me, you smug bastards! I beat you!!" Then I thought again, fuck all that and just get up on the dock. You're not finished yet. You haven't even begun.

Swimming to the dock itself, I tried to wrap my arm around one of the heavy pilings. Every time I'd lock my weary arms around it, they would slowly slide down to the water. The seaweed and muck made me feel like I was tackling a giant eel! Shit, don't drown now! I laughed and leaped up out of the water. I extended my right arm full length, trying to grasp the flat edge of piling supporting the dock at its corners, and came away just a few inches short. I stopped trying for about five minutes, treading the water with as little motion as was needed to stay afloat, and regained some strength to try again. On the first try my fingers caught, my body swinging unsteady, half out of the water. Then bringing my other arm up, gripping and steadying myself, and finally pulling my body up high enough to a point where I could hook the flat surface with my chin. That enabled me to get both my arms up on the dock and pull my body up onto the platform. I laid on the dock blowing and wheezing like a fish out of water in its death throes. I opened my eyes and looked into the clear blue sky above me. It was completely daylight! Still lying on my back, I just rolled my head as I heard movement of what sounded to be some type of construction work. There was nothing happening other than some early birds getting on the job. I watched as three or four guys were throwing planks from about the fifth floor of a project that was going up about a hundred yards away from where I lay. As I got to my feet and started to walk away from the dock area, I figured they must at least have MP cars out on patrol for insurance, in view of the possibility that I did get off the island. I walked faster now with that thought in mind, not even a damn subway around! People started to come out of the woodwork now, rushing for buses, etc. No subway! In my anxiety to get out of the immediate area, I never stopped to think of the picture I presented until the first person approached me on his way to work. He was an elderly man in his sixties and was carrying a lunch bucket, obviously putting in his last few years to retirement.

He was about ten yards away, walking towards me when he suddenly stepped sideways and off into the gutter, looking at me as if I were some kind of freak. He wasn't really looking at me as much as he was at the deadly looking butcher knife. It was still tucked beneath my belt to my surprise. Christ! No wonder he was frightened! What the hell do I look like? I know one thing; I've got to get off the street NOW!!! Suppose that was a cop instead of that old man, then what? That old geezer is probably on the phone right now. I spotted a guy coming out of a diner across the street with what looked like a container in one hand and a bag in the other. I loped across the street keeping the only truck outside the diner between the two of us. As I was a few yards from the truck, I bent down quickly and looked underneath. He was coming this way. It was his truck! My mind spun furiously. I couldn't think. My hand went instinctively to the knife, pulling it out and behind me as the guy came around to the driver's side. Big bastard! I thought, as I stood frozen in front of the cab of the truck. He stopped only a few feet from me, sensing trouble. His eyes, his face, nothing about him showed a sign of fear. "What's up, kid?" he said almost offhandedly, the container and bag still in front of him; never did he bat an eye.

"I need a ride, mister," I said in the same matter of fact voice with its shoddily veiled threat.

"That ain't necessary, kid." He spoke softly, poking his chin out to indicate he knew I had some sort of a weapon. He still held the container and bag, not trembling, nothing. This guy didn't have a nerve in this body.

"Alright!" I said, putting the knife inside my shirt this time.

"That's better," he smiled and shook his head. "Get in the cab."

"Thanks, mister." I answered happily and wasted no time getting in there. He came in right behind me, handing me the bag and container as he climbed abroad.

"There's some donuts in the bag. Drink the coffee too. It's good and hot. You need it."

"I'm alright," I started to protest.

"Never mind the crap, drink the coffee before you freeze to death!" he ordered, his voice harsh but caring.

What a rotten, sick feeling I had. I didn't like to think that I possibly could have hurt a guy like this! He leaned back in the seat, eyeing me as I sipped the steaming coffee. I was beginning to feel warm again. He had also turned the heater on full blast.

"Where'd you come from, kid? The island?" he pointed off toward the water.

"Yeah!" I mumbled, not looking at him.

"You swam off there?" he asked in amazement.

"Yeah."

"With those big ass boots on?" he shook his head in amazement, laughing now. His humor was contagious.

"Well they didn't help matters any. I just forgot to take them off." I smiled back at him.

"Lucky you didn't freeze your balls off. How the hell did you stand it?" He questioned good-naturedly.

"I didn't stand it. I just got numb after awhile, I guess."

His face became serious all of a sudden. I thought something was wrong.

"Can I ask you a personal question, kid? I don't mean to be nosy--" he said very soberly. His quick change surprised me.

"That's alright, I don't mind mister, what is it?"

"Why did you do such a thing? What made you take such a risk? Were things that bad?" He asked, his eyes seeming to be looking right through me.

I was really tongue-tied. Why did I take such a risk? I mean REALLY WHY? I just looked at him, feeling I owed him some kind of explanation. I didn't want to bullshit him though as I have so many other people in the past. He's a REAL person. The kind I could respect, maybe even listen to.

"I don't know, mister." He just stared at me.

"Really, I don't know." I said, dropping my eyes from his penetrating stare. I hated pity and I didn't want that to start.

"I believe you, kid," he said softly, patting my shoulder.

"Where do you want to go?" He laughed again with suddenness and released the brakes and started the motor.

"I'd like to get to East New York, Broadway Junction. Do you--?"

"Yep, we're on our way." He yelled jovially, over the roar of the motor.

Neither of us spoke the whole way. I thought it strange how people draw within themselves when confronted with something they can't understand. I would have liked to ask him what he was thinking, maybe he could help me to understand, but he looked so far away. He pulled the big trailer right outside the entrance to the subway. As I was about to get out, he motioned me back and coming out of his pocket with a roll of bills, he peeled off two tens, saying emotionally, "I wish you luck, kid. Next time I meet you in Manhattan, I hope the conditions are different." He stuck out his big hand, grasping mine till I thought it was surely broken. "Be good, huh kid?" he whispered.

"I will mister, and --uh--t-thanks." I offered, feeling embarrassed as I thought of how we met.

I shot down into the subway and onto the train, suffering under the contemptuous and pitying stares of the early morning riders. I ran the six block distance to my house and went in through the cellar door, which was always open. My brother Jerry was the only one awake. My sister, Ellen had already gone to work. Damn!! I needed a few dollars, at least. Jerry didn't have any but he got me clothes to wear and fixed me something to eat. I didn't waste anytime in the house. They would be coming here any minute.

"What happened, Joe?" my brother asked as he watched me wolf down the food. He was only about thirteen at the time and really in awe of it all.

"I escaped. I swam off the island!!'

"WOW!" he laughed.

"Listen, Jerry, I gotta get outta here. If anybody comes, you haven't seen me, O.K.?"

"Yeah, Joe, you know I won't say nothing."

"Damn, I need some money," I was talking more to myself than him.

"I-I haven't got any," he said, feeling hurt, as if he had let me down.

"I know you don't Jerry, what time does Ellen get home from work?"

"Usually about five o'clock Joe, but she don't have much."

"I know, all I need is a few dollars. What train does she come home on, do you know?"

"Oh, yeah," he was glad to help, "she gets off at Liberty Avenue."

"Which way does she walk home?" I asked.

"Gee, I'm not sure, Joe. I met her a few times and we always walked down Woodhaven Boulevard to Atlantic Avenue."

"Thanks, Jerry, I gotta go. I'll see ya. OK?" I loved this kid. He was so tough but yet so wide openly honest. Nothing sneaky about him. My being the oldest brother, he had always looked up to me. At times, I felt ashamed that he did because I was his idol to some degree and I knew I was not worthy of the trust and love he placed in me. I never told him anything that I thought would be harmful to him; I also never gave him any constructive advice either. Just, "Be tough! Fight! Don't ever let nobody walk over you!" He never did!! He would have fought a gorilla as long as I was standing there, and beat him too! Why couldn't I have banged better things into his head like, "Go to school, Jerry! Learn! Don't quit." This is the way I should have taught him to fight. But I didn't. Only because I was too young and foolish to know that this was the right way. The only way. I'm sorry Jerry. For both of us. But, we must keep striving ahead. It is not too late. It's never too late!

"I'll see you, Joe," he mumbled, looking very confused and worried about me.

"Don't worry, I'll be alright!" I said, laughing and feigning like I was gonna throw a punch. We used to have some real playful rumbles together and even at thirteen he was strong as a bull. Since he thought I was unbeatable, I always played the part, even under the worst of conditions. Like the time he charged me with his head down, catching me high in the middle of the chest. Instantly, upon contact, I thought I heard the bones crack. Holy Christ! He had me, flipping me to the ground. I just lay there about five seconds, fighting unconsciousness, trying to draw air into my lungs. Jerry was still squeezing me in a head lock till I thought my eyes would pop out of their sockets like grapes from their skins.

"C'mon, Joe! This ain't no fun. You always let me win!" he moaned.

"Yeah, heh! Heh!" I laughed feebly. I could almost open my eyes now, which had been closed tightly in pain. The little bastard almost killed me, I thought. I still had a hard time breathing three months later and had pains in my chest for about a year. I left him standing there, as I did so many times before, feeling sorry for myself. I didn't belong in that house anyway!

***

Forest Park, Queens, N.Y.

Since I had about seven hours to wait before I could meet my sister,

I walked up to Forest Park where I always went as a kid whenever I ran away from home or any other place. There was a giant crater, which was now all dried up and dead looking. It was once a pretty pond where all the kids used to go fishing for cat fish or guppies along the pond's edge with their mother's strainer. Mom used to have the cloth-type strainer. It really worked well because the guppies wouldn't pop back out as they did with the shallow metal ones. I always managed to get it cleaned (those guppies really smelled) and back in the kitchen cabinet before it would be needed the following morning. I sat on the embankment that surrounded this moon-like crater. I recall the strange sense of loss I felt looking down on that empty space that was slowly beginning to fill up with broken bottles, cans, and all types of garbage. What happened to all the water? What became of all the guppies and catfish? Why must everything change? Why does everything have to die? I thought of my father who, at thirteen, I had just begun to know and emulate. He was still a young man and the best looking man in the whole neighborhood. He wasn't old! Why didn't nobody else's father die? It all happened so fast. It seemed like only a month before we were supposed to go to Yankee Stadium but he got sick and couldn't go. I didn't feel too bad because he told me there would be plenty of other times, "You just wait!" I never thought of people dying, especially my father who, in my mind, was the closest thing to Superman that there was. I never even thought about death, so how was I to know it was a serious thing?

***

13 Years Old - 1952 Parochial School

About two weeks after my father got a "little sick", I was playing baseball in a vacant lot across from St. Elizabeth's, where I attended grammar school. It was supposed to be my turn to bat next, so I was really upset and embarrassed when I heard my mother call my name. I wanted to run up to the plate quickly and get my swings, but when Mom spoke in authority everything was dropped.

"Joseph, come over here!" She commanded, leaving no doubt in my mind that she meant NOW!

"Aw, Mom--" I started to protest, but when I looked up and saw that tears were coming from her eyes I was speechless. I never saw my mother cry before.

"What's wrong, Mom?" I asked, feeling so helpless standing before her, watching her cry.

"What's wrong?" she hissed. "Well, I'm glad you're happy and enjoying yourself, because while you're here playing baseball your father is in the hospital in critical condition!" she barked and walked away.

"T-Tommy, what's a critical condition m-mean?"

"I don't know, Joey! Hey, you gonna bat? It's getting late!"

"Y'yeah, yeah!" I began when I saw Sister Eugene Catherine leaving the convent across the street from the empty lot where we played baseball and head for the side door of St. Elizabeth's Church. This led into the sacristy where I had spent many hours the past four years as an altar boy, laying out the priests' vestments and preparing the altar for Mass, which was said in Latin in those years.

"Sister Eugene!" I cried out, dropping the bat and dashing across the street and down the alleyway between the school and rectory. The St. Elizabeth complex of church, school, rectory and convent was laid out to form a perfect square; the church and school facing Atlantic Avenue in Ozone Park; the convent and rectory directly in the rear of each.

Sister Eugene instinctively opened her arms and I ducked within their welcome embrace, burying my face between the soft warmth of her breasts, smelling the clean black and white linen habit I had come to associate with love and safety for the past two years.

"Hush now, Joseph. Hush." she cooed, rocking me gently to that soft melodic voice that had first attracted me to her, and with which she led our choir so adroitly. A humming bird's voice, which I've never heard, duplicated, but I am reminded of each time I hear Anne Murray sing "Snowbird."

I had fallen in love with Sister Eugene. After six years of poor marks and daily fist fights after school in the lot across the street, I suddenly became an altar boy in her class, the 6th and 7th grades. I also became, in her words, "her little lover" in a very real sense. And even now, so many years later, I do not speak in hypocritical indignation or condemnation of Sister Eugene's action, but solely with warmth and a lasting affection for the moments we shared together. If anything, I can now better understand the "needs" of a healthy, beautiful woman in her early thirties in conflict with her natural, physical, and human proclivities, while trying desperately to adhere to the vows of an unnatural vocation, made so by man. I have never believed that loving another person or oneself is in conflict with ones' love for ones' Creator. For such union was the very purpose of our creation as separate and unique genders. Any man or woman can serve God's children without such unnatural sacrifice being imposed upon them in this day of enlightenment--as can be attested to by the decimated pool of girls for sisterhood, and the given fact that priesthood has become a vocation where latent homosexuals can ply

their assorted deviations behind the guise of "The Cloth," particularly
on unsuspecting young boys in awe of their god-like authority. Marriage
would alleviate the need for perfectly decent young men and women to
fulfill their worldly needs of the flesh by having to sneak about in the
shadow like some leper or religious felon.

Personally, I would scoff at the thought of some who would think
I was taken unfair advantage of due to my still-tender age. At the age
of twelve and thirteen a young boy is in his birth stages of transition to
manhood, and is in search of his own sexuality. This happened to be
a stage in my life when the simple, vibrant humming of a bus ride or
a strong wind against my pant's front was sufficient to induce lasting,
painful erections that I needed to work off, whether it was by mounting
and rubbing against a pillow in the dark of night until I experienced that
frightening but glorious release, or by rubbing myself against a table,
doorknob or whatever was available. So I was not exactly a wide-eyed
hayseed to my dilemma. And if I was a "victim," I was certainly as happy
as a pig in shit to be one!

I had always been the "class clown," shooting spitballs and pulling the
hair of the girls seated in front of me. I was a sharpshooter when it came
to hitting kids in the ass with my rubber band and paper clips while they
were working on the blackboard and the sister's head was momentarily
turned. The normal punitive measure for such an infraction of the rules
was to have a kid stand in the corner of the classroom, facing the wall,
for hours. But even when I was caught red-handed and accorded this
punishment, Sister Eugene saw how I continued to disrupt the class by
making faces or sticking my tongue out at the girls and boys, who were
giggling at my predicament. She wasn't having any of this and ordered
me to get under the opening of the huge oak desk, at which she sat facing
the class and that had a completely closed front that settled on the plank
wooden floor.

"I'm not going to--" I started to protest, until I saw the angry glint
in her eyes. I scurried like a little rodent to obey. Having been raised in
a strict Catholic family, I dare not go home with a report stating I had
disobeyed or been disrespectful to a nun. I'd have been better off running
away from home, or simply placing a gun to my head and getting it over
with quickly. In my parent's eyes, it would have been as much a sacrilege
as spitting in God's face!

Sitting in the semi-darkness with my back against the inside of the
wooden desk-front, I was pondering my latest debacle when to my
dismay, shock, and finally petrified fright, I saw Sister Eugene, from the

waist down, standing in front of me, gather her black habit and rosary beads in her hands, lifting them to just below the knees, before she sat down and pulled herself and the chair beneath the desk. What nice legs, I thought. And that was my last thought before scuttling backward in stark horror, away from the sacred relics, mashed back against the desk-front, knees tightly drawn up under my chin. "Oh my God! Oh shit!!" my mind screamed.

I moaned softly in pain fifteen minutes later, just knowing my spine would snap like a piece of peanut brittle if I held this excruciating position a moment longer! Finally, I dare to slide my ass forward on the splintery floor to take some of the weight off my lower back.

"Joseph!" came the sharp authoritarian voice from heaven above. "Stop moving around under there, be still!" This, of course, brought a titter of laughter from the kids who cruelly revel in the humiliation of others.

"Sons-a-bitches," I cursed under my breath. "I'll get you." I vowed silently, groggily, before my head fell forward on Sister Eugene's lap in a dead sleep, my arms unknowingly wrapped around her black cotton-clad legs.

I could have barely been asleep minutes when I awoke in a state of arousal, thanks to the feather-like touch of Sister Eugene's hand who's fingers ran gently through my hair and caressed my neck and face in a symphony of erotic delight. My cheek lie shockingly against the warm velvety softness of her inner-thigh, chin resting on the roll of cotton just inches above her knee, secured in place by an elastic garter. Breathlessly, I did not flinch or move away from her loving touch, instead, shivering in this sweet agony of sexual awakening, reacted instinctively upon smelling the unique essence of a woman and paid homage to my exotic antagonist by kissing and licking her thighs in the ancient rote inbred in man. My heart beat wildly as I dared to slide my hands beneath her hiked up gown, feeling her wiggle to give my hands access to her full soft buttocks which I clung to like a drowning man and kneaded in rhythm to my lips that worked like some carnivorous animal against the moist fragrant mound of her cotton-encased vagina. My body went perfectly still in wonder as Sister Eugene's hands clasped tightly behind my head and her body began to twitch convulsively lasting only a few short moments, then suddenly pushing me away and lowering her gown at the same time. Sitting frightened once again I listened to the hoarse voice of a stranger dismiss the children for lunch hour.

"I-I think you've been under there long enough Joseph, you may come out!" She said, though in a not unkindly manner as she pushed away from the desk, and allowed me to stagger from my cave into the bright, blinding light of the classroom, aware of the sticky wetness in my pants.

"I-uh .. Sister E-Eugene--" I was tongue tied.

"It's alright Joseph," she whispered softly, her back to me as she wrote on the blackboard. "Thank you -- but I hope this will be our secret".

"S-Sure, Sister Eugene ---I--I would nev--- Yes! Its our secret." I vowed and wanted to add, "I love you Sister Eugene," but just stumbled out of the classroom, and school, into a seemingly less mysterious world.

For the next few weeks, Sister Eugene barely spoke to me, unless it was in direct relation to a study lesson. I didn't look at her for fear she could read lascivious thoughts! But my manner in the classroom became more subdued and studious, which the other kids attributed to my recent humiliation. A lesson learned, etc.

One afternoon in the schoolyard, situated between the church and school, Sister Eugene approached and beckoned me from where I was standing with my friends. Her eyes were a deep blue-green, I first noticed, beneath silky eyebrows of strawberry-blonde. Her sharp features would have been patrician were it not for the full blown, sharply defined lips of her mouth that exposed the white pearls of her perfect teeth when she smiled.

"Joseph, are you listening to me?" she smiled coyly. I thought how she would always be my favorite "penguin," an affectionate nickname for sisters of the Dominican order, due to their black and white habits.

"I said," she continued, "that I was talking to your mother (my heart flipped) yesterday, and she was telling me you had a wonderful voice-- which you never told me. I had hopes that you might give consideration to joining our choir group. Would you, Joseph?"

"Gee, Sister Eugene." I blushed, "I don't know. I'd love to, but with my Sunday Masses, sometimes morning Masses, and now 'The Stations of the Cross' during Lent, I--I don't know how I--"

"Well," she interrupted, "I'll just have to speak with the Monsignor! We have more than enough altar boys, but far too few good voices in our choir! What do you think, Joseph?" she smiled, melting me completely.

"Yeah," I beamed, "I'd like that!"

"Good, it's settled! Practices are Mondays, Wednesdays and Fridays in the choir loft."

I had always had a pretty good falsetto tenor voice as a young boy, and sang such Irish songs as "Danny Boy" and "My Wild Irish Rose" whenever we had a family gathering for the holidays and other occasions. That is, until my voice changed at seventeen years of age and I awoke one morning with the sound of a frog emanating from my throat, my boyhood behind me.

So at that earlier stage of my life, I became the proud star of Sister Eugene's popularly acclaimed choir, singing not only with the choir for Sunday Mass but singing solo from atop the choir loft, while she accompanied me at the organ. I could really hit and hold the notes in those days. I especially loved midnight mass on Christmas Eve, my highlight being when I was given the chance to sing my two favorite songs; "Our Father," having been a great admirer of Mario Lanza, and "O Come All Ye Faithful," which I would sing in Latin as "Adeste Fidelis". Both songs gave me goose-bumps and I derived a great deal of spiritual gratification whenever I felt I had done these beautiful songs a degree of musical justice and such affirmation came solely in a nod or smile of approval from my mentor, Sister Eugene.

During our weekday practices Sister Eugene would run over to the convent and change into her lightweight working smock, with a matching white Arafat type headdress. It only increased her ethereal beauty. After each session with the other boys, she would keep me behind so we could work on my "solos" together in undisturbed harmony after locking the stairwell door, so that the intrusive eyes of the enemy were not offended by our innocent human frailties. To my trembling delight she would shed the headdress and allow me to run my fingers through her choppy reddish-blonde hair as she disrobed me and introduced me to heavens true wonders. But the main course came when would lie back on the thickly carpeted floor of the choir-loft and allow me to feast my eyes on the virtual forest of fiery red pubic hair between her wantonly spread thighs where I bowed and knelt at the altar of her womanhood, and lost all sense of time -- hearing nothing but her keening impassioned pleas and loving praise as we basked in the scented delight of the human body.

But all that, and life as I had known it then, had all come to an end with my mothers foreboding words. "Your father is in critical condition."

"You must be strong Joseph -- for God has his reason for the life he gives us -- just as he does when he chooses to bring us back home to his kingdom." Sister Eugene whispered softly, holding me tightly in the middle of the deserted school yard.

"But -- It isn't fair!" I protested angrily.

"It never is Joseph ... it never is." She sighed. "Maybe everything will turn out alright. But please remember, whatever happens, and wherever you might go in life ... my love and my prayers go with you." She choked, tears running down her beautiful cheeks. "I love you Joseph!"

"A--and I love you, Sister Eugene!" I uttered to my own shock and amazement, before spinning away and running from the schoolyard --- never to see her again. I attempted to do so many years later, only to be told by a new Mother Superior after flipping through pages of a huge log book, that Sister Eugene Catherine had been transferred to an unrecorded location in 1953 -- Just months after I had run from the schoolyard.

***
Forest Park, Queens, N.Y.

Damn! I thought. It's starting to get cold. It must be at least three o'clock by now. My sister Ellen should be coming home from work! I walked up the embankment, stopping at the top, to look down at the fishing hole one more time. Maybe, it will fill up again--Why does everything have to change? Maybe we'll have some rainstorms and it will fill up again. But then I remembered all the fat catfish and thousands of little guppies that used to be there. I realized that even if it did fill up, it would never be the same again... they're gone, and can't come back!!

As I walked down Woodhaven Blvd. to meet my sister, I wondered who was looking for me. I knew the M.P.s would be, but I wasn't worried about them. Most of them were my age and not exactly what one could think of as mental giants, cause if they were, they would have set the ring of M.P.s on the other side of the river as a precautionary measure, and also a Coast Guard boat patrolling the water. If they had either one I couldn't have gotten away. Maybe the C.I.D. will be called in. I don't know what their function is exactly but this could concern them. But I didn't have much respect for them either, knowing what one had to go through just to get a pair of government issued socks. They couldn't be much more progressive in their methods. Besides, I've only been gone about twelve hours and they couldn't possibly have gotten so far in their investigation where they would be thinking of me trying to meet my sister coming home from work. But I better keep my eyes open, just the same.

I was standing on the corner of Jamaica Ave., waiting for the light to change, when out of the corner of my eye, I saw a car suddenly slow down. It was a gray Chevy. The guy in the passenger seat was turned completely around, looking back in my direction, but then it took off again. Was that guy looking at me? There were five or six other people standing behind me, who were waiting for the bus. The car did have an aerial though! Detectives!? No, those fools would have jumped from the car shooting. Anybody they catch, it is rarely through intelligent investigative work, but either through an informer or the criminals own stupidity. So when they set eyes on their prey, the morons go all out; insensitive to any bystanders who are unfortunate enough to be in the line of fire. Knowing in their hearts *this* was it. For due to their lack of training and limited intelligence, on the whole, there was no second chance for them. I shrugged off the bad feeling and kept walking. When I reached Atlantic Ave., I took my position and stood between two garages. From that vantage point, I would be able to see the two possible routes my sister could take. I recognized her when she was still three blocks away, but I didn't want to walk out into the wide-open Boulevard to meet her! When she was only about ten yards away from me, I stepped out in front of her!

"Hi Ellen!" I said as she came up to me.

"Joe, what are you doing around here?" she said immediately. "They're looking for you!" She looked around worriedly in all directions.

"C'mon, take it easy Ellen. Let's walk. Who's looking for me? The M.P.s? Detectives?" I asked, not overly concerned.

"No Joe! I was talking to Mom on the phone from work. Mom told me they were asking all kinds of questions about you. Where you'd go, things like that. T-They even asked about me. They wanted to know what time I got off from work, and..."

"Who were they, Ellen?" I asked. But I already knew. Gray Chevys they all drove them.

"The FBI, Joe. You better go..." It was too late. I turned around just slightly, enough to see the gray Chevy coming up on the inside lane slowly. I felt like I was going to throw up.

"What's wrong, Joe?" Ellen asked worriedly, seeing my features change. Maybe I can still make it. The Feds will let a guy get away before opening fire around innocent people. They know there's a tomorrow for them! But God! Suppose they did fire!

"Get out of here, Ellen, go on home!" I pleaded with my lovely, red-headed sister.

"No!" her lips trembled. "I won't leave you!"

"Alright Ellen, just walk then, everything is gonna be alright." I said as the gray Chevy slowly passed along the curb, coming to a stop about thirty yards ahead. There were four guys inside who never glanced our way. The two guys that I saw in the other car, must be behind us, I thought. Three of the men got out of the car in front of us, as Ellen and I closed the distance to about twenty yards. They waved to the driver as he slowly pulled away. They were laughing and joking with each other. When they were about ten yards away from us, they began to close in, never looking our way! I stopped and stepped away from my sister.

"That's them, Ellen," I nodded. "Please go.."

"Joe," she started...

"Hold it, Sullivan!!" One screamed, as they all rushed toward me with their guns drawn. They grabbed me and, as they lifted me parallel to the ground, they began to frisk me, "He's clean," one spoke as another, snapped the cuffs on me. The second car had pulled right behind us. My heart hurt seeing my sister standing there very frightened for me, crying brokenly.

"I'm alright, Ellen." I tried to comfort her as they were putting me in the car. One of the agents was real decent. When he saw that my sister was completely distraught as she stood on the sidewalk, he got out of the front seat, telling the driver to wait a few minutes, and calmed her down. He assured her that everything would be all right. They were mainly concerned about the whereabouts of the knife, which didn't mean anything to me, so I took them up to Forest Park where they recovered it. They treated me pretty good while they held me in the Federal Building in Manhattan, where I waited for the Army official to come for me. These men left a lasting impression on me. Not so much that of an awed young man, though I did feel a certain admiration. But my impression was one of respect for the dignity with which they carried themselves, and more so the sensitivity they showed toward the few prisoners I watched them escort in and out of the different offices for questioning. No loudmouth bluster, no threats and cursing. No blackjacks sticking out of every pocket or blood stained floors. I thought I was sitting in some Wall Street office; my captors were young college-type executives. They were dangerous just the same, more mentally than physically. They did not ask one question without a well thought out reason for asking it. They won't ask one blunt question for an answer, but instead will ask a hundred seemingly harmless questions, and piece together their own answers and conclusions. I've known quite a few guys who had done Federal time, and they all said the same thing. "Sully, these guys treat you pretty decent, but don't let them engage you in a seemingly routine conversation, even if they only want to talk about the weather!"

As I sat there drinking, a young boyish looking agent walked in. "You're Sullivan, huh?" he asked good naturedly, giving me the once over then sitting down across from me. "You know who's coming for you?"

"No sir...I guess the M.P.s or somebody!"

He laughed, saying, "Not a chance! This calls for a General, kid, you're a celebrity!"

"A-A General?" I stuttered.

"Yep! The whole works." He said becoming serious. "Did you really swim that freezing river, kid?"

"Y-Yes Sir."

"What happened to the life-preserver you took from the boat on the Island side?" he asked, holding me with his steely eyes.

"I-I don't know, I lost it when I first started out on the other side."

"I know!" he laughed again. "We found it."

The dirty bastard, I thought.

"Listen kid, if you decide to do it again, give us a call, okay?" He smiled.

"What for?" I asked not knowing what he was getting at.

"No, No," he threw his hands up, "I don't want to arrest you. I just want to watch you, okay?" he chuckled.

"Yeah, Okay!" I chuckled back.

After all the hullabaloo was over I was escorted down to the waiting cars. Trailing behind me were a General, a Colonel, and three M.P.s. Naturally, I was cuffed. They said they didn't want to cuff me, but felt I still had a lot of "rabbit" in my blood. It was dark as we left the Federal Building, heading for South Street, to get the Governor's Island Ferry. I was just beginning to realize that I was captured and where they were taking me. I was really feeling evil and was already beginning to think of my next escape plan!

"Listen son," the General was speaking in that condescending tone. "It isn't over yet. You can still make a good soldier. The army needs men like you. You've had a good record, other than this incident. I see no reason why we can't straighten this out." He smiled at me looking very proud of himself.

"Sir, I don't want to stay in the army." I said with a politeness that I didn't feel.

"W-What?" he blustered. "Don't you know what we can do with you Boy? Why we...."

"Fuck y-o-u! And fuck the Army, General!!" I hissed glaring into his shocked face.

"That's no way to talk to a Gene," the Colonel began to defensively say.

"Fuck you too! Mister!!" The Colonel raised his hand to slap me.

"Colonel!! This boy is obviously sick!" I think we've said enough," sighed the General.

We rode the rest of the way to the ferry in complete silence. I was feeling very bad for having cursed them out, and worse for not knowing how to apologize to them. They were only trying to help me. But, shit, I said it, didn't I? It's too late to apologize; they would never be able to forget my words. "The hell with it!" I thought.

I was thrown in segregation, which was actually a tin box with a slot in it for food to be passed through. I was up there for about six days when my Sergeant friend from the kitchen came up to see me. He gave me cigarettes and matches, and informed me that I would probably be court-martialed and sent to Leavenworth, the Federal Prison in Kansas. He figured the best thing I could do was "Bug-out" and try to get to a hospital. This way, when they did bring me back, they couldn't try me, that's if I didn't get a discharge from the hospital. About three o'clock that morning, I woke up every living ass on Governor's Island. I set my mattress on fire, smashed the thick glass covering my light bulb. Then commenced kicking on that tin wall, and screaming at the top of my lungs until the building shook. I guess that I would have to be half-a-nut to go through this shit anyway, so I really got in the groove, until *I* believed I was for real. A male nurse came into my cell behind six M.P.s, grunting and cursing, trying to hold me down while the nurse popped me with the needle. They didn't want to hurt me to subdue me, but I could see they were becoming extremely angry.

"Shit, man, just knock the little bastard out!" One of the guys grunted sourly, and that's when I decided to poop out, and let them do their thing!

The following morning, when I woke up, I was immediately taken to the psychologist. I giggled incoherently for the two hours I spent with him. When he got on the phone, whispering low and secretively, smiling at me as I giggled and waved at him from where I sat on the floor in the far corner of his office, I thought I had it made. But when two M.P.s came in and led me out of the office, I figured I had blown my 'screen-test.' "Back to the box." I thought mournfully. But there it was! Sitting right at the curb waiting for me with a long, shiny tan and brown army ambulance. They had me strapped down to a stretcher inside the ambulance in a matter of seconds. I was saying, "Hi, How are you?" to everybody...like I was the Democratic candidate for Mayor of New York. The psychiatrist got into the ambulance and held my hand, and we giggled together like morons all the way to Valley Forge Army Hospital in Pennsylvania.

"Wow," I thought as we rolled up outside the gates to the hospital grounds. This looks like a Country Club! Spacious green lawns, beautiful trees, beautiful army and civilian nurses running around. "This is gonna be alright!" And it was, but giggling to myself every time I heard footsteps, became tiresome real quick. After about thirty days I began to ease out of my "bag" gradually. Unfortunately, the medical personnel began to see through my smoke screen of insanity. One day, I was called before a panel of the Psychiatric Department and deemed sane. They didn't want to give me a medical discharge because that would hold the Army responsible for me. Instead, they decided to give a Bad Conduct Discharge (BCD) and sent me back to Governor's Island to muster out.

***
Attica, 1971 - 9:20 A.M.

A shrill whistle brought me quickly to a crouch from where I lay in the coal pile, protected from view by the railroad tracks that ran in from the rear gate of the prison. Mike wouldn't have whistled unless something was wrong. I watched him bending down as if to tie his shoelaces. What was wrong?

The guard walked out from behind the front of the building and glanced in the direction of the coal pile. I swore he had looked right into my eyes but he kept walking to the gate that led to the yard of the powerhouse. Swinging it shut, he snapped the padlock on it. This gate was supposed to be locked at all times, but since garbage trucks came through pretty regularly it was much easier for the guards to leave it open. They didn't like having to walk from the powerhouse to the gate every time a truck came.

But why lock it today? My mind raced. Do they know something? Did they miss me already and know I'm in here? He's going back inside now. He didn't even glance my way! Nothing about him looks like he's on to something.

Mike was standing up with his broom again, like some cigar store Indian. How long have you been there, Mike, a thousand years? 9:20? . I brought the watch to my ear. It's still working. I could tell that by the second hand. God damn, you're a genius, Sully!

Take it easy, breathe deeply. You've got to be cool, it could be any second now! C'mon, you've got to laugh. What on this earth is worth being serious about? You're 32 years old and haven't lived at all--but you **have** lived. Look at those poor bastards in Vietnam. Kids, seventeen and eighteen years old, getting "whacked out" and never knowing what for. You've lived double their lifespan already, and you're a criminal. Where's the justice in that? Shit!! I'd take one of those kid's place in a hot second. At least I'd have a shot at getting laid before I die.

If the government cared at all about those kids, then why don't they let so-called waste products like us replace them and let those kids live, go to college, marry their childhood sweethearts, and really be "all that they can be"? All they can be in the Army is filler for body bags! But then, I forgot about the black and white hat philosophy, the good guys and bad guys. The so-called "criminal type" isn't supposed to have the courage to fight. Try telling that to a French legionnaire! But, shit, the only way I'd fight in that political war is if they imported it.

Prisons, like drugs, have become a major industry. People have got to have jobs, and need clowns like myself to fill the human warehouses. But those kids, half of 'em, who never had the chance to get laid yet, are expendable pawns to political prostitutes who have dodged the draft themselves and never had a bloody nose in their lives. I'd love to see half those so-called "hawks" (boy killers) on their bony knees, scurrying down Pennsylvania Ave. like the low-life rodents they are. At one time it took a man to speak for his people, but now all it takes is a snake. And the more powerful a politician, the higher he climbs, the bigger snake he is- -nice guys do not have the imbued sense of immorality to compete. As a country we're only holding on desperately now, even the simplest of men and women sense this.

Just think, Joe, if you stayed in the Army you'd probably be dead by now anyway, so this shit here is a small thing. I fought in the battles of Trenton, Rahway, Sing-Sing, Attica, and almost got "iced" (killed) in those places a few times. Some of those naive kids got a better shot of surviving Nam than they would have in these jungles! Jeez! I feel faint... can't even keep my eyes open. "Some tough guy you are, Sully!" I smiled as I drifted away from my immediate plight.

***

Home - 1959

I was home from Valley Forge Army Hospital about a week when I decided it was time to look for a job. I would have liked something in the line of construction work, since the pay is good and I work outdoors most of the time. But I quickly found out that if you don't know anybody, getting into a union was tougher than getting an audience with the Pope.

A friend informed me that "Squibbs" in Brooklyn was hiring, so I shot over there to their employment office and got in line behind two butchers, who must have slept outside the joint overnight to get there that early.

The interviewer was a young black woman about twenty-six, very pretty and soft-spoken. She gave out forms to the two butchers and gave a run-down on how they should be filled out.

"May I help you, sir," she chirped.

"Yes, ma'am, I'm looking for employment," I smiled, thinking that that would automatically win a job by itself. Was I ever mistaken!

"Is there any particular field you have in mind, sir?"

"Yeah, center field," I was tempted to retort, but checked myself. "Uh, what have you got?" I couldn't think of anything better to say, but by her immediate ear-to-ear grin I knew she peeped my whole car. "Another retard," I could hear her thinking.

"Hmmm," she said, playing cat-and mouse now. "Were you thinking of something in the executive department?" she questioned seriously. This bitch must have gone to Vassar or Smith. She sounded like Lady Churchill--the bitch was "out-whiting" me.

"Listen, lady," I quit pretending. All I wanted was a fucking job. "I was thinking of something more in the line of a bucket and mop, a porter's job." Her eyes flitted around the room, pausing momentarily on the offices to her left. I started to understand what the deal was and felt bad about putting her in this uncomfortable position because, behind the bullshit facade she had built around her, she really was a nice person.

"What's wrong, miss," I asked with warmth, letting her see that I had followed her eyes and flashing thoughts.

"Uh, listen, mister," she was talking personal now, down to earth. "About this uh, maintenance wor--"

"Porter's job," I corrected her, smiling.

"Yes, well..." she said, grinning again. "Isn't there something you're... skilled in?" she whispered seriously.

"Well, no!" I laughed. "Just give me one of those forms for a mop and bucket, and I'll work my way to the top of the company!" she didn't laugh.

"I could give you the form, Mr.... uh, Sullivan, but I'd just be wasting your time." She couldn't look at me. I should have stopped, but I was determined to hear it with my own ears.

"Why would I be wasting my time? I need a job. I like to eat. Why should I be different?" She stood up ramrod straight and looked eyeball-to-eyeball, proud, I thought.

"This," she said in disgust, "Company does not like to hire whites for maintenance work if at all possible," she managed to get out quickly. I was seething mad and ready to continue, but I looked into sad eyes that said my feeling of defeat was also her own.

"In other words, your function here is simply to hire porters, your brothers, *for* whitey, huh?"

I should have cut my tongue out at the expression of hurt that was brought to her face by my words.

"I--I'm s-sorry, I didn't mean it to come out like that." I could feel my own eyes beginning to fog up on me. "B-but you're better than those bastards. I just want you to know."

"Thank you," she said, and meant it!

As I turned and was walking away towards the door, feeling a sense of relief to be getting out of the building, my mind was filled with thoughts concerning my brief encounter with that lady. But like everything else that bothers me, I just forced it to the back of my mind. Not out of it, never out of it!

I bought a paper then shot down into the subway for Manhattan. Eighteen West 75th, the paper said in my hand. It was an old address a friend of mine had given me in Coxsackie a year before.

"Don't forget to come see me, Sully, we can do some 'work' together." Burglary was his bag.

"Yeah, all right," I promised, never expecting to see him again.

I was tired of all the job-hunting and the bullshit it entailed. I had only about nine bucks in my pocket and couldn't remember who gave me that. I was tired of all the excuses, too, though my mother and sister never asked me for any. It was for me, I felt so damned useless.

It was one of those old "brownstones" right off Central Park. I rang the doorbell in the vestibule that had his name on it, but got no response. The way the joint looked, I figured they were out-of-order. Everything's probably out-of-order in this dump! I laughed to myself, stepping inside and walking down a littered, stinking hallway to the rear of the ground floor. Smells like someone pissed on the radiator. Damn! I almost gagged.

I banged on the door about five times before it was opened. Some young dude about twenty-four opened the door. His eyebrows had been recently shaved and he had one of those permanent pouts on his mug. A fuckin' fag! I must have the wrong address.

"You looking for someone?" The punk preened his feathers.

"Yeah! I was looking for a friend, but I guess I got the wrong address."

I started to turn away.

"What's his name, baby?" It squeaked in its most effeminate manner.

"Johnny Michaels," I said offhandedly, about three steps away. "But you wouldn't know hi---"

"He's inside baby!" It said, and walked away, leaving the door open.

"Hey, Sully, what's happening?" Johnny roared good-naturedly looking quite embarrassed.

"Yeah, what's happening?" I asked him looking all around me.

"Well Sully, I – I," he didn't know what to say since he knew I couldn't forget how he was always the first one to down homosexuals when we were in the joint.

"You don't have to explain to me, Johnny. If that's your thing, well -- what can I say?"

"What are you doing, Sully, you working or what?" He asked, trying to keep things going.

"No, I was thinking maybe we could do something. Remember?" I asked, putting him on the spot.

"Oh -- Oh yeah," he said uncomfortably.

"Don't you want to do nothing? You can do better than this, so can I," I offered.

"Yeah -- sure, but I ain't ready yet!" He wasn't ever going to be ready anymore.

"Listen, man, I need a place to stay for a while, till I can get straight," I said.

"Sully, you can stay here as long as you want. We ain't got much but it's yours."

"Thanks, Johnny."

Johnny went on to explain that the whole five stories of the building were homosexuals, with a few lesbian couples thrown in for camouflage. Even the landlord was "stuff". I was treated like a king for the time I spent with them. I learned a great deal about people, all kinds of people. I pretty much stayed to myself, when I wasn't in the house listening to records.

I was in Central Park walking, trying to think! What was I going to do? I couldn't live like this all my life. He may go for this scene, but it wasn't my thing. I was tired of it and needed to move on.

"Sully, they're having a party upstairs tonight. Wanna go up, break up the monotony a little?" he offered trying to get through the wall I had thrown up around me.

"What kind' a party?" I asked suspiciously.

"Christ!" he sounded offended. "What's it matter? There'll be drinks, some hash and stuff!!"

"Yeah, alright!" I had smoked some pot a few times before and had liked what it had done for me. I had never smoked any hash before, though I heard it was good!!

I heard the soft music in the background as I worked my way in the front door through the smoke-filled room, and withering mass of humanity! Taking refuge finally in the far corner of the room, free from the sighing, moaning herd, I accepted a reefer from the human-vending machine that flitted around making everybody happy with the world.

"Hi, Baby."

"Hi, good looking." I heard as I began to float away from it all, feeling very evil instead of carefree.

"That brunette with the long hair! Big thighs -- big ass -- she's out' a sight! At least *she's* dancing with a man," I thought.

I was hawking her like some kind of hungry wolf, when she walked over with the guy she was with. He looked kind of strange, I thought, watching them sit down on the couch in front of me. A little while later, when the guy excused himself to go to the bathroom, I moved in. I was really out of my tree!!

"Hi Baby", I smiled, sitting on the arm of the couch. She couldn't move away because she was hemmed in as somebody sat down. She turned and looked up at me, her beautiful face twisted in a mask of sheer hatred. Goddamn! I couldn't be that bad to look at! What did I say that was so bad, I wondered. Nothing!! I had just put my hand on her shoulder when something hit me on the side of my face, knocking me completely over the couch. I almost went out!

"Stay away from my woman," a voice snarled at me as my eyes began to focus more clearly. It was the little creep with the greasy "duck-ass" haircut and motorcycle jacket. I didn't even want to fight as I looked up at him stunned. Just staring at him as he stood with his hands on his hips, gloating!! I wanted to kill him!!! In one quick motion I pulled the hunting knife from the leather case inside my waist-jacket, and in one bound was on the bastard who suddenly collapsed on the ground crying out in a soprano voice, "Oh -- Please!" The voice wailed. I was very confused, something was wrong here!

"Joe!!" Johnny had now stepped in between us.

Everything seemed deadly quiet. Where was everybody? Where were all the shrieking freaks? This hash got me fucked up, what am I doing with this knife! I looked at Johnny, but I didn't really know him any more. He was my friend, wasn't he?

"Joe," his voice seemed very strange. "This ain't no guy, look at her close, it's a girl! Put that thing away, she didn't know what she was doing!"

"No! No! She didn't mean it!" her girlfriend moaned. I looked down into the girls broken contorted features in disgust, staring hatefully at her.

"What happened to the deep voice, Baby?" I whispered viciously, then spit full in her face.

I walked back to the corner where I had been standing, and gradually the people started easing out of the apartment in twos and threes like I was the social leper. I was but, at that time, I didn't care about what people thought of me.

A couple of minutes (or hours) passed when some slim redheaded guy approached me, handing me a drink. I could see right away, he didn't belong in this company. He had about a five-days growth of beard, and his eyeballs were bloodshot!!

"What's happening, man? What the hell was that all about?" he asked trying to make conversation.

"What's your story?" I snapped tiredly at him.

"There ain't no story," he snapped back with a shitty attitude. I liked him.

"Let's get out of here and go somewhere, huh?"

"Yeah," he smiled knowingly. "That's a great idea."

"I ain't got a fuckin' dime, you buying?"

"Sure!" he laughed. "Let's go!"

There were still some joints with dime beers left and we walked down Amsterdam Avenue until we found one, somewhere in the 60's, around St. Nick's Arena. We figured we could blow a whole two dollars and still have enough left for the subway, should we need it.

After a few beers we started feeling each other out, and as he gained confidence in me, he ran down his story. He had "jumped bail" over in Jersey City for Arson and Robbery; he didn't mention what kind. And, since he knew they were all on the take over there (which came out later) he figured if he got three or four grand he could buy the cases. And he could have!!

After listening to him, I ran down my dismal financial situation. The fifty dollars a week factory jobs and everything that went with it.

"What do you want to do?" he asked.

"I don't know -- Maybe we could *both* do something, huh!"

"You ever pull any heists?"

"Yeah", I lied. "A few, nothing big though."

The biggest thing I had ever stolen was that car when I ran away from Warwick, and didn't even get the satisfaction of driving it. I didn't know how!

In truth, I spent the last seven years of my life in reformatories, for running away from home and playing hooky. A real dangerous criminal! No wonder they put vicious kids like that away -- to rehabilitate them! They sure did a good job of it; those places simply do wonders for young boys!

So I'm twenty now, and now the rabbit got the gun. "Turns go around," as they say.

"I think I can get a few pieces over in Jersey. Want to come over with me?" he asked.

"Sure, why not!" I laughed.

"Okay, but we'd be better off going tonight, while its still dark. Every Bull in Jersey City and Bayonne knows my face."

"Where we gonna stay?" I asked.

"At my girls. Only her and the kid live there. It'll be alright," Red assured me.

We grabbed the Tubes that ran to Jersey City, and then grabbed a bus for Bayonne where his girl lived.

"Are you sure there's nobody else up here with her?" I asked, a little concerned as we entered the private, two-story house and felt our way up the dark stairway leading to her apartment.

A slim sleepy-eyed girl opened the door, grabbing and hugging Red as he walked in first. I followed peeping warily about me into the three other rooms.

I lay on the sofa in the living room, falling slowly asleep with the sound of sighs, moans and musical bedsprings dancing in my head. Red had graciously offered to make it a threesome (not even bothering to ask the girl how she would feel about the extra company, though she looked capable of handling it)! Feeling the blood rushing to my face, I claimed an astounding headache and retired for the night. A loud crashing sound awaked me, like that of a door being kicked from its hinges.

"Sully?" I heard Red call.

"Sully!!" I looked around quickly. Then, grabbing a bronze statuette from the end table I ran out into the kitchen.

The girl was crying, "Don't let him take my baby!" As she huddled in a far corner, her mouth gaped wide in terror. Red was punching vainly at the short, squat built gorilla, as he backed a step at a time for the doorway, the baby cradled beneath one arm, trying to ward off Red's blows with the other. My mind was very confused and racing wildly as I took in the scene. What was this guy taking the baby for?

"C'mon, Sully, help me!" Red gasped, unable to do anything with the gorilla. He was backing out the doorway now.

"Get out of the way!" I yelled covering the kitchen in about three quick strides, grabbing the baby's pajama top in my left fist. In the same motion, I brought the statuette almost from floor level, crashing into the gorilla's nose and mouth, leaving the baby dangling and crying wildly in my left hand, as I watched the figure disappear from sight, crashing down the stairwell. Putting the baby down on the floor, I stepped into the hallway and looked over the banister. This fuckin' guy must be strong as a bull, I thought, watching him struggle to his knees, cupping his broken face in both hands, as if he were trying to keep it form falling apart completely, making strange strangling sounds as he rose shakily to his feet and staggered blindly out the door. I ran back inside.

"C'mon Red, we gotta get outta here!" I yelled pulling on my pants, starting to put my shoes on.

"Fuck the shoes!" Red yelled.

"There's always a cop right on the corner, bring 'em wit' ya, c'mon let's go!"

"I'll catch ya later, Baby!" he called to the frightened girl on the dead run as we shot down the stairs three at a time.

"The side door!" Red yelled, as he spotted the blue uniform through the glass door out front. We shot out the side door, across a large empty lot littered with what seemed to be a million broken bottles. I was running damn near on my toenails. I was cursing myself, Red, the cop, and the useless shoes I carried in each hand. I was still cursing, as I sat on a curb about ten blocks away checking out my feet to see how bad the damage was, unbelievably, none, other than some dog crap I stepped in when I went to sit down on the curb. Red was in tears, he was laughing so hard, as he watched me trying to clean the shit from between my toes. It was freshly dropped and stunk so bad, I almost puked. I didn't even have any Goddamn socks to put on; I forgot to grab them when we left.

"What the hell's so funny, Red?" I asked in disgust at the whole damn situation. When I looked up seeing him bent over laughing noiselessly, I had to laugh myself. What the hell, we got away didn't we? That's all that really matters.

"Alright," I smiled. "What are we going to do now, we ain't got a dime, I ain't even got no socks now!"

"Let's go get them pieces. We got to do something!"

We went to some bar in Bayonne. I waited outside while Red went in to rap with some guy about the guns. I watched through the window outside, seeing Red almost pleading with some greasy creep for about ten minutes. This type of shit embarrassed me. Why don't he just slap that mutt in his face! Oh, yeah, I forgot. Red told me he was supposed to be a "Big Man" in Bayonne. He was connected. Big fuckin' deal! I'd like to go in there and really hook him up. I guess he just wanted to see Red squirm a little, let him know who he was, or remind him.

I watched the dude slide out of the booth and walk into the men's room. He came out a few minutes later with a paper bag in his hand. They talked for a few more minutes and then Red came out.

"You got them?" I asked, looking at the bag.

"He only had one," Red shrugged his shoulders.

"All that bullshit for one stinking piece," I spat out. "The way he was carrying on, I thought you were asking him for his fuckin' life!"

"Yeah, but you know how these guys like to play the part, Sully."

"No, I don't know!" I said angrily.

"Forget it," Red urged. "Let's split up." I was still staring into the bar at this so-called big shot.

"Didn't you tell me all the 'runners' turn money into this guy, Red?"

"Yeah, but--"

"Ain't his money any good, Red?" I asked wanting to make him mad and realize how the creep treated him.

"Yeah-- but he gave me this piece-- he's my friend, he--"

"He's shit, Red, a real piece of shit! And that's how he thinks of you; no man puts a friend through the changes he put you through. You know what I mean?"

"Damn, I know the guy all my life -- we can't -- just --"

"Alright, forget it!" I said seeing that in some way he felt he owed the bird a little loyalty, maybe they went to different schools together, who knows?

"So, what now?" I asked hotly.

"Listen, I know this bar that--"

"Bar?" I asked stunned. "What can we get out of a bar -- fifty -- sixty dollars? Shit! And half the customers in them bars are off duty cops, you got to be kidding!" I exclaimed.

"Wait a minute, listen, will ya!" Red protested. "This joint does a good business on Friday and Saturday. Real good! They don't do too bad on Sunday either."

"So?" I asked not wanting any part of this bar action.

"So?" Red was becoming upset. "We need money, don't we?"

"Dig, these people don't take the money to a night deposit, and they don't take it upstairs over the bar where they live. I figure there must be a couple a grand there! All we got to do is wait till the joints ready to close, there'll only be a few people left and I know all the cops around here! No trouble, in and out. A real quickie, okay?" he explained.

"Where's the money Red?" I asked still persistent and very skeptical.

"It's in a wooden drawer directly beneath the cash register, and it's only locked when they close for the night."

"You're sure, the money's there?" I asked again.

"I'm sure, I'm sure!" Red sighed. "I been in there enough I should know, shouldn't I?"

"Yeah, you should know!" I just looked at him.

It was about 1:30 a.m.! We stood in the dark shadow of a garage across the street watching the bar slowly emptying. There were about four people still seated in the bar when Red spoke.

"You ready, Joe?" he whispered to me, pulling the gray silk stocking down over his face from under the lid of his stingy-brim type-hat. I felt like I had to take a crap real bad, and my legs felt like they were going to buckle on me.

"Shit! I ain't going in there without a gun!" I got a mental picture of the bartender coming up from behind the bar with a big forty-five and putting about three slugs in my chest while I was trying to say I didn't really have a gun.

"Let me have the gun, Red!" I demanded, and he knew exactly what I was feeling.

"C'mon Sully, don't worry, I'll watch them real close. You just jump over the bar and get the bread."

"Jump over, my ass!! I'll choose you for the gun!" I persisted.

"Alright." Red sighed resignedly. "Odds!!" he called nervously.

"Best two out of three, okay?" I asked.

"God damn!" He cursed looking worriedly toward the bar.

"Yeah! Yeah! Best two out of three." He rasped worrying that the bar would close any second.

Whip--Whop! Got me two in a row!

"Let's go!" He ordered commandingly. I followed him across the street toward the dimly lit bar, trying to squeeze the cheeks of my ass together so I wouldn't shit my pants, I had lost control over my bowels!

Red opened the door stepping inside about five steps. I followed taking about two steps to the left of the door, just standing there with my hand in my pocket, and my heart in my mouth, trying to look as fearsome as possible. Red made me jump when he snarled viciously:

"Alright you mother-fuckers, this is a heist. Put your hands on the bar and freeze." I winced at the word motherfucker! No class I thought. No class at all! "That wasn't necessary," I thought, looking at the lady sitting at the bar and feeling embarrassed, when I caught a movement from my left and ducked, throwing up my left arm. My eyes had been riveted on Red's actions from the second we walked in. So I hadn't bothered to look around me, or I would have seen the smaller alcove just to my left, barely large enough for a pool table and its players. Red hadn't told me about it either. I never saw this "Instant-hero" until I felt the searing pain bite into my back. It left my whole left side numb; I looked up from the crouch I had balled up into instinctively. I saw some big baby-fat nineteen-year-old kid standing almost directly over me with the broken pool stick in his hand. He knew he had blown his shot and he stood wide-eyed, trembling like a jellyfish! I came out of my crouch, hitting him dead in his quivering lips. The big instant-hero didn't even go down, but he threw his hands up in front of his face protectively like a little bitch! Red was at my side as soon as it happened.

"Ya alright?" he whispered worriedly still covering the people with the gun.

"Yeah, I think so, but I can't lift my arm. Give me the gun and go get the money!" I winced at the waves of pain rolling around in my head.

Red was pulling out all the drawers and dumping them on the floor. I sensed something was wrong. He snatched the bartender by the collar.

"Where's the money!" He screamed at the already cowering bartender.

"I-It's gone!" He wailed.

"Gone where, you lying bastard!!" Red growled drawing back his fist.

"The-The B-Bank, w-we take-- it to the B-Bank now!" he pleaded.

"Come on! Get what's there, and let's get out of here!" I yelled in pain, watching as he emptied the register and the people's wallets. He told the woman to empty her purse but she held it to her breast with both arms wrapped around it, her chin poked out in stubborn defiance. She was frightened, but she wouldn't be bullied.

"Let her go, boss!" I called to Red who really didn't want to force the issue anyway. I was standing by the door waiting for Red to go out before me.

"Wait a minute!" He yelled jumping over the bar and back again, with a half filled bottle of "Four Roses" in his hand. "He's got to be crazy," I thought, dashing out the door a few seconds behind him.

We had to run down some side streets, about ten blocks for a bus stop. It was killing me to walk, no less run. And here's this son-of-a-bitch partner of mine uncorking the bottle and tipping it up to drink from on a dead run. I yanked it from his hand, whiskey splashing onto his face and shirt front. If I had stopped to argue with him about it, I had no doubt he would have shot me. But I kept running, pulling him along saying, "There's plenty of time for that later, you nut." I said with a big smile. "Let's get away from here first, huh?"

We just caught a bus as it was pulling out and were on our way to Perth Amboy, New Jersey; to some girl's pad that he said was a friend of his friends. The bitch was one of those hundred dollar a trick hustlers, and was supposed to be "good people" (meaning closed mouth and stand-up). Between the bus ride and walking all over Perth Amboy looking for the address, we finally found the house about eight o'clock in the morning. So we decided to go for something to eat and walk around till a movie opened, since he told me the girl held a legitimate job and only worked on her back nights!! After sleeping through some insignificant double feature, it was about four o'clock and we decided to try her again. She still wasn't home! And as bad as my back was hurting, I was determined to lie down somewhere.

"There any other way to get in there, Red?" She had the upstairs apartment.

"Yeah, I was here once before with my friend, Tony. There's a stairway in the back," he said.

"Alright, you sit here on the stoop. This way we'll draw less attraction. I'll try to get in the back way. If I do, I'll come down and let you in the front."

"Good enough!" He said tiredly, we were both almost out on our feet.

The stairs in the back leading up to the second floor reminded me of the kind I used to see in the old Western Movies; steep, wooden, singular foot steps with a worn wooden railing. The only difference was that the small landing on top was enclosed with some type of awning that gave it the appearance of a porch. And I was glad for the cover, because the kitchen window was inside the closed-off porch. It was the old type

window with the regular clasp. All that was needed was a little pressure
on the window, just to widen the space enough to slide the blade of my
knife in and ease the clasp back.

I had myself a nice cold glass of milk and some homemade cookies
that were in a bowl on the kitchen table. "Nice pad! Think I'll stay here
a while," I thought testing the big roomy double bed with my hand. On
the way down to let Red in—"wonder what she looks like?"

"Damn, what took you so long!" Red grumbled as I let him in.

"Sorry partner, but I had to stop for a little snack!" I smiled.

"You dirty bastard!!" He laughed.

Red didn't waste any time, he went right into the bedroom and
feel out! Didn't even ask me if *I* was tired. "Shit, we both can't sleep.
Supposing somebody walked in?" I thought.

Figuring I had to keep busy, or fall asleep, I began to take a complete
inventory of the premises. Finding a big bundle of mail in the bottom
bureau drawer beneath a neat pile of multicolored, crotch less panties, I
decided to get a little background on this Helga. Needless to say, those
hot looking panties gave me the additional incentive needed for some
heavy reading. I got myself some more milk and cookies, and settled
down on the couch, opening the first of the many sensuous letters from
her numerous "Johns"! If I hadn't taken so many "Benny's" to stay awake
the last ten days, I would have probably ran into the bedroom and raped
Red! "Fanny Hill", "Tropic of Cancer", etc. could be put in libraries
for kiddies, like Tom Sawyer or something. The shit these freaks were
writing made good old American smut look like the skinny guy in a
Charles Atlas advertisement (who gets the sand kicked in his face all the
time). In a separate envelope there was about twenty Polaroid photos of
her in such unbelievable positions that I just had to try to get into them
myself. Being pretty limber and in good shape, I figured, "if she could
do it, I could do it!" Having failed on about the first twelve positions,
I was in the process of a small victory, lying on my back in the middle
of the carpet, my eyeballs bulging out. I almost had the heels of both
feet hooked behind my neck, telling myself it would be easy if I didn't
have my shoes on! Damn! If she could do it -- she had thighs like some
defensive lineman for the N.Y. Giants. Just when I felt my heels lock
into place, I heard a key click into the lock downstairs. I almost broke
my neck trying to leap to my feet, forgetting the absurd position I had
accomplished.

"Who was it?" I thought, seated upon the couch again. Sweating
profusely and trying to gain my composure, I slipped the bundle of letters

beneath the sofa, grabbed a magazine, and opened it up, as if reading, the gun in my right hand behind it. The key fitted itself in the apartment door and opened! She looked better than her pictures, like one of those big healthy German barmaids; big all over without being fat, she was also blonde all over. I knew, and I'm not her hairdresser.

"Oh!" she startled, "w-who are y-you?" She was just surprised and didn't appear frightened.

"Come on in and close the door, Red's inside." I tried to smile, I was really tired.

"Who are you?" She said nastily getting real loud. The door wasn't closed yet so I had to be careful. Putting the gun beside me on the sofa and the magazine over it in one motion, I rose slowly still smiling.

"Don't get excited, miss!" I was saying until I reached her.

"Get inside you dirty bitch," I hissed at her. "Before I kick your nose off your face!" I grabbed a fistful of her thick blonde hair and hurled her to the living room floor, locking the door behind me. She looked up at me from her knees, hair all disarrayed and very frightened now. She was hard though, never even thought of crying. She just looked up at me, her full, red lower lip trembling. I was standing almost over her and couldn't help smiling, seeing that she couldn't keep her fluttering eyes above my belt-buckle. "You got anything to say, bitch?" I asked nastily, smiling down in her nervous eyes with a nasty sneer, caressing the back of her neck in an insinuating way.

"Uh -- oh! N-no -- no!!" She gasped in a little girl like voice, raising one hand hesitantly to the inside of my thigh, eyes cast down, caressing me lightly and knowingly, but looking up at me with hurt in her eyes when she finally acknowledged I was "out to lunch"! I felt like crawling under the rug in my embarrassment, cursing those lousy Bennys and myself! Look at this, I thought. And I can't even get it up!! Sheeet!! Pulling her to her feet gently, I kissed her cheek and smiled.

"Can you cook, Baby? Maybe I need a good meal or something!" I laughed, feeling sick. She was completely at ease with me already.

"Sure, Honey!" She laughed playfully. "I'll take good care of you!"

Damn! These bitches always had a way of turning the table on you, once they found out you carried your brains in your jock! The lovely fat butt bitch just hopped off gaily toward the kitchen, figuring a steak dinner would bring me back from the graveyard.

I immediately went in and woke up Red figuring he'd bail me out of my dilemma.

"C'mon, Red, the girl's here, get up and rap with her, huh?" I persisted.

"Shit, I'm beat!" He said, rising groggily with my helping hand.

"Yeah, I know." I said sarcastically. "But this coming here was your bright idea, so the least you can do is talk to this broad. We don't want her getting unhappy, you know what I mean?"

"Yeah! Yeah! Alright," Red said tiredly.

Helga went all out, steak, baked potatoes, salad, and rolls. It really looked good and I really appreciated her efforts; but all I was concerned about was wolfing it down and hitting the bed for some sleep. I knew Red was thinking the same thing. They were getting on very well when I excused myself on the pretence of going to the bathroom. I tripped over the bed on my way there and was working on my second hour of dead, blissful sleep when Red woke me up whispering, "C'mon Sully, you got to do something for this bitch. She's been rubbing that hot pussy of hers against me for the last hour, a-and and I-I can't d-do a thing!" He stuttered nervously. "It must be those fuckin' Benny's!" he grated.

"Why the hell do you think I woke you up?" I said, laughing and rolling over to cut more wood.

"Well -- what am I supposed to do? She -- wants some **action**!!" He wailed.

"For Christ's sake, Red, just tuck a napkin in your shirt and enjoy yourself huh?" I muttered, burying my face in the pillow to muffle my laughter.

"You're a dirty dude, Sully. That ain't no shit either!" He said seriously, before going back into the living room to take care of business.

I awoke about five hours later, still very tired, but restless, Red was asleep on the living room couch, buck-naked. Helga was sitting, legs crossed, on the love seat reading some women's magazine in her panties and bra! My eyes almost popped out, gazing between her heavy widespread thighs seeing the thick tufts of curly blonde hair poked out through the slit in the shimmering black, silk bikini type drawers. She looked up over her magazine in disgust, looking quite mad and evil.

"You had enough sleep yet, Honey?" She asked sarcastically.

"Just read your magazine and shut up!" I retorted hotly, sitting in an armchair across from her, drooling like some kid looking through a candy store window with no money to spend!

We were both sitting there uncomfortably for about fifteen minutes when the phone rang. She answered the phone, almost whispering as she spoke, her eyes darting warily in my direction as I sat glaring at her. She finally hung up.

"T-That was one of my John's. I-I have to go out!" She said uneasily, not looking at me. "I'll be back in an hour!" She said, walking toward the bedroom, her heavy buttocks rolling liquidly, shimmering beneath the silk wispy covering.

"Something's wrong here," I thought. She couldn't even look in my eyes and her voice was very shaky. Something about that phone call frightened her. That wasn't no John!

"Red! Red! Wake up! She's getting ready to leave!" I spoke urgently. Red sat up looking wide-awake, startled by the sound of my voice.

"What for?" he asked.

"She said some John called and she had to meet him!"

"So! What's wrong with that, she's got to make a living!" He yawned.

"Red!" I said speaking slowly. "I watched her talking. That wasn't no John on the phone! She ain't acting right -- something's wrong!"

"What do you wanna do, Sully?"

"Let's tie her up and get out of here!" I whispered, trying to convince him. If he could have seen her actions himself, he would have seen what I meant.

"No, listen, maybe you're just jumpy. Let her go. We'll just watch from the windows, okay?"

I didn't say anything, I was too tired to argue or even think. Helga came into the living room, ready to go out, apprehension in her every step. Even in the short trench-type raincoat, her big breasts stood out high and proud, accentuated even more so by the wraparound belt tied tightly around her waist. She carried a beach-type handbag with a long strap slung over her shoulder. She just stood there, guilty, not knowing what to say, or how to just walk out the door.

"Where ya going, Baby?" Red asked, still not really thinking anything was wrong.

"I-I got to leave R-Red," she said trying to force a smile. "One of my 'Sugar-Daddy's' is waiting for me!" But she wasn't looking at Red as she spoke. Her eyes darted to meet mine and, in their guilt, could not look for more than a second at a time. I didn't say anything until she was opening the door.

"It was nice meeting you, Helga!" I called to her softly, freezing her for a moment.

"Uh -- Oh! Y-yes!!" She whispered sounding as if she were about to cry.

As soon as I heard the downstairs door close, I spoke to Red. We had both been sitting in silence.

"She said she'd only be gone an hour, Red. Let's play it safe and wait in one of those alleys across the street. If everything's okay, we haven't lost anything anyway!"

"Shit. We're just tired, Sully, and jumpy. She's alright, and she wouldn't rat on us!"

"How did she find out about us messing that guy up in Bayonne?" I asked.

"I don't know! Some guy told her that the cops were looking for me, and for another guy for assault, besides, my bail jumping. Shit! I'm going back to sleep. She's alright!" Red said, wearily going back into the bedroom to lay down.

I was going to leave the house and wait in the alley myself, but it wouldn't be right to leave Red sleeping like this. I could never warn him! I turned off the lights in the living room, leaving only the light in the bathroom on to see by. I double-checked both the back and front doors, and made sure all the windows were locked. Bringing a straight-backed chair in from the kitchen, I placed it to the side of the window where I had a complete view of the street.

About forty-five minutes later, I was still sitting in the chair barely able to keep my eyes open when I heard a sound. A creaking sound! I was up and alert. I was cursing Red silently for not listening to me, and myself for not making him listen. I moved into the doorway of the bedroom, holding my breath, waiting for the next sound to come. Creak!! The back stairway!! My heart pounded like a hammer. I looked at the German Luger in my hand, only five slugs in the slip. Damn! If it's the cops -- I know game. Right! They're probably surrounding the house. I'd need a sawed-off shotgun to stand a chance getting out of here. I was one step into the kitchen now. Thirty seconds passed -- no sounds. Then, a soft tapping on the French-windows of the kitchen door -- "Helga!" "Helga!!!" A man's voice called softly. Moving quickly and silently, I was in the bedroom.

"Red -- Red!! The Bulls are here!" He was up on his feet eyes looking wild.

"Let's get out of here." He whispered, desperately starting for the door.

"Come 'ere," I grabbed his arm. "We can't get out, they're all around the place. We ain't got a chance ---!!"

Spotlights hit the house from all sides, almost completely lighting the rooms. The front and back doors came crashing down simultaneously, as I dove under the bed with Red hot on my ass. All I could feel was embarrassment, the blood rushing hotly to my face.

"Diving under a bed? Ain't this a bitch?" I thought, as the room was full of hard voices.

"Check the bathroom! Look in the closet -- a foot!! Watch it -- don't move you bastards, or we'll kill you right through the bed!" A voice shouted viciously.

Someone had me by both ankles, trying to pull me from under the bed. But I was holding onto a bed leg with both hands.

"Come on, you son-of-a-bitch". The voice screamed. He yanked so hard; I thought he dislocated my kneecaps!

"Alright, Alright! Take it easy!" I yelled.

"I'm coming!!" I said, releasing the bed leg and sliding out.

The one bastard continued to hold my ankles tightly as the mad-dogs closed in, pulling one another out of the way to get their kicks in. All I could do was throw my arms over my head, so they wouldn't kill me. I remember seeing the terribly large brogue-type shoes being drawn back for delivery from all sides. I don't think there was a size nine in the whole crowd! The last thing I saw when I peeped between my crossed arms was Red. He was in the far corner by the bathroom, cringing with both arms protectively over his head as two Bulls with blackjacks were swinging for the fences, trying to get to his skull.

As they took us down the front stairs of the house, I wasn't even concerned that all the people were staring at me, some even laughing. The cops had ripped my pants off me and I had to walk out into street in my drawers. I had spotted the pale face of that rat-bitch, Helga, before she ducked down out of sight in the back seat of the patrol car across the street. I wanted to run over and spit in the Judas bitch's face! I wanted to scream to all her neighbors what a low-life bitch this "good girl" really was, but I said nothing and looked forward to everything.

I found out later that she was a professional "stool-pigeon". She would give up cats like myself to keep the weight off of her! Since her prostitution activities included a number of police sergeants, captains, etc, she was well known in that particular circle of super-freaks!

Both Red and I were taken to headquarters, booked, and questioned for almost two days. Neither of us had lawyers and advising one of his right's was unheard of by them. The only thing these bastards would advise you of was when they'd be coming in your cell again to kick your guts out!!

Some self-righteous, good Catholic, Irish police captain by the name of Thomas Whelan handcuffed my hands behind a straight back chair, slapping me in the face for about five minutes before reaching in my drawers to squeeze my balls in his rage to make me talk. I realized the "good man" was only doing his job. But it is hard to accept, especially when you are the recipient of such action. Gagging and choking on your own vomit, wondering how this man could become even more angry and indignant, just because a bit of your insides splashed on the cuff of his white shirt! Strange indeed, since a friend told me dear Mr. Whelan is in a Federal Penitentiary now, with the rest of his respected fellow politicians of Jersey City; the church-goers, hand shakers, baby-kissers, ball-squeezing, undercover perverts. It's a shame that I could not have been in the Federal Penitentiary to give them their just welcome!! How times have changed, that men like this will live to come out again. These little garden snakes, which have been swallowed whole by their fellow anacondas, whose instincts for survival is greater than their own.

Jersey City, Hudson County, Warden McFarland? Yes, he's in the Federal Penitentiary now too, isn't he? Such a shame, that all these good Irish-Catholic men should be sacrificed in such a common manner. Men of such stature loved and trusted by the public. Shouldn't the public also vote upon the fate of those who they have deceived? These dogs pilfer millions of dollars from the poor and workingmen, and also sit in judgment of those same people.

"A stolen car?" -- "Five Years." -- "You snatched a purse?" "That's grand larceny boy, -- Five years!!"

I was in Hudson County Jail about a week when I was called to the bars by a captain.

"You, Sullivan?" He asked.

"Yes, Sir!" I answered trying to search my mind for something I might have done wrong that would demand his presence.

"How you feeling, Kid?" He asked jovially enough to relax me a little.

"I'm doing alright," I shrugged, still wondering what he was after.

"What's your beef?" He asked.

"Robbery," I answered. The captain looked around, and then came closer to the bars.

"You got any money, Kid?" He whispered, conspiratorially.

"No, Sir!" I said.

"How about your people, your family? They must want to help you?"

Damn, I thought, this guy's offering me an out. I wonder how much he wants?

"Yes," I lied. "They'd help me, but how much would I need?" I asked.

"Well," he looked around again. "Would fifteen-hundred be too much?" He offered quickly.

"I-I don't know," I said. "How can I be sure I'll get out?"

"Don't worry about that, there's no funny business. This goes right through McFarland!"

"A-Alright, how can I get you if I get the money?"

"Just tell anyone of the officers you want to see Captain R. right away, and I'll be up, okay?" He smiled.

"Y-Yeah -- sure – thanks, Captain." I said, like some sorry son-of-a-bitch, thinking, "Wow! This guy must want to help me, offering me an out like this!" Not knowing at the time that he would sell his mother's eyeballs for five hundred a piece! Why should he bother with me if he didn't mean good? I'm a nobody! Why take a chance on me for a lousy fifteen hundred? Not thinking about the other four hundred guys who they haven't really got a good case on anyway, and can afford to be gracious with their deals. It runs into millions of dollars. Then, of course, Hudson County offered all the conveniences of home for those who could afford it. Special cells up in the Penthouse with TV and, in special cases, a telephone line installed. For the ordinary peasants, like myself, with a ten-dollar bill to spare, they'd lock you in a private counsel room with your wife or girlfriend for twenty minutes to do your thing! The sturdy, long, oak counsel table saw a lot of action during the McFarland era, and none of it was legal-action! Not only would these bastards pimp your own women to you, but also had the audacity to ask guys, "Was it good?" or, "Was it worth the ten?" Because I was not fortunate enough to be able to acquire fifteen hundred dollars, I was to spend almost six years of a five to seven year sentence in the New Jersey Prisons -- Trenton and Rahway! And, later on in their butcher shop for the criminally insane, Trenton State Hospital.

As I mentioned before, the state had no concrete evidence that we committed this robbery. But what they did have was Red's younger brother (who was about seventeen) for burglarizing a Safeway Supermarket. So, in turn, they told Red they would cut his brother loose, if we would both "cop-out" to the robbery charge. Red felt really bad. He had a sister who had died recently, he already was in jail, and he was thinking about his mother. This is all she would need. The other son in jail too!!

Red never asked me outright (he wasn't that kind of guy), he just explained what the D.A. had told him, and told me.

"But you do what you want, Sully. If you want to go to bat, I'll go with you!"

I knew how he really felt inside, but when I asked him what he wanted to do, he just shrugged his shoulders helplessly. "What can I do? Either way it's bad!"

What the hell, I thought, making up my mind, I'm only nineteen now, I could get out on parole in two or two and a half years. I ain't got nothing to go out to anyway, so what difference will a few more years make. I also felt a strong loyalty to Red and he was deserving of it! Though I went through a lot of changes in those six years, he also did. I have never had reason to regret our friendship.

I was sentenced to five to seven years in Trenton State Prison. I didn't see Red again until about a year later. He got seven to twelve years, including the charges he had pending before I met him.

***

Trenton Prison - 1960

When I first walked into Trenton, I could feel the tension and sense the ever-ready potential for violence that existed throughout the five years I spent there; it more often than not exploded into pure physical savagery. This was early in the year 1960, when prisoners both black and white (in all prisons) were still ignorant of their own plight. Hate! Though ignorance and mistrust was the prevailing factor, hate was fed and encouraged by the administration itself. "Keep them apart, keep them divided, keep them weak!" Knifings, pipings, rapes, and the widespread homosexuality was virtually ignored. The only way any of this gets to a newspaper is when the assaulted person dies, and even then it is no big thing!

"The administration breeds homosexuality!" I had been told on numerous occasions, by the "brass" -- "Why don't you get yourself a 'kid' and settle down, Sully?" They would say it laughingly, but were dead serious. They figured if you became "involved" with some homo, you would be one less potential troublemaker. They were actually relieved to see the tougher inmates getting hooked on these punks. No "Playboy" or girly magazines are permitted as a form of relief.

One guy put it perfectly clear to me. "Sully," he snarled, "these people would rather see us sucking a dick, than reading a Playboy Magazine! Their objective is to break us completely! Physically, spiritually and morally. Don't you ever believe no differently! I've seen guys go to the box for sixty days for pornographic pocket books. And I've seen other guys get reprimands for raping some young kids! Animals aren't even supposed to think of having women, and this is how they think of us. These are the same people who then condemn us and get indignant when we get out of here after 5,10,20 years of their debasing treatment and rape their women in dark alleys and jump from tree limbs on dark streets and in the parks! The same with all the recidivists, their murders, rapes, robberies are all simply a product of their own making. You might say that which one sows, so shall he reap in return. Undoubtedly, these mutts are under the impression that this shit only works one way! These people have two faces, Sully! One for the public and one for us!"

I was only in Trenton about a month, and I witnessed two rapes. They were young kids, nineteen or twenty, who had just come in. They were forced to commit acts of sodomy. Force was not necessary 90% of the time. Just the threat of physical violence, like the flash of a knife or pipe was enough to make them drop instantly to their knees in uncontrollable fear. These are the men referred to as "punks" because they were made into temporary women, simply because of their own cowardice and fear.

In 1960, in Trenton, there were actually regular "crews" of the "asshole bandits" in seven-wing. They would have different kids cells cracked and run in and rip them off, regardless of the outcome. Most of the time these kids would be too embarrassed or frightened to report it. They didn't have enough heart to kill a few of these birds, so it just went on from there. It became a regular thing! One kid, I understand, fought feebly everyday for the first two weeks! Then all of a sudden started to "dig it", he had a wife and two kids. He left the joint a few years later, more woman than his wife.

Being only nineteen myself and barely shaving, I immediately put in an order for a big shank!! I'd much prefer the cops to catch me with it, than have these bandits catch me without it! During the first couple of weeks I was in "idle co." We didn't have a shop assignment yet, so we could stay in the cells all morning and sleep. The levers above the gates opened so silently that you couldn't hear them open and many dudes who got shived and piped can give testimony to this! If I were going to sleep all morning, I would tie two empty cans together and set them on the toilet bowl in the rear of my cell with a piece of strong black thread. It led to and was tied to a bar on the bottom of my door (where it couldn't be seen)! This way there wasn't any surprise visits!

I knew quite a few guys who always had three knives stashed! One in the shop where they worked, one in the cell, and one buried in the yard! More often than not, these guys always seemed to run into trouble between these given localities and, whatever their beef, ended up in big trouble! So I just kept one and it went everywhere I went, even to bed. Though I learned soon enough that nobody is too quick to jump on you when there's a good chance of dying. Why go after the shark, when there are so many smaller fish around? I have never seen anyone more adept at spotting weaknesses in people than a convict. If you have one, he'll find it!

***

Rahway - 1961

After only a month, I was shipped to Rahway prison, right into the midst of a riot in the making. Being from New York, I knew nobody in Jersey, until I finally ran into a few guys that were good friends of Red's. One of the guys named Sonny C., turned to me in the mess hall one morning (about two weeks after I was there).

"Do you know what's supposed to go down Wednesday morning, Sully?" he whispered.

"No, I don't." I'd seen a lot of talking and whispering going on, I knew something was happening, but I didn't know what it was all about.

"What's happening?" I asked.

"Listen, you just came and I figured maybe you wouldn't want no part of it. But the way it's going down, you ain't got much choice!"

"No choice about what?" I asked.

"The Riot! The dudes are gonna turn this joint out --"

"You mean the mess hall?" I asked feeling a strange excitement.

"The mess hall, commissary, officer's Barber Shop -- they're gonna rip up everything they can get to!"

"Who's 'they', Sonny? What are they asking for, what are they trying to gain by it?" I asked.

"There isn't any list of demands that I know of, at least I haven't seen one. We just want better treatment, better chow, hospital care, etcetera. Dig, you haven't been here long enough. Look at the shit they feed us, Sully! They cook it for the pigs out there on the farm, and give us first crack at it!! Just the overall treatment, Sully!!" Sonny said.

"Do all these guys know about it?" I asked looking around our table.

"Yeah, they know!" he nodded.

"How about the Black dudes? Are they down with it?" I asked.

"Well - uh! -- I don't know -- I --" He started and I couldn't help laughing.

"Are you serious, Sonny?" I was shocked at how nonchalantly he was taking a very serious matter.

"You mean to tell me that there's supposed to be a riot Wednesday and you don't know if the Blacks are down with it? Who are the leaders? Haven't they spoken to each other? Who's supposed to be doing the talking, Sonny?" I asked incredulously.

"Uh! I-I'm supposed to be one of the leaders --" he said sheepishly.

"Christ!!" I was amazed. "Damn, Sonny! If you're one of the leaders and you don't know what the Black dudes want to do, who does?"

"Dig, Sully," he said very seriously. "This riot shit ain't my bag, I mean, I don't know how to handle these things!"

"Damn." I felt sorry for him.

"Then how did you get hooked up as a spokesman? You know all these guys that you say know about it are relying on you to get things together, don't you? This could turn into a race riot if everybody isn't aware of what is going on! It could get real bad, Sonny?"

"I-I've thought about that!"

"Thought about!? One misdirected tray or pitcher, one fool who can't pass a chance to knife somebody, and it's all over! Who else is supposed to be with you, Sonny?"

"Tony, Mike, about six other guys, they're getting the white dudes together. They left it up to me to talk to the brothers. I was in Bordentown Reformatory with a lot of them, so they figured I could rap with them!"

"Did you?" I asked.

"Yeah!" He said indignantly. "I talked to Rubin C., Nubby and a few other brothers!"

"What do they feel about it?" I kept at him persistently.

"They're down with it. Rubin and the others will have to get out of the kitchen though!" He said.

"Who's this Rubin you keep mentioning, Sonny?" I asked curiously.

"Rubin Carter! The guy we was watching workout yesterday."

"Oh Yeah." I said, remembering the devastating puncher I had seen the day before. He was a middleweight, but built like a heavyweight from the waist up! This same Rubin Carter, later known as Rubin "Hurricane" Carter, left prison the following year. He went on to knock out Emile Griffith in one round, and fight for the middleweight championship. He blew the fight. I understand he was doing too much drinking and partying. He must have, because the guy I remembered, they couldn't beat.

"How's this thing suppose to start? Who's gonna start it?" I smiled at him, wondering who was fool enough. Sonny almost fell off the seat, he was laughing so hard, tears were running down his cheeks.

"S-ome -- gu-y a-t the front table!" He gasped going into another fit of laughter.

"Wow, he can't help but be seen as the guy who started it, all the fuckin' 'brass' standup there!" I exclaimed.

"Ye-eah - ye-eah", Sonny laughed even harder. "But that's who he's supposed to hit!"

"Hit? -- With what?"

"Listen, Sully, to hear this guy talk would actually throw fright into you. We didn't ask him, he *wants* to be the one to start it! When I give him the nod, he's going to throw over the front table and throw one of these stainless steel pitchers in the Hack's face. Whoever's closest, Captain, Lieutenant, he says it doesn't matter to him!" Sonny smiled.

"Damn Sonny. Either this guy's got to be insane, or he's got the heart of a lion. But even then, he's still got to be crazy. I can see ten, fifteen guys going into action on a given signal -- but one guy jumping up like that?" I shook my head.

"Are you down with it, Sully?" Sonny asked looking at me serious now.

"Listen, Sonny. I'm not anxious to get my head cracked, but like you said, I'm going to be in here when it happens. So, if I'm going to catch a beating with those clubs, I may as well be guilty of what I'm being clubbed for, maybe it won't hurt as much. When is this supposed to go down, in the morning or afternoon?"

"At night, Sully!"

"B-but half of the guys will be in their cells, they feed two different messes!"

"Yeah, I know," he said shrugging again. "We're supposed to try and get those guys out of the cells!"

"Sonny, when we go up to the gym tonight, get Mike and as many guys as you can. Get them into pairs and send them to talk to any of the brothers you know are respected by the others. As good as this Rubin is, he's only one man. He can't talk to everybody! Listen, as far as I'm concerned, this whole thing is a mess, no organization between black and white. No definite plan of action. No definite assignments. No definite set of demands! It's self-defeating, and really a waste! All most of these guys want is to get their shit off! Break the place up, etc. I bet three-quarters of them aren't even aware of what they are really doing, or what the kick back is going to be. A lot of guys are going to be hurt, Sonny, maybe even killed. I'm not saying they are wrong in what they're doing.

I've only been here a couple of weeks! But I do know they're wrong in how they're going about it! Doesn't it make sense; that if your going to pay for something, even if that payment is only blood, that you would like to know that you are getting something in return for it? But it's gone too far now to stop it -- even if that fool at the front table doesn't start it -- the next fight in the mess hall will! And then **nobody** will know who's after who. So this shit here may as well run its course. I only wish I knew most of these guys, Sonny, because it's really a wasted action. It's a shame. But the least we can do is try to insure that this will not be passed off by the administration as *just* another race riot. You know what I mean, Sonny?"

"Yeah, Sully, I know," Sonny said, looking as if he had just finally woke up to the catastrophe that was building around him.

That night in the Gym, we walked around casually talking to different guys. I was shocked at how many guys really didn't know about a riot that was only a night's sleep away, and how quickly they jumped into it with both feet, as if they were accepting an invitation to a tea-party! Well, at least everyone was aware that they were not to cut each others throats the following night.

When I walked into the mess hall that night and got in line to get my chow, it was dead silent, almost eerie. There was no loud talk, no laughter; every man was alone within himself for these last few minutes. As I walked to the line and stuck my tray out for the beans, I looked into the eyes of the guys serving the chow. They all knew! Some smiled, others nodded acknowledging. All were tense and serious, ready for whatever was to come! I really felt a closeness to every man I saw with this look of readiness. They didn't have to be here. For many, they weren't in here to prove they were tough-guys. They were here because they believed they were doing the only thing they could to get the administration to stop and look at them, not through them as if they were just another piece of furniture (a chair, a table, a number)!

As I looked into the guys face at the first table, that was supposed to start it off, I thought he looked terribly ill. His face was chalky-white, but when I looked into his eyes he could not conceal the stark terror he was feeling. For some reason I became terribly angry. This loudmouthed mutt must have thought this wasn't really going to come off.

As I walked by his table, I bent over and whispered in his ear , "You ready, Killer?" I sneered. "It's almost curtain time!" He jumped, hearing the disdain that dripped from my voice and turned his head, but could not hold my eyes.

"Y-yeah, I-I'm ready," he mumbled shakily, looking under the table somewhere. Maybe he had dropped that big heart of his under there. I continued to walk looking at the table immediately around the one where I always sat and couldn't help but notice all the unoccupied seats of the guys who had stayed in their cells. The table where I sat was completely filled, everybody was here. I felt pride in just this alone.

"Give me a little room. Let me hide somewhere too!" I said forcing a smile, but not really feeling it. "Anybody want my beans?" I asked looking around me, still smiling, a few guys laughed, and everyone at least grinned, breaking the deadly tension. The mess hall was full now and the officer was locking the gate. The cops were aware *something* was wrong. It was too quiet, they all had moved out of the aisles and were standing with their backs against the walls. They were all fidgety, scared, unable to look any inmate in the eye without coughing, or bending down to tie a shoelace. Anything, not to have to look into the hate filled faces of the "animals" around them.

"Yes look! You motherfucker! Look at them! Look at them and see yourself, for they only reflect the treatment you have given them!"

"When is this guy supposed to move Sonny?" I asked impatiently, strung tight as a wire.

"Sh-it," Sonny hissed. "I've been trying to motion to one of the guys at the table! The mutt hasn't turned around once. They're gonna be opening the doors in a few minutes. Shit! -- Shit! -- Shit!!" He cursed angrily to himself.

I looked around the mess hall. Everybody was waiting. They didn't know where it was to start. All they knew was that at the first commotion, tables, trays, pitchers, everything went at once. The guys were starting to look around the mess hall at each other now. Shaking their heads, lifting their hands as if to ask, "What's happening?"

"I'm gonna talk to this guy, Sonny!" I said, getting up from my seat. "What's his name anyway?"

"Tommy -- but don't do nothing to him, Sully!" he whispered. I walked up to the serving table to get more bread, which we were allowed to do. On the way back I stopped for a few seconds by his table. Not bothering to bend down, I spoke low so it would not carry to the officers standing behind me.

"What are you gonna do, Tough-guy?" I hissed at him. He didn't even look up. He just sat there, his whole body trembling, his hands clasped between his thighs, his head bowed. I hated him at that moment, creeps like this with all their false bravado, until the shit hits the fan!

"C'mon, Punk, everybody's waiting!" I rasped and hearing him make some sobbing incoherent sound, I started back for my table. They were opening the doors now!

"Sully, what's happen ---" he started as I sat down straddling the bench.

"Nothing!" I snapped. "He froze up like an ice-cube."

"God – Damn!" Sonny cursed, looking around. The Guards were trying to get the Brothers in the last row on the other side of the mess hall to start filing out! I saw a few brothers rise, only to be pulled back down by the others who knew.

"Sully, we got to do something!" Sonny pleaded, looking desperate.

"Give me that pitcher, the full one. Hurry up!" I was shaking now.

"But ---" Sonny started.

"Just give me the fucking pitcher, fuck all this bullshit!"

"Here!" He gave me the pitcher.

"Alright!" I said still straddling the bench, talking to the whole table. "As soon as you guys see the pitcher coming up from behind me, turn this whole row of tables over and scream at the top of your lungs. Sonny, take that empty pitcher and throw it through the window right after I let mine go, okay?"

"Y-yeah – yeah, Sully!" He said nervously, and I couldn't help but wonder if my face looked as strange to him as his did to me at that second.

"Alright -- Alright!" I said, bringing the pitcher behind me, lining up the lieutenant and sergeant about three rows away.

"You ready!" I said looking around the table seeing them all nod at once. "Now!!" I screamed leaping up quickly and throwing the hot pitcher of tea with everything I had. But I had thrown it too hard, and the handle had twisted in my hand as I released it. I watched its flight. I was shocked as I saw it hurtle downward almost immediately crashing sickeningly into the face of a man two rows away. He disappeared beneath the table screaming, holding his broken face in both hands! I started to move toward him, but the air was now filled with trays and any object that could be thrown. I hit the floor and watched as the scaling trays ripped into the faces of those still standing, watched as they staggered around the mess hall moaning, the blood blinding their vision. One of the civilian cooks was trying to break for the door, when one of the guys behind the counter poured a huge pot of the boiling sticky beans over his bald head. He screamed like a Banshee, jumping three feet off the floor. When he landed, he shot out the door as if jet-propelled, "Yieeee!

-- Yieee! -- Yieee!!" I could still hear his echo as he moved down the corridor, outside.

The mess hall was completely destroyed within two minutes. I was moving through the screaming, cursing mass of men toward the front of the mess hall when I saw something. At first it caused me to laugh, but then turned sour on my stomach. Some young sergeant was standing in the middle of five hundred raging men who were bent on destroying every "State-made" thing in sight. Here he was like some Keystone Comedy Cop, trying to direct the traffic!

"Tweet!" with his whistle.

Then, "Alright you guys, that's enough!"

I couldn't believe I was really seeing it. Was this guy for real? He repeated this scene about three times, when some guy shot out of the crowd behind him and teed off on his head with a stainless steel pitcher.

"B-o-n-g!!" The sergeant's hat flew off and his legs went rubbery, but he didn't go down.

"Tw-ee-t!" He blew the whistle, his eyes all glassy-looking. Here came his friend again, but this time from the other side!

"B-o-n-g!!" It was a sickening sound. The sergeant went to his knees, looking out of unseeing eyes. The hurt look on his face was more of confusion than pain as if he couldn't believe anybody would want to do something like this. He had lost his whistle and he crawled about ten feet to retrieve it. "No, you fool!" I thought still trying to fight through the tight circle of men that enclosed this spectacle. Here comes that nut again! Raising the pitcher high above his head, as I broke through the crowd about fifteen feet away.

"That's it!" Some big dude yelled, stepping in front of the kneeling sergeant. The guy came to a halt glaring hatefully at the guy who was taking away his recreation.

"Who the fucks side are you on, man?" The nut screamed.

"You had your fun man. He's had enough!" The big guy said softly not budging and ready to fight. Stepping past the big guy, I walked over to the nut smiling.

"Forget it Baby," I laughed. "He's fucked up. You did a real good job on him!" I said holding my breath.

"Yeah – man," the nut was giggling. "But who's this punk think he is?" He said glaring over my shoulder at the big guy.

"Forget it, everybody's excited, he don't mean nothing. He just don't want you killing the guy. You know what I mean, Baby?"

"Y-yeah -- yeah, I guess so." He muttered, moving away sulking.

Everyone moved out of the mess hall. Sonny and a few other guys were trying to scream the running herd into some kind of order.

"To the Blocks!" Sonny was screaming. "Take the Blocks!!"

The mob, unable to hear above the din and no longer capable of a constructive thought- just continued on their way. The officer's barbershop went in about eight seconds. As I turned the corner toward the center (which is a barred enclosure for the officers), I saw Rubin C. kick the commissary door in like it was plywood or something and the herd streamed in. As I stood with my back against the wall, I watch them empty it out in a matter of minutes. Guys were running in all directions, some with as much as twenty cartons of cigarettes loaded in their arms. That's all they want! Look at them running for their cells with them smokes! What the fuck do they expect to do with them? I was actually laughing, when Sonny ran over with about eight other guys.

"Sully ---"

"Look! -- Look!" I laughed, pointing to some old guy running down the hallway toward the cellblock. He must have had forty pints of ice cream stacked up in his arms. He had to peep around the side to see where he was going. Sonny failed to see the humor in it.

"Fuck that shit, Sully. He's lucky if he gets to eat a pint. Stupid bastard!" He screamed at no one in particular. The center was packed with cops now, straining against the bars like mad dogs. Each one was personally affronted by our wanton destruction. There was murder dripping from their eyes.

"Alright, fellas! Let's go back to the blocks now!" A captain was speaking through a bullhorn.

"You've got your point across. There'll be no retaliation. Just go back to your cells and everything will be alright," he said soothingly.

"Yoo-hoo!!" Some moron yelled. "We got a win! We got a win. Let's go back!" He yelled happily.

Sonny covered the distance in an instant, lashing the dude across the mouth with his open hand, sliding him across the floor.

"Listen to me!" He screamed pleading to the crowd that was already moving slowly but steadily toward the different blocks. "If you lock in them fuckin' cells, you're finished! You're all alone! This is how they want us -- alone! This is our only strength! We must stay together --" The guys hesitated momentarily, a few at a time, thinking, then drifting back by our side.

"That's --- it, fellas!" Came the captain's voice again, dripping honey. "Just keep moving toward the blocks. It's all over, nobody wants to hurt you!"

"How ya doing, Cap?" "Everything alright, Captain?" Some of these guys said, smiling nervously as they passed the center.

"Yeah, don't worry, fellas! Ha! Ha! You guys sure did some job, huh? Heh! Heh!"

We were standing in the hallway, just barely out of sight of the center, taking a quick head-count. I turned to Sonny and the others.

"We're lucky if we got forty guys here. We got to get out of here, NOW!!"

"We got to pass the center!" one of the guys said. "They'll see our faces, and WE'RE the ones they'll really want!"

My instincts for survival were working overtime. Taking my gray shirt off quickly, I buttoned it completely up again, except for the second button from the top, to see through. The others immediately followed suit, laughing.

"Yeah -- this is more like it! Yeah!!"

"Alright, are you all ready? We all got to move at once, and move fast. Ready!" I lifted my hand like a starter for the hundred-yard dash.

"Go!" I yelled shooting around the corner like the "Road Runner" moving past the startled cops inside the center cage.

"There's the bastards." I heard a guttural voice growl deeply.

"Stop!" he yelled.

Yeah, I'll stop! At the first brick wall I run into! That guy's got to be crazy, I thought. Sonny, a guy named Mike and myself shot up the stairs to our galleries. Sonny locked on the other side and Mike locked a few cells from me. The tiers were deserted. Everybody was locked in already. We were standing by the lock-box waiting for a guard to show up.

"We're in big trouble if they catch us like this, Mike. We got to get in the cells!" I whispered urgently.

"Let's go back down and get Mr. B. He's a good dude. He'll let us in!"

"You sure? You know him?"

"Yeah, c'mon. Let's go!" As we were racing down the stairs, Sonny's head popped over the railing from the gallery above.

"S-Sully, I can't g-get in!" he squawked.

"No shit, Dick Tracy!" I yelled up. "Wait there, we'll try to get the man!! Mr. B was sitting at his desk smoking his pipe like he didn't have a care in the world. The building could be caving in and he'd just sit there and smoke his pipe. Sonny told me they were going to fire him a few month's back for refusing to take a "club" while breaking up a fight.

"Mr. B.? You got to let us in!" Mike gasped, as we came to a stop in front of his desk, looking back over our shoulders toward the center, they'd be rolling in any second.

"Why?" Mike squeaked, looking trapped. "C'mon -- Mr. B, huh?" He really sounded pitiful.

"Let's go!" He roared, coming to life like some big cat, moving gracefully up the stairs three at a time.

"Sonny's on the other side!" I yelled, as he opened the lock-box and cracked our cells.

"I seen him," he smiled, "get inside they're coming!" he snapped suddenly. I lay down on my bunk trying to breathe normally, listening to the feet pounding up the stairs. I looked out through the big barred windows in front of my cell. The National Guard had encircled the prison, and big vans were pulling into the parking lot. They were the cops from Trenton, Damn! Looked like hundreds of them.

"Hit 15! Hit 18! Hit 25!" Harsh voices screamed and the cells on the tier below me were opening. For the next seven hours I lay trembling, my clothes soaked with perspiration. I couldn't close my ears to the piercing screams, nor the sickening cracking sound the clubs made, striking the flesh and bone of the men. The grunting animal sounds coming from the cops as they crushed the skulls down below me filled me with an unbelievable horror. As time went on it turned into a pure quiet hatred. I watched the reflection in the window. It was dark now.

They cracked a cell just below me. About six cops were crowded around the poor bastard's cell.

"Take your clothes off, Punk!" Hissed some fat-bellied cop who under ordinary circumstances couldn't beat my sister in a fair fight. Most of these types take these jobs simply because it fits their sick, sadistic personalities. They have a license with their badge to harass and beat on men. They can work their frustrations off.

"Outside!" The fat pig screamed. I couldn't see clearly, but I knew this pig had to be frothing from the mouth. The cringing figure stepped from the cell and was hit viciously from behind on the head. I thought surely it killed him. The man moaned, trying to put his hands over his head as he hit the gate, sliding slowly to the floor.

"Kick his balls off!" The fat pig grunted as they kicked the man into peaceful unconsciousness. Another man was running naked down the cell-block tier with his tormentors in pursuit. He saw he was to be trapped by the six dogs below me, and without hesitation, leaped over the railing to the concrete floor below, breaking his leg. I imagine this scene was one of the highlights in these sick guards' minds. It was something to remember in their older years, something to tell their grandchildren. How they single-handedly fought hand to hand with some dirty convict and luckily escaped being thrown off a tier as they both teetered on the edge in deadly combat! (Well, let me tell you something children. If your grandfather was a prison-guard, chances are good that you're looking at a real low-life piece of shit, a moral and physical coward, who could not make it anywhere else in life. But fortunately enough, because of dregs like us, there are jobs for dregs such as these. Though there are the decent men, they are too few, and their calm voices cannot be heard over the loud self-righteous, right wing sadists. These are the same breed of men who were hand picked to run the Nazi death camps, the same men who would oversee plantations in the South -- not because the pay was good -- but because a whip went with the job! A whip and an unlimited number of defenseless backs to beat upon! But only today they get a regulation club, with a shiny regulation badge that authorizes their actions.)

But today, men are no longer as humble as the Jews, or as ignorant as the Black's of the past. Many of us are not sleeping through the Revolution! We are fighting it daily, if not with our bodies, then with our minds. We are fighting the sick fascist philosophy of the conservative mind, the dehumanization of the human being. I only hope to God that I will always be able to be merciful, and man enough to step between my tormentor and my fellow inmate and say: "That's it, that's enough!" Even at the cost of my own life, like that big guy in the mess hall. Would that officer have done the same with their positions reversed? It is very doubtful. Not that I don't think that the sergeant had the decency in him, but he also has unknowingly become his job. He can no longer see that there is decency and fairness in the men he looks upon as animals. A cop is killed and they scream, "He's one of us." Who do they mean by *us*, God? Didn't You teach people that we were all made in Your same image and likeness. Surely, You didn't teach them this Holier than Thou way of thinking? Is there a special place for them up there, God? Or is it just that unknowingly murderous train of thought again? That conservative mind which was State raised, State trained and State paid. Will the meek really inherit the earth, my God?

"Ple--ease! -- Help M-me!" The elderly man moaned, withering naked on the cold concrete floor. He was battered and bleeding from his nose, mouth and ears. One leg was bent at a grotesque angle with about six inches of stark white bone gleaming sharply from his pant leg. This poor bastard wasn't even in the mess hall, I thought, looking down at his face.

"We'll help you, Punk!!" yelled one of the cops down on the flats, grabbing him by both ankles and dragging him screaming down the hallway out of sight. He must have passed out, I thought, as his voice ceased suddenly. They were up on my gallery, but I was too numb and sick to care about being clubbed anymore. I just watched and stood by my gate in silence. My mind had already passed beyond this, not to more days like this, but to the ending of it. Was it only wishful thinking?

"Crack 8, Crack 11!" More screaming, more grunting pig-like sounds. Isn't there an end to this? Some young cop was standing in front of my cell, and I can't even recall his face now. He was just staring at me. He had been in the mess hall when it first started. He couldn't be more than twenty-two years old. They were sending him around to pick out the faces he remembered seeing doing any actual destruction, etc. I saw the recognition in his eyes and I just nodded in confirmation to it! He actually blushed in embarrassment that I remembered him too! He had been in the rear of the mess hall when the shit first broke out, six or seven cops were getting punched around, but nothing serious. He made a break for the door but had got caught up in the mob around our tables. He wasn't touched, but just seeing the cops across the way being set upon made him shake in terror. He'd looked around at me, Sonny and the rest of the guys, expecting us to beat on him. He looked guilty, as if he deserved a beating. We were just standing there waiting for the confusion to clear up a little. He grabbed me by the forearm, his lips quivering.

"I-I I've always been pretty good w-with y-you guys, h-haven't I?" I just looked at the sad figure I had never seen before, trying hard not to laugh.

"Yeah, I guess so, why?" I smiled, feeling very uncomfortable seeing the guy like this.

"A-Are t-they going to b-beat all of us?" He choked.

I had felt sorry for him, but not in the same way I felt for the sergeant who insisted on blowing his whistle, stupidly but courageously! This was a weak man, who had to look in the mirror and see a coward. I pitied him. I did not pity the sergeant. But I did feel an outrageous anger at seeing a man being treated and ridiculed in such a lowly manner. Regardless of whether or not we wear gray pants and they wear blue, a man recognizes and respects another man! It is sad that this is true, more so with the so-called dangerous convicts (the bad ones)! Again I have seen it with guards, but they are so far and few between. I imagine their code of ethics does not allow much room for the common cop to turn around and tell his sergeant or captain: "This is wrong! That's enough!" And the decent guys never seem to wear the stripes or don the bars. They very rarely get in a position to dictate policy.

The young officer must have been standing there in front of my cell for eight seconds. I could see the battle going on within him. He was probably remembering how I had escorted him through the gate, telling about six different dudes that he was an epileptic and felt a seizure coming on.

"You got one down there, what cell?" The guard down by the lock-box yelled impatiently.

"Do what you gotta do, Mister. I'm not going to beg you," I said softly.

"N-no -- D-Don't worry, it's alright!" He smiled sheepishly, starting to move away.

"A couple of my friends lock down there, Mister!" I whispered after him. I listened with my heart in my mouth. He had to be past Mike's cell already. He didn't call out even one cell! Damn!!

"There ain't no more on this tier!" He yelled up to the lock-box, as he passed my cell again giving me a big wink. He even felt better for what he had just done.

"My God!" I felt myself growing faint. I fell on the bunk, burying my face in the pillow to muffle the wracking sobs that were burning in my chest and tearing through my throat. I closed my mind on the screams that still drifted to my ears from the blocks far away. I felt somehow I was a deserter, a coward. I should be sharing the pain. I didn't think of the beatings so much. All I could see was the men's nakedness and I could feel the terrible humiliation they were feeling. Knowing that these cops would act no differently under the same circumstances gave me no consolation at all. Officials will tell you they do this to men because it gives them a defenseless feeling. How much more defenseless need they become? There is something purely sexual in this demented, degrading abuse. Even when the men were naked, I have seen these pigs fondle the cowering men's genitals with their crazed eyes, with their sticks, and even go so far as to jab their clubs at the men's hind parts. What message are they actually trying to deliver by this sick sexual abuse?

"You call yourself a man, tough-guy! Why, you're so frightened. We could fuck you if we so desired."

During the city riots years ago in Long Island City Jail, naked men were beaten beyond endurance with clubs, pick-handles and baseball bats! But this wasn't enough, the officers, both city and prison guards, forced the inmates to line up in single file with a man's penis between the buttocks of the man in front of him. Those who defied this order had their heads split open instantly. Laughing, they would make such comments as: "C'mon Punk, don't jump. You've had one before," or "C'mon, get it in there!"

I had heard this from at least six different guys who spoke of it with great reluctance. One cried with the shame of it and has turned into a real hate monger because of it. None of these men were aware of the reasons, as if there could ever be a reason to justify such a sick action. "Why?" I kept asking. They didn't know. I found out **why** when I was in the Tombs from a Black Officer! We were discussing the riots. He was trying to justify the excessive brutality used on the "Long Island City" inmates.

"You don't know the story, Sully!" He said shaking his head.

"I don't care what the story was, Mr. W! The hostages were released unharmed, not one of them was touched! Mayor Lindsay gave his word, so did Shirley Chisholm and all the rest! So what happens? These guys release all the hostages and file out into the courtyard with their hands behind their heads. Pick-handles!! These cops were using, smashing down on their skull as they came out one at a time ---"

"Sully, you don't know the whole s---" he started.

"Are you kidding me?" I sneered.

"Those guys killed two officers, Sully ----" He stopped suddenly.

"What two officers? No cops were killed, or it would have been splashed in the Daily News for the next ten years!" I retorted.

He was a big man, a nice man, a tough man and he was feeling embarrassed about something. I just looked at him.

"What happened, Mr. W?" I asked him. "I want to know!" I said sincerely. He looked at me hard for some time and then lowered his voice.

"I-It isn't something you talk about, Sully -- no less publicize." He said quietly.

"What happened?" I repeated.

"When I said they killed them -- I didn't mean in that way, t-they destroyed their lives -- as -- men!"

"You serious?" I asked shocked. "How come I never heard nor read about it?"

"Like I said, these aren't things that you tell the papers -- those guys had families."

"Okay! Okay!" I said feeling sick. "But did they know the guys who committed these acts. They had to!"

"Yeah, they knew who they were!"

"Were there many of them?" I whispered.

"Just a few!"

"Alright!" I said. "That type of shit makes me and many like myself just as sick as you must feel about it. But why -- because of three or four perverts, did they do what they did to those men, simply because some of them may have witnessed it? The majority of the men in there, at least the ones I spoke with, weren't even aware this happened. Why should they have been put through such degrading acts? Why didn't they just break-up those responsible? You speak of two men's lives being destroyed, Mr. W I'm speaking of hundreds! When these guys came to Attica telling the Long Island City story, do you realize how it heightened the already growing hatred? Those guys saw the pictures in the Daily News, and how they were coming out with their hands behind their heads. Do you know what the general reaction was after seeing this? There had been a lot of tension that year and a few close riots. The guys felt that if this was the treatment we could expect, then there could be "no giving up" if something were to happen. Don't you see why no kind of negotiating could have got these guys to put their hands behind their heads and walkout? If we cannot believe the word of the Mayor and others, then whom could they believe? Who could they trust? The inmates in all these incidents have been true to their word. But just like in all those Indian Treaties of years ago, 'Great White Father Speak With Forked Tongue'! So now it is clear for all to see, their true feelings, their hidden hatreds! Don't talk with them. Don't barter with those animals. Kill them! So be it. But never again in this life should any dare mention the synthetic word, compassion, in their presence."

Mr. W. sighed deeply, there was a terrible look of hurt and confusion in his eyes.

"I know Sully -- I know!" He said simply. "But look at this place Sully! (The Tombs) I know it's no place for men to live, regardless of the crime he has committed. A man can't take one step in any direction without somebody breathing on him. I would like to help you guys. I know you got a legitimate beef! But I'm in no better shape than you guys are, except that I can leave every night. What do you think eight hours a day does to me in here? I watch guys burning themselves alive, hanging-up, cutting their wrists and throats! Don't you think this affects me and most of the other officers? Don't you think we'd like to work with you guys under more humane conditions? Christ!! We hate this fucking place as much as you guys." He said in disgust. "They ripped down the Women's House of Detention, Damn! This is the place that should be destroyed. This is the modern day black hole of Calcutta!"

"Hey, you don't have to convince *me*!" I said and we both laughed.

I walked away with a better understanding of the average officers position. In the overall scheme of things, he had no position! He was the pawn that risked his life on a daily basis. Always up front during times of duress, yet he had no voice. His sole job was to save the King and Queen from the angry people, his own people! But Mr. and Mrs. King Wasp up there in the state house pay his salary, so how can he tell them, "You're a parasite, Mr. Wasp and your wife isn't really 'happy' with you sucker. She's in love with the material things you can offer her. Have they blood on them too?"

I awoke at the bell the following morning. The usual talking and laughter could not be heard. The only sounds were those of a toilet, a sink, or the brushing of teeth. Otherwise, it was deadly quiet. "Who did they get? Sonny? -- Tony? -- Johnny? -- I hope they're not hurt bad -- or dead!"

"Alright," a voice of authority yelled, breaking the peaceful silence. Here we go again, I thought. I didn't even want to look into those ugly hate-filled faces again. "When we crack the cells, everybody comes out. You'll move to the mess hall in single file. There'll be no talking, no looking around. You'll look straight ahead, and when you get in the mess hall, the same applies there. Understand?" He barked like some master sergeant that had been demoted and had just gotten his stripes back. A little pompous ass-hole, a nobody trying to be a somebody. Nobody as much as acknowledged they even heard him.

"Alright!" The little mutt gloated, accepting our silence as some kind of personal triumph. As I walked by, I could see his half-sneering, half-smiling face from the corner of my eye. I wanted so bad to just spin around and spit a clam in the mutts face and stomp his rotten body right through the pores of his rotten outer skin. But since I was aware that these people fully reciprocated my own feelings, I succumbed quickly to my better judgment.

I walked along the temporary serving-counter they had quickly installed. Taking only the coffee, the guy pouring it whispered, "They got Sonny!" I looked up quickly but his eyes were glued to the counter. The mess hall was jammed with cops and civilians. They were only feeding one tier at a time. There were only thirty of us! The cops began to come around the tables trying to find the faces they knew they had missed.

As each one passed, I would drop my head to the coffee cup, sipping, exaggerating its hotness.

"You." A voice barked, almost made me bite the heavy mug in half.

"Y-yes, Sir?" I said putting on my best wide eyed innocent, pitiful stare as I look up at the lieutenant standing beside me.

"What's your name?" He said very crisp and business like. There was no harshness in his voice. I guess they're tired; *they'd* had a rough night.

"M-my -- n-name?" I stuttered with pretended nervousness. Trying to gain a few seconds to think. He didn't know my name? Makes sense, since I've only been here a few weeks.

"McBride!" I said holding my breath, using an old alias.

"First name?" He snapped.

"John, Sir, but why are ----"

"What's your number, McBride?" He said ignoring me. I gave him a number in the general vicinity of my own and a cell location from the tier below me. This was the answer I didn't want him thinking about since all the guys who were in here were from only one tier.

"B-ut w-what's wrong, lieutenant? Have I-I done something wrong?" I began to even feel sorry for myself, and the lieutenant wasn't that bad a guy.

"It's just routine, McBride. We'll call you down this afternoon. It's nothing serious." He said trying to soothe my obvious frayed nerves.

"Oh!" a sigh of relief. "Thank -- Thank you, lieutenant!!" I simpered disgustingly.

Mike, who was sitting right next to me and all the other guys almost spilled their coffee. They were shaking in silent laughter. Mike whispered into his hands that were cupped over his mouth.

"Damn, Sully, I felt like puking. You should get an Oscar for that shit!"

"Your lucky you ain't getting the Oscar wise-guy," I whispered back, "because the first name that came to my mind was yours!"

"W-What?"

"Yeah! But the only reason I didn't do it was because I didn't want to have to sit here next to you when you shit your pants!!"

"Fuck you, Sully!" Mike hissed.

Everybody cracked up, laughing loudly, including Mike and myself. About five more hacks ran over. "Shut up! Shut up!" They yelled, which made us all laugh even harder. It really wasn't what passed between Mike and I that we were laughing about. That was simply an excuse to relieve all the pent-up tensions, fears and hopes that we all secretly harbored.

"You guys are finished eating!" We weren't, but we weren't about to argue either. "Let's move out!"

I was on the administrations "ten most wanted" list for about three days. After a prison wide intensive investigation, I was finally apprehended. I surrendered meekly in the mess hall.

"That's him!" A high-pitched woman-like voice pierced through the mess hall chatter, which was back to normal now. Everybody looked up immediately. The lieutenant was on the other side of the mess hall waving frantically to the guard standing closest to our table.

"Get out of this one!" Mike laughed. I put my head damn near in my tray as the guard was pointing to different guys at the table. The lieutenant was shaking his head from side to side with an impatient, negative gesture. When the guard pointed his finger down at me, I peeped at the lieutenant across the mess hall. I thought he was going to break his neck the way he was shaking it up and down, motioning for him to take me out.

"Let's go." The guard said, raising his eyebrows as if to say, "What can I do?" Mike turned to me as I was getting up to leave, grasping my hand and shaking it firmly.

"I'm sorry, Sully, but you be cool, huh? If you go back to Trenton, tell Sonny and the rest I said hello, okay?"

"Sure thing, Mike. You be good too, huh?" I smiled walking away with the cop, waving goodbye to the different dudes (both black and white) I had shared another part of my life with. No regrets! I thought. They would be worth it all over again, even at the most terrible price.

The lieutenant was waiting out in the hallway with about five cops with their clubs, naturally. I felt good now, no more ducking, no more slipping and sliding! Here it is!! I felt even better knowing what I was going to do if they swung them clubs at me. I knew I wouldn't win, but there wasn't going to be a "naked runner" for them to laugh at today. I've been beat before. I couldn't believe my eyes as I walked up to him. He was just standing there with his fists on his hips, smiling sardonically, still shaking his head.

"So your McBride, huh?" he said. He looked so congenial. It was catching.

"No, Sir!" I grinned myself.

"Then you must be Sullivan, right?" He arched his brows.

"Right." I laughed.

"Alright, Sullivan, I probably would have done the same myself, if I could have thought of it!" he laughed. "These officers will take you to your cell. You'll be going back to Trenton, in the morning probably!"

"Could I ask you a question, lieutenant?"

"Of course, go ahead." he said.

"To be truthful, I don't understand how or by whom I was picked out or for exactly what. I'm not going to lie and say I wasn't in the mess hall. Of course I was, and I admit to my share of the action. But how did you get it out of so many?"

He just laughed. "You been around long enough, Sully, to know we have our informers. We tallied up all the 'rat notes' we received the following morning. You polled about number three in the popular vote, and we had close to two hundred notes. As the saying goes, 'a million Frenchmen can't be wrong', huh?" he smiled.

"Damn! Yeah, I guess so."

So it was back to the "snake pit," as we often referred to the sun-baked piece of earth that served as the "yard" in Trenton State Prison for eighteen hundred men. The ground became so dry and cracked in the summer that at times we wore bandannas to cover our noses and mouths. Big drums of oil were poured over this parched earth, and huge rollers were constantly being driven across it in an effort to keep the dirt and dust packed down. But when the sun beat down on it, by mid-afternoon one could not breathe too deeply for fear the rising oil fumes would burn his lungs out.

This oil-slicked piece of turf also served as our softball field. In order to play a game, the rest of Trenton's entire population had to stand in about a ten foot area against the yard's four walls. Everyone who came to Trenton soon became adept at pulling his head in between his shoulders like a turtle every time he heard the solid crack of the bat. Those who didn't, took the ten count with broken jaws and noses. This would teach them the cost of not paying close attention to our national past-time. Being a left fielder, I not only ran the hazard of the cement wall, but also the "brick shithouse" which jutted out dangerously from left-center. What I was most conscious of and always aware of were the chess, domino and card games going on against the left and center field walls. Every time a ball was hit hard, my first thought was, "Oh shit! Who am I gonna have to fight this time?"

It was a choice of either stepping in the middle of someone's Pawns and Knights and catching the ball with a good risk of a fight; or pulling up short before the crowd and playing the ball off the wall, with a good chance of blowing the game. But, if I were to choose not stepping in somebody's mug, just to catch a ball, then the popular feeling, often expressed verbally, was that I had no heart! I was told that if I were going to play left or center-field on that team, "The Black Sox", then I had better get used to stepping on people and knocking them down. So, since I had a weak stick, all I had to rely upon was my fielding ability and a strong throwing arm. I learned to dodge and duck and, when I couldn't run around people, I ran over them. I had to play exceptionally hard because I was the only regular starter who didn't have a life sentence, and this team was used to being a winner. The two biggest sports in Trenton were softball and boxing, also quite a bit of handball. So any time that I did not have a scheduled league game, I would work out. That included running six to ten miles every other day, calisthenics, and the heavy bag on alternate days, along with some light sparring. Outside of a few white guys, most of the fighters were Black, and all of them were good. There were a few "short-stops," but they were lifetime "shadowboxers!" Every time a dude like Rubin Carter, Chuck Carter, Brady Howard, Caponegra, Hank Sheely, Jingles, Edwards, or Louie Vandyne came to work up a sweat, they couldn't find anybody to work out with. All the so-called fighters claimed fatigue, bad back, sprained wrists, etc. Frankie DiPaula who, also like Rubin, had had a championship fight in Madison Square Garden (light-heavyweight title) wouldn't even lace the gloves on against these dudes. There were two Italian guys, both from Newark that could have been champions in their own weight divisions. A guy named Caponegra "Cappy" and a good friend of mine, Jerry Naive. Jerry was Frankie DiPaula's partner on an assault charge in which Frankie opened up on them. The guy was a top-notch stool-pigeon and he was deathly afraid of Jerry. So naturally, when I heard Frankie fighting for the light-heavyweight championship of the world, I couldn't help but crack up in laughter. Remembering how Jerry, 145 pounds, slapped the shit out of him on a stairway in seven-wing.

I worked out hard and trained for about two years religiously. Though I never became exceptional, I was better than average. Just the physical condition I attained was worth all the hard work.

I was going pretty well for a while until I ran into some static with the so-called "Nazi-party." I was never even aware that such a group existed. One day a few of these guys approached me in the yard. I had just finished running about eight miles, and was putting on my sweater and jacket to protect my overheated body against the biting cold. I always walked the track for about ten minutes, until my body came back to it's normal temperature. I had just pulled my navy, wool watch cap over my ears and was pulling on big leather mittens when somebody called me.

"Hey, you!" The voice called again, I turned around to the sound of the voices and saw three guys huddled over in the corner, away form the blowing gusts of snow. One of them was motioning in my direction to come over. I had never seen any of the three before, but if they wanted me they could walk over here. So I turned my back to them pretending not to hear.

"Hey man, didn't you see me waving to you?" Said some short, stubby dark haired guy with earmuffs on. There has always been something about people who wear earmuffs that bothers me, and this guy was a snotty little creep! As the creep was talking, I was trying hard to place his face. I remembered seeing him somewhere! The other two guys had stayed over on the wall.

"Yeah, Man," he said opening his jacket collar to expose a giant-black swastika dangling from a chain around his neck.

"You work in that diet kitchen, don't you?" He said putting a sneering emphasis on "that."

"Yes," I said nicely, "I do!"

"I-I don't know, man," he was shaking his head in displeasure. "I just don't understand it!"

"What don't you understand?" I said, knowing what he was getting at.

I remembered this punk now! It was in Rahway, just before the riot. I had just finished playing a game of handball out in the big yard, and was walking into the bathroom to wash-up a little. I had only seen the face momentarily, because the quick look I took was between the legs of three different black dudes who had their guns exposed, cocked, and primed for action. This creep here (his name was "Bello") was on his knees, licking his trembling lower lip trying to decide which to tackle first. I just splashed some water on my face and got out of there quickly.

"You know!" he was saying, as I just stood there smiling, deciding which side of his jaw I would break.

"I mean -- it don't look right, six 'shines' in there -- and your the only white guy -- y-you know --" he started to stutter.

"No, I don't know!" I said nastily, still smiling at this phony creep.

"Dig, Man!" He puffed up fondling his swastika. You can see where I'm at, right? You know how I feel about them! A lot of guys don't like the idea of you working in---"

"Hold it right there!" I said stepping up real close to him. "First of all, whatever I do is my business. I don't care what nobody thinks understand?! I know what I am, and those I call my friends know what I am. That's all that matters. I took the job in that diet room because I can cook my own shit, and eat halfway decent. I wouldn't care if there were fifty Brothers working in there, as long as I get the same respect that I give. Am I supposed to be afraid of the terrible Black Rapists? That's all they think of, you know! Isn't it true that anytime you see a white guy and black guy who are friends, one of them must be a homosexual? Isn't this the general consensus? But you know why I don't worry about it, why I don't worry about walking into a shower-room full of Brothers, or anyplace else? Because I'm a man, Punk! That's the way I try to carry myself, with *everybody* and that's the way I am treated. Now get the fuck out of my face!" I shot at him, starting to turn away.

"I got friends, I-I ---" he started.

"Were your friends in the shithouse down Rahway, Punk? Were you wearing your swastika then, too?" Bello's eyes flew open and he was looking back to where his friends were standing, wondering whether they had overheard our conversation. He just stood there staring at me, trying to figure out if I had really seen him!

"What's wrong, Mama? You ain't got nothing to say? You got a lot of heart Punk. You know that? Out here in the yard you preach all this racist bullshit, this Nazi-Party superman philosophy -- and all the time you can't wait to get back to the block, or the nearest shithouse to suck a black dick! Who do you think you're bullshitting? You're a sick bastard, do you know that?" I laughed in his face as he was trying to work up his nerve to make some feeble retort.

"Don't say another word, Punk. Just walk away while you can and don't worry about me pulling the covers off you! I won't say nothing to your friends. Who knows!? I may even want a shot of that hot-head you got! I'm really surprised that a racist such as yourself doesn't prefer his meat on the light side!" I said, laughing, trying to goad him into swinging on me. But he just stood there, his eyes darting nervously in all directions, wanting to get away from me, but not knowing how.

"Alright, Mama!" I sneered. "You can leave now."

"I--I--" he started to mumble.

"Don't say anything!!" I said walking away, starting to jog again to get my blood running.

About three weeks had passed since I had words with this guy, Bello. He never as much as glanced at me when I passed him in the yard, or in the hallways. But meantime, unknown by me, he was trying to pump heart into a few of the creeps that hung around with him. There were about twenty guys in this so-called Nazi-Party and most of them were impressed by this guys glib tongue. They were also under the impression that he had guts to match it! About seven of these guys worked in the kitchen. Whenever they were all sitting together during "early-chow" for the kitchen help, they would glare at me menacingly as I went about my work in the diet-room preparing the different meals for the men with Ulcers, Colitis, etc. Naturally, I had access to all the special foods and, naturally, I looked out for all **my** friends. Fixing up special trays for them and sneaking them out to them when they came in to eat with the regular mess. I have never been a jail house peddler with food, clothes, or anything else. This shit was all "State" stuff and, if I had access to it, I gave it away! To my friends first and then to anybody else! It's amazing, and also very sad, how men in prison can build up such petty jealousy and animosity over an extra piece of chicken, a bowl of peaches, or even a "job" itself, and then direct their hatred at you under a completely different pretence.

I pretended I was unaware of their baleful glances, and as long as nobody said nothing to me personally, or put their hands on me, I would ignore it.

I was carrying some trays over to the hospital one morning when Tommy Barker, a friend of mine, stopped me in the hallway.

"Sully, what's going on with you and those Nazi creeps?" He asked looking very serious.

"Nothing, Tommy. It's all just petty shit. They're frustrated tough-guys, that's all!"

"Do you know that Joey C. asked some guy for a shiv yesterday?" he asked.

"So, what's that got to do with me?" I asked.

"Well, the guy that this Joey asked is a friend of mine, and he told me that the guy said he wanted it for you!"

"And of course your 'friend' gave it to him," I said sarcastically.

"He didn't know it was you 'till after he had already given it to him, Sully. That's why he came right to me."

"Well, it doesn't make much difference, Tom. He would only have gotten it some place else anyway. It's better this way, at least I know! Thanks."

"Is this Joey C., the guy who's always hyped up on pills, Sully?"

"Yeah, he don't know where he's at half the time. Them creeps probably been pumping his heart up the last few weeks! How many more of them you figure want some action? I'll get Louie, Jerry, Cody, and a few of the guys. We can catch them in the yard this afternoon and---"

"Forget it Tom. It's only this one guy, so why start a big thing when it ain't necessary?" I said.

"It ain't gonna be no big thing, Sully. We'll run right through these mutts in a matter of seconds. We can---"

"Forget it!" I laughed. "I appreciate what you want to do, but I got to take care of my own trouble. If it was more than just this guy, I'd say 'yeah,' but I'll be okay, Tom!"

"You sure?" He persisted.

"Yeah," I laughed. "I'm sure. I'll catch you later, huh? I got to get these trays to the hospital."

"Alright, Hoss. Take care, huh?"

That afternoon, when everybody was in the mess hall eating, this Joey C. walked by the diet-room window. His eyes were glazed and the pupils dilated. It didn't appear that he could even see me when he spoke.

"Hey, Sully, I'd like to talk with you in the back when you get a chance. It's important!" He said with a forced sickly smile.

"Alright, I'll be back in a few minutes, as soon as I finish wiping this counter off. Okay?" I smiled back at him openly and dumbly.

"Yeah, sure, I'll wait," he said.

The blood was rushing hotly through my body as I reached into the drawer beneath the counter for one of the butcher knives. But deciding against it, I walked back toward the iceboxes. Every muscle in my body was tense and hurting, my eyes started to burn, and my temples pounded thunderously. I took a wide turn going around the corner out of the kitchen area. I spotted him immediately, standing in the far corner between the two big iceboxes. He was talking to some red headed dude who, upon my approach, scurried away quickly. Both his hands were in sight as I came to stand right up in front of him.

"You want to see me?" I smiled.

"Yeah," His hand started to move.

"Bang!" I caught him with a left hook. It was only a glancing blow, but enough to slam him straight up against the icebox. Then I leaned on him hard, hearing the bridge of his nose snap as I drove my right hand hard into his face. I stepped back as I watched him bounce off the box and drop to his knees. He was moaning, the blood gushing in spurts through his broken nose and out between the fingers clutching his face. I didn't stomp him, figuring he had enough. He was on one knee and completely bent over. I was standing directly above his balled up body, so I never saw his hand snake inside his shirt. He came to life suddenly, and I felt a searing, burning pain. I had his hair gripped in one fist, looking down into his frightened animal-like eyes. I wanted to move, but I couldn't! Something was terribly wrong! He made some strange choking sound and his body moved again. The terrible pain flashed to my brain again, as my grasp on his hair loosened. I staggered back a step, feeling almost paralyzed. Was he punching me in the groin? Is that what I felt? Then I saw it! He was coming up out of a crouch. His right arm was drawn back, and at the end of it was the longest ice pick I ever laid eyes on. My mind screamed, "He's killing you!" But I couldn't move. He lunged upward to thrust the knife into my belly. A friend of mine, named Hank, came from nowhere falling on his arm and getting stabbed in the side himself. Though he didn't know it until afterward, the knife skidded across the floor. He started to move toward it, when everything came back to me! Just as he laid his hand on it, I kicked him viciously in the belly, lifting him off the ground. He was gagging, and then puking, as he lay on his back, his feet kicking in the air spasmodically. I stomped his face till the solid thudding sound turned wet and gushy. Someone pulled me back off him. There were ten or fifteen guys around now.

"You alright, Sully?" Somebody asked.

"Where are you stuck?" Another asked.

"I -- don't know." I muttered. Feeling faint as the pain began to sweep through me. I looked down at my white kitchen pants, and they were a bright, wet red from the waist to the knees. I pulled my shirt up running my hand over my belly, trying to feel for any puncture holes. If he got me in the stomach, I was in big trouble. I could be bleeding internally. I spit on the back of my hand but it was white, no blood coming up at all.

"There they are, Sully!" Exclaimed one of the guys kneeling in front of me, pointing to two small punctures on either side of my groin. They were barely visible. I opened my pants up quickly; worried that he may have got to the "money"! But the two jagged punctures were barely a half-inch to either side of my testicles. The blood was oozing out slowly, but steadily. I could hardly stand up any longer.

"You gotta get to the hospital, Man!" Somebody said.

"Yeah!" Voiced another.

"Son-of-a-bitch!" I murmured looking at the still figure of the hophead the guys had dragged him over in the corner, behind some pots and pans that were stacked by the icebox.

"Hank, walk with me over the hospital, huh?"

"Yeah, sure. Let's go!" He said holding me under one arm as I staggered out of the kitchen into the mess hall. Chow was still going on. As soon as I walked out and guys saw my pants, a number of them got up from the tables, which is against the rules. Asking who did it? Not caring about the guards shouts to sit down. My friends Tommy and Peppy slid up to my side.

"Was it that guy, Sully?" Tommy asked.

I just nodded yes and continued walking from the mess hall.

"Where's he at?" Peppy demanded.

"In back -- But forget it, he's already fucked up!"

As I lay stripped from the waist down on some outdated operating table, biting my lip damn near through against the pain, some homo inmate nurse was more concerned with playing with my balls than cleaning the wounds.

"Get away from me, Punk, and get the doctor in here!" I snapped at him, raising up on one elbow.

"Oh, yes!" He squeaked and ran out of the room.

The doctor said there really wasn't much he could do with these type of wounds, other than pack sulfur on them and wrap them tightly. A few minutes later, the Warden came in asking if I wanted to press charges and to sign papers.

"I don't know who did it, how can I press charges?" I said.

"Don't give us that crap, Sullivan. We got the guy who assaulted you in the other room. You know who he is!" the warden rasped.

"Sorry, but I didn't see who did it--happened too fast."

"Well, he's going to sign papers against you. Doesn't that make a difference?" he asked.

"Nope. I don't know the guy. How can he sign papers against me?"

"All right, but you think about it. Don't you be the fall guy. We'll talk with you again tomorrow, okay?"

"Yeah, sure. I don't mind," I smiled at the warden, knowing he was wishing that I were dying slowly.

The doctor came back in as I was being helped into a wheelchair. "Damn, kid, that's the worst beating I've seen in thirty years! What did you use, a pipe?" he laughed.

"No, I didn't beat anybody. That guy's really messed up, huh?" I asked, feeling a lot better.

"He just came in a minute ago. His head's the size of a basketball--all broken up." the doctor was laughing, a real sadistic bastard.

"You mean he wasn't awake when the warden was here? Didn't he sign no papers?"

"Nope," the doctor said, "just woke up."

"So you didn't see him sign no papers, huh?"

"Nope," the doctor laughed.

The outcome of this incident was sixty days on bread and water for both of us, for refusing to sign papers on each other. They threw me in a dark, rat-infested cell in South Hall, giving me one rotten meal every third day. The puncture holes were running green and yellow pus; sometimes black, and they refused to change the filthy bandages. I had to rip up the only shirt I had and use that to keep the dirt out of the still open wounds. I used the bottom half of the pajama-type outfit we were issued in the box. I cut it off from the knees down and used these portions to clog up the toilet bowl at night, so the rats couldn't come up through the pipes. All that was in the cell was a huge concrete slab, a grimy lice infested mattress to cover it, one thin blanket (that never managed to cover my freezing body regardless how I managed to ball myself up), and a toilet bowl without tissue paper. They had always "just ran out" of it. I would use little squares ripped out of my blanket each day. By the time twenty days were up, I had a blanket the size of a napkin! There was no need for a sink since we were given a cup of water three times a day with our bread. And in the heat of the summer, if things really got bad you could always dip your cup in the shit-bowl (providing you were thirsty enough).

I got out of the box sixty days later and twelve pounds lighter. But in two weeks, I was in the groove again working out, boxing, etc.

The year was 1963, Trenton was starting to get real bad. Not only was the racial tension bad enough already, it was getting worse because of the overall conditions of the prison, the attitudes of the cops, lousy meals, improper medical care, unreasonable wages, poor visitation facilities, etc. Leaflets made up in the print shop were being passed around the yard. Every man was made aware. I couldn't help but think of the Rahway affair and wonder if it was to be the same thing all over again.

My friend, Tommy Barker, and three Brothers approached me in the yard that afternoon. They wanted me to be part of the committee, which would put forth the demands to the administration Sunday afternoon, while the "Outside" softball team was still inside the yard. This way, the guys figured our plight would not go unheard.

"There ain't gonna be no violence, Sully, unless they provoke it!" Tommy was saying. "This is just gonna be a sit-down strike. Everything stops. Except for the guys in the hospital, I mean everything. If they want to lock us in, we lock in. If they want us to lock out, we lock out! Everybody keeps eating, just as always. To turn this into a hunger strike would only hurt us, since we want to hold out for months, if necessary.

We want to hit them in their pockets because it's the only thing they are sensitive to."

"I can understand this Tom. Are all the demands written on paper? How many guys are on this committee?" I asked.

"About fifteen, Sully!" A Brother named "Doc" offered. "I talked with Chuck Carter and most of the other brothers. I can't say what the Muslim Brothers want to do. They haven't decided yet!"

"Wait a minute. If I'm not mistaken, one of the demands is for facilities to allow Muslim services; [*Muslim services were outlawed in New Jersey and New York in prison in 1961. Muslim services was one of the demands.*] and for a Muslim minister on a regular basis, which I am in agreement with. But why the indecision on their part, as far as backing this strike is concerned? They must have some reason, Doc!"

"Listen, Sully," Doc spoke, throwing up his hands in mock resignation, "I can't speak for them. But my feeling is this: first of all, they didn't initiate the strike. They feel they would just be going for a ride without any real voice in the matter. Secondly--"

"What's the real issue, Doc?" I smiled, and he knew what I was talking about.

"They don't want any part of anything you devils helped start. It might be some kind of trick!" Doc said, feeling stupid.

"Ain't that a bitch!" I could only shake my head. "Are they serious? How the hell are we ever gonna get anything if we can't even get together ourselves? There are times when differences should be put aside, Doc. And this is one of them!"

"I know," Doc said softly. "I'll get Chuck and try to talk with Brother John again this afternoon."

"I like that dude, Tom," I said, watching Doc make his way across the yard.

"He's a man, Sully. And don't let his age fool you, he's a bad piece of work."

"How old is he?"

"About fifty, I guess. He's been here about twenty-two years," Tom said.

"When's he going to the Parole Board?"

"He should go back again this year. He got hit with eighteen months last trip. That must have been fourteen months ago!"

"And he's fucking around in this thing, Tom?" I was drugged.

"He's been through a lot in here, Sully. He believes in what we're trying to do, the things we're trying to get. He says, 'If we just get one of our demands, it will be worth it.' He figures we got to start somewhere."

The administration was well aware that some type of strike was in the making by the leaflets, and by their "requests" boxes that were jammed to the bursting point with rat notes! But they didn't know what type of strike it was to be, or where it would take place.

The Outside softball team came in as usual that Sunday afternoon to play the Prison Varsity Team, which was comprised of the four best players from each of the six regular league teams. The ball-players were always allowed out in the yard for batting practice etc., about twenty minutes before the rest of the population. All the players were tense and their minds preoccupied. When the Outside team offered us the field to start warming up, we refused. They began looking very strangely at one another. I figured the "Brass" might have told them that they were expecting possible trouble. Everybody was coming into the yard now, packing tightly against the four walls. To the Outside players, it appeared that everything was normal, but to those who lived in there, the atmosphere was electric! There was talking and horseplay, but it was forced and strained. The umpires signaled our bench to take the field. Since we were always the home team, we jogged out to our position. No sooner had their first batter walked to the plate, then guys began to drift away from the walls and onto the playing field, until there were five or six hundred guys out there.

"Clear the field! Clear the field!" The yard sergeant ordered over the speaker from his booth by the center field wall. "Clear the field!!" He barked as the guys took sitting positions, their hands wrapped around their knees. About ten guards rushed to the visitors' bench to usher them through the field of sitting men. They hurled obscenities at them, such as, "You come in here fat and healthy looking. We wanna eat too!" and "Yeah, tell them we wanna eat when you go out there, you fat bastards!" Another chimed in, "The hospital's a Butcher Shop!"

The whole yard was screaming after them as they left the yard hurriedly. Though the men were screaming their threats at the Outside ball players, their stares and all the venom was directed at the guards who stood cowered against the walls.

Doc, Tommy, Peppy, Chuck, and finally myself rose above the sitting men to speak and tell them exactly what we wanted to do -- what we expected to gain. Even if we gained nothing in the material sense, we could at least salvage the little bit of pride every man should retain, regardless of the physical and mental abuse he must endure.

The men roared their approval as one, upon each demand that was voiced openly and clearly for all to hear. They were also told that if the men who spoke here today were locked-up, there were four smaller back-up committees who in turn would step forward should the need arise. We also explained how, once they were locked in their individual cells, they would be preyed upon, harassed, threatened and possibly beaten. If this was to be the case, I explained, it was no longer a demand for material things, it became a group fight. It became the fight of each individual man to follow that small part of his mind, which screamed in hunger for pride and dignity.

Under duress, it becomes extremely simple for each individual to justify in his own mind a thousand seemingly good reasons why he should capitulate and just become one of the mindless herd. But I imagine the biggest factor that changes a man's mind is to listen to the agonizing screams of your friends as they slowly work their way to your cell. Though twenty men might be beaten, and only one succumb to their way of thinking, your mind will tend to grasp at this one man, as a means of your own salvation. You will not want to remember the nineteen others who were beaten, but still unbroken! "He's doing as they say," your mind will scream, as the click of the cells, the screams and thudding of clubs draws closer. "Why shouldn't I?" This is what you will ask yourselves when you lock in your cells! There will be no "leaders" in there to talk to you and comfort you. But when you ask yourself this question, ask it of yourself only! For what the next man does (or the next hundred do) will be no reflection on you. For at this final moment, you will stand alone!

I can only hope when this is all over, we may all look upon one another with the same pride and self-respect that I see in the eyes, and carriage of every man here today. And regardless of what we might gain or lose here today, let us all (both black and white) maintain and nourish this newly found closeness of spirit. It has risen from our mutual sufferings. Let us never again be used as ignorant tools of an uncompassionate administration, that cares not whether we live or die. The days where they could pit black man against white, in any prison crisis, are ending. A new day is nearing, where men are intelligent enough to recognize a common cause, where color, religious beliefs, and political ideals should play no major part.

We, here today, are the pathfinders, merely leading the way for those to come after us. This new day I speak of may be a long time coming, but as my friend, "Doc" here believes, we must start somewhere! And I can't think of a better place. The yard was thundering and shaking as Doc,

Peppy, Tommy and Chuck C. spoke their minds, humorously, bitterly, matter-of-factly, but always truthfully. I thought I was in Yankee Stadium watching one of the old Yankee-Dodger games during the World Series. It was that hysterical and deafening.

"Look up over the wall!" Tommy whispered in my ear.

The roof of the warden's house, which was just outside the prison, rose to a peak and jutted above the prison wall. It was high enough so that anybody looking from the attic windows had an unobstructed view of the prison yard. There were two windows and both were occupied. There were three or four pairs of binoculars trained on us. All I could make out from where I stood were the gold bands on what were obviously officers' hats.

"They probably got all the names already, huh, Tom?" I asked.

"Yeah, but it don't make no difference. Look at them sergeants over in the corner with their pads out, writing a mile a minute!"

"Hey Doc! Chuck!" I called.

"What's happening, Sully?" Doc said grinning from ear to ear.

"Listen, Doc, they'll probably be grabbing us as soon as we walk in the blocks. Let them guys on the first back-up committee know what's happening, okay?

"Yeah, don't worry. They already know. But I'll go over it with them again."

"Good. How much time left before we go in?" My belly was in knots.

"About ten minutes!" Doc laughed sensing my uneasiness.

We walked into the blocks. Nothing happened! Everybody went to the mess hall for supper. Nothing happened! The guards were behind the counters serving the food, looking mean and embarrassed.

About 5:30 that evening, my cell door cracked open and four guards came to escort me to the Warden's office.

"Fold your arms across your chest and look straight ahead when you walk." The one guard motioned with his stick. As I passed through the center on my way, I saw that all the guards from the other shifts were being called in. When I reached the Warden's office; Tommy, Doc, Chuck, Peppy, and about eight others were already there; facing the wall, their arms folded in front of them, encircled by about twenty guards. As we approached the Warden's office I was put up against the wall and frisked thoroughly.

"Is that Sullivan?" A captain asked standing in the now open door.

"Yes, Sir!" The guard answered nervously.

"Alright, bring him in. The Warden will see him now!"

I walked into the office and stopped before the long table, at which sat Warden Yeager, an assistant warden and two captains. I almost laughed aloud at the silly game they were playing. I must have stood before them for five minutes before anybody looked up from the papers they pretended to be so involved in. The Warden looked up first in mock surprise.

"You're Sullivan?" He asked.

"Yes, Sir." I answered.

"Alright, Sullivan, I'm not going to play games with you, I haven't the time for it. Just what is it you men want?" he asked offhandedly.

"Have you seen the list of demands, Sir?" I asked looking into his eyes.

"Uh – Why, yes, as a matter of fact, I have one right here before me." He said picking up a sheet of paper between his thumb and forefinger disdainfully. It angered me. Just by the simple action, I knew his complete attitude toward the men in general.

"Then you know what we want." I answered, trying to hide the bitterness I felt.

"Don't you think they're a bit unreasonable?" He was smiling now.

"Which one, Sir?" I smiled back at him.

"Well, uh -- how about this food thing. I ---"

"It's garbage, Sir, mo----"

"What!!? Who do you think your talking to? I -- I --"

He was on his feet now leaning across the table shaking his finger at me. I just stood there smiling at him, seeing this so called intelligent, reasonable man almost frothing at the mouth. With the help of the captains and their coaxing, he finally sat down again, and regained his false composure.

"So! -- I gather you don't care for the menu?" He smiled evilly.

"As I was going to say, Sir. If you were to weigh the slop cans that go out to the pigs after every meal, as ordered by the state law, you would realize that almost three-quarters of the food is not being consumed by inmates. What would this lead *you* to believe, Sir?" I asked trying to talk sense to him.

"Humph," he snorted. "What's this about medical care? What's wrong with our hospital, if I may ask?" He said like a snotty little kid.

"You haven't got a hospital, Sir, nor the staff to run one if you did. Neither nurses nor competent doctors! There are too many guys dying who shouldn't be. Not so much from the butcher-like surgery being performed, but from the complete lack of after care. In many cases is the most critical point. If ---"

"What else is there that doesn't meet with your approval, Sullivan?" He said gritting his teeth.

"Do you really want to know, Sir?" I asked wondering just how far I could go before he jumps across the table and sinks his fangs into my jugular vein.

"Yes, I'm dying to know!" He sneered.

"Disregarding the demands we have listed, Sir, the biggest hurdle that lies in our path is the complete insensitivity on the part of the entire administration, from you on down. Even now, you don't understand a thing I'm trying to say, or you don't want to understand. I really don't know which!"

"What do you want, Sullivan?" The Warden said again, throwing his hands up.

"I've already told you what 'we' want Sir, the list of demands is --"

"I asked what *you* wanted, Sullivan. How much time are you doing?"

"Five to seven years!" I said.

"Have you ever thought about putting in a request for Jones Farm? The food's very good, you can visit with your family on the grounds, and there's only about 150 men there, not overcrowded at all!" He smiled, dangling his bait.

"What would I have to do for this?" I smiled back at him.

"Now your talking reasonable," he guffawed. "You don't have to do a thing, Sullivan. I just want you and your friends to work together with me. Just tell the men to return to work. Meanwhile, we'll work out the demands in a democratic way, the white man's way!" He smiled as if we had shared some big secret.

"Which way is that, Sir?" I was still grinning stupidly at him. This brought him up a little, but he gathered nothing from my facial expression and continued.

"These people don't think the same as us, Sully. These black bastards are only trying to use you." He sighed. "I only wish there were some way to separate them from you, but it's not in my power. Will you pull together with me? You'll find it worth your while!"

"You say the Blacks are trying to use us, Sir?" I laughed aloud. "What gives you the impression that the white men in here are less hungry than the Black men? What leads you to believe that we are not suffering the same indignities as the Black man? To use the base word "nigger!" You could apply it to all the men in here. We're all niggers of the State! You'd crush my skull just as quick as you would theirs! So let's not talk about 'us and them'. That shit's played itself out!"

I expected him to jump up raving like a mad dog, but he kept the dog restrained inside himself.

"Is this the way you want it?" he said, his voice hard and cold.

"No, Sir, it's the way you want it. The way people like yourself have made it! All I can do is try to live with it. And maybe some day help to change it!"

"You and the likes of you will never change anything, Sullivan, as long as there are decent people in this world!" he whispered.

"Do you consider yourself one of the 'decent' people, Sir?" I smiled.

"That will be all, Sullivan!!" He quipped.

"May I ask one more question, Sir?" He nodded his assent.

"From what you have said to me, I know what you told the other white guys, but what kind of story did you give those black bastards you speak about? Did you tell them how treacherous the white guys in the yard were? How we were tying to set them up? Or did you tel- -----"

"Get him out of here!!" the Warden screamed, his face livid with rage!

I was taken back to my cell, where I waited in apprehension, wondering what the next move would be. They didn't bring in over two hundred cops to just stand by idly. I was working my way through my third pack of cigarettes. My stomach was really messed up between all the smoking and coffee.

"On the phones!" someone shouted.

"The Warden's on!" said somebody else.

I reached over my head, grabbing my earphones off the wall. It went something like:

"Men! This is the Warden speaking. I am talking to you tonight because I have a problem, a problem that I am unable to solve without the help and cooperation of every man in this institution, and I am asking you for this help men! I think every man is aware of that which I am speaking. I have received a list of the demands put forth by the members of the committee and agreed upon by the population in general. Needless to say, I fully agree with a good portion of them. Even before this unfortunate incident, I had planned an overall change in the menu that would be instituted this coming week. I have been working hard for you men, but I am only one man and I need help. I need your help! I need time men, and I am asking you to give me that time. Just this evening

I spoke with each individual member of the committee. Thankfully, all agreed and came to the realization that you men had nothing to gain by a strike of this nature. They also felt that the only way to better conditions in this institution was for us all to work together. They also gave me their assurance that there would be no further disruptions of the institutional schedule. During this interim, the inmates and administration alike will strive together to meet the demands, as well as the needs of all the men.

Thank you for listening, and good night!" he chirped pleasantly.

I lay there in the darkness of my cell listening to the soft buzzing of voices up and down the tiers. Some of the guys were actually going for that crap! Child psychology! This is the straw for the weak to grasp! A way out for them in which they could save face. I knew it was only a matter of minutes before they came for me, and pick up the rest of the guys. After that speech, they couldn't keep us here. "Probably put us in the box!" I thought.

"Sully!" The guy next door tapped on my wall.

"What do you think of that shit? He got a lot of heart, huh?" he whispered. It was very quiet so I spoke in my normal voice, which I knew could carry the length of the block.

"Listen, Tony, everything that had to be said, was said in the yard this afternoon. But it seems by the whispering I hear, there are a lot of guys who don't want to remember it. The principles the men of the committee are standing up for have not changed. And for those who are not men enough to bring their own personal fears under control, I have nothing more to say."

"What's wrong, Sully?" Tony asked.

"What's wrong? I'm sick of all this bullshit. You talk till you're blue in the face, for what? So some lying piece of shit can come behind you with false promises of sugar and honey that amounts to nothing but veiled threats? These dudes aren't ignorant of these lies, Tony. But they would rather pretend ignorance and crawl on their bellies, than stand up on their hind legs like human beings. Shit!! It's normal to feel fear. But it's not normal for a man to cringe in terror every time it rears its ugly head! I've been scared by one thing or another my whole fucking life, Tony. Each time is as frightening as the last. It isn't something you grow accustomed to, you know what I mean, Hoss!?"

"Do I know what you mean?" he laughed nervously. "I've been sitting on this shit-bowl for the last three hours. I think by now I must have shit out everything, my fright too!!"

"Be cool, Tony!" I whispered. "Somebody's coming up the stairs!"

I was expecting the guards to come up and take me to the box, but when I looked up and saw the three State Troopers in front of my cell I was shocked. "Damn!" I thought. "What the hell's going on here?"

"You Sullivan?" one of them asked politely.

"Yes, I am!" I said, looking for an answer to what was going on. A million thoughts were flashing through my brain, all bad.

"Get dressed." He said, motioning up front to whoever was working the control box for the gates.

"If you don't mind," I said as sweetly as possible. "May I ask where I'm being taken, and what I might bring with me?"

The trooper looked at me with indecision in his eyes, then came around.

"You got some cigarettes and a few changes of underwear? You'll need them!" He said, I knew that's all he could tell me, he was pretty decent.

"Thanks!" I mumbled, pulling on my socks and shoes, and throwing some soap, toothpaste and smokes in a paper bag. "I'm ready." I said, but not before taking a deep breath to face whatever awaited me.

I walked out of the block and into the center, where I was greeted with shackles for both my hands and feet. A short chain was run from hand to ankles, which hindered me from standing straight. I was then led over to face the wall, where the rest of my friends were already lined up.

Hundreds of guards, about twenty State Troopers and all the bigwigs from the state house in Trenton were all there to see that the ungrateful animals who dared ask for better food and more humane living conditions were promptly dealt with. These were the same good Christians who many years ago were persecuted and died in similar arenas for daring to stand up for what they believed. But today, they are the Romans, and no longer need religion for a crutch. For what better crutch is there than power? Power has replaced Christianity. Power and greed. Yes! They are pigs, in every sense of the word, the hogs of the earth.

It was almost midnight by the time they were ready to take us out of the prison. We were all told to turn around. One long chain was looped through the rings of the shackles on our feet, tying us together in one long line. Some little scrawny captain strutted up and stood before us. His fists were balled up on his hips and his weak jaw jutted out daringly, mentally I pictured how many places I could crack it in with one punch! I wanted to laugh, but I knew he'd turn killer, not caring that I was all chained. Look at that little rooster with his little chest all puffed out!

"Alright," he snarled, his eyes darting over for a split second to where the Commissioner of Correction stood nodding his saintly approval.

This really turned him on and he came out of his James Cagney bag, speaking harshly through clenched teeth. Rotten ones at that! His lips curled outward in a devastating snarl, for added effect, I imagine.

"When I give the order, you will move out slowly -- understand?" he paused, walking up and down the line with his hands clasped behind his back, Gestapo style. All this mutt needed was a swagger stick!

"There will be no talking -- you will look nowhere but at the man's back in front of you. Understand?" he pronounced each world slowly and perfectly.

"Do you understand?" he shouted.

Nobody said a word, or as much as nodded their head in recognition of this fool. He just stood there trying to think of something to get a response, when a Deputy Warden whispered from behind him, "Move them out, Captain!"

As we moved out the front gate to the waiting van, about ten yards away, I could see people outside the lights of the barricades that blocked the entrance from both ends of the street. There were State Troopers inside the barricades, and three or four of them had Thompson Sub-Machine Guns cocked on their hips. As we made our way up the two steep steps into the van, I looked at a young State Trooper only a few feet away. He also carried a Thompson. He was down in a crouch with it pointed directly at us. I think if I had farted, fifteen men would have died. I couldn't believe this shit was really happening.

It was pitch black in the van and we were packed in like sardines. No one dared talk until we were well on our way. Everyone was alone with his own thoughts. "Would they really kill us?" I thought listening to the deep breathing of the men around me. My heart skipped a beat every time the van came to a momentary stop. "Maybe they're just going to stop on the side of the road somewhere, near some woods. It's possible, and we can't even run chained together like this." I couldn't help but think of the many books I had read by "Leon Uris", especially "Mila 18." The way the Nazi's would take people in the middle of the night for transportation to death; the cattle cars, the walks in the forests. I knew in my heart, right then, that even if it did not happen, they were more than capable and willing to carry out such orders. I could see how Nazi's were able to kill millions of people, before anyone could really believe such a horrifying atrocity was being wreaked upon them.

"What do you think, Tommy?" Doc's voice whispered, but it had the affect of a sledgehammer, bringing us all to our senses.

"I don't – know, Doc." Tommy whispered back. "How long do you think we been riding now?" He asked.

"Almost an hour, it seems like." Doc said.

"What direction did we leave the prison in?" Asked a voice I didn't recognize.

"I don't know," Chuck Carter broke in. "But if we were being transferred to Rahway Prison, we'd have been there already!"

"Yeah, you're right!" Somebody muttered so dejectedly that we all broke up laughing. "This was more like it," I thought, as a muffled voice came from the cab up front. Sounded like "knock it off!" or something. Without a thought, all fifteen men answered almost in unison -- "fuck you!" Then came more nervous laughter. We were riding so long I felt we were out of the State of New Jersey. I was beginning to feel like we must be leaving the country, when the truck pulled slowly to a stop. The motor was turned off, and the truck rocked slightly as the cops climbed from the cab, the doors slamming. We were expecting anything. At the last second before the door swung open, Tommy burst out in his pent up anxiety. "What are we gonna do, just sit here?" He croaked.

"What can we do, Tom, but wait and see?" Doc answered softly. We were backed up to the doorway of some building. Not until the door was opened and four or five guards came out, did I realize it was a county jail. The State Troopers must have lead and followed the van in their own cars because they were still with us, brandishing their rifles and Thompsons. Five names were called. One of the troopers gave his guns to another. He climbed in the van with a flashlight to unlock the long chain in order to take these men out. Chuck was the one I knew personally out of the five.

"Be cool, Chuck, take care huh?" I said feeling a strange sense of loss at this sudden separation.

"Alright, Sully. You take it easy too. I'll catch you later!" Everybody said their hurried farewells before the door was slammed shut again, sending us back to the heavy silent darkness.

We rode in silence for another thirty minutes before pulling into a dark alleyway beside yet another small, unknown county jail. Five more were taken out, leaving Tommy, Doc, Peppy, Joe and myself to continue on to our final destination.

I figured it must have been 3:30 in the morning when we pulled into the parking lot just behind the Salem County Jail, at the farthest tip of New Jersey. Another mile across the bridge and we would have been in Delaware. So I wasn't too far off in my feelings that we were being taken out of the state.

We were sitting in the "Bull-Pen" (large cell) surrounded by State Troopers, who were still taking off our shackles, when some big beefy dude came up to the bars outside the pen.

"Hello, Tom!" He said smiling at my friend Tommy Barker, who was sitting next to me. Tommy stared hard for about ten seconds before answering.

"Hello, Sheriff." he said softly, his features turned rock hard.

"It's been a long time," the Sheriff whispered, pausing momentarily, looking, thinking. "W-We don't want no trouble with you guys, Tom -- I d-didn't even want you guys here. But it's orders!"

"What the hell is going on here?" I thought looking from Tom to the Sheriff.

"You guys act decently and I'll go out of my way for you, I mean this!" He finished abruptly looking only at Tommy.

"There'll be no trouble, Sheriff!" Tommy said, and I could feel he really meant what he was saying. We had no ideas of causing trouble anyway.

"Alright, Tom." He said and walked away.

"What was that all about, Tom?" I asked, unable to suppress my curiosity.

"Remember that escape I told you about, and how I got the time?" He whispered.

"You mean this is the jail?" I asked incredulously.

"Yeah, this is Salem County Jail, only it's a new one. I was in the old joint, in the same spot!"

"Alright!" I asked still confused. "But where does this guy come into the picture? He's the Sheriff. How come he knows you?"

"Eleven years ago he was just a turnkey, a regular guard. He was one of the two guards on duty the night I tried to escape. The other guard was a good friend of his, the one who died."

"Damn, you'd think this guy would want to kill you!" I said.

"What for? I could have killed him, but didn't, even when it meant my getting out. He hasn't forgotten this."

"You had already killed one guy. What difference would he have made?" I asked.

"I didn't want to kill him. He just had a soft head! I only tapped him with that bar to take him out and the bum croaks on me, sh-it!!" He spit out.

"Oh well!!" I smiled at him. The Sheriff treated us very well. We were put on a special tier of the jail and prison guards were sent from

Trenton to watch us while we were there. Even though, the Sheriff saw to it we lacked nothing, food, clean-linen, cigarettes, books, etc. We were still kept incommunicado the whole two weeks we were there. A few unidentified creatures slid in to see us three or four times, threatening us with charges of rioting and being responsible for inciting. We were the ringleaders they said, and we did not deny it. Telling them in turn that we more than welcomed any court action that would enable us to bring to light the existing inhumane conditions of Trenton State Prison (which, no doubt, still remain to this day).

One of the prison guards revealed to us that they "had no intention of bringing us to court. This was the last thing they wanted," he laughed. He also went on to say that "they only wanted us out of the prison. Feeling that without us there, they could crush the strike."

Which they did within three days after we left. The backup committees we relied upon never did materialize. After they cracked a dozen skulls or more, they opened all the cells asking whether anybody felt like going to work. "They almost trampled each other to death that morning, Sully! You wouldn't believe it. You'd have thought they were just told everybody would be getting five bucks an hour!" Some guy told me about five months later. When I inquired even further, later on, I found out that the same guy who told me this was one of the forerunners in the race to work.

***

Rahway Prison - 1962

After our forced two week vacation in Salem County Jail, we were again shackled and herded into a waiting van that would take us to Rahway State Prison, about 150 miles away. Immediately upon arrival, we were taken to one of the blocks. At first I thought we were going to be put on a regular tier like anybody else, but we were marched up the stairway past what I thought to be the top tier. There was an iron spiral staircase that led up into the roof of the block. There to my surprise, was a real dungeon type of lock- up that hadn't been used in twenty years! The other ten guys, who had originally made the trip out of Trenton, were already there. The cells we were put in had a bed, wooden table, and wooden straight-backed chair. We were to remain in these cells almost eight months, being allowed out once a month for a shower and shave, which we were given fifteen minutes to accomplish. During this eight-month period, inmates and outside workers alike were busy constructing a special yard to put us in. The twelve-foot walls were cinder block with triple strands of barbed wire on top. The yard itself was about fifty yards both in width and length, with one of the gun towers directly overlooking it.

Early in the sixth month of this lock up things took a drastic change. Doc, Chuck and about six other brothers (all who had come from Trenton) were sent back there along with the other guys. All that remained was Tommy B, Joey A, and myself. It remained like this for about a week, until they brought up eleven Muslim brothers who had refused to break a prayer meeting in the yard. Contrary to the Muslim brothers of today, both in and out of prison, these so-called Muslims in Trenton Prison in the early 1960's carried themselves no better than any common street gang. This was the time of Malcolm X and the fiery inciting speeches. Many of these people were attracted to what they believed to be this man's philosophy, violence! For many, it was just something to cling to and feel pride in identifying. There was very little time given to religious teachings in the true sense of the word. The true believers of Islam, when it came to prayers, dieting and abstinence from pork in any form, constituted a small minority. These men were respectful and commanded respect simply by their bearing of dignity. The phonies and others who used Islam as a guise for their own individual fears and treacheries brought only shame and mockery upon the others. I felt nothing but contempt!

From the very beginning, until the first day the yard opened, which was a little better than two months, we laid in those cells listening to the indirect verbal abuse, the constant moronic signifying that went on for hours at a time every day. They had already decided that the yard presently being built was theirs and that any "blue-eyed devils" who step out there would die! In so many words, they were telling us indirectly that they were barring us from the yard. What bothered me more than the threats was their complete ignorance to the mutual dilemma we were all undergoing. In a close-quartered lock-up such as the one we were confined to, I felt we should be pulling together to better the outrageous conditions we were forced to live. Why couldn't they direct this burning hatred toward their real tormentors? Obviously, they were choosing the safer path in which to vent their anger and frustration. For seventy-two days I never said a word to them, though I wanted to scream out and curse them for their insensitive stupidity. Though I hate even to write this, one night, a short time before we went to the yard, I could no longer suppress the terrible hurt I felt inside me. I cried silently and uncontrollably at the thought of what all this was leading to. Wasn't it enough that we all had to be subjected to this treatment? Why must we do this to one another? I cannot hate you -- I have never even seen you, nor you I! I am not going to die easily. I want to live -- for what? I don't know. I have never had anything in this world either. But -- someday I hope to -- I hope only for the simple, but good things. A good woman, a child, and maybe, if I'm lucky, a house and a second hand car. It ain't much, but it's all I need, and all I live for. No! I'm not black like you, but my being white has not made me immune from suffering, brother, and I must come to the yard. Of course I'm afraid! But I'm more afraid of showing cowardice. I cannot allow myself to bask in such a comfort, for I'm sure it would be habit-forming. I know that whether I live or die, you will still not accept me as a fellow human being, but you will respect me as a man! Is this all any of us have left in these cesspools? This foolish pride? Someday I hope we shall rise above this.

The day before the yard was to open, Tommy, before going to the shower, asked the guard if he could bring a book down to my cell. He was in the first cell and I was in the last. He stood in front of my cell looking tense, but bitter and full of hate.

"What's happening, Tommy?" I managed a weak smile. I hadn't seen him but four times in the last eight months. He really looked bad.

"What are you gonna do, Sully?" he whispered coming close to the bars. No doubt he had been listening to his fate being decided also.

"I'm going out, Tom!" I said looking at him as if for the first time, and possibly the last. Tommy was a bad piece of work, very unpredictable and extremely dangerous. We differed on many things, but on the whole, we had formed a close relationship over the last three years. He was thirty-nine years old at the time, but in great physical shape. Always running and doing calisthenics everyday was something he held over from the old days. He had been in the Marine Corps during the Second World War, and was in from beginning to end. He hit damn near every island in the Pacific. He was shot up bad coming ashore at Tarawa. Luckily enough, he came in on the second wave, for the first was virtually wiped out. The stories he had to tell would make my hair stand on end. Mai-Lai was a mercy killing compared to the atrocities these dudes committed. When Tom came back to the states, he was a D.I. on Paris Island for about four years before he decided to pack it in. Now! Outwardly, this situation didn't seem to bother him to any great degree.

"You don't have to go out, Hoss. Nobody would think less of you!" he said softly trying to give me a way out.

"I would, Tom."

"Alright, listen! See those rungs on your chair," I looked at the chair. Funny, I never notice them before. "Just take the nuts off and the chair will come apart. As soon as you get them off, put the chair back together again so it won't be noticed. File them down on the floor until they're like needlepoints. Wrap the handles with strips of sheet and then bind them tightly with shoelaces. Okay? I would have done it myself, but my cell's right in front of the man's desk!"

"How many should I make, Tom, there's four rungs?"

"Four other white guys came up a few days ago. They lock up in front by me and they're frightened to death. So just make three-- you, me, and Joey A!"

"How will I get them to you and Joey?" I asked.

"You won't be able to." he smiled. "You'll have to bring them out!" he laughed. "You ever stuck anyone before?" he asked it like it was such a natural thing that I felt embarrassed saying no.

"No!!?" he really sounded surprised.

"Yeah, 'no'!" I answered sarcastically. "I had toys to play with when I was a kid. My mother wouldn't even give me a paring knife when I helped her peel potatoes. She always made us use a carrot scraper, so I wouldn't nick myself!" I laughed nervously.

"I wasn't trying to be smart, I just figured as long as you been in jail ---"

"I've always used my hands, Tom, and on certain occasions, a pipe!" I said.

"Well, let me tell you something, Sully, last year you almost died because you wanted to use your hands! That creep who stuck you didn't care that you were unarmed. He didn't want to fight. He wanted to kill you!! He wanted to pull your heart out!!" Tom grated viciously. "Don't you understand what I'm trying to say!" he said softly. "I can use my hands pretty good, Hoss! But I haven't in years and never expect that I will again. I have learned to come 'firstest with the mostest' and I don't care how I get there. Front! Back! It doesn't really matter how you kill a man. He's still just as dead either way. You'll be nervous at first, but just follow your instincts and you'll be all right."

"Shit, I felt much better before you came!" I laughed. "But don't worry, I'll have the things ready if I have to work all night."

"You probably will. But keep your ears open, huh? And pour a little water on the floor. It will cut down on the noise. I gotta go, this dude's getting impatient. Be cool, huh?"

"You too. And don't worry, I'll have them," I promised.

Tom hadn't been gone five minutes before I had the chair disassembled and the four rungs off and under my pillow. I worked at getting the chair back together--I've never been much of a handyman--It took me damn near an hour to get it to stand at attention, with the help of the wall and table support. Since my turn for shower would be coming, I decided to wait until after supper to begin working on them.

Just before the count, at two o'clock that morning, I finally finished. I inspected and felt the fine points of the pick with my forefinger. It was as good as possible. Not counting the time I had taken to rest and have a smoke, it had taken a good seven hours. My hands were blistered and bleeding. I wrapped the handles quickly and tightly with strips of sheet, and put them under the mattress at the foot of my bed. I was too tired to even bother undressing, so I just lied on top of the covers and went to sleep ready-rolled.

"R-i-n-g! R-i-n-g!" the bell pierced through my deep sleep. Damn, I thought, rising up on one elbow, trying to shake the sleep from my head. I just closed my eyes! I finally managed to roll off the bed, and was splashing water on my face, as the guard rolled up in front of my cell with the food wagon.

"Just the coffee!" I muttered, drying my face and hands.

"What's wrong, Sullivan? You sick? Normally you're ready to eat everything but the wheels on the wagon!" he said laughingly.

"Naw, I just don't feel hungry this morning." I managed a smile.

"Can't wait to get out in that yard for some fresh air and exercise, huh?"

"Yeah," I smiled widely again, wishing the hell he'd just stop talking and leave me alone.

"Don't blame you, eight months is a long time in the cell without getting out."

"Sure is!" I said. Only you don't really know how long and you don't care, you phony bastard!

"Alright, Sully, enjoy yourself!" he said handing me my bowl of coffee and started moving away.

"Say, do you have any idea what time we'll be going out this morning?" I asked.

"From what I understand, it's supposed to be from nine to eleven in the morning, and from one to three-thirty in the afternoon!" he said.

"Alright! Thank you!"

I figured I'd lay down for a while since I still had better than two hours before nine o'clock. It passed very quickly, too quickly! I heard what sounded like three or four guards coming up the back stairway, which led out to the yard. I jumped from the bed quickly, my heart racing wildly.

Reaching under the mattress, I grabbed the three ice picks and slid them down into the cup of the jockey-shorts, letting them puncture all the way through till the steel lay pressed against my inner thigh, held secure by the makeshift handles. If the guards frisked me, they would have to grab me by the balls to discover them! The ice picks, that is!! And from experience, I knew that it was very rare that they cared to linger in that area. Of course there were always those few who had a real picnic on general frisks! Where else could a fag get to caress five hundred (on a good day) dicks in one day!?

The door opened and I thought the Marines had landed. The Warden, Assistant Warden, two captains and three or four guards walked in nodding and smiling like they were doing a hell of a thing, just letting us animals out of the cages. Phony cocksuckers! Eight months we've been in these stinking cells and they never had the decency to come up and even ask how we were feeling. But here they are for the "grand-opening," expecting us to fall on our knees and gaze up at them in adoration. These self-righteous smiles were soon to be turned to masks of horror. The long bar above the gates was pulled back, now they would use a key to open each individual cell.

"You may as well start back here by the door, Captain, and work toward the front. It will save walking and time." The Warden spoke directing the flustered officers and guards.

"Good idea!" The Captain nodded.

"Yeah, ain't he a genius!" I thought.

"Well, Sullivan, looks like you'll be the first to Christen the new yard!" He said jovially opening the door. "Just cross your arms in front of you. These officers will bring you down."

I preceded the two officers down the stairs. Christ, I actually felt dizzy by the time I reached the third landing. When I reached the door leading to the yard, another guard told me to put my hands on the wall. I stopped breathing momentarily as his hands ran around my chest and back, down the outside of my legs from the hips and down the inside from the knees. He finished by running his thumbs around the waistband of my pants.

"Alright!" he said swinging the yard door open. I felt like I was going home after being locked in that cell so long. For a short lived minute, I forgot what lay ahead, just happy being able to breathe the crisp cold air. The blue patch of sky above me was clear and beautiful.

"This alone was enough to continue living for." I said aloud to myself, coming back to my senses. I tried to run once around the yard to loosen up, but I felt weak and nauseous. I wondered how the hell I was going to be able to move when I had to. Walking away from the tower looking down on me, I pretended to be pushing my shirt down inside my pants. I removed the picks to my right hand pocket, punching them through the material so they would fit in without being noticeable. I was throwing a handball up against the wall when the first Muslim brother came into the yard. I held the handball momentarily, staring at him as he walked down the steps and toward the far corner. He stood there with his arms crossed. Standing very straight, his eyes had flickered across mine momentarily, but did not hold. Out of the next ten that followed, I only saw two who (my instincts told me) were to be reckoned with. A certain look -- a certain way, a certain magnetism that almost nodded in recognition.

These two are the strength, the backbone, for eleven men. Those are the two we must hit first! The other four Muslims they had brought up must have gone out already, I was thinking, still throwing the ball against the wall. Every nerve in me was tingling with apprehension, ever conscious of the group of men whispering in the corner.

Joey A. came out, and I could tell just by the way he was walking and looking that he was going to be of no use to us. I could see it had taken everything in his power just to walk out here, but I couldn't feel angry with him. I suddenly felt very sorry and protective toward him, though he was almost twenty years my senior.

Tom finally came out looking like the mean ol' bulldog he was. His head was high and his chin jutted outward, daring the world. I couldn't help but smile.

"You got the things?" He said, all business now

"Yeah!" I whispered. "But let's wait a while, huh? If they're not gonna fuck with us, we'll leave well enough alone. Personally, I can do without it!" Tom was strung too tight, and death was in his eyes and rolled from his snarling lips.

"What's wrong?" he grated. "Your feet getting cold? You gonna wait for these black mother-fuckers to stab us?"

"No." I whispered nastily. "But I ain't gonna panic either! When the time comes, I'll be ready to move. Let's give this thing a chance. I know we haven't been having delusions, that all that graveyard talk wasn't just in our minds, but let's wait. We'll know soon enough and whatever happens, don't react to it. Just walk away defeated. We can't win on these terms, and losing in this situation means dying. If we can get two guys right-off, we'll get them. We've got to still their voices immediately!"

"Who!?" Tom asked confusedly. "What are you talking about?"

"Don't look, Tom! Let's walk around once. As I'm talking, just keep smiling, even laugh like I'm telling a joke or something. Glance, but don't gape at them, you dig?"

As we went around and started walking toward them I was talking to Tom, but aware of the positions in which they stood. "You see the real heavy set black dude, about 220 pounds? You can't miss him. He's got glasses on." Tom must have looked toward them and back five times. "Damn, be cool, huh?" I said.

"I see who you mean, he's talking now, right?"

"Yeah." I laughed nervously, looking at the sky above them.

"Let's walk around again. I want you to look at the tall brown skinned dude. He's the tallest one th--"

"I seen him." Tom broke in. "He was the first one I noticed and not because he's tall!"

"Then you know what I mean, huh?" I asked.

"Yeah, you want these guys first, right?"

"Yes, I'd bet anything that these are the two that have been doing all the rapping. The others are just parrots. 'Yes, man! No, Brother! Yes, Brother! Goodnight Brother! And Good morning, Brother!' is all they can manage to say. They aren't given the time to talk, no less think! Let's fool around with the handball and try to ride this out, okay?" I asked.

"Yes, Brother!" Tom mimicked.

"Fuck you, too!!" I laughed.

"C'mon, Joe!" Tommy motioned, throwing the ball on the wall.

"Uh--who--wh?" The poor bastard was in another world, his face was chalk white and he was shivering.

"Why don't you go over and stand in the sun, Joe?" I pointed. "Maybe you'll warm up a little."

"Uh-Ye-yeah -- good idea, Sully." Tommy was staring as I turned back to him. "I hadn't even noticed before, he's not going to be any help, is he?"

"No," I shrugged. "But at least there was something left in him. He came out!"

"You're right," he said softly, probably thinking of those four mutts sitting up in their cells, as I was.

The Brothers started walking around the yard in three different groups, spaced about twenty yards apart, so that one group or another would pass in front of us every minute or so, making us stop our play in order to avoid hitting them. After about ten minutes or so, when they tired of this harassment, one group stopped in the middle of the handball court, then the second, and third. They just stood there carrying on meaningless conversations, as if unaware of our presence. I just dropped the ball and let it roll away. I walked toward the steps by the door motioning Tom with my eyes to follow. Before we had even sat down on the steps, four of the Muslims had already begun a game on the court we had been forced to vacate. Tom was sitting next to me seething with hatred and anger.

"Give me the fuckin' knife!" he hissed, talking into his hands that were cupped over his face.

"I'll give it to you when you cool down, not before!" I looked over at Joe still sitting in the sun, oblivious to everything around him. "Your hate will do us no more good than the catatonic state he has worked himself into. I want to go over this with you sensibly. I thought common sense would be our biggest advantage, but it doesn't seem to be the case."

"Alright." Tom looked up at me pulling himself together, his face was still flushed and the veins in his forehead were visibly pounding, but he was smiling calmly now, icily. "What do you want to do?" He asked.

"That big brother, the black one, they're calling him Brother John. He must be their preacher or minister. Whatever. I want you to walk over there and call him aside. I want you to try to talk sense to him, try to make him understand the position we have all been put in. You--"

"Talk!?" Tom's lips curled in disgust. "You can't talk to them! You seen how their action----"

"I know, Tom, and I don't expect them to be receptive to you. I just want you to position them. You will already have this Brother John in front of you. He's yours! I am not going to walk over until that tall one joins the crowd around you, and there will be a crowd!" I laughed. "You're gonna become popular very quickly. You move when you're ready, not before. I'll be waiting on you. How do you feel about it? You know we got to get these two and this is the only way we can catch them. Right?! Put them out of action on the first shot!"

"Sounds good to me." He murmured. "But try to keep your back to the wall. They have chairs in their cells too you know! What do they intend to snuff us with?"

"We are not going to be the defenders, Tom. We are doing the attacking. This is the best defence we have. Just keep sticking and tearing, even scream. Stick and move, don't stay on one guy over five seconds. Keep them scattered and don't let them get together. If you see a man coming to the aid of the dude you're working on, leave him immediately and attack your attacker. Don't take a step backward and don't let yourself be cornered. That fighting from a corner or back to back action is bullshit! Keep spinning and moving, even when you think there's no one in striking distance. If you're in bad trouble, scream my name, and if it's at all possible, I'll be there. I'll do the same, and will expect the same. If we botch this thing right at the start, run right for this stoop. The sides are high and the widths of these steps are only an arms distance. We could do alright here, if necessary. Here's the shiv!" I whispered, passing it under his leg. "Just put it in your coat pocket and keep your hand right around the handle. It's cold, so they won't think nothing if you keep both hands in your pockets. Especially if you hunch over and shiver a little!" I smiled.

"You got this whole thing figured out, huh?" he laughed.

"Not quite, Tom, but I do know we're going to need every advantage we can get, no matter how small or inconsequential it may seem now. You ready, Hoss?" I whispered, squeezing his arm in my need to feel he was really there. This was all like a bad dream. I never really awoke until long after it was over.

"I'm ready!" he whispered, squeezing my leg in return. Before strolling casually to the middle of the yard, I watched from the corner of my eyes as he motioned for Brother John. He walked over to Tom and stood about an arms length away with his arms folded, listening. The other brothers moved over one at a time, until Tom and Brother John were in a complete circle. The tall Muslim was in the circle directly to Tom's right. I moved off the stoop slowly, both hands in my pockets, my shoulders hunched forward as if fighting the cold. My right hand clenched tightly around the handle of one of the two shivs in my pocket. As I approached the circle almost directly behind the tall Muslim, he looked over his shoulder at me, glaring. I dropped my eyes smiling uncertainly and weakly at him, as if to say, "I'm with you. I just want to see what's going on!" And this was exactly how he took my charade. He turned back to face the two men in the circle. I stepped right up by his side. He wasn't concerned about me.

"As I said before," Tom was saying, but I could see he was at the end of the line. "all we want is the same respect we give you. We have listened to your insinuations for two months. Yet we have not spoken back in return. We have given you more respect than you give yourselves. We have not abused you, your people, or the God you believe in. All we ask is the same treatment. What's it gonna be?" Tom asked with a ring of finality.

I knew this was it! I could feel my whole body shaking. My legs felt as if they were going to give way under me. I felt hot, then extremely cold. My whole body was hurting, every nerve screeching for release. My God, I feel as if I'm frozen. Will I be able to move? Will I move?

"We don't give a fuck what you want, cracker," he was saying as he took a step toward Tom threateningly. "We--" he had started to say when Tom uncoiled, driving the ice pick deep in his chest. The man staggered back, pulling himself off the knife, his eyes wide in fear, his mouth open wide, trying to speak. But nothing came out. Tom lunged again. Brother John blocked its path to his heart, screaming as the pick punctured completely through his thick forearm. The rest of us had been completely shocked at the initial attack. The suddenness of it had even shocked me, and I knew it was coming. Brother John's scream brought the tall Muslim beside me to life. Just as he stepped across me, his hand going into his pocket to come up behind Tom, I hit him just above the belt line, in his right side. I hit him so hard and went in so deep that I broke my thumb. I could hear his breath hiss, and it was the only sound he made as his body arched backward. I yoked him around the neck hitting him up high in the back this time. His body was jumping and convulsing wildly against me. When I released my grip, he slid off the knife slowly and hit the ground. As soon as I felt the arm go around my neck, I expected to feel something hit my back. I stabbed back wildly and got the dude through the thigh. He fell back away from me. As I spun to meet him, he was backing away, his palms up in front of him trying to placate me.

"I -I -- was j-just t-trying t--to---"

I leaped forward quickly, thrusting out my right arm in full length. I hit him in the side, but the fuckin' ice pick curled up around my fist like a wet noodle. I must have hit a bone, I thought, looking at the useless twisted shiv in my fist, spinning around, looking, and remembering the third knife in my pocket. Six of the Muslims were huddled in one corner of the yard and had no intention of moving. That was just fine with me. When I looked around again, Tom was rolling around on the ground with Brother John. He had lost his knife and they were clawing, punching and choking each other like two grizzly bears. As I ran the length of the yard toward them, I heard a horse choking from above me scream.

"Stop!--St--op!! O-Or I-I'll f-fire!" he squealed excitedly. He had the riot gun pointed directly on me, but I was too far gone to care. I stopped for about five seconds and just stared up at him. He finally just lowered the gun and turned his back. I could hear the riot bell ringing inside the block as I pulled Tom and Brother John apart. I still had the knife in my hand and Brother John was looking up at me, not saying a word. He wasn't afraid, even now! But I could see he was wondering why I hadn't stabbed him. I had the perfect opportunity to do so while he and Tom were locked together. I looked over toward the door expecting the riot squad to burst out any second. Cuddled up in the corner of the stoop was a small young brother, who couldn't have been more than nineteen. His head was down between his knees in a fetal position. His wracking sobs could be clearly heard.

"I don't want no more of this." I said to John "I want to throw these knives over the wall!" I said softly, feeling drained. He understood that I was concerned about being jumped once I got rid of the knives. I didn't want the guards to come out and catch me with them.

He looked over at the wall at the six, now seven brothers huddled in the corner, with disgust and complete loathing. "Throw them away," he smiled in pain, still looking at his cowering brothers. "You have nothing to worry about."

"Thanks," I said, quickly gathering up the other two knives and throwing them all over the wall. I'd seen from where we locked upstairs, that directly across the road from the wall was swamp land.

The riot squad broke through the door, screaming harsh orders and demands. "Up against the wall, strip down. Get them all off!" one sergeant screamed.

Outside of the three brothers lying on the ground and the young kid huddled by the stoop, unable to move, we were all made to strip naked and spread-eagle against the wall. Facing the wall, my heart pounding rapidly, I listened to them screaming like bitches for the doctor, stretchers, etc.

"All right you, bastards, turn around and face the tower!" The sergeant shook with rage, pointing his finger to the guard on the wall. "This is it," I thought.

"Who had the knives? Where are the knives?" he yelled up to the tower guard. I almost gaped in disbelief when the guard raised his hands and said, "I don't k- know!"

"W--hat?" The sergeant gasped in dismay. "You heard him, you mutt!" I thought, smiling inwardly at his bewilderment. He almost ran over to Brother John, who was now standing holding one hand over his chest where the blood was slowly seeping out.

"Who did this to you?" He asked in his now kind and fatherly voice.

"Get away from me!" Brother John whispered viciously, leaving no doubt as to how he felt about him. The sergeant cringed backward, away from the pure undistilled hatred that confronted him.

Brother John and the two other brothers were taken on stretchers to the hospital, and the young kid was taken inside somewhere.

The sergeant tried to talk to Joey A. Seeing he was completely incoherent, they took him away somewhere. We stood there freezing our asses off for about fifteen minutes before we were allowed to put our clothes back on. As I was tying my shoes, I saw some guard come through the door almost running, trouble! He called the Sergeant over and was whispering in a low vice, but their eyes were darting daggers over to where Tom and I were standing. I knew the young kid must have talked.

"You!--and You!" He growled, pointing to Tom and myself.

"M-Me?" I stammered, looking around behind me and staring back at him innocently, as if he must be making a mistake.

"Yeah, you! Get out here!"

We were told to face up to the tower again.

"Officer." The Sergeant yelled. "Two white men stabbed those three black men. I want you to look at these two very closely now. Were these the ones?" The officer up there looked down at us for about ten seconds. I knew he was probably thinking about his job and the family he had to support.

"I-I don't know!" he croaked.

"What? -- You don't -- they're the only two white gu--."

He caught himself. "Are you sure, officer?" The Sergeant asked, a definite threat in his voice.

"I-I can't tell!" he answered.

We were all taken inside, but Tommy and I were taken to the box. As the Sergeant and a few guards were putting me in a cell, I saw the Warden and a few Captains coming down the tier with the guard who had been in the tower. They had stopped at Tommy's cell first. When they stopped in front of me, I was sitting on the edge of my bunk.

"Stand up, Sullivan!" The Warden said, taking a mug shot of me out of his jacket pocket. He stuck it up in front of the guard's eyes. He was a real young guy. I could see in his eyes he remembered me when he had pointed the riot gun. He couldn't help but remember. "Is this one of the men, officer?" the Warden asked him.

"I-I'm not s-sure. E-everything happened so fast!" he stuttered, the beads of perspiration glistening on his forehead. This guy was one in a million. I thought. I was at the point where I wished he would say "yes" and save himself. He didn't owe me a damn thing. I've never seen anyone like him before. He had everything to lose and nothing to gain. "Yes or no?" the Warden snapped.

"No!" He snapped, just as nastily, spinning on his heel, leaving the Warden there looking at me.

"Did you hear him, Warden?" I smiled sweetly.

"This doesn't change a thing, Sullivan!" the Warden answered, his eyeballs bulging out like a frog.

"Why not, sir? If he had said yes, you would have believed that. Wouldn't you?"

"This isn't over yet!" he said indignantly, walking away. About six-thirty that evening I was taken up to the hospital and paraded before the beds where the three brothers lie. They all looked pretty good as far as I could tell, stopping in front of the first bed.

"Do you recognize this man?" the Warden demanded. The brother just nodded his head negatively. When I stopped in front of the tall brother's bed (his name was Abdul, I had learned) the Warden asked the same question.

"Never saw him before!" Abdul said weakly. I later learned that he was in bad shape for a while. When I walked up to the foot of Brother John's bed, he spoke even before the Warden did.

"How are you feeling, Sully?" he asked with a sincerity that made me feel like shit.

"Alright, --you, John?" I whispered.

"Everything's everything!!" he laughed.

"I see there's no need in asking you anything?!" the Warden said, speaking to John, wondering what the hell was going on.

"That's right!" John answered, not bothering to look at him. I wanted to say many things, but I couldn't say anything with all the people behind me.

"Maybe I'll see you later on!" John said, offering his hand.

"I hope so!" I mumbled trying to fight back the tears and the terrible rage I felt against everything that brings these tragic incidents about.

***

Trenton State Prison - 1964

A year later, I was sent from the box in Rahway to one-left, the segregation facility in Trenton State Prison. I was only in Trenton about five days when they had a shakedown. They came in with a steel-detector, something like a small "mine finder'" which we all referred to as "the rat." You couldn't hide a knife anywhere without that detector picking it up. I knew I had been set up, because as soon as they rolled in, the guy with the "the rat" came directly to my cell. I stood outside watching while they took the mattress off the bunk and put it on the cement floor, because the bunk itself is steel.

As soon as the guard ran the hard instrument over my mattress, "the rat" started buzzing and jumping like a frustrated bitch! "Give me a knife!" the guard called. "I think I got something!"

I was so mad, I couldn't check myself. "You think you got something!" I sneered. "You mean you 'know' you got something! Whatever it is you bastards planted it there!! You snakes are all the same," I hissed. "Pure Pussy!" I screamed in anger.

"Say another word and we'll split your head open!" one of the guards said, stepping in front of me.

"Here it is!" the cop inside my cell yelled holding up a knife. I had never seen it before.

"Lieutenant!" one of the cops called down the tier.

"What is it?" he asked as he approached. As if he didn't know!

"We found this knife in Sullivan's cell, Lieutenant," the guard said.

"What have you got to say, Sullivan?" the lieutenant clucked sympathetically.

"Why should I have anything to say? You put it there." I said, trying to hold myself together.

"Take him to the Box!" the lieutenant sighed wearily.

"Yeah, take me to the box!" In all my time in jails I had always tried to avoid static with guards, as much as I felt humiliated at times. It was not the idea of the "box" that made me throw all caution to the wind. I knew they were doing this for what happened at Rahway, the spiteful petty creeps! My nerves had become very bad over the last four years, but they had good reason to be bad. I had been in the "box" for four of the six years I did in Jersey. If that knife had been mine, I would have went to the box with no beef, as I always had. But this shit made me sick, physically and mentally.

"You gonna give us a hard time, Sullivan?" the Lieutenant asked, taking a step toward me.

"Me, give you a hard time? If you want to kill me, do it now, you rotten bastards --I'm tired of listening to your phony bullshit!" I was raving like a maniac and was really unaware of it. This is all they wanted from me. I reacted just as they expected I would on this trumped up charge.

"Alright! Alright! Take it easy, Sullivan. Just go in your cell and take it easy. Would you like to see a doctor?" he said soothingly.

"I-I don't need a-anyone." I muttered trembling. "J-just leave me alone, huh?"

"Alright -- But just lay down for a while --you'll be alright Sully!"

"Sully! Hey Sully! You alright?" My friend Bob called from the next cell.

"Yeah, I'm alright." Wouldn't anybody leave me alone? Just six more months and I will be home. Don't they want me to get out?

"Sully, please listen to me. Will ya? They're trying to make you 'bug-out' man. God Damn!! Don't help them, just watch! They'll be calling you out for the 'Bug Doctor' tomorrow. If they told him they want you committed to the hospital, then you're as good as gone. Don't help it along. You know what they did to Andy and Billy over there, don't you?"

"Yeah, I remember. Listen, I want to try to get a little sleep okay, Hoss?"

"Listen, Sully, I was just tryi--"

"I know you meant well, Bob. I just feel so weak and tired. I-I'm sorry."

"That's alright, Sully, but just be cool, huh?"

"I'll try, Bob, but it gets harder all the time." I said closing my eyes trying to rest.

Andy and Billy's faces flashed to my mind. Both of them had been so full of life; healthy, witty and really nice guys. Sure! They were tough, didn't let people walk on them. Simply because the administration couldn't break their defiant spirits, they had them committed to the State Hospital. They were turned into vegetables by a bunch of "wet-back" quack doctors. They burnt Andy's brain out completely with their shock treatments. Therapy, they called it. Andy came back to the prison two years later like a five-year-old kid, and knew nobody he had previously. He had to think for two or three minutes before he could tell me his name was "A-n--dy!" I couldn't even talk with him without wanting to cry, and shied away from him as did the other guys who had known him "before". But we always made sure he had plenty of cigarettes, toilet articles, etc., because he was no longer capable of taking care of himself.

The first time his people came to visit him, they hadn't seen him in three years (he was originally from Boston) his mother screamed and fainted in the visiting room. It took six guards to hold his father down on the floor. I'm surprised they didn't diagnose him right there and send him for shock treatments, his mother too. They shouldn't be reacting like that!!

Billy, I don't like to think about, he went away one of the tougher guys in the prison. He was a real lady's man outside. When he came back, he was a lady himself, switching and batting his eyelashes. He spent most of the time in the shithouse, eyeing prospective lovers! He didn't remember me either. I didn't bother to refresh his memory, thought it wouldn't have done any good. He was a vegetable too! There were many cases, but I wasn't bothered as much by them because they did not hit close to home. These two guys were my friends.

The following morning, about ten-thirty, two guards came up to my cell.

"You got a pass for the hospital, Sully!" One of them said.

"The hospital? I didn't put in any slips for sick call, or the dentist!"

"I don't know what it's for. I was only told to bring you over," he said.

"Alright, let me change my shirt first." I had completely forgotten about the incident the day before, until I stepped out of my cell and my friend in the cell next to me whispered, "Remember, hold your head, Sully!" Then it hit me, and I turned around to face the two guards. One I knew pretty well.

"Is this for the head-shrinker, Mitch?"

"Yeah, Sully." he mumbled, not able to look at me.

"Have they got you believing I'm crazy too, Mitch?" I smiled.

"No-- I was --told not to tell you!" Mitch said, feeling embarrassed by the whole scene.

"I understand."

I walked into the psychiatrist's office. The doctor was a senile old man who had worked in different prisons the last thirty years, and looked like he was in desperate need of therapy himself!

"When are they gonna get some new ones?" I pointed to the same old "Blocks and ink-blots" that lay on the desk before him. I had played with them a thousand times before, seeing whatever I thought "they" expected me to see in them. I remember one sick head-shrinker jumping up and down by my side while he was showing me a particular Ink-blot.

"Look --Look at that. What do you see?" I didn't see a fucking thing! "Don't it look like a bat?" He squealed excitedly.

"I better not cause this bird any displeasure," I thought.

"Oh, yes! Yes!" I exclaimed childishly. "You're right! You're right!" These sick son-of-a-bitches loved nothing more than to have you sing their praises and tell them the wonders they were doing for you. My favorite line, which used to make them ejaculate in their pants was,

"Oh Doctor, how did you know what I was thinking!?" But now I was very tired of the fun and games, and only wanted to be left alone. They couldn't understand this. The old bastard slid the blocks across the desk to me, taking a stopwatch from the top drawer.

"For this first problem, you will have two minutes, and--"

"Forget it!" I said wearily.

"Uh --what did you say?" he appeared astounded.

"You heard me, I said forget it! Let's do away with all the pretensions. You've already got your orders concerning me."

"What!-- I don't--"

"You've been committing guys to the 'funny farm' on the States orders for thirty years, you fuckin' robot. I've seen enough bats, elephants, tigers and bloody vaginas in your 'ink-blots' to last me a lifetime. I'm through playing games with you demented old perverts!" I rose from my chair to leave and the old bug-doctor, thinking I was coming at him, pressed a button or something, because just as I was reaching for the door handle, Mitch and two other cops burst in almost knocking me down.

"What's going on, Sully?" Mitch asked.

"Nothing, not a thing, Mitch! Take me back to my cell." I stopped in front on Tommy B's cell on my way to my own.

"How'd you do, Sully?" Tommy asked, looking very concerned.

"I'm on my way, Hoss!" I smiled. "Have your girl call my mother right away or write. Have her tell my mother not to sign any papers that come from either the Warden or the State hospital. No matter how sick they tell her I am, they can't give me shock treatments unless she signs, giving her permission. Please, make sure this is done or I'm in big trouble!"

"Don't worry, Sully. I'm supposed to get a visit tomorrow afternoon. I'll have her make the call as soon as she leaves."

"Thanks, Tom."

***

The Cuckoo's Nest - 1964

Early the following morning, right after breakfast, they rolled up in front of my cell--about six guards! They were expecting action. They wouldn't even open my cell before they put the cuffs on me. I was told to put both my hands through the opening where the food trays were passed through, and only then was I shackled. The cops then started with the small talk, phony smiles and false good wishes. I just looked at them and they took the hint.

I said my good-byes to the guys on the tier as I passed their cells.

They all looked at me as if I were going to "The Chair!" Their salutations could barely be heard. My good friend Tommy B. couldn't even look at me when I passed. He just sat on his bed, deeply involved in some magazine. "That call will be made," he managed to choke out.

"All right, Tom." There was nothing to say. As we pulled into the parking lot before the special section for the criminally insane, the cop who had driven the station wagon turned to me.

"Listen, Sully, I know this ain't right. You don't belong here but just go along with their program -- and -- maybe you'll come out of this okay."

"Thanks." I said dryly, thinking, here's another guy just doing his job.

I was stripped of my clothes down in the receiving room and given a pair of pajamas, a robe and cloth slippers, all stamped "State Hospital." I was then brought up to the second floor where the cell blocks were. Right then I realized I wasn't in a hospital. The only indifference was the attendants (guards) wore white uniforms instead of blue. In place of the "club," they had a hypodermic needle, which they were not qualified or authorized to use. These sadistic attendants called *all* the shots in this wing of New Jersey State Hospital, not the doctors, the psychiatrists or psychologists. I got my first bad beating after I had only been on the floor an hour. I was standing in the day room (so called recreation room) up against the wall looking on in horror at what were once people! There was no intelligence, or the slightest sign that these mummies were even aware of who they were, or where they were. Everybody was moving in a zombie-like state, slow motion. I felt cold, alone and very much afraid, trying to smile and speak to every attendant that went by. If I could only speak with them they would know I was not like the others! I had to show them I was just like them, that there was nothing wrong with me, before they did something to me. I was really in a state of panic. What made these men appear as if they were already dead? They all couldn't have come here like this.

"Alright, on the medication!" Some burly attendant called out. Rolling a cart off the elevator stacked with a hundred different types of bottles.

I watched intently, frozen to the wall, as the zombies shuffled up to the cart eagerly with silly smiles on their faces. There were three attendants busy calling names and pouring different types of liquids into small cups. What the hell were these men getting?

"Sullivan!" the attendant called. I just stood on the wall, getting angrier by the second.

"Sullivan! Who's Sullivan?" the attendant snapped, looking around then spotting a new face.

"You Sullivan?" he asked nastily. I just stood there not answering. He put down the bottle he had been holding and walked toward me. When he got close, I stepped away from the wall to face him. My mind was made up.

"Didn't you hear me call you?" He snarled towering over me, feeling very secure with the height and weight advantage (mostly pig-fat) over me. I wished he were the only one I had to worry about.

"I heard you." I said very low.

"Well? Get over there and get your medication!" he said.

"I don't take medication, Mister. I don't even like taking aspirins!"

"You're a tough-guy, huh!" he sneered.

"No, I'm not a tough-guy, Mister, but I'm not sick either. I don't need your medication!" I answered.

"Well your gonna get it whether you need it or not. We got ways to handle guys like you." He was breathing heavy now.

"That's the way it's gonna have to be, Mister. I'm not a wise-guy, but there's no way you're gonna get me to drink your poison, as long as I can move."

He looked in my eyes trying to decide whether he could just slap me around like he did the rest of the poor, sorry bastards, but thought better of it.

"Put all these guys in their cells and leave this one out here!" he said moving toward the elevator. "I'll be right back!"

I was standing alone in the rec room when one of the two remaining guards walked over to me. He was a young guy and seemed pretty hip.

"Why didn't you take the medicine, Sullivan?" he said shaking his head, looking towards the elevator.

"Why should I?" I asked.

"No good reason really, except that it will save you a beating, and the stuff they're gonna hit you with is brutal!"

"Yeah, what is it?' I asked him.

"Compozine, ties you up in knots. Every joint in your body tightens up on you. I seen it, Sully. It's bad!" And I could tell he meant well.

"What's the stuff in the cups?"

"Liquid Thorazine, it's not too bad!" he shrugged.

"It ain't? You had some?" I smiled.

"NO--" He turned red in the face.

"Is that the stuff most of them guys are getting?" I asked.

"Yeah, but ---" The elevator door opened and five guys came in, along with a female nurse trailing behind them with a spike in her hand. I pulled off my robe and shirt as they approached me warily, putting their watches in their pockets and moving in slowly around me. There was no more talk. I just wanted the "big guy." I didn't care what happened afterward. I wished I were able to kill him with just one punch. He came in at me slowly from the front, while the others eased around to my sides. I moved just as he was taking another step toward me, moving to his left quickly, but feinting a right hand to his belly to bring his hands down to protect himself. He did! And I leaped at him with all my weight driving up behind the left hook that caught him solidly on the hinge of his jaw. He came right up off his feet and hit the floor on his back. "Big stiff!" I thought. As someone hit me in the back of the neck driving me forward, almost knocking me unconscious, someone kicked me in the groin. I fell to the floor moaning, both hands holding my crotch. They just kept kicking me in the head, ribs, and back. "Hold him still!" I heard a woman's voice as I lost consciousness. When I awoke some time later, lying on the cold marble floor of a cell, I knew immediately that something was terribly wrong. I tried to move but couldn't! Had they tied me up? I can't move my arms or legs. What's wrong with my neck? It felt like it was at a grotesque angle. As my eyes became accustomed to the dark, with only the light of the moon shining into my cell, I stared down at my arms, especially the fingers of my hands, all curled up like two claws and locked tightly against my chest. My legs were drawn up and frozen in the same manner. I could move nothing but my eyes. Once during the night, I heard footsteps outside my door. I tried to talk, to ask for help, but nothing would come out. Whoever it was walked away. I just wanted a blanket -- the floor was awfully cold -- I lay awake long into the night. It was starting to snow -- I thought of Christmas -- my family -- we hadn't had a Christmas completely together for fifteen years now -- I wondered if they missed me. Would they feel hurt if they saw me like this? -- I hope Mom doesn't sign any papers. -- But she doesn't know -- she, like so many others, puts too much confidence in those with authority. She couldn't believe they would hurt me! -- How long am I going to be like this? -- My neck hurts real bad.

On the third day, my legs started to regain their feeling, enough so I could put them flat on the ground and push my body away from the pool of urine I had been lying in (my bowels had also moved as I had no control over myself). There was a bowl sitting just inside my door that someone had put down during the night. I managed to work my way over to it. It was right beside my head now, but the only way I could get to it was to rock my body back and forth until I built up enough momentum to roll over on my stomach. My face settling directly in the bowl, I couldn't see what it was. It smelled like some kind of stew. There were two pieces of bread settled on top, so I had to gnaw through the center of the bread to get at the stew! I tried lifting the bread out of a bowl with my teeth, but I couldn't lift my head high enough to get it out of the bowl. Every once in a while my nostrils clogged up with stew, and I had to blow my breath through to clear them out! The stew was stuck to my eye leashes and in my eyes, but I was too hungry to care.

The first two days, I cried in the self-pity from what they were doing to me, but it turned suddenly to a bitter, burning hatred. Hatred kept me going -- I dreamed and schemed of how I would kill them all! I kept picturing their faces in my mind. I wanted to remember them! I thought of the worst and slowest deaths imaginable, and how their faces contorted in their fear and pain. They would all lie in their own filth, just as I am now. But with one difference, they would die in it!! The afternoon of the fourth day, a doctor came in with two attendants and knelt down by my side. He looked up at the attendants.

"How long has this man been here?" he demanded.

"Uh, I don't know. I just came on duty," one of them said.

The doctor put his arm under me, cradling my head.

"You'll be alright, son," he whispered reassuring me. When I opened my mouth to thank him, I found I still couldn't speak, nor could I hold back the tears that ran hotly down my cheeks into my mouth. This one man's simple gesture of affection for ten seconds washed away four days of death and hatred.

I was given an injection by him and soaked in hot baths to relax my shaking body. He then gave me some hot broth and later sleeping pills. He said he would be back to see me. I awoke late the following day feeling a little groggy, with every muscle in my body sore as hell, but I felt good simply being able to roll out of bed and stand up. There were windows in the cells with bars on the outside. A window of my own was a luxury after five years in Trenton and Rahway. I felt like I was in a penthouse on Central Park West, but the view was drastically different. The walls I looked upon were very high, even higher than those in the prison, I thought, trying to measure them visually. Since this was supposed to be a "hospital", there were no manned towers on the walls, but I noticed high wooden life-guard type chairs spread about twenty yards apart, set against the walls around the whole yard. I counted nine of them.

"Sully! You son-of-a-bitch!" I spun around quickly. A face was pressed against the square glass plate in my door.

"C-Cody! God Damn! - Damn!" I couldn't believe that I was seeing him, a human being -- a friend.

"Be cool, Sully," he whispered through the crack in the side of the door. "I ain't supposed to be up here. I snuck up. I got to leave in a minute so listen. Tony P. and Eddie S. said to say 'hello.' Here's some cigarettes!" He slid them under the door. "We got something going, Sully. It has been for months, but we can't seem to get it off the ground. You got to get out! Listen, I heard what happened, but take the regular medicine. It only slows you down and makes you sleepy. As soon as you get with the regular population, which will be about another week, I'll show you how to beat taking it at all!"

"Are you taking it?"

"Yeah!" He laughed. "Can't you see, I'm twisted now?"

"You always look like that!" I smiled.

"Are you gonna do as I asked, Sully? These people don't care nothing about killing you. You're probably lined up for 'shocks' too, we haven't got much time." He said looking drawn and old all of a sudden.

"I'll take the medicine, but tell Tony and Eddie not to make any more moves until I get out. It looks that good, huh?"

"I think it's a sure pop!" Cody answered.

"Then how come you guys haven't moved already, if it's that good? You said you've had it for a couple of month's didn't you?"

"I don't know, Sully. We just can't seem to get it all together. Nobody can seem to agree on anything! Listen, I got to go, okay?" He smiled happily.

"Yeah," I laughed, "and thank the guys for the cigarettes!"

It was a beautiful day, sunny and very warm, June 1965. Tony, Eddie, and Cody were waiting for me as I walked out the door into the yard.

"Am I safe out here?" I laughed, shaking hands with friends I hadn't seen in three years.

"Most of these birds are harmless, Sully," Tony was saying. "Anybody that's violent is shot up so full of shit, or on Thorazine, that he can't stand up. There's a few 'swinging bugs' around, but they're mostly old men and can't do no real harm!"

"Swinging Bugs? What the hell are they?" I asked.

"Aw-- They ain't nothing! Every once in a while some Bug will run up and punch you in the face for no reason. Most times they like to punch ya in the back of the head."

"Are you serious?" I asked amazed how calmly he talked about it.

"Yeah!" He laughed. "But like I said, they're mostly old cats, and they don't do damage. I got hit three, four times last week." He smiled.

"Oh boy, big fun!" I laughed. "Where can we all talk without ears." I suddenly asked.

"Let's sit out in the middle of the yard, on the grass, pretend we're playing cards. This way nobody can slide up near us!"

"Good idea, Tony!"

"So, what kind of shot are you guys thinking of taking?" I asked Tony, shuffling then dealing the cards slowly.

"The Wall!" He said it quickly, looking up from his cards to see my reaction. I just sat there waiting and he continued. "Listen, Sully, this thing may slip through our fingers within a week if we don't move soon!" he pleaded.

"Why?" I asked.

"They just finished painting over here and they should be taking the ladder out of there any day, I --"

"What ladder, Tony? Out of where? I can't read your mind, you know!"

"There's a ladder locked up in a big cell in the T.V. room, which is to the left of where you walk in that door. It's one of those tripod type of ladders!"

"Never heard of it. How do they work, Tony?"

"The thing opens up like a small step-ladder, only it's big!" he whispered!

"Big? How big?" I just couldn't imagine that type of ladder being built that big!"

"Listen, the ladder itself is only about twelve feet, but there is an extension that is pushed up in the middle. It's about another twelve feet. That's a brand new wall, Sully, and if you look at it close, you can see that it's built in three sections. It only looks like one section, but it's been sprayed with cement, about a half-inch thick, look! Can't you see the lines? They show up even better when it rains!"

"Yeah, I can see them." They were just barely visible.

"But that wall's better than twenty-four feet, a lot better!" I looked at him quizzically.

"No way!" He burst out indignantly. "I measured the lower section and it was eight feet, the other two are the same!"

"Did you measure them?" I said. Cody caught my eye and raised his eyes to the sky, as if looking for help. I could see now what he meant about them not being able to get together.

"Damn, Sully, the bottom one's eight foot. Look at the top two! Are they the same or what?" He said with exasperation in his voice. "Have you ever stood on a shore and looked out across a lake, or any body of water? It's deceiving, Tony. I'm not saying you're wrong, looking at those portions individually, they all look the same! Cody, how tall are you?" I asked.

"Just six foot, why?"

"Go over and stand up straight by that wall, without being obvious."

"Alright!" Cody smiled, moving away.

"Tony, Eddie, let's get on the other side of the yard. We're up too close to the wall."

"Damn!" Tony whispered, looking at Cody's figure across the yard. "He could be stacked up at least -- five times-- maybe more!"

"You said that ladder's twenty-four feet. We got to make up at least six feet. How?" I asked, as much to myself, as to Tony.

"I know a way!" Cody exclaimed after we had been sitting there about five minutes. He just sat there a few seconds before he spoke, smiling, obviously impressed with his brainstorm.

"What is it, genius?" I laughed.

"Yeah. Why don't you share this treasure, you mental-giant!" We all cracked up, laughing, rolling in the grass and Cody's very serious countenance made it worse. I finally managed to pull myself together.

"Okay! Okay! Let's try to be serious, huh?"

"Yeah!" Piped Tony trembling, tears rolling down his cheeks. "L-Let's --be--serious!"

"Listen, Sully, if we put this ladder flush up against the wall, even if one of us were to stand on the very top rung with our palms up and against the wall, we'd still fall short, right?"

"Right! About six foot short!"

"Okay," he nodded. "You're still in pretty good shape, aren't you?"

"Sure, but what are you talking about?" I wondered.

"This! Tony's the lightest one here. He's damn close to six foot, with his arms extended over his head, about seven and a half feet. We let him go up the ladder first, his feet on the top rung, face pressed to the wall, and his arms above his head, palms on the wall to steady him. Then you come up beneath him, let him put both feet on your shoulders--"

"God Damn!!" Tony hissed.

"Beautiful! Beautiful!" Eddie sighed.

Cody went on. "Just bring him up one step at a time Sully, real slow, no jerky movements. Do you think you can do it?" Cody asked, hopefully.

"I think I can do it, if he can hold on!" I said, looking at Tony.

"Hold on to what? That wall's as smooth as a baby's ass!" he said defensively.

"He's right, Sully. All he'll be able to do is try to balance himself. The way you bring him up determines the outcome. He'll have no control over the movement."

"I like it, it's worth the shot!" Tony and Eddie nodded their agreement.

"How's the rest of it go, Tony?" I asked.

"Well, you can see for yourself what the yard looks like. There are twelve cops. Sorry, *Attendants*, out here. They aren't allowed clubs in the yard, but they all have those wooden bed slats behind the chairs! This isn't what we have to worry about though, Sully. There are three attendants inside, two in the TV room where the cell with the ladder is and the yard marshal who sits just inside the door there. All three sit within reach of the button that rings for the riot-squad. If one of them ever got to the button, it's all over. You worry about shock treatments now! If they nip this break in the bud, and nobody manages to get out, they'll hit us with so much voltage, we'll be walking G.E. Plants!" Tony said wryly, but there was no more laughter. "That big yard marshal is a real prejudiced bastard, Sully. Him and Eddie talk about us dirty honkies all day! Right, Eddie?" Tony laughed. Tony and Eddie were inseparable, like Mutt and Jeff. Tony was doing thirty years and Eddie had life, plus thirty-five! Cody had twenty years! And I had six months before the expiration of my sentence.

"Fuck you, Tony!" Eddie laughed good-naturedly.

"Yeah, he calls me 'brother' then *lets* me shine his shoes before he goes home every night! Just one wrong move and I'll rip his mother-fuckin' heart out." Eddie was hissing through clenched teeth, his dark brown face tight and glistening with sweat.

"Alright, so you went through a lot of shit the last few months, but we got what we wanted, didn't we?" Tony persisted. Eddie had learned the use of every key on the big steel ring the yard marshal carried, and there were sixty-three keys! We decided that Eddie and Tony would take the marshal, since this was the most strategic point. There were a number of things to be done, and be done quickly! After grabbing the marshal, Tony would lock him in the bathroom, while Eddie locked two doors. One leading from upstairs where the goon-squad hung around and the other leading to the yard, so the attendants out there couldn't get in. We didn't want them to know what was really happening till the last possible second. Let them think there was a riot, anything, but not a break. We needed every second we could get. Cody and I would take the two attendants in the TV room. We would have to act like nuts in order to sit by them without raising their suspicions. Just one ring of that bell!! I shivered at the thought. We all had ice picks to use as persuaders, and to be used if absolutely necessary. We figured to grab a car from a house just outside the high cyclone fence surrounding the hospital. Cody was from Trenton. He knew the woods and every back road in the entire area, and a place we could lay up for awhile.

"What do you think, Sully?" Tony said when he was finished.

"Sounds good to me! But we're counting on an awful lot of things going just right!"

"Like what?" Tony asked.

"First of all, like fifteen attendants doing as we say, without any heroics. Secondly, this *is* a nuthouse. We don't know how these bugs are gonna react, anything can happen! Let's just 'suppose' the riot bell did go off, can we still get over the wall in time?" I asked.

"We're gonna get that door locked, Sully? They can't get out in this yard any other way. If they do see us pass and go out into the yard with the ladder, it will take them at least five minutes on foot to get around to this wall. They'll have to run upstairs through the administration building, then damn near a half mile around all the buildings to get here!"

"Alright, I'm with you!"

"Beautiful!" Tony smiled. "We haven't got much time, I--"

"Tomorrow, Tony, I'm not waiting another day, not the way they scoop guys up suddenly for the brain wave tests, and shocks right behind them."

"Alright." he said looking at Cody and Eddie, who nodded their confirmations. "When do you want to go, morning or afternoon?"

"This yard always stays open till seven in the evening, Tony?" "Yeah, just for the summer months."

"Then we'll start moving at a quarter to seven! This way there'll only be two hours of daylight left. If things go wrong, we'll need no help from Mr. Sun!"

That following evening at 6:30, we dug up the ice picks we had wrapped in plastic and buried just under the surface in one corner of the yard. We hurriedly went over a few last minute details. At exactly five minutes to seven, Cody and I walked inside and back to the TV room. Tony and Eddie would walk in down front a few minutes later, Neither I, nor Cody had any trouble positioning ourselves within striking distance of the two attendants, we were as close to the bells as they were. The minute it took Tony and Eddie to walk in seemed an eternity. Cody could not see them from where he sat a good twenty yards across the big room, but I could see straight down the hallway by just turning my head slightly. As soon as they made the grab, I went into action and Cody was waiting on me! Eddie walked in first with Tony about three steps behind, acting as if he weren't with him. The yard marshal was sitting in a chair with one leg propped up on the desk as Eddie approached saying something and laughing. His hand flashed out of his pocket with the pick and in the same movement snatched the marshal around the neck, but instead of being cool, he jumped straight up lifting Eddie off the floor with him. His call for help turned into a piercing scream as Eddie drove the long pick down between his collarbone and into his chest. I was transfixed by the weird scene, until the scream brought the attendant next to me to his feet. I spun around quickly pulling my sticker, jumping between him and the bell. The young attendant's face was frozen in terror.

"How do you want to do this?" I said softly, looking up at him from my crouch. His eyes darted around nervously, and I thought his teeth were going to bite his lower lip in half.

"I-I won't m-ove!" he stuttered.

"On the floor! On your stomach! Don't look up and don't move! You understand?"

"Y-y-yes!" his voice shook. I looked over at Cody and he was standing up straddling the attendant on the floor.

"Watch them both, Cody!" I yelled running out into the hallway to help Tony and Eddie. They already had the marshal under control, but he was balking about being locked in the bathroom, pleading that he would die from the knife wound. But, when Eddie drew back the pick to hit him again, he jumped into the shithouse with both feet off the ground. Eddie laughed crazily at this, yelling as he was closing the door.

"Too bad I ain't got the time 'brother' he emphasized or I'd let you shine my shoes for me!" He started giggling when the riot bell went off! Three hearts almost stopped simultaneously as we gaped at each other for a second. I looked at Eddie.

"Did you lock the doors?"

"No!" he said quickly. "Didn't have a chance."

"Lock them!" I screamed on the run for the front desk, and when I turned the corner, I was shocked. Some nut still had his thumb on the riot bell giggling, his eyes opened but seemingly sightless in their crazed state, screaming: "Their coming! -- Their coming! -- Their co---" Bang! I hit him right between his funny looking eyes! Eddie no sooner put his key in the door and turned it when the riot squad came rumbling down the steps. "Eddie, this one! This one!" I yelled seeing the attendants coming across the yard on the run. He locked it quickly. And we stood in the hallway between the two doors as the withering, frothing, mass of so-called human beings clawed and beat against the steel doors, wide eyed! They were no different from most of the patients, worse! I thought.

"Eddie!!" I screamed again as I spotted one of the attendants easing a key out of his pocket. "Put the key in the lock, hurry!" I screeched. I was in pure terror. If these animals ever got in, I knew we were dead, but Eddie was having big fun, pressing his nose against the thick bullet-proof glass, and sticking out his tongue.

"Sully!" I spun around, Tony and Cody were standing just out of sight in the hallway with the ladder. "You ready?" Tony asked.

"Yeah." Was I ready? I couldn't get out of this horror house fast enough.

"Where's those two attendants?" I asked.

"In the cell!" Cody answered, quickly.

"Good! Eddie, twist that key in the lock, just try to jam it in there good! Then open the door to the yard and step to the side. Listen!" I said speaking to Tony and Cody now. "When he opens that door, just ram right into them with that ladder. Scream crazily, and lift those knives above your heads as if to stab them. They think we're all coconuts anyway. Ready?" I asked. Cody and Tony held the long ladder like a battering ram.

"Open it up, Eddie! K-I-L-L!!! I let out in a blood curdling scream as the door swung open. There was no need for a battering ram. As soon as they heard the screams, and saw the knives and the faces behind them, they were climbing each others back trying to get away. They ran clear to the other end of the yard. As I followed the others through the door to the yard, I looked back at the other door. The "goon squad" was already gone, and on their way around.

"Hurry! Hurry!" I urged Cody and Tony, running along side them with Eddie on the other side to keep the curious and eager bugs from blocking our path. We set the ladder up quickly against the wall and

Tony pushed the middle section up and locked it in place. The damn thing was shaking and there wasn't even anyone on it yet, shit!

"Alright, go on up, Tony! - Eddie! - Cody! Hold the damn thing steady, huh!?"

I went up right behind Tony as the big whistle from the powerhouse outside blew its warning! My skin became very cold. I stopped moving completely as Tony stepped on the top rung and braced his hands against the wall. I moved up one more rung so my head was directly in the back of Tony's knees.

"Alright, Tony, step on my shoulders. Easy!! -- Don't shake the ladder!" I grunted as I felt his full weight settle on me. My hip felt like it was going to come out of its socket as I lifted one leg to step up, taking the whole weight on the other, while at the same time, trying to keep my shoulders level and steady. These were the hardest, longest, four steps of my life.

"C'mon, baby, one more step! He's almost there!" Eddie coaxed from below.

"Come on, Sully! You're almost there!" Cody whispered chokingly. Just as my foot settled on the last rung, something jolted the ladder and almost threw Tony and me off.

"What's go---" I started to say as the ladder swayed precariously for three or four seconds.

"It's alright, Sully! Go on! Just some Bug trying to go up the ladder. Sick bastard!" Cody muttered.

"Can't be that sick, if he wants outta here!" I was thinking, when Tony's voice came down to me.

"Just a couple more inches, Sully!" He gasped. "Let me get a good grip! -- I got it!!" He grunted pulling himself up, then straddling the wall and reaching down to me.

"Grip my wrist, Tony, I'll grab yours!" I yelled. He pulled and I dangled in mid-air, my feet off the ladder.

"I-I can't pull y-you, Sully!" Tony gasped, starting to tremble his grip slipping. "Slide over the side then. Your weight will put me up enough for me to reach the top -- go on over!" I said desperately feeling my own grip on his wrist begin to slide from the sweat.

"They're coming!!" Tony screamed up to me from the ground below. I looked over my shoulder from where I sat atop the wall, taking in the attendants, the woods and cornfield all in one glance.

"Start coming up, Eddie, they're almost here!" I groaned, pulling Cody right up to a sitting position next to me. Cody's eyes were wide when he looked down and saw the mob of attendants barely a hundred yards away.

"Sully!" He gasped, his eyes looking wild and desperate.

"You got him?" I asked.

"Yeah!" He nodded, pulling Eddie up as I hung, then pushed outward and away from the wall. I turned in the air as I was going down and hit the grass leaning forward with my knees slightly bent, rolling three or four times. Coming up on a dead run, two or three of the younger, faster attendants were out in front of the rest of the pack and were only twenty yards away from me when I put my foot in the gas tank.

"Stop! Stop!!" They actually had the nerve to yell. I had run about two hundred yards and was really starting to leave them behind when I spotted Tony just to my right about twenty yards away. He was down on one knee under a scattering of pine trees. I ran over to him, looking back over my shoulder.

"C'mon, Tony! What are you stopping here for?" I screamed pulling him to his feet. "Run! Run! Run!"

"I - I c-can't -- can't hard -- b-breathe, that fucking medication," he wheezed. "I can't hardly move!" They were about forty yards away now!

"I gotta go, Tony!" What could I say?

"God damn!" I thought. I ran almost directly across their path trying to draw them away from Tony and I looked so close and tempting that the three took out after me. I came to the end of the grounds and a cyclone fence about fifteen feet high, with three strands of barbed-wire on top, looking left and right. I saw no opening in the fence, so I picked up speed hitting the fence on the run. Hitting it with one foot damn near midway up, and grabbing hold of the top strand of barbed-wire (one barb went deep into the palm of my right hand) as I pulled upward in the same motion I hit the fence with. The wire was new and tight! Only a few barbs sliced and popped through my skin as I rolled across it to the ground. The cornfields were right across the highway, only twenty yards away, so I slowed down to a walk trying to look just like anybody else to the passing cars. I was thinking of State Police cars in particular. I knew the attendants were watching me from behind the fence, so when I crossed the highway, I darted sharply to my left into the cornfield. After I was in deep enough, and hidden by the high stalks, I cut back completely to my right again, knowing that the woods lay in that direction about another mile away. Running against the furrows of a cornfield is like running a gauntlet of straight razors! As I ran, feeling the leaves whipping against my face, I paid them no mind until my forehead and cheeks felt like they were on fire. I passed my palm over my forehead to wipe away what I thought was sweat and it came away sticky and wet with blood, so I turned up one of the furrows and ran along the soft freshly turned earth. It was very hard running and put a great strain on my legs, tiring them much more quickly than they normally would. I had ran about two miles when I heard what sounded like a helicopter approaching. It was! And it was flying extremely low. I fell face down in the deep furrow, arms stretched out in front of me, tasting the black dirt that half-filled my mouth. My clothes were soaking wet. I wanted to move to scratch the open cuts that burned and itched. My heart was beating so hard that I thought even those in the helicopter could hear it. I needed this rest anyway, I thought, closing my eyes for a short time while the chopper passed over the field four or five more times before going away.

I continued running until I couldn't take another step. When I fell to the ground, I started crawling. I crawled until it became unbearable. The cloth of my pants was completely gone at the knees, and my knees themselves were swollen and bloody. The blood ran steadily down my legs, even through the black dirt that had turned into bloody-mud. I couldn't stop! I knew all the local farmers would be swarming through this field in a matter of minutes! I knew it couldn't be much further to the woods. I dropped back to the ground and resigned myself to moving a yard at a time, dragging my body along the furrow by putting both my forearms out in front of me and pulling myself forward; my toes scraping through the dirt in order to elevate my legs enough so that my knees wouldn't come in contact with the ground. Even as soft as the dirt was, it hurt. I heard the motor of a truck and the sound of voices not too far away. They were coming closer! I lay the side of my face in the dirt, staring breathlessly in the direction of the sound. It sounded as if the truck were coming right through the cornfield. The motor became deafening and the loud, boisterous voices grew louder, laughing. I was shocked as I lay watching the open-rack truck pass not twenty yards from me. I saw about eight or ten farmers in the back of it, their shotguns and rifles silhouetted against the clear blue sky, peering intently into the field. My heart leaped as one of them seemed to look right into my eyes where I lay on the ground. I expected to hear a yell! Then the gunfire! But it did not come, they continued along the road. They were laughing! I thought lying still trying to fight the sleepiness I felt.

"Big Sport! The poor man's fox hunt!" I wonder how anxious and brave those blue bloods would be if someone armed all the foxes? I wonder how many manhunts these farmers would be willing to volunteer for in the future, if I had leaped out onto the road with a Thompson, and hit them with a couple of bursts! But then that wouldn't be according to "Hoyle" by their standards! Some of your better cowards have gained fame riding with posses! Ten, twenty and thirty men riding out armed and tall in the saddle to capture, but preferably kill, one unarmed man -- or fox, same thing! You would think a "man" would find it embarrassing to even be present at such an action.

I crossed the road running slowly towards the thick woods ahead. It was getting dark fast, so I decided to keep toward the road as I walked about another three miles before coming out of the woods onto what appeared to be some small type of town or village. I laid down in some bushes across from a line of five or six ranch style houses, just on the other side of the road.

Two teenagers walked slowly by, arms around each other's waists. They were whispering and giggling. The boy bent to kiss her on the neck, and she cringed away unconvincingly, as though she didn't like it, but blushing and smiling shyly as they continued on. This was the most beautiful thing I had seen in five years of violence and mayhem. "That it what life's all about." I thought -- man and woman, nothing else matters -- money, flashy cars, fancy clothes. That's all I want -- that loving glance -- the tender affection! Am I only twenty-four? Why do I feel so much older, so different from them? Would they have been terribly frightened had they seen me? No, I mean even if I were clean and dressed up. Could they tell what kind of person I have been? My eyes maybe? They've made me an animal, animal!! Waiting to pounce -- but beautiful people like that don't deserve to be pounced upon!

I awoke some time later, shivering and cold. I need clothes, food and some money. I had to go in one of those houses. Spotting a Coca-Cola bottle a few feet away, I picked it up and filled it with dirt to give it weight. I darted across the dark road, across somebody's front lawn and stood in the dark shadow along the side of a house. I crawled through the pitch-black yards behind the houses. I had tried the doors on three different houses. None of them were open. Finally, I got desperate and walked to the front of one of the houses. Stepping upon the brick porch quietly, I grasped the doorknob tightly and turned slowly. It clicked and I pushed inward, it opened! I stepped into the vestibule closing the door behind me, but not completely. I stood there about ten seconds listening intently. Nothing! The kitchen was directly ahead. The lights were out, but there was light coming from another room. I walked very softly looking around a partition into the living room. The first thing I noticed was the T.V. The picture was on, but the sound was off. A cigarette had been put out, but it was still smoking faintly in an ashtray on the coffee table. Somebody was here! I stood still listening, but still heard nothing. The smokes on the coffee table almost tempted me, as did the comfort of the long couch. But I thought better of it. I better see what's going on here, before somebody runs out and shoots me.

I walked quietly from the living room down a short narrow hallway, stopping as I heard the low whispering voices. I was just outside the doorway now, and it was almost completely open.

"Oh Henry! Oh Henry! Ooooh Henry!! A woman's voice was moaning softly over and over. I almost laughed aloud thinking this would be a good pitch for "O'Henry" candy bars. She was definitely convincing.

It was dark in the room as I peeped inside, but the light from the hallway carried far enough inside to illuminate and bathe in a startling glow; the heavy, milk-white buttocks of the lovely lady in question. They quivered, trembled, and shook violently as she moved and worked upon her straddled lover. This was too good to interrupt, I thought, much better than those lifeless Playboy magazines I had become engaged to! The nightgown that had been hiked up around her waist had slid down covering her fat, lush butt and I felt cheated as she leaned forward to put it in high gear. Jiggling and thrashing, grasping and grunting, like a fish out of water, finally crying out and twitching spasmodically as she reached her climax! Another minute of this and I would have reached mine! *O'Henry* still hadn't said a word, moaned, groaned, nothing!! Damn!!

They were still lying like that when I ran my hand up along the wall inside the door.

"Click!"

I leaped to the middle of the room as the room lit up. The guy looked up at me in horror as the woman rolled away pulling her nightgown down around her. The poor guy didn't know whether to charge at me or cover his nakedness. He decided on the latter, pulling the sheet onto his lap cringing on the end of the bed, still deciding whether to leap at me.

"Take it easy, Mister, and you won't get hurt. I'm not going to bother either one of you, I just want some clothes, a few dollars and something to eat!" I said.

"Who do you think -- What --" He started to bluster, beginning to rise from the bed. The lady had come around from the other side now. She stood right in front of me, staring frightened, but in full control of herself. She had a lot of heart!

"I meant what I said, lady. I don't want to hurt either of you!"

"Please -- Henry! Sit down! He isn't going to harm us. Don't worry!" She said softly, pleading with here husband.

"Humph!" He grunted and settled back down, as if she had twisted his arm. Some protector he is! I laughed inwardly. She's got more balls than him!

I put the bottle down on the floor.

"I hope you don't hit me with it now!" I smiled trying to show my good intentions and put them at ease.

"I won't!" she actually laughed.

"May I use the bathroom, Ma'am?"

"Of course, it's right in here!" she said leading me out of the bedroom and across the hallway. I turned on the light and looked in the mirror. What an ugly, horrible sight! I just stared for long seconds at the wild mask that was my face, which was just a mass of mud and congealed blood!

"I'll get some towels and things. Would you like to shower?" she asked nicely.

"No, Ma'am. I'll just wash up!" I could just picture them on the phone with me in the shower. She came back into the bathroom with towels, iodine, a pair of pants, underwear and shirt.

"They your husbands?" I pointed to the clothes she held out to me.

"No. They're my sons. He's in the service. He's about your size, they should fit."

"Thank you!" I said. She put iodine on my face, and hand and back where the barbed wire had punctured me.

"Is that place as bad as people say?" she whispered, looking very concerned.

"W-what place?" I asked.

"I know where you came from." She waved her hand as if it didn't matter. "It was on the T.V. an hour ago and the State Police were going from house to house!"

"Were they here?" I asked.

"Yes, about two hours ago."

"That place is *worse* than you heard, Ma'am, I don't even like to think about it!"

"I don't blame you for running away. You hungry? That's a silly question," she laughed.

"Yes, Ma'am!" I smiled, she was a nice woman and she made me feel nice.

She made some sandwiches and brought a bottle of milk, sitting down across from me at the kitchen table.

"You better not go out on the highway!" She offered, as I wolfed down the sandwiches and emptied the bottle of milk.

"Why not?" I smiled.

"Because, the State Police have been passing by every fifteen minutes."

"Who's car is that in the driveway, your husbands?" I asked suddenly.

"No! I m-mean y-yes, but it's not running, it's --!"

"Forget it!" I knew she was lying, but I couldn't blame here for worrying about her husband. "How do I get to Trenton? How far is it?"

"About a mile and a half!" she said. "You can go in the back way, nobody will see you!"

"Which way is the back way?" I laughed.

"I'll show you!" she said getting up from the chair. I followed her out the back door into the yard. She pointed to a narrow dirt road some fifty yards away.

"Just follow that road," she whispered. "And it will take you right into the city."

"Is it used very much?" I asked.

"No, just by the people who live around here, that's all."

About an hour later, I stood on the back stoop, ready to leave.

"I'm sorry I broke in on you like I did, Miss. I really appreciate how you have acted!"

"Oh, that all right!" She smiled, puttering around, straightening my collar like she was my mother sending me to school. I got all choked up when I saw the tears brimming in her eyes.

"Well," I said embarrassed scuffling the ground with my feet. "G-good-bye!" I managed to get out, turning away.

"Remember, stay on that road!" She called softly after me. I was walking for about ten minutes, when suddenly I thought of the last words she said to me. "Remember, stay on that road!" Why? I thought suspiciously. So she can get on the phone and call the State Police?

I veered off the road, figuring to cross the highway about a hundred yards away and follow the woods on that side. I climbed the steep bank. No sooner had I started across the highway when a pickup truck came around the bend. "Probably some farmer," I thought reaching the other side. The truck swerved suddenly, pulling into the oncoming cars and screeching to a halt.

"Where you going, Boy?" Some big beefy guy asked through the window of the cab as I spotted the insignia on the door of the cab "Sheriffs Dept."

"Oh, I'm going home, Mister!" I said in my little boy's voice, full of innocence. "What's wrong? I asked trying to get his mind off me as I stepped away from the glare of the headlights. "If he had seen a picture of me, he wouldn't be talking now," I thought. There was a big dog sitting at attention in the cab beside him, though I paid it no mind at the time.

"Where do you live?" the guy persisted, ignoring my question. I didn't even know the name of a street around here.

"I said I'm going home!" I answered indignantly. The door of the cab opened and he leaned out now trying to get a better look at me.

"Where's that?" he demanded gruffly, reaching to his hip. I had to move fast.

"Right over there!" I said pointing my finger behind him, moving quickly, as his eyes flashed momentarily behind him for an instant.

"Stop! Halt!" he screamed as I dove down the side embankment.

"Boom!! Boom!! Boom!!" I felt I could make it! There were just ten more yards to the pitch blackness of the woods. Just as I rose up to run, a terrific blow caught me in the back, driving me to the ground again. My first thought upon contact was that I had caught a slug. But that was soon dispelled when I heard the snarling roar in my ear and felt the hot wet breath on my neck, swapping, digging in, trying to lock it's jaws on me. That dog! My mind screamed as I rolled over, lashing out at him with my fist and trying to rise at the same time. The man!! I had to get away! But the vicious bastard hunched its muscles, the sickly yellowish eyes like twin beacons in the darkness. I gave up all thought of escape. My immediate concern was to stay alive. The animal sprung, catching me in the chest. Falling backward, I slid my hands through the thick bristly hairs, locking my fingers in the heavy pulsing muscles of his neck. His long ugly stark white teeth were bared in insane hatred, but he ceased to snarl, as my fingers squeezed unmercifully at whatever it is a canine dog breathes through. It seemed like hours, but was just a few seconds. He jumped and quaked, his tongue lolling, the warm saliva dripping in my face, making terrible low guttural sounds. I felt the heavy limp weight of his body sag down on me as something struck me in the head! When I came to, after what must have been just a few seconds, the deputy sheriff was sitting astride my chest in place of the dog (who lie right beside me choking and whimpering as he tried to get himself together). The Pig above me was snarling and rolling over me worse than the dog had, pressing the barrel of his gun under my chin.

"I ought'a kill you, boy! You liked to kill ma dog!!" he grunted.

"Fuck you -- and your dog!" I hissed up at him with hatred, almost hoping he would just pull the trigger. I'd never know what happened, and it would be all over. No more cells, no more box, no more doctors to use me as an experiment, no more hopes for a better tomorrow -- but my will to live was still stronger than the frightening thought of returning to the hospital, and possible shock treatments!

He made me roll over on my stomach, and after cuffing my hands behind me, dragged me by my feet back up the embankment and across the highway to his truck. A lot of people had gotten out of their cars and walked up close for a better look. The pig had one foot pressed on my spine, his gun pointed at my head while he called for help on the extension he had in the pick-up. My chest was throbbing and burning from being dragged across the cement.

"What did he do, officer?" One of the spectators asked, looking down at me matter of factly.

"Stay back!" the deputy growled. "Just a nut. Escaped from the hospital!"

"Oh!" the woman said, then turned and walked away, her curiosity satisfied.

"Just a nut!" I pressed my forehead to the cement, my eyes filled with tears of humiliation. "Just a nut!" I remembered this cruel instant diagnosis for a long time afterward.

I was brought back to the hospital from the Trooper Barracks about two hours later. Immediately upon my arrival, I was brought before a staff of medical hypocrites who gave me papers, certifying that I was mentally sane. Nobody seemed to know why I had been brought there in the first place. They cringed before my tirade, as I told them something about themselves in a layman's vocabulary of four letter words, filthy ones at that! They were frightened to death of any further investigations of the hospital. Two attendants were already in prison, for raping the mentally retarded female patients in Graystone Hospital, and some state senator was pressing the investigation into Trenton State Hospital after receiving numerous tales of horror.

I was put on a special tier called "Shit-Row" while I awaited my return to the prison. Eddie was over in the civil part of the hospital. He had broken both his ankles when he jumped from the wall. Tony and Cody were only a few cells away, but they weren't in any condition to be talking. The attendants had kicked most of Cody's teeth out and his nose was broken. They caught Tony in the cornfield and had stomped him; breaking a few ribs and knocking his face out of shape. They told me that the only reason they stopped beating them was because I had gotten away. That caused them to put out an alert bringing publicity.

We all agreed that we would all be vegetables now, had they caught us all within the grounds. Nobody would have ever heard about it.

Since Cody and Tony were temporarily out of action, I spent the last two days in the hospital rapping with a young eighteen year old kid who had come in the day before from Rahway Prison. Having been there myself for three years, we found something in common to talk about. After talking for about three hours, he finally blurted out why he actually was sent here. As I said, he was young, and a real good-looking kid. He had been in Rahway just one month and from the very first day the "asshole bandits" were after him. Giving him candy, magazines; writing love letters, and leaving them on his bed, or sliding them under his door. When they found that none of this worked, they resorted to threats and finally to physical violence; catching him in the hallways and smacking him around. He explained to me that he never had a fight in his life and was deathly afraid of violence, whether receiving it or dishing it out. He said he was no homosexual, but that the physical and mental harassment had driven him to the point where he was weakening. So rather than be made somebody's "old lady", he went in his cell one evening and slashed both his wrists figuring it was the only way to escape the bandits. One wrist was cut so severely that he will never use that hand again. When the cops ran in his cell, he kept screaming until they gave him a needle to put him out. When he told me he was going for shock treatments, I felt sick. He was such a nice kid, completely normal (whatever that is)! All he was trying to do was escape a brutal, perverted environment, and stay a man. And for this his penalty was death.

"Do these people know your reasons for coming here, Kenny?" I asked him late that night.

"No!" He whispered almost as if he were afraid someone would overhear, and send him back.

"No!?" I exclaimed in anger. "Why the hell didn't you tell them?"

"I - I couldn't." he said very softly.

"Do you want me to tell them? Maybe they'll change their minds, if they knew your motive for cutting up like you did".

"No! No! -- Don't!!" his voice went high.

"They're gonna hurt you, Kenny! They're gonna hurt you real bad! You got to do something, anything --"

"I - I don't care," he said in a sobbing voice. I just couldn't understand or accept his defeated way of thinking. I couldn't understand how any man could stop fighting and give up so easily.

"Don't speak to me any more, you make me want to puke." I snarled unwarrantedly at him.

"Sully, I --" he started.

"Shut up! And get ready for your shock treatments, you meek little bitch! You don't need that seed you have for a brain anyway!" He was silent the rest of the night and I felt like a real dog. Why did I hurt him like that? About four o'clock the following morning I woke up still thinking about what I had said to the kid. I finally couldn't stand it any longer and knocked lightly on his wall.

"Kenny!" I called.

"Y-yeah, Sully?"

"I-I'm sorry, I didn't mean what I said."

"T-That's alright, Sully!" he whispered.

"I shouldn't have said something like that!" I admonished myself.

"Really, I k-know y-you didn't mean it!" he said shakily.

"Goodnight, Kenny. I'll catch you in the morning, okay."

"S-sure, Goodnight, Sully."

They took the kid out of his cell right after breakfast that morning and I just couldn't keep my mouth shut. Seeing Kenny looking so content and unaware of what awaited him: it infuriated me.

"Why don't you mutts try finding out why he cut his wrists before you burn his brains out? You mutt bastards! You know that kid ain't crazy!" I snarled through the bars at them. One of the attendants dropped his head, but the other one who was a real sadistic bastard, who took great pleasure in his work, turned to me.

"I wish this were you, Sullivan!" he snarled coming up to my bars, his face twisted, saliva bubbling on his lips.

"Why?" I sneered with a rotten smile. "So after they knock me out with the shocks you can satisfy your homosexual appetite -- you are a homo, aren't you?" I asked innocently.

He screamed in rage, jumping up on my cell door with both hands and feet, his eyes protruding wildly, his beefy face pumped full of blood. I fell back on the real wall of my cell, doubled up in laughter.

"I'll kill you! I'll kill you!" He continued to scream, until three attendants pried him loose from my bars and led him away mumbling incoherently.

I had packed my few things and was being brought downstairs, when

I saw Kenny being led back between two attendants. He was staggering and they were half carrying him. I stopped as he approached, ignoring the attendants command to keep moving.

"K-Kenny!?" I whispered hoarsely, the tears stinging my eyes until they just ran freely down my face. His eyes were open, but he looked through me, with that emptiness. Thin trickles of blood ran from his nostrils into his blubbering mouth, and there was blood on the collar of his shirt where it had ran from his ears. The attendants that were leading him actually stopped and turned him to face me, trying to conceal their evil sadistic smiles. It was almost as if they were showing me myself, or what they wished had been me.

"Goodbye, Kenny!" I choked, and walked away. I wanted to turn around. I wanted to run back and help my short-lived friend, but it was done and like everything else, to look back would only be to relive a terrible experience.

I was released from the "box" and Trenton State prison in September, 1965. I had been indicted for escape, robbery, and assault relating to the incident at Trenton State Hospital. The charges were later dropped, only because if they were to try me, the only way they could convict me was to admit I was mentally competent at the time I was sent there.

I was placed in Mercer County in lieu of seventy-five hundred dollars and was released two months later, in November. I had a hard time getting a bonds-man who would take me out, the reason being I would be leaving the state. Finally, upon hearing of my situation, a friend of mine in the "death house" in Trenton sent his bonds-man to see me. All he wanted was three hundred dollars, which my brother and sister-in-law sent me a few days later.

***
RELEASED TRENTON - 1965

When I walked out onto the street, I really didn't know who I was or where I was going. I was suspicious of everyone and very withdrawn, still thinking everyone who spoke or smiled at me had an ulterior motive. My sisters, my brothers and my sister-in-law were all very good to me, but I always felt bitter at the thought that they were not there when I needed them the most! Failing to understand that they had their own lives to live and families to raise. I felt that just the fact that I had survived all these years of inhuman experiences, somebody owed me a living. "It's all over now!" They would tell me, and I felt even more sorry for myself. I imagined I could have done my time much easier, by reacting like one of the "Pavlov experiments." I could have looked the other way and pretended not to see, every time a friend was in trouble. I could have slipped and dodged every time some so-called tough-guy raised his voice, lowered my eyes shyly in submission like a little bitch in the face of any threat of danger. I could have pretended to like people I didn't like, and hate people I didn't hate. I never tried to be a tough-guy, but I always strived to be a man, with all men! But to act like a man in prison, is to be branded a rebel, militant, or troublemaker in the eyes of the administration. The price of being a man is very costly in prison. The results are harassment, keep-locks in the cell, the box, beatings, gassings and ultimately, if you are in prison long enough, death, a violent one! Although, people outside today are being made more aware of, through the daily publications and T.V. media, nothing has changed over the years, other than a few titles that are used as cheap psychology to mislead and dupe the tax payers into believing their money is being spent wisely, for so-called progressive prison reforms. Oh, excuse me. These places are no longer *prisons*. They have been renamed correctional facilities! And our cells are to be referred to as "cubicles" in the future! As is the title "guard" being changed to "rehabilitative experts!" If this all weren't so sadly true, it could be extremely amusing. The term "progressive reform" obviously was born with constructive rehabilitative measures in mind. But as always, mealy-mouthed, lying, two-faced politicians have turned one of the nations more vital and long needed programs into a game of semantics while men wait, fight and die for the fulfillment of these promises that are their only shred of hope for a better life in the future, both in prison and when they return to society outside. Hope alone is the sole beacon that strengthens the spirit in the prisoners' tomb-like style of existence from day to day. To shatter this hope is to invite disaster, to kindle anew the dormant fires of bitterness and distrust.

***

Return to the Willow Bar & Grill - December 1965

Coming out of Trenton State Prison at 25 years old after heavy box time, stabbings, riots and barely escaping shock treatment in the Cuckoo's Nest, I was definitely an accident looking for a place to happen. I had about twenty bucks in my pocket and no real place to go, although my brother Jerry and his wife were kind enough to take me in. But they were just getting by themselves, and with Terry due to give birth any day, I felt it best I move on. I was working a bullshit job where my sole function in a factory that made artificial Christmas trees, was to stand by some machine with my gloved hand wrapped tightly around a thin wire that ran through the item, fluffing up the green nylon shit on the wire, giving it the appearance of pine branches. For eight hours a day, I stood there like a fucking robot until my eyes burned and my shoulders felt like they were dislocated.

This shit went on for weeks until one afternoon, while holding the wire and watching all the other ants scurrying about as busy as bees, seemingly mindless and contented with their menial $2.50 an hour tasks, I just started giggling and thought, "Hey, I look like that, too! Oh, man! What the fuck are you doing, Joe?" I began laughing so hard I had to release the wire, which of course brought angry glares from my fellow ants. Unlike myself, they were the elite "piece-workers" who made anywhere up to 50 cents an hour extra if they really broke their humps and "produced" for the company.

"Hey, buddy! Grab that wire! You're wasting material and holding up production!" some faceless foreman called out.

"Yeah," I laughed, removing my glove, "but it won't happen again!" I quipped and walked out of the factory into the bar across the street. During the course of an hour drinking in there, I bought a gun from some guy and began barhopping in down Jamaica Avenue until late in the evening.

At about ten o'clock that night, I found myself in a strange bar on Jamaica Ave. and Van Wyck Expressway. Some strong inner voice was telling me to go home. "But I don't have a home," I retorted silently.

"Of course you do," the voice whispered silkily. "Your brother and his wife still have your mother's house right around the corner from Willow Bar. You remember the Willow Bar, don't you?"

"Yes, I remember the Willow Bar," I confirmed.

"Well, go there and have one last drink. Then you can walk right around the corner and go to sleep."

"Yeah. The Willow Bar..." Some distant graveyard chorus seemed to echo in my soul, lifting me off the stool and directing me out into the cold night on a journey that led me through the darkened side-streets, finally bringing me to the same bar window I had stood up on my toes to peer through twelve years before. Through the alcoholic haze, the people somehow looked different...

"Do as I say, Joseph. Your father's friends have taken up a collection..."

"I'll get it. Mom!" The now-grown, drunken man whispered his promise and walked into the Willow Bar & Grill as if for the first time. I went to the small end of the bar where the cardboard beer container had sat with its quarters, dimes and nickels. Only now, in its place was a

"March of Dimes" canister for children with polio. It didn't say "Sullivan Kids" on it, but I knew better and smiled secretly, dropping some change into the slot as if I were in church where one must make an offering before lighting a candle.

"Can I help you, buddy?" a fat, jowly-faced bartender asked with a plastic smile. I didn't remember him.

"Yeah, give me a Piel's draft," I said. My eyes drifted to the two guys playing pool in the far corner of the bar. The younger kid, about eighteen, looked familiar, I thought.

Sipping my beer, my attention was now drawn to the two unfamiliar faces a few stools from me. Were they there that night?

"Go home and go to sleep," a voice warned.

"Hey, are you one of the Sullivan boys?" One of the two middle-aged men asked, sliding onto a stool next to me. I didn't recognize him or the warmth in his voice.

"Why do you ask? Do you remember me?"

"Uh, no, you look like one of the Sullivan boys. I know your Mom, and knew your Dad," he offered.

"You knew my father? D-did you every put any money in that container?!"

"Huh? Oh, the March of Dimes, " he smiled. "Sure, once in awhile. Why do you as--"

"Have you ever taken any money out?" I hissed, unaware of anybody else's presence.

"Hey, what are you talking abou--"

"You KNOW what I mean, you piece of shit!" My fingers curled around the butt of the gun in my jacket pocket as a voice screamed "He wasn't one of them!!!"

"For phone calls! For the jukebox!!" I snarled. He saw me draw the gun from my pocket and tried to spin on the stool to get away.

"You're ALL guilty!" I said just before the shot shattered the quiet of the bar, and brought three heads spinning on their necks to gape in frozen horror at the hideous scene their minds had trouble absorbing (as did mine). Seeing myself reflected in their eyes, seeing how I must have looked sitting there, the gun still smoking in my hand. I tried to understand what it meant in relation to the man slumped on the stool against the bar in front of me, blood bubbling and gurgling from a gaping wound in his head.

"I killed him!" the seriousness of the senseless crime just dawning on my quickly sobering mind. Somebody moved and so did I.

"Get behind the bar and on your knees. All of you!" I ordered and they obeyed. My mind was already dictating that I must kill them all as I leaned over the bar and pointed the pistol inches from the bartender's lowered head, watching his shoulders shake with a convulsive sob as he sensed the end coming.

"N-no, J-Joe, Don---don't!" It was the voice of the young kid. Tears spilled from the dark eyes that looked directly at me, more in confusion than fear. My resolve melted as I recognized him. Richie! He was a nice little kid whose father owned the barbershop down the street. He could only have been seven or eight in 1953, a really nice kid.

"You!" I pointed the gun at the bartender, never looking at Richie again. "Get up and give me the money in the register, and after you do that, lie down until you hear the door close behind me." Which he did without any further words.

I ran out into the cold, rainy night, no more exorcised of my demons than I had been when I walked in. If anything, I had only gained another.

When my sister Ellen came to see me in the 102nd Precinct, after I had been captured in Evergreen, Alabama two months later and brought back to New York, I was in a bull-pen type cage awaiting transfer to the Queens House of Detention, and the cops let her step up to the cage and speak to me for a moment. The fact that she looked at me as if seeing me for the first time was even worse then what she had to say.

"Joe, why? Why did you do this?" she cried softly.

"I--I don't know, Ellen," I lied. "I w-was drunk."

"D-do you remember B-Bill-Billy Campbell...who you used to go to school with?" her eyes implored.

"Y-yes, I remember him."

"That man you k-killed, Joe, was Mr. C-Campbell, Billy's father. He was a good friend of Mom and Dad!" she keened like a wounded animal and ran from the room leaving me totally crushed and disorientated in the cage.

"I didn't know, Ellen! I didn't know!! I though he was one of them." I whispered to the empty doorway.

After being tried and convicted in Queens Criminal Court of manslaughter in the 2nd degree, I was sentenced to 20 to 30 years.

**

SING-SING - ATTICA - 1967

I was sent to Sing-Sing Prison in 1967, which is a reception center for the upstate prisons. After about three months I was sent to Attica and, like every man to walk through those gates, was awed by the overpowering sense of finality, the high, steep walls, electrically controlled gates, and the regimented military type regime. The place simply reeked of security, and most men who harbored thoughts of escape left them on the bus when they got off.

On the bus that I approached the prison in, all shackled down, there were forty-four men. Upon first sight of the prison, all voices were suddenly stilled, including my own, as we paid our silent respect to this unbelievable fortress. It was definitely the ultimate in concrete and steel.

Attica! The Mecca of all prisons. The lone forty-year old virgin in the New York State Prison System, if not the entire United States. Alcatraz, San Quentin, Devil's Island, they were all whores in comparison. I knew that to deflower this grand lady, I must not look upon her in awe as did so many others, but instead treat her with the cunning respect if I was to be rewarded. I'm going to make you part those lovely legs you bitch, you Mona Lisa! I know you've got an opening somewhere, and I'm going to find it beneath all your fancy frills and lace!

I spent three years looking, thinking, seeing nothing but the smug faces of the guards, who counted the men three times a day, just walking down straight corridors from the cells to the mess hall, not including the other dozen counts throughout the course of the day and night. We couldn't walk fifty yards in any direction, other than the yard without a pass. So most guys vented their pent up anger and excess energy on the football field.

***

The Longest Yard - ATTICA STYLE 1968

This was a far cry from South Bend and the Golden Dome of Notre Dame, I thought. I was shivering noticeably, trembling, while trying to control a bout of diarrhea that had been plaguing me since each morning and listening to the guttural chant of "Kill! Kill! Kill!" in rhythm to the sharp clacking sound of our football cleats upon the cement floor of the long hallway leading out in to B-Block yard to play "The Brown Bombers." It did not tighten my loose bowels. The Brown Bombers vs. The Centurions. The first time ever in Attica's history the black and white leagues would play against each other. I felt like I was jogging the last mile to the death house instead of what was supposed to be a football game. I wanted to go off in a corner and cry, piss, and shit at the same time. And almost did, as coming out the door and onto the field the team had to run through a virtual gauntlet...a sea of venomous, sneering black faces...and the "trash talk" momentarily made me doubt my sanity for putting myself in this position. "Here come de Clan!" one asshole started it off and dozens picked up on it.

"We gonna bust you soft crackers up!" cackled another.

"Hey, white boy. Yeah! You hear me, number 21?" a voice screeched with hateful emphasis. "You think you look fly? You think you look pretty in that there un-e-form? We gonna bust yo motha-fuckin lungs!" Which of course brought a roar of laughter and high-fives from the brothers. But made my nut-sack draw up momentarily in pure fright. Where was I...the fucking Congo? As it dawned on me I was No. 21. Jesus Christ!! For the past forty odd years there had always been two separate leagues in Attica, black and white. And although each would watch the others games with interest, they'd never played each other, firstly, for fear of a race riot on the part of the administration. Even though the cops betted heavily on the games in those days. And secondly, for the very real racist feelings by a certain number of hate mongers on both sides, though very rarely athletes themselves. But in spite of the fact that times they were a changing in the 60's, a lot of mean-spirited trash talk had built up over the years. Which, in spite of a few of the old timers, had gotten together and buried a forty year old hatchet, and somehow convinced the administration to allow the separate leagues to play each other in 1968, with the idea of combining both leagues, black and white the following year if it proved successful. Meaning no riots or killings that were football related that we did in 1969. But, on this brisk, sunny September afternoon in 1968, I didn't see any signs of brotherly love as I looked around the yard and up on the walls while our team went through its ritual pre-game limbering up exercises on the fifty-yard line. I felt we were all on the brink of some Christian Muslim war. The entire sidelines were all black and all white on our respective sides of the field without exception. The surrounding walls above us were dotted with prison guards in tear-gas attire, while blacks and whites climbed the bars on the cell block for a better view of the upcoming spectacle, but with the thought in mind of being in a safe perch if hell broke loose!

After looking at the size of our opponents, many who worked in the steel mill, I took some degree of comfort in the size and heft of our own animals---who went 260 lbs. or better along the line offensively and defensively. I was a 28-year-old rookie and at 5'10" tall and 175 lbs., I did not exactly strike fear into anybody's heart. It was because of my speed, good moves, and hard work that allowed me to make this squad of hard-nosed lifers and long-timers at all. These guys had played together in the white league for 8 - 10 and some as much as fifteen years. And they were very protective of each other's positions against outsiders, "New Jacks" ---as they referred to new arrivals. So to say cronyism and favoritism was practiced would be an understatement. But I respected the older guys and kept my mouth shut and waited for my shot. I knew that although I wasn't starting this game, **they** meaning "Don Nemire" a great football player, middle linebacker in the Jack Lambert mode, and whom the blacks referred to as "The Grand Wizard" (Ku-Klux-Klan) would soon turn to me. Because I believed none of the pre-season hype and pervasive attitude that what our team lacked in overall speed, we would make up with brains, "Cause them niggers can't think!" Nor did I subscribe to the black attitude that was prevalent that they were going to destroy us, "cause whitey's soft, and ain't got no heart!" I knew this was going to be a brutal dogfight.

So to me personally, it was more a matter of self-pride that gassed me up, rather than hatred I could not feel. My heart was pounding as I knelt by the bench on the sideline with my own thoughts---thinking of my father who's memory alone had guided me through some hard times in prison as a young man. Whenever I doubted myself or felt fear and even after fifteen years, I felt he was watching this day and smiling. It was not Notre Dame, and I was not Paul Horning. But in my mind, he has never stopped being my father: a resounding roar ripped from a thousand throats, and I came back down to earth as we kicked off to the Brown Bombers, and the sound of crunching bodies meeting helmet to helmet with each team's refusal to take a safer, saner angle was sickening.

"God-damn, baby!" Some black dude screamed ecstatically as one of our guys in such a collision had his helmet split-open like an eggshell and was carried to the hospital unconscious. But his voice was quieted when one of the black player's was clipped and lay on the ground moaning in agony. Finally, the game settled down and both sides forgot the forty years of bullshit and concentrated on playing football. We were holding our own, until midway through the second quarter after we were scored on once in spite of the valiant defensive play --- we were not moving the ball on offense. The line was doing their job --- but that old leather helmet approach of three yards and a cloud of dust was not paying dividends. Not against the big, quick, Brown Bomber Defensive Line, and even quicker defensive backs. Legs and arms continued to pop like chicken-bones on both sides.

Nothing dirty -- just fierce hitting, and as I watched guys getting tossed into the wheelbarrows standing by on both side-lines, I wanted to run out on the field and stab Nemire for his thick-headedness, who himself was playing with a cracked sternum and broken nose received in the first quarter. I was raging inside. As I knew what I could do, but needed a shot! And my heart swelled with hope, when with about four minutes left to half-time, and trailing 6-0. The Christians finally gave up on the slow trudging war-horses.

"Sully! Sully! Sully!" The chant started by a few and was taken up by all when we received a fumble after a hard hit on our own 30-yard line. The chant grew so loud that even my own teammates looked toward the bench where I was confidently strapping on my helmet and limbering up, while staring out at them arrogantly. Taylor and Fat Charlie knew I could run and prevailed upon the Grand Wizard that enough was enough! It was time for a changing of the guard. So when Nemire screamed toward the sideline like a fucking Emperor, "Sullivan!!" I raced out to the huddle no longer aware of the crowd. But when I reached the huddle and looked into Nemire's eyes and stubborn battered face attained by his macho refusal to use those new-fangled facemasks on his helmet. I didn't know which I wanted more; the ball, or to break his nose a second time. He knew my strengths and weaknesses. Off tackle and sweeps were my bread and butter.

"I'm gonna run you till you drop." he sneered in a nasal tone, gagging on his own blood.

"Give me the fucking ball!!" I snarled back to the delight of the offensive linemen, who grinned knowingly when I looked up and said. "Just screen block them, give me a crack, just a little daylight --- we can run on them!"

"26 Power on Three! And I want that fuckin' hole wide open!" Nemire bellowed as we headed toward the line. I always run best left to right and played two-back in the pro-formation we used. I had complete confidence in the line, that also featured a great blocking tight end, and our flanker right was not afraid to sacrifice his body.

"Hut--Hut--Hut!" There's no nicer sound when you're young and healthy. No better feeling when you believe in your God given physical ability. Re-enforced with endless hours of hard work. Weights—sprints-- push-ups-- sit-ups -- jumping jacks -- long after everybody else has left the practice field. My heart raced in exultance immediately upon taking the handoff going to my right--- seeing the hole open after a cross-block wide enough to drive a herd of goats through --- stutter stepping just long enough to allow my flanker to crush the outside line-backer. Cutting back across the middle of the field against the traffic and brought down on the Brown Bomber nine yard line.

"You got that one, Bro! But don't come back!" Their free safety gasped laying on top of me, our face masks mashed against each other.

"Sorry 'bout that!" I grinned, watching his dark countenance soften then break into a laugh while helping me to my feet.

"No," I thought right then, "it's not about hate, just pride-- and a need for mutual respect." And as good as I felt about myself, it was more fulfilling for me to see that shot of adrenalin the run had been for the confidence of my teammates, and all the guys on the side-lines I felt I was representing. Even the Grand Wizard gave a grin of approval when I went in on the following play from nine yards out. It was the hardest game I was ever to play in throughout the following ten years. Because it was more about a hard grudging change, about some men who went into it hating mindlessly, because it was expected of them. And came away after a hard fought 20-20 tie hugging their foes and looking at each other in a different light -- if just for the moment. And the fact that neither team won became a secondary thought. There was no need for the gas or clubs as we had beat on each other enough on the playing field, each coming away with his own conclusions and understanding. I do know that I was deeply saddened when many of these same guys died in the Attica uprising a few years later along with a handful of guards- - a few who were real decent guys, also. And all because of a lack of that same understanding and dialogue. Who we are, or what we are, does not negate ones humanity on either side of a human equation.

I left Attica to go to Auburn almost three years later, and was there about nine months when I learned from my sister-in-law, not my sister, that my mother was in New York Hospital and dying of cancer. My first reaction was no reaction, I felt cold, numb. I had only seen my mother on possibly four occasions, since I was a young boy at the time of my father's death. And now, even fifteen years later I had still not forgotten how she had pointed her finger at me as the cause of his death. Nor the many times when I ran away from different places as a youngster and she refused to take me into the warmth of what I always thought was "our" house, nor the time I had snuck into the cellar out of the cold blowing snow, after running away from Warwick Reformatory, only to be woken in the morning by Police Officers. There were so many things that happened after my father's death, which I took very personally as a denial of her love.

If it were not for Warden Deegan, I never would have been able to visit my mother, as there were others that tried to convince him I would escape, or try to, but he gave the order to send me anyway. He is the only Warden I have seen in seventeen years whom the men actually liked and respected, all personal, petty grievances aside. Had he remained as warden in Auburn, there would have been no riot. Because he was forced into retirement by the rest of the administration, guards and officers alike, who felt he was coddling the inmates (simply treating us like human beings) the prison population showed their great displeasure.

For security reasons we were met by two New York City Detectives, who drove us to New York Hospital. I was taken through a back entrance, and down into the cellar, taking a freight elevator up to the eleventh floor. My sisters, Maureen and Ellen, were not inside with my mother because they had heard I was coming and were waiting outside the front of the hospital for me to arrive. A nurse came into the hall while the officers were uncuffing me.

"You can go in now sir," she said politely.

There were about six beds in the room. I walked past the first bed, my eyes passing over a very old woman lying deathly still in the bed. "Oh my God!" I thought after taking another step. "Those eyes!" I turned around slowly looking back into the ravaged face of the woman who was my mother. I was a little boy again and I loved her. Though I tried very hard to control myself, I cried like a baby. The love that shone in her eyes was for me! I knew now that she had always loved me! I continued to cry begging for her forgiveness, but her eyes flashed in anger as she tried to rise away from her pillow, she couldn't but she did manage to point a hand toward the end of the bed. There was a pencil and pad there on the nightstand.

"This Mom?" I held them up for her to see.

"Yes!" she nodded.

My sisters came into the room and she motioned to Ellen to wind the bed up so she could be in a sitting position. I kissed my sisters and they left me alone with my mother. She couldn't even raise her arms to take the pad and pencil, so I placed them in her hand on her lap.

"That's all over!" She scratched painfully referring to my pleas for forgiveness. "I love you!" She wrote looking at me, the tears welling in her beautiful eyes. The eyes were all that was left of the beautiful women I knew as a young boy. There was a white sling covering the lower half of her face, and when I reached my hand and touched it tenderly she tried to cringe away, but was physically unable to. She didn't want me to see how her tongue protruded through her lips, swollen five times its normal size, and leaking the cancerous poisons that were taking her life.

The strength in her weakened body shocked me as she squeezed my hand pulling it to her body, as I bent and kissed her lips. The only way she could hear was when I came close and whispered directly in her ear.

"Mom, I've lied to you all my life. I don't ever want to again! There's got to be a God up there somewhere, Mom. If you see Dad, I want you to tell him I'm sorry for the heartache I've caused you. He must be mad, huh, Mom?" I asked through blurred eyes. Her head barely nodded, but her eyes smiled lovingly and impishly at me.

"I've done some terrible things, Mom, but never nothing really bad, u-until this time -- remember how I cried for two days when 'Tabby' (my cat) disappeared? I've changed so much, Mom. I--I'm not the same. I wish we could go back again." I cried softly.

Mom scratched painfully again. "When will they let you out?"

With a straight face, I lied to my mother for the last time. "I'm all right, Mom. With a little luck I'll be home next year," I smiled through tears of love. Who else but a mother would put the welfare of another before themselves, even on their deathbed?

I was unaware that my sisters had come into the room and were standing by the bed, as were the prison guards.

"Time's up, Sullivan. We got to go," one of the guards said softly.

The panic in my mother's eyes and the grip of her hand was more than I could bear.

"I love y-you Mom, b-but I have to go. I--I've always loved y-you. Ellen, p-please help me," I sobbed uncontrollably as she gently pried Mom's fingers from my hand.

I stumbled blindly out of the room into the hallway, gasping for breath.

"You all right, Sully?" a guard offered.

"Y-yeah, I'm fine. Thanks," I gagged.

"God damn, I hate to take you to the Tombs after this---" the big cop said. "That place is a cesspool!"

"How bad can it be? One's as bad as the next," I said, not knowing this was the Tombs two months before the first riot.

"Well, we'll be here early in the morning to get you," he said.

***

Tombs - 1969

When I walked into the receiving room it was 8:30 in the evening. Normally, the receiving room is empty at this time of night, but all the "bull-pens" were packed tightly. One of the guys told me they had been standing up in there since ten o'clock that morning because the people were trying to find space for them up on the floors. Most of them in the pen I was in were winos, lying on the floor in their own puddle of urine. The drug addicts were lying beside them, curled up in pain and kicking unattended. The guards paid no attention whatsoever to the pitiful moans of neither pain, nor the pleas for help. They had become immune to such human weaknesses.

Finally, after about three hours of standing, pressed tightly against the bars, a cop opened the gate and called about twelve names to go upstairs. I was one of them. On my way into the elevator I wondered if they passed out the sheets and blankets upstairs now. They had always done this in the receiving room before.

"All right, get up against the wall and stay there!" Snapped one of the guards, a slim black dude with a big Afro. These types killed me, these "brothers" who wanted to be looked upon as "militant" by their own, yet wanted to be cops, too. These were the type of frustrated "Toms" who would walk around with a pocketbook sticking out of their hip pocket, usually "George Jackson's" or "Malcolm X!" As if to say, "Look at me brothers, I'm down with the movement! This blue shirt and badge is just a stuff-off!" But in reality these are the puppets who will run in a brother's cell upon command and kill him even quicker than whitey will.

"Alright!" this killer yelled, calling off cell locations. The other guard, a big fat pig about six foot five, just stood there like a moron. He was the robot's robot. The half live winos and junkies started to move off as the militant called their locations. Something's terribly wrong here! I could feel it.

"Are there sheets and blankets in the cells, officer?" I asked politely trying to halt their movement. He didn't even look up at me and just kept calling names until only three of us were left.

"Sullivan!" He called, and when he didn't get any answer, he looked around at me.

"You Sullivan?" he asked.

"Yes!" I answered.

"Here's your card, you're in lower A-6!" he held out the card. And when I didn't move, but just stared at him, he laid the cards on the desk and walked over to me.

"What are you, a wise-guy?" he said leaning forward on the balls of his feet.

"No, all I asked you was about sheets and blankets!" I said facing him.

"You gonna go in the cell?" he whispered viciously. He turned to the fat guy. "Let's lock these guys in!"

While they were gone, I took off my overcoat and jacket and stuck it through the bars, but when they came back they had both taken off their shirts and they had black-jacks in their hands. "What the hell is going on here?" I thought. These guys are ready to kill me without a thought in the world. God Joe! Not for just one night! You'll be gone in the morning anyway.

"What are you gonna do, Baby?!" The brother said sliding up on one side, the big white guy on the other.

"All this because I asked for sheets and a blanket man!?" I tried to reason with him.

"We ain't got none. If we had them you'd have got them downstairs. Now, how do you want this? You're going in that cell one way or another," he hissed hatefully.

"Since you put it so nicely, I'll walk in!" I smiled hating myself. When they opened the gate leading to the cells I couldn't believe my eyes. There was a bare space of floor without a mattress on it! I guess I was lucky to be getting a cell, I thought, as I stepped over and picked my way between the sleeping bodies, and those that were awake didn't even bother to move. I had stepped into the pitch darkness of the cell and shut the door, before my eyes had grown accustomed to the darkness and I realized there was already guys in both the bottom and top bunks. I took another step forward and jumped back instinctively having stepped on someone on the floor. We were all in a cell no bigger than six by nine feet.

"Is this shit for real?" I said in disbelief, looking into the eyes of a dark face whose eyes were trying to pierce the darkness. "How many fucking guys are in here?"

"You make four, brother!" said a weary voice. "You from upstate?" he asked.

"Yeah, Auburn!" I answered. "How long has this been like it is?" I asked incredulously.

"Well, I been here six months like this. We ain't been out of the cells in the last three weeks. No showers, no soap, no clothes, nothing! We're lucky they're feeding us."

"What have the guys done? Aren't they going to do something about this? How do you take it? I couldn't stand this if I thought I had to be here longer than just tonight. How can that dude just lie on the cold floor like that without a mattress, not even a blanket?"

"We been filling out some forms from Senator Dunne, he's investigating--"

"Shit!" I broke in.

"What are we supposed to do man!?" the young brother said defensively.

"Die!!" I hissed. "It's better than this --anything's better."

"That's easy to say, brother. I ain't ready to give it up just yet."

"Neither am I!" I confessed meekly. "But something's got to be done. Somebody's got to get these guys together, get them angry, make them aware of the terrible indignities being perpetrated upon them -- like corpses!"

"I know. I know." he answered softly, and fell asleep a short while later, the other two black dudes, in the lower bunk, and on the floor were not talking, they were too much in pain to speak, kicking some bad habits, cold turkey. About two that morning the young brother awoke claiming he couldn't sleep. I had been leaning against the bars, trying to support myself, I was damn near drained and to the point where I thought I was gonna fall out. All the tension of the day had really wore me out. I think the only thing that stopped from curling up on the floor was the synthetic militant I had the trouble with. He came by every half hour hoping to see me lying on the floor like a dog. If I did get on the floor, he'd never see it, that much was for sure. On his next count the young brother called to him as he passed by.

"Why don't you bring the guy a blanket?"

"No, forget it," I started feeling embarrassed that he was taking my part.

"You just mind your business brother!" the cop started.

"Brother?!" he exclaimed. "Why you stinking Uncle Tom ass mother-fucker!" he grated, sticking his face through the bars.

"Forget it man!" I said pulling him away from the bars.

"Don't even waste your breath on these people. Forget it!" I tried to soothe him.

"Why don't you climb up there and get some sleep. You must be tired?"

"No!" I protested weakly. "I'll be leaving early!"

"Go on, man!" he insisted. "I ain't been doing nothing but sleeping the last three weeks."

"Alright, t-thanks!" I said giving him my overcoat before I climbed up on the bunk. "Wake me up in a couple of hours okay? That's all I need!"

"Sure!" he said sitting half in the sink, his foot propped in the bars. He never woke me, and when the bell rang the following morning and woke me, I found him shivering, curled up in a ball on the floor, my overcoat was folded up on the table, he didn't want to get it dirty. I shook him lightly waking him up and helping him back onto the top bunk, he was shivering like a leaf.

"Stay in there till you warm up, I'll get your coffee and stuff!" Son-of-a-bitches! I thought watching him tremble every couple of seconds.

I left the Tombs that morning in haste, but I took something with me, a lesson. I learned that in times of suffering, friendship has no color barriers. It was very humble experience and I feel richer for having lived it.

I returned to Auburn, and was doing pretty good time, lifting weights and playing softball. I was voted unanimously "manager" of our softball team only because nobody else wanted the unpopular assignment. My good friends, Daryl, Gary, Roger, and Tony blew my head up telling me how I was the only one qualified, blah, blah, blah... They were the first ones to give me the evil eye if I dared have the audacity and pull them for a pinch-hitter or something. But we all had fun, as we all got along very well on the whole. Being the manager of the crew of madmen had a great deal to do with about ten of us getting "shipped" out of Auburn to different prisons. Daryl, Gary, Sally and myself were sent to Attica. Peanuts and Joe D. to Clinton; Tony D. to Comstock, etc. Sadly enough, we were guilty of nothing other than "hanging out" together and doing a good bid!

Obviously, some "rats" felt we had it too easy! At the time we were shipped out there was some pot in circulation and though it was common knowledge not one of the guys I knew were directly involved, the petty, jealous, vicious rats went to work! Since the authorities didn't know what to believe, they just scooped up every one of us to "make sure" they got the right one. Yet, the "right ones" were left behind. I was so angry and bitter. Even when I'm not guilty, they're just going to *make* me guilty!

I was really doing well in Auburn. It was a decent joint; the sports, the chow, even the cops were pretty fair, overall! There was a lot lacking, but at least we had a Warden who was making great efforts on our behalf. But they shipped him out too! He was doing *too* well! "Alright!" I felt after that. "I'll play your way!"

***
ATTICA: 1971 - 9:25 a.m.

The roaring sound of a distant motor brought me up away from the comfort of the coal-pile, instantly alert! 9:26! It's late I thought, listening to the heavy beat of my heart pounding at my temples, as I gripped the pipe firmly in my hands, squatting crouched over, looking, listening! Looking at Mike and Lenny as their bodies tightened up. They heard it too! I waited for Mike's signal with my ears as I turned to face the wall, looking to the top now between the heavy timber of the tracks above me.

"God! It's high! You can do it Joe! -- You can do it! -- Just don't look at the towers! --You'll swear they're looking even if they aren't! -- Don't break your stride! -- Keep your rhythm! If they see you, you'll never know about it anyway, you won't feel a thing!"

Crack! Crack! Crack! The broom hit the concrete and deep in my guts at the same time. I moved the short distance to the wall quickly, hugging the solid concrete with my shoulder and raising the pipe quickly, but smoothly till I rested straight up not five yards from the gun-tower. I rose to my feet quickly, easing the long prongs over the top. "Move!" My mind screeched and every muscle in my body trembled then sprung to its command.

My eyes saw nothing but the top where the wall and sky came together, and my ears heard nothing but the silent voice inside urging that I move faster! As I neared the top and all my weight came directly to bear on the couplings, I heard the first sounds of tearing metal -- but I was grabbing hold now, I couldn't grasp the top with my hand because it was beveled roundly. I had to drape and catch it with the crook of my arm. I couldn't bother to hang and drop, I didn't have time! So I just rolled over pushing away as I went, feeling a sharp pain in my elbow. I hit something! What, I didn't know. I hurtled through the air hitting something reasonably soft. Grass? Dirt? Hot white flashes shot through my head upon impact, as my knees were driven into my chest partially glancing my jaw. I had to get up -- get up! -- Couldn't lay here -- m-my hat! -- Where's my hat? I finally saw it through my half-unconscious state, moving away toward the parking lot in a wide circle, far enough away so that my face could not be distinguished, nor the shiny tin badges on my blue denim shirt and makeshift hat. I walked at a normal pace, restraining my body from the urge to run. I paused a few times, looking around on the ground as if I had lost something out here. I passed five towers, two times, returning the waves that came from above.

My eyes took in the parking lot in a brief glance as I approached it almost from the front. I breathed a sigh of relief as I neared the cars. There were no officers or guards around, but I had to hurry. Five cars had occupants in them. Three cars had single white guys sitting behind the wheel. They could be guards! Off duty, picking up a paycheck, anything!

I was directly beneath the front tower now, about forty yards away. There were two women in one car and a single black guy in the other. I got to try him! He sure ain't no cop! Isn't a black one in the whole prison. He's got to be visiting and if that's the case, he has no special love for these people. I came up from the rear of the car and stopped before the open window. He was a young guy, about twenty-five, dressed mod, chains around his neck, the whole thing. I knew I had a winner.

"What's happening?" He asked matter of factly, thinking I was a guard. But when his eyes fell on the badge on my chest, he looked up at me quickly and quizzically.

"I need help!" I said desperately, but without fear in my voice.

"You---" he nodded toward the wall as it hit him.

"Can you get me out of here, just to Batavia? Ten minutes!!" I whispered, holding my breath.

He looked around uncertainly for about ten seconds, then gasped. "Get in!" Reaching for the key in the ignition.

"Wait! Look over my shoulder, is the guard watching us?!"

"No!" he answered. His eyes barely flickering as he looked. I climbed into the back seat. "Move it, Baby! Move it!"

I laughed nervously glowing with exhilaration, taking the tin can off my chest, and ripping the hat to shreds. We made one stop to deposit them and continued into town.

"Where do you want to go?" he asked.

"I'd like to get to a bus or train station and catch the first thing smoking!" I smiled.

"I can dig that!" he laughed. "Hey, bro!" he called to some black dude passing by. "Where's the hound run out of around here?"

"About four blocks down on the right, brother," he answered.

"Right on!" the brother saving me waved.

We passed a clothing store about a block back from the Grayhound bus station. He had suggested that I stop and get some clothes. He was thinking.

"No, I want that ticket first. I don't stand out anyway. Everybody dresses like this up here."

"You got bread?" he asked.

"Yeah, I'm all right."

"Don't get hung up in this town," he said sincerely, shaking my hand when I stepped from the back of the car.

"I'm leaving now, don't worry!" I laughed.

"Right on!" he called as he pulled away. I turned and walked into the bus station.

"When's the next bus for Rochester, mister?" I asked feeling that I had "Attica" written all over me, wondering if I looked as strange and out of place as I felt. I was ready to bolt and run at the first and smallest sign.

The man's eyes passed over me casually before he answered.

"Just missed one. The next one doesn't leave till 11:20." Damn! Almost an hour and a half! I wanted to ask if one was leaving for Buffalo any earlier, but I didn't want to raise any suspicion.

"Oh well!" I tried hard to smile. "I guess I'll just have to wait! One, please!"

"Yes, sir!" he said stamping and sliding me my ticket as I paid him. There were only three or four people sitting inside the station, nobody that looked like trouble, though. I realized I still had my black jacket with me with a homemade shiv in the pocket. I put it down on one of the benches in the waiting room, and then went into the men's room. I rinsed some of the sweat and grime off my face and upper body standing stripped to the waist before the big mirror over the sink, grinning at the gaunt hollow-eyed reflections, and not believing that it were really me standing there. I better get moving, get some clothes, can't hang around here! I had taken three steps out of the bathroom and was moving toward the side entrance.

"Sully!?" A voice called. My heart froze, I looked and retreated into the bathroom and locked the door quickly behind me, my back against the door, no windows!! I thought looking around. Why hadn't I thought that this could happen? Why wasn't I more alert! I cursed myself silently, waiting for the pounding to come at the door. Of all mornings, I got to run into six parolees going home from the prison. The guard who had brought them to the station had his back when Sammy called me without thinking. I don't know if the guard had paid any attention to this exclamation since I had spun on my heels almost instantly. I was standing against the door for a good five minutes, sweating profusely, trying to pull myself together. "He couldn't have heard Sammy!" I thought. "If he did he paid no mind to it or he would have been on me by now!" How many other guards were there? I had to go out though, couldn't stay in here like this. I'm trapped! Easing open the door I glanced around the corner looking out toward the side-entrance. Sammy was seated facing me, his eyes as big as saucers, but otherwise very calm. I just stared at him and he nodded, giving a slight movement with his hand to go. I walked with my head down, my handkerchief over my face, sneezing fitfully. I walked down the street and walked into a small men's clothing and picked out a pair of light flare slacks and sports shirt. The old man was very nice, so I spent about twenty minutes talking with him. I sat in the back of the shop with him as he tailored the pants for me at no extra charge.

"Your from around here?" he asked cordially, just making conversation.

"No, sir. Work over in Buffalo, just passing through." I answered. We chatted on, mostly about the beautiful weather, the coin collection he had on the wall, etc. He told me there was supposed to be a "double" at Batavia downtown, -- "was it that night or the coming week? I don't remember." But I told him I had a bus to catch and couldn't make it.

"Stop by again, young man!" He waved as I started to leave.

"If I'm ever through this way again, I'll drop in and thank you!" I waved goodbye. I walked about four blocks down from the bus station and came to the main street. I was surprised seeing the heavy traffic of people. This was a nice sized town. I stepped into a drug store and bought a pair of those round-lensed, psychedelic sunglasses, with an orange tint to them. I stood before a narrow full-length mirror in the drug store and nearly laughed aloud at the picture I presented. All you need is the long hair and you'll look just like all the rest of those mod-dressed cats. I walked up and down the main street taking in all the voluptuous female figures sliding by me gracefully; tall, short, thin, plump, they were all fine! Just being around women again was worth everything! This is what men live and die for. This is what life's all about! There is nothing more rewarding.

I kept a close eye on the time, giving myself ten minutes to get back to the station. I didn't want to hang around that terminal a minute longer than necessary. As I walked up the side of the main street and down the other very slowly, two times I had to duck into a doorway twice and pretend I was window-shopping as a prison guard passed. Once with a wife and daughter, the other time with a young boy, probably a son. And both would have known me on sight!

I watched from the rear of the parking lot, as about fifteen people filed out the front door of the station, standing in front of the bus waiting to board. "I have to get on that bus!" I thought desperately, looking at the six parolees mingled with the waiting people, and the guard who was seeing that they got on. It was only about ten yards from the front entrance of the station to the door of the bus! I walked quickly through the side entrance and eased out the front door into the people crowded around the door of the bus, my back to the guard. I saw Sammy, and another guy I knew well, move up to shield me as I moved toward the open door, waiting to hear an outburst behind me. I moved toward the back of the bus and took a seat, pushing it back and closing my eyes. My friends took seats close up front realizing I was in no frame of mind for conversation. A few times between Batavia and Rochester they came back to the bathroom to nip on the bottle they had bought somewhere in Batavia. As they passed me, they just looked down at me and winked patting me on the shoulder. I returned their smiles, but my smile left no opening for further talk. They understood my very precarious situation.

"Rochester!" the bus driver called. As Sammy and John prepared to leave the bus they glanced at me and I nodded that I would follow.

"Damn, Sully! I'm sorry! It just came out." Sammy started to say when I caught up with them about two blocks away.

"Forget it, Sammy. Everything turned out alright, that's all that matters." I said shaking their hands.

"Where ya going, Sully? Ya got any money?" Sammy asked. His forehead creased with concern.

"Yeah, I got a little, but I can use more!" They went in their pockets and came up with thirty dollars between them. We rapped a few minutes longer, talking about old times, none of them good, which neither of us really wanted to remember. I gave them both my heartfelt thanks and said good-bye.

I arrived in Utica, New York a week later, where I met some old friends who supplied me with funds and a place to live for a while. They also gave me an offer and good solid advice as to leaving the country but, stubbornly, for very special reasons of my own, I did not wish to leave at that time. Though they might feel I was very foolish, and perhaps I was, I doubt that I shall ever live long enough to regret it. I have learned my head is harder than my heart, my sole vice!

About five weeks later I repeated an old mistake and made a phone call to a person I had known in New York for some time. Not only did I talk to the person the call was intended for, but unknown to me at the time, I was speaking to the switchboard operator in the office building who had been schooled to be on the alert some two weeks earlier. I told my friend that I would be in the city about three days later but I packed my things that night and took the bus. I figured if anything were wrong, they wouldn't expect me so soon.

It was about 9:30 in the morning when I reached East 12th Street and began to walk toward University Place. I was walking slowly, enjoying the sunshine and what can be considered fresh air early in the

morning in New York. It's the best you'll get all day! I was about fifty
yards away from the office building on the opposite side of the street,
when suddenly I stopped! I didn't see anything unusual--but something
was wrong--terribly wrong-- my happy early mood had suddenly turned
to one of foreboding. I continued walking, although very slowly now. I
had planned to cross the street and enter the building. There were old
Brownstone apartments to my right. The thought flashed quickly across
my mind to drop my suitcase and dash into one of the doorways. There
must be back entrances! But I shrugged it off, angry with myself for
being so jittery. I'll just go in that restaurant on the corner and tell my
friend to meet me in a bar down the block. I would watch from there,
this way if anyone followed, I would know!

I reached the corner of University Place diagonally across from the
restaurant. There was a Catholic Church right on the corner with a
wrought-iron picket fence about six feet high running around it. Why
was I stopping here? There was a graduation ceremony going on. It was
a Catholic girls school and they were all fluttering around happily in
their caps and gowns. "You could jump over this fence and cut through
the crowd, they wouldn't shoot into them! Who wouldn't shoot!?" My
mind screamed! I turned away from the fence suddenly. As I did some
guy across the street to my left flipped a paper up in front of his face. I
stared waiting to see if he would bring it down again. He did, and was
looking directly in my eyes for a split second. Suddenly, he turned away
and walked across the street toward the restaurant. He then turned, and
crossed again to get to the opposite side, directly across from where I
was standing, but kept walking until I lost sight of him behind a parked
truck. "No!!" That's too funny and obvious to be real. Maybe he was a
queer or some kind of nut. After all, I am in the "village!" I laughed aloud
at my own nervousness, but for some reason couldn't take my eyes off
that truck. I put my suitcase down again on that corner and bent over
pretending to knock the lint off my pants, looking beneath the truck
about twenty yards down the street. Nothing! He must have gone into
the building down there. I was right. My mind's just playing tricks on me.
My eyes swept the four corners in all directions. Hippies, truck drivers,
bums and just plain people, nothing else!

I had just stepped onto the sidewalk in front of the University
Restaurant when something hit me hard in the lower spine driving me
forward. I tried to regain my balance and spin off it, but the weight
dragged me to the ground. I watched my suitcase skid away as I hit the
ground on my hands and belly. Guns were being jammed in my back,

neck, head and face, as the voices screeched.

"Don't move a muscle or we'll kill you!" -- "We got him!" -- "We got him!" -- "Don't let him move! Watch him, hold him down, careful!"

One of the "hippies" got down on his hands and knees.

"You're Sullivan, aren't you?" he demanded.

"What's going on? Who are you people?" I started, trying to sound bewildered and indignant, but feeling sick and empty as my whole world caved in on me.

The head man leading the investigation was named McCarthy. He approached where I lay with his right hand man, DiFilipis.

"Pull up his sleeves," McCarthy ordered. Looking at the tattoos on my arms brought a smile to his lips.

"That's him all right!"

When they finally had me cuffed and on my feet, I looked at the faces around me. Ten? Twelve? I had seen every one of these guys! I had thought them to be hippies, bums, and truck drivers. The guy I had seen with the newspaper was standing in front of me. He just smiled and nodded, and I nodded back sickly.

Everything to follow is only more of everything I have seen and heard for the last seventeen years, with the exception of maybe five months on the streets; fingerprints, mug shots, bullpens, more fingerprints. "Strip! Open your mouth! Lift your arms --pull your nuts up--bend over and spread 'em! Back in the bullpen--wait! Wait! All right, upstairs! Clank! Bang! Clank! Ring! Ring!! Ring!!! Wake up! Eat--sleep--shit--cry--and die!"

DAILY ⊡ NEWS

Mad dog killer who fled Attica in '71 is caught

By NEAL HIRSCHFELD

Joseph (Mad Dog) Sullivan—the only man ever to escape from Attica prison and a suspect in at least seven murders, three assaults and numerous bank robberies—was surprised and captured yesterday by 10 FBI agents as he and his girlfriend strolled out of a motel near Rochester.

Sullivan, 42, a reputed mob hitman, was wearing a bulletproof vest and was armed with a .38-caliber revolver and an M-16 automatic rifle. But when the agents moved in, "he just smiled" and surrendered, said Clinton Van-Zant, acting agent in charge of the FBI's Rochester office.

Following a tip, the FBI set up surveillance on the Denonville Inn in Penfield, a Rochester suburb, about 9 a.m. An hour later, agents grabbed Sullivan and his girlfriend, Theresa Palmieri, 25, of Avenue X in Brooklyn, as they loaded their belongings in a truck parked outside their room.

Sullivan, of Richmond Hill, Queens, gained notoriety in 1971 by becoming the only man to escape from maximum-security Attica, where he was serving time on a manslaughter conviction. Sullivan, who threw a rope over a wall to make his getaway, had kept himself in shape by running 10 miles and doing 1,000 pushups every day. His father, Jeremiah, was a decorated New York City police detective who died in 1951.

SULLIVAN IS WANTED for a double homicide in Suffolk County last Dec. 8, the shotgun assassination in December of a mob-connected Teamsters union official outside Rochester

Joseph (Mad Dog) Sullivan in a 1971 photograph.

and a homicide in Manhattan in January. He was indicted for an attempted double homicide in Greenwich Village last June, law enforcement officials said. He is suspected of commiting several murders at the behest of organized crime.

Sullivan was held in lieu of $500,000 bail at his arraignment yesterday in a $10,000 bank robbery in Utica. Palmieri was charged with harboring a federal fugitive.

Daily News, Wednesday, February 24, 1982

'Mad Dog' guilty in slaying

Alleged hit man Joseph John (Mad Dog) Sullivan (center), 43, of Richmond Hill, Queens, leaves court in Rochester after being convicted of second-degree murder in the slaying of Teamsters official John Fiorino. Sullivan, a suspect in about a dozen murders across the state, is the only man ever to escape from Attica prison.

TONIGHT
Snow, low 20s

TOMORROW
Clear, windy, cold, 20s

Details, Page 2

TV listings: P. 59

NEW YORK POST

WEDNESDAY, FEBRUARY 24, 1982   **25** CENTS   © 1982 News Group Publications Inc.   Vol. 181, No. 86
AMERICA'S FASTEST-GROWING NEWSPAPER

FINAL
SPORTS EXTRA

AVERAGE DAILY
SALES EXCEED
910,000

HOW COPS PUT LEASH ON 'MAD DOG'

This is Joseph "Mad Dog" Sullivan, the most wanted hitman in the country. The extraordinary photo shows the bizarre side of the man who, police say, snuffed out 30 lives as a gun for hire. He is posing in almost comic book, Bonnie-and-Clyde fashion with his flapper girlfriend, Theresa Palmieri, complete with machine gun, pistol and money bag as he was on the lam from one of the biggest dragnets in history. Sullivan was nabbed with his girlfriend in upstate Rochester yesterday.

PART TWO

1975–1994

Beyond the Pale

"A little I'm hurt, but not slain. I'll lie down and
bleed awhile, and then I'll rise and fight again!"
-Anon-

There are too many things happening on the sands of a prison's coliseum floor for the stranger or novice to survive. The weak body or dull and unprepared mind, surrounded by the ever-present mass of hostile bodies and feral scent of danger can quickly lose its strength of will to act on natural impulse.

I can't help but laugh at the false bravado of certain prison guards. They sit high above in their ivory tower of complacency staring down with twisted, sneering lips of contempt at the waste products of humanity in the arena of heartache, desperation and despair below, observing the physical abuse and horrors without truly understanding the reality of the very world they so gleefully impose upon their fellow man.

That is, until one day, during the course of an uprising, they somehow fall from their perch of safety on the wall to the bloody sands of the arena below, finding themselves in a totally frightening and alien world they have never seen before. Then, for the first time in their lives, they find themselves looking beyond the scarred, time-hardened faces, whose eyes betray no sign of compassion or empathy, in search of that one sensitive and forgiving heart whose sense of humanity has stood the test of Hell on Earth and will deliver them in spite of their own sins against humanity. Many times, during my thirty-five years of incarceration, I have looked into such eyes of dawning recognition. Some are weak and cowardly, others strong and determinedly proud, but all aware of their sudden precarious mortality-- a prisoner's daily fare in the arena.

"Hello," their hearts whisper silently.

"I know now... I understand your plight, as I never have before. I love my wife and my sons as you love yours. I do not want to die here! Not like this! Can you -- will you help me?"

And my soul would capitulate, but not without the awareness that I would need the aid and support of others. In prison, loyalty has a lifespan that lasts only as long as a common self-interest exists. Honor exists solely when victory can be tasted on ones palate. But there are exceptions: friends and equals of mind and soul, sharing something that transcends even barriers of racial, ethnic and religious prejudices, friends of kindred spirits who share not only like principles, but more so the laughter, tears and fears that make an otherwise hideous existence bearable. Men who will die with you because the fear of losing you would be tantamount to losing ones sense of self, that simple veneer of human pride and dignity that one clings to after all thoughts and hopes of a shared common civility between antagonists has been banished from the platter.

Now, as I sit in my cell in April of 1994, feeling like some old damned fool, I look around me and see that nothing has changed since I first heard a steel door clang shut behind me when I was a *young* fool in 1954. When I was paroled from Clinton in 1975, after my escape from Attica in 1971, I was 36 years old and considered myself very fortunate to have received a parole so soon after that escape.

The fact that I became heavily involved in the educational programs available in prisons, for the first time in all my years of incarceration, my growth was conducive to the parole board rendering a favorable decision. Although the reason for my seeking more intellectual pursuits was not particularly a noble one. For the past twenty years in prison, I had been doing my "Time" lifting weights and playing softball and football, while using the hours in my cell reading or writing, rather than becoming involved in evening programs that required classroom situations. In my eyes, that spelled unnecessary exposure to the herd, and the possibility of random confrontations.

But at thirty-four years old the "weights" seem to get heavier, and the aches and pains from football games didn't wear off until the end of the season. That strongly suggested it was time for me to accept the passing years gracefully, and seek a gentler form of entertainment to occupy the endless hours that weigh heavily upon ones mind in an 8X10 cell (it feels more like an incubator after a couple of decades). I had been in the "Drama class" which came in from Potsdam University three afternoons a week. I found it extremely stimulating and enjoyable. Some months later, in 1973, I joined a photography class at the insistence of my good friend, Al Haber. I'd spend endless hours in the darkroom learning the art of developing black and white film. But in spite of all this, I still had three evenings a week in my cell with nothing to do and a guy can only do so much reading before he burns out. How I came to find relief, and fill in those three non-productive evenings, came about in the most surprising manner, but one that would give me more gratification than anything else I had ever been involved in, including sports.

It was a Friday afternoon and I had just come from the drama class with a load of books under my arm. We had been rehearsing Eugene

O'Neil's "The Moon for the Misbegotten," but I also had football practice. Rather than returning to my cell to drop off the books, I went directly to the yard and left the books on a bench on the sideline close to the football field. In reality, the "field" was no more than a hundred yards of hard-packed dirt, which we called the rock garden, as after each heavy rain a new crop of jagged slate rock seemed to spring up making each step or fall a deadly venture. I had walked down to the far end of the bench to talk to my friends Gyp and Sal Calcagno, our quarterback, about plays we'd be running in preparation for a playoff game the following day. When out of the corner of my eye I saw "Jack the Iceman." He was a 270-pound, defensive tackle, sitting on the bench and looking through the books I had left there. When I finished putting on my cleats and kneepads over my pants I walked over to him.

"See anything you like, Jack?" I asked, thinking maybe he found something interesting. I wasn't prepared for his startled look and stuttering response, nor how he quickly put the book down as if he had been caught stealing something.

"Uh...N...NO! I was j-just looking." This gentle giant (until the whistle blew) muttered softly.

"You like Eugene O'Neil?" I asked.

"Who 's Eugene O'Neil?" He asked almost defensively.

"The playwright. The guy in the book you were just browsing through I..." God Damn! How ignorant can I be I thought, looking at him standing there with his head bowed. Here was a guy I thought I knew for the better part of ten years, one of the best chess players in the joint, I was tongue-tied.

"I can't read, Sully." He looked down at me defiantly with tears in his eyes, looking up and down the bench thinking he had been heard.

"You can read, Jack." I answered softly, confused as to how to handle his volatile mood.

"I said I CAN'T read!" he almost shouted, as if I were suggesting he were lying.

"Hey, relax," I smiled.

"I know you can't read at this moment. What I meant was you CAN *learn* to read. You're not one of the better chess-players in the joint because you're a mental retard! I can't play chess, Jack, but it's not because I'm too dumb to learn. I've just never had a real interest. Football has always been my chess game. Obviously you have a reason, and an interest to learn now because it's eating you up inside. What is it?"

"I--I've got a daughter, Sully. She's eight years old. Writes me every week now and is hurt because I don't write her back."

"So why not go to school, Jack?"

"I can't," he shook his head.

"I'd feel like a big dummy sitting there. And, if anybody said something, well you know what the outcome would be. I just thought, seeing your books that you were one of those tutors with the Literacy Volunteers of America Program they started here. They teach guy's one on one..." his voice trailed off dejectedly.

"Would it have made a difference if I was one of them, Jack?"

"Yeah, I felt I could trust you."

"What's trust got to do with it, Jack!?"

"Y-you know how most of these assholes are. They ain't happy unless they got somebody to put down or laugh at." The whistle blew for practice, and we stood there looking at each other.

"Listen Jack," I said coming to a firm decision, "I ain't no fucking genius or some pseudo intellectual and I don't belong to the Literacy Volunteers Program. But, if you care that much about your daughter that you're willing to swallow that stupid pride that's been choking you for years, and you really want to learn, then I'll sign up as a tutor Monday morning. Is it a deal?" Jack was too emotionally wound up to answer without crying, but simply shook his head affirmatively.

"Let's go play ball, student!" I smiled.

"Alright, Teach!" he laughed good-naturedly.

My time with Jack (and eventually others) was truly a gratifying feeling. And after ten months, Jack had made great gains. He went from a 3rd grade reading level to the 7th. My greatest reward came in the form of a letter Jack showed me from his daughter. Telling him how much it meant to her to hear from Daddy.

"Jesus H. Christ," I exclaimed, thrusting the letter at him in mock disgust. "I can't stand this tear-jerking crap!" Though we both grinned misty-eyed, in awe of simple human communication, between ourselves, as well as his little girl.

I can honestly say that my plans upon being released were good ones. All I thought about were a decent job, a good woman and a couple of kids to enjoy the remainder of my life with. Well, I have no excuses, as I had all a man could ask of life, including two good friends in Kenny Jackson and Ramsey Clark. They did everything humanly possible to redirect twenty-five years of arrested development. They never failed me. I failed myself.

I also failed a woman that many men dream of having but never know, my wife Gail. She brought two beautiful boys into my world, making her love a three-fold treasure that should have sated the emotional needs of any man. Her words haunt me now. How she implored me time and again: "Joe, you've made enough waves in your life. I want you to be here to help guide your sons through the troubled waters they will face in theirs. My God, life is not a game!"

And that was it, in a nutshell. Life for me in prison for the 25 years prior to my meeting Gail had been just that, a game. I just didn't know how, or was too selfish or too frightened, to switch gears. I think I preferred being a Big Fish in the microcosm of life's pond that is prison, than to being relegated to the insignificant status of a guppy in the ocean of sharks I saw and felt around me on the outside. The only way I felt I could maintain my former status quo was to apply the only "trade" I had years of training in, violence and surviving in the arena.

***

New York - December 1975

New York City: the Barnum & Bailey of organized crime. I was finally in the main ring of the Big Top, where there were but a few emperors and many enemies of their domain to slay. In return for sacrificing my individual thought and human empathy with my services, I was awarded "freedom" from the everyday struggles of providing for my family in the manner I admire so much in hard-working men and women but cringe at, myself.

I was out of the joint about a month when I first met Gail, again, on 75th and Central Park West. I had been living in a brownstone apartment that my friend Kenny Jackson had gotten me upon my arrival in New York. Kenny had also gotten me a job as a counselor working with juvenile delinquents in an organization he started called O.A.R. "Offender Aid and Restoration." For the first six weeks until I met Gail, he virtually stayed with me day and night like some guardian angel. He showed me the thousand different every day things those twenty-five years of prison had made me completely ignorant of. Everything from dialing a phone, eating with a fork, ordering and tipping in a restaurant, getting to and from simple destinations on a bus or train, to virtually wiping my ass! It was as if I were from Mars. Men don't grow up in the joint like they do when they are on the streets--time stands still in there in a way, but the years still tick away. This re-entry was both an exhilarating and humbling experience. He took me by the hand like a big brother and guided me around the early pitfalls that are the recently released prisoner's greatest danger to himself. They are even more so to those around him, as so many of the little discourtesies and disrespectful remarks, such as one may get from the average cab driver or even a harried, hard-working clerk in a store, are seen as felony offences, reasons to kill, by a "long timer" in prison. These things can, and do, happen before a man gets a chance to adjust, and realize such disrespect is not personal but is merely the way of the "rat-race." Everybody is scurrying around too quickly and does not have time to pause and give thought to social amenities.

A blue and white '76 Oldsmobile Cutlass pulled to the curb where I stood. Gail, even with her head in curlers, a scarf wrapped around the unsightly pile of plastic, still looked as beautiful as I remembered her looking in 1965. She had been seeing my brother, Jimmy. She later married a friend of mine named Robert, who sadly had allowed drugs to destroy their marriage, and eventually his life.

"What was she, thirty now?" I thought, drinking in her big brown eyes and the perfect teeth her generous smile presented. We had been talking to each other on the phone for a few hours each day for weeks. We spoke mostly of her life-- or more accurately, her lack of life-- and the trials and tribulations her husband's use of drugs had presented. I had always loved her as a bouncy, intelligent, humorous and good-hearted human being, but now, seeing her again, looking into her eyes of this sensuous, lush-bodied apparition, I wanted her totally as my woman. I knew instinctively that this ride was forever, and my heart pounded in my ears when she said,

"Hi, Joe. Nice to see you again."

She took me home to her quaint little cottage-like apartment under the El on Etna Street, off Jamaica Avenue in Cypress Hills, New York. For the next year we spent the passions of a new-found love, moving to the sounds of the "J train" rumbling above us throughout the late night and early mornings, unaware of how it virtually shook the apartment building because in those early days we were shaking, rumbling and exhorting each other to greater speeds ourselves! Though it's been a "ghost train" to Gail for far too many years, she refuses to change lines and punch the ticket of another conductor--which *is* the bottom line in my eyes.

This brings to mind the words of a poetic verse: "When two stones meet, they create fire. When two lovers meet, they create flame." This verse, in turn, reminds me of a few words of an old 1930's song my dad would teasingly sing to my mother whenever he was trying to butter her up, or get back in her good graces after a short stint in the doghouse. "I don't want to set the world on fire, " he'd coo softly, "I just want to start a flame in your heart."

As good as my life was with Gail, by mid-1976 my enthusiasm for my work with "Offender Aid and Restoration" began to wane. I've never been an "office type" guy and wanted to work directly with the kids on Rikers Island. I was denied for security reasons due to my escape from Attica and a few other places. I just couldn't get excited about computer printouts and the clerical crap that accompanied them.

My friend Kenny saw the discomfort in me. I was really of little use to the organization, but he kept me on until I made a decision one way or another. He realized he'd taken me as far as he could. I remember one day he had to call Ramsey Clark, a close friend of his (and former United States Attorney General under Lyndon Johnson), to save my ass from being extradited to Houston, Texas on a fifteen year old outstanding warrant for the hold-up of a Western Union Office there.

I had walked into the Parole Office (on 40th St. and 8th Avenue) to make my weekly report and was immediately cuffed by two gargantuan tobacco-chewing state troopers, who had produced a warrant stating, in essence, "Y'all deliver the body (mine) forthwith to the Sheriff's office of Harris County, etc." I was offered one phone call, which I used in desperation to call Kenny. Besides being the president of O.A.R., he had been the president of the Fortune Society for ten years. He had also been appointed to the prison watchdog Commission of Prisons in the city by the Department of Corrections, as one of the Commissioners. This in itself may not have been a big accomplishment, but as a sixteen-year-old kid Kenny and I had done "time" together in Coxsackie Correctional Facility. I have always been proud of the way he turned his life around. He did this by using his own inner courage and strength and with the help of Lorraine, his wife, the only woman who could possibly put up with him!

"Hold on, Sully, don't sign anything and tell them your lawyer.."

"Kenny, I ain't got no lawyer--" I interrupted.

"Shut up and listen, huh? Tell them your lawyer, Ramsey Clark, will be there in thirty minutes. You got it?" he urged.

"I got it. I love you, Daddy!" I said, half jesting.

"Damn! Can't I leave you alone for a minute?" he laughed.

When Kenny walked in with Ramsey, my first, and lasting impression of Ramsey was of his quiet dignity and gentlemanly ways. Even while standing before him I had to strain to hear his voice. He spoke so softly in his inherited Texas drawl. Even more surprising though, was how people listened. They listened in spite of how they might have been in conflict with his humanistic politics and deep-seated beliefs--much of which, incidentally, I do not share. His innate sense of decency was too glaring for any man to question his commitment or doubt his integrity. No matter how contrary his beliefs and ideas might be to their own.

Despite the fact that Ramsey got me out of that jam and was always there for me to talk to, I've nevertheless always found a way to self-destruct.

It was a warm, mid-May afternoon in 1976 when I walked into the Coliseum Restaurant on 59th Street and Columbus Circle. J.J. was a slender middle-aged man. He smiled and waved to me from a corner table as I entered the room. Neither of us being much for small talk, we got right to brass tacks.

"I'm glad you called, Joe," J.J. started, patting his lips with a silk handkerchief after each sip of Michelob, "but are you sure this is what you want to do? I could always put you to work across the street (in the Coliseum). You can make a good buck and--"

"That isn't why I came down here, J.J. Can you use me?" I asked, looking into his piercing blue eyes.

J.J. was a stylish dresser and was still a good-looking man, with his silver-black hair and almost quaint pale face. I first met him in Queens House of Detention in 1965 while I was awaiting trial for manslaughter. We hit it off well. I didn't see him again until 1971 when I escaped from Attica, after doing about five years on my 20-30 year bid. I was hot as a pistol, the whole world seemed to be hunting me, but J.J. never shut his door. He looked out for me with money and a place to stay, and I never forgot that.

"Yeah, I can use ya," he smiled. "I know you're capable and handled yourself well all those years in the joint. And your escapes show me you have ingenuity and are daring. But I just want you to know, it's one thing fighting with your hands, or even using a pipe or a knife to defend yourself when you got no choice. A lot of guys do that everyday in prison. But, see that guy sitting by the door?" he pointed.

"Yeah, what about him?" I was puzzled

"Never seen him before?" he smiled.

I looked at the guy closer, "N-no, never."

"Well, then would it bother you if I passed you a piece beneath the table and asked you to blow his brains out before we walked out the door?" he whispered softly.

"Just like that, huh?" I couldn't help but grin.

"Yeah, my friend, just like that," he replied.

"Damn!" I laughed. "Is he the butcher, baker, candlestick maker, or somebody like us?"

"Does it matter to you who or what he is, Joe? He's not one of us," J.J. spoke with finality as our eyes searched, and finally nodded in agreement.

"No, J.J., it doesn't really matter. It doesn't really matter at all," I sighed, burying any shred of feeling left for my fellow man.

"Well, his name is Tommy Devore. He's with Mickey Spillane's crew, the last remnants of the old Irish mob--and nothing to do with the younger guys; these so-called "Westies" who have hooked up with the Pope (Castellano) in Brooklyn. These guys have been snatching wise guys from both the Gambino and Genovese crews and demanding anywhere up to two hundred grand to get them back. Only problem is they don't come back. These bums have been chopping them up!" J.J. snapped angrily.

"What do you want to do, J.J.?" I offered.

"This ain't the place, Joe. Go home and get a good night's sleep, and pick me up outside this joint at eight tomorrow morning. I've been trying to pin this cocksucker down for six months. He's back and forth between New York and Montreal, and only in for a friend's funeral over on Lexington Avenue. I'll have everything we'll need. You all right?" he smiled.

"I'm fine, J.J., don't worry about me."

Racing across the 59th Street Bridge from Queens the following morning, I felt all pumped up, like I was going to a high school prom. I wasn't nervous, but a bit high-strung in my desire to make my debut in a dramatic and successful fashion. I hadn't the slightest doubt as to the outcome. I had complete faith in my condition, stealth, ability and chutzpah! As far as I was concerned, this bird was already history. And I looked forward to dispatching that entire crew!

My first surprise in this new life was learning that J.J., being Irish, was with "The Fat Guy" and the Genovese Family, and had been for thirty years. Having been in the can all my life, I was unaware that there was no longer a singular, solidified Irish crew left in Hell's Kitchen's west side. There were a dozen or so dinosaurs--ethnic remnants and offspring of a past era whose history dated back to Owney Madden and his famous Cotton Club, whose own genesis derived from the Irish immigrant gangs which sprang up to claw for survival in a hostile new world upon reaching these shores at the turn of the century. A donkey's options were severely limited in those days--strong back, but no brains.

So along came the infamous Gophers, Hudson Dusters, and Arsenal gangs who made it known that they were here to stay, and would get their fair dole by hook or by crook.

Mickey Spillane led the older of the remaining remnants during the gentrification period of Hell's Kitchen during the 1970's. The "young lions" detectives in the neighborhood precinct dubbed the "Westies" were a separate entity, and bitter rivals for whatever scraps were left from the Roman Banquet. The Westies, in essence, were a conglomeration of the displaced Irish left behind in the changing ethnic mean-streets of Hell's Kitchen (now referred to as "Clinton"). They were a band of childhood friends whose two common denominators were the hunger from a shared prison experience and Jimmy Coonan. Coonan was "one of theirs," while unlike themselves his prison experience allowed him to rise above, or better yet, put aside the old ethnic prejudices (Irish vs. Italian). Because of a personal feud between his family and Mickey Spillane (in spite of the innate distrust he and his followers held for the Italians, who they referred to as the "linguini mob"), Jimmy finally saw the futility of it all. He offered the olive branch to Paulie Castellano and the Gambino Family--or so he thought. In a nutshell, he proposed that if Big Paulie would help him get rid of the "old-timers," Spillane and Company, he and his Westies would protect mob interests on all of Manhattan's west side against the ever-growing insurgence of new ethnic groups (Puerto Ricans, Colombians, etc.) that now dominated the neighborhoods. Of course, he expected a steady piece of the pie from numbers and loan-sharking, specifically.

What Coonan didn't know, however, was that both Castellano (Gambino) and the Fat Guy (Genovese) were acting in concert to rid the West Side of *both* Irish factions, considering them too wild, unmanageable and bad for business. Their "game plan" was: once the small number of "old-timers" were dispatched, then both families would focus their attention on the Westies, specifically Jimmy C. and a half dozen other "thinkers." What I felt was of little consequence, as I had committed myself to J.J. and would play out my hand.

J. J. was waiting by the curb when I pulled up. He was dressed in light slacks, a windbreaker, and a floppy sun hat.

"W-What--who?" he started in shock. Then his face lit up with a smile of amazement.

"What do you think?" I laughed.

"Son of a bitch!" he exclaimed. "You could have passed me on the street and I wouldn't have known you! Where did you --"

"Compliments of the drama class I joined from Potsdam University while I was in Clinton Prison in the early-70's. We put on a lot of shows, a few things for Channel 13, the "educational" channel," I laughed, "and make-up, wardrobe, ya know, came with the territory."

"Great, Joe, just great! But does that shit come off easy?" he asked, referring to my hazelnut coloring beneath the medium-sized Afro wig that gave me the appearance of a dark Hispanic. I also penciled my eyebrows and mustache.

"No problem, buddy. I got a half-wet towel in a plastic bag on the back floor. This light-base grease comes off as quick as the Afro. The suit and tie is simply to give me a touch of respectability. Don't want nobody thinking I'm some common street-mugger that bears watching."

J.J. and I shared a light breakfast. Then he directed me to a bar on Lexington Avenue, right across the street from a funeral parlor where Devore would be attending a wake.

"Listen, Joe, you sure you don't need me in there with you?" he sounded worried.

"No, don't worry, J.J. I can move better if I'm alone. Just park around the corner and don't forget to slap those dealer's plates with the magnets over the back license plate. I'll find you," I said, breathing deeply.

"All right. But remember, he may stop in the bar before he goes to the wake. You might have to wait a few minutes, so drink real slowly. Also, he may be with a few friends. So..."

"Enough yet!" I laughed, feeling the weight of the .38 snub-nosed in my right-hand jacket pocket as I slid out of the car and crossed the pavement into the dimly-lit bar, not looking back.

A long Formica-topped bar ran along the wall to my left. There was a cigarette machine, a phone, and a jukebox on my right. The pool table was directly to the rear. There wasn't much of anybody to see except an old-timer seated midway down the bar, and a stocky, beefy-faced guy behind the bar, wearing an open-necked white shirt and an apron tied around his waist. He was polishing some beer glasses while bullshitting with the old-timer.

"Hi, buddy," I nodded as I passed them. "Let me have a Michelob, huh?" I said, finally settling on the stool farthest from the door.

I faced the door as I seated myself at an angle, pretending interest in their gossip. I was in there about twenty minutes sipping from my second draft, when the door opened and Devore walked in with three other guys. I glanced their way purposely as it's a person's natural curiosity to do. I would have tipped my hand if not, especially with a fellow predator. After glancing in their direction, I casually returned to my beer.

Damn! I know the little bald-headed guy from Attica. I looked right at him but he didn't recognize me! No wonder--I smiled at the dark-skinned Latino with the Afro in the mirror behind the bar.

They didn't sit down, but ordered shots and beers while standing around the short-end of the bar about ten feet from the door. Probably just a quick drink and out... Showtime!

I wiped the glass with my napkin, and did the same with two single bills beneath the edge of the bar before setting them down, and eased the .38 out of my pocket, holding it down along my leg and slightly behind as I walked close to the stools on my way out.

"Take care, buddy," I called to the bartender as I passed him and the old-timer. At the same time I was watching the foursome to see if they were alert to my leaving. They were not.

Devore had just lifted the beer to his lips when I brought my arm straight up, stopping inches from his ear as I pulled the trigger. The dull roar of the weapon echoed in one part of my mind while the other concentrated on the three men that had been facing him--all now wearing the same looks of fear as the shattered bits of bone and blood sprayed their horrified faces. I hadn't broken stride on my way to the door, and never took my eyes off them as I stepped outside onto the deserted street. I broke into a slow jog that wouldn't attract any attention.

"All right, buddy, let's roll!" I smiled, sliding into the front seat and then reaching over it to get the plastic bag with the wet towel in it.

"You got him already?! He's dead?" J.J. gasped.

"Does a bear shit in the woods? If he's alive, buddy, he's going to have a lifetime migraine!" I laughed as he drove away using one hand while pounding me congratulatory on the shoulder as I wiped the make-up from my face, neck and hands.

"Sons of bitches!" he shouted gleefully. "We'll kill all those low-life cocksuckers! All of them!"

"No problem, J.J. But first I've got a long delayed vacation to go on with Gail. A cruise to Nassau--we've planned it for months--and I look forward to my Love Boat."

"Great--good for you. I hope you both enjoy yourself," he said sincerely. "I'll have some money for you in a few days."

We never discussed how much I would make for my work, after all I felt J.J. would be fair with me. This was not the case, as I got a few thousand once in awhile and a no-show job. "They" kept the hundreds of thousands that the contracts were going for. I was the fool, but didn't think of it at the time. Like everything else, I thought eventually "they" would be loyal and good to me because I was that way with them, but it never came about.

Gail and I were always at our best, and happiest, when traveling alone together and were left to our leisure. The ship we sailed on from Pier 52 was in all respects our "Love Boat." It was called the Oceanic and sailed under Panamanian colors, but with an Italian crew that promised a gourmet menu around the clock. That cruise outdid all of our expectations; for three days going, three days sailing back, and the three days spend on land in Nassau, we had the time of our lives. We sunbathed and drank Pina Coladas on the lower deck by day (when I wasn't in the pool trying to teach Gail to swim, though to this day she's a human rock!), and late in the evening we'd sneak off to the upper deck like two kids ducking out of school and make love to the soft lapping sounds of the water as the huge steel fish ploughed its way toward Nassau.

The white sand and blue-green waters of the island were equally enticing. But the biggest highlight of our stay, a debacle really, happened when we first docked and I saw all the different couples renting mopeds to get around on the island.

"Y-you sure you know how to drive one of these, Joe?" Gail looked at me cautiously, probably recalling how she had just taught me to drive a car a few months before.

"Sure, no problem!" I blustered.

"I mean, how fast can this thing go, 40, maybe 50 miles per hour? Ain't no different than a bike, right?"

"Oh, Joe," she sighed in surrender, "we'll get one."

I forgot exactly what I did wrong the first time, but no sooner did I fly off the dock--Gail screaming in my ear--and take the highway that circled the island, I met a curve I thought I'd have no problem maneuvering through. But I twisted the handgrip for the gas instead of the break and we went off the highway into some wooded area of pine trees, sliding on the soft blanket of pine needles until we crashed.

"Gail! G-Gail, you all right, honey?" I felt terrible. She was shaken but okay.

"Oh, Joe, " she gasped. "I thought you knew how to drive this thing?" she glared at me accusingly.

"I do! I do! It's j-just been so long. I thought the gas was the break!" I started grinning, and then we both burst out laughing.

My second accident, about ten minutes later, wasn't humorous at all. Somehow, going down a perfectly straight highway I kept veering to the left. Despite Gail's calm directions on how to rectify my error, I was mesmerized like a mosquito to a "zapper" and went off the road onto a grassy area. I started my, seemingly graceful, hook-slide into second base. When we hit the ground on our left side, I thought I had held the moped up off our bodies with my outstretched arms, but then I turned and saw Gail lying on the grass holding her left calf. She was moaning softly because of a deep three-inch burn that had been inflicted by the hot engine that had pressed against her on impact. Tears just ran quickly from my eyes--all this because I was too "macho" to allow her to do the driving while I sat behind her, holding on like some wimp.

She looked up at me and hissed like a cobra. "You--son--of --a -- bitch!" she spat out one word at a time, each with great emphasis.

"G-Gail, listen. I'm sorry," I began weakly.

"Get on the back," she snapped, lifting the seemingly harmless moped from the ground.

"I'm doing the driving!" she glared at me defiantly.

"Okay, okay!" I held up my hands, smiling weakly as I pointed to all the couples zipping past with the traditional male driving, the female holding on to her hero for dear life.

"All right, Gail but you know what this will do to my image?"

"Fuck your image, Sully, look what it did to my leg!"

She was right. What could I do? I spent the rest of the day with my hands holding onto her waist, daring anybody to question my manhood with malevolent glares. My sons still laugh at this story eighteen years later.

We had a wonderful time during our vacation. I dreaded returning to the life I had embarked upon and to that other person I've never dared to analyze, but could turn on and off at will like a hot and cold water faucet.

**

Queens, New York -- November 1976

"Joe, I--I think I'm pregnant." Gail said offhandedly one morning, having been a few weeks past her period.

"Hey, damn, that's great!" I lit up like a Christmas tree.

"When?" I asked eagerly.

"Hold on! Hold on!" she smiled.

"I said I *think* I'm pregnant. I'll make an appointment with the doctor this week."

We had always intended to get married, but always felt that we had a lot of time to plan. Everything started happening too quickly. I look back now and see how selfish I was, how immature and unfit to accept the heavy responsibility of a family when my own life was in such chaos and jeopardy, whether by sudden death or a life behind bars. Had I truly cared as a husband and father-to-be, I would have, should have, ceased all the senseless insanity I had chosen to become involved in. Instead, I shrugged off the feelings of guilt, thinking that I was somehow different, that I could somehow isolate and polarize one life from the other.

I had "taken down" three or four miscellaneous tough guys since Devore and had that "no-show" job with a container company for the parole officer's benefit, first at the Meadowlands and then at some joint in Port Newark, where they repaired containers off the ships. Life, also, was becoming a job. The thrill of the hunt was not all it was cracked up to be once the novelty had worn off. It was a study in patient stalking, as a human prey knowing his name surfaced in the lottery of death moves like a fox and is a difficult target to corner. So most of our days J.J. and I spent in the sweltering heat of summer nights or frigid cold of winter mornings, drinking gallons of coffee in our car like any detective would on a stake-out of a target's house, apartment building or social club. We always stayed at a distance of a few blocks so that we would not be "made" first, and end up in a dumpster somewhere ourselves.

Usually by the time I got home in the early evening, or picked Gail up on Madison Avenue where she was an Account Executive for a small advertising agency and drove home with her, we were both perfectly ready for a nice quiet evening together. We'd make plans for our wedding, the baby, sip Amaretto and Seltzer while watching Night Line and have our little late night pregnancy snacks. Those simple times were the good times, and what life is truly all about. I even attended Lamaze childbirth classes with Gail at Long Island Jewish Hospital, and began to act like I was the one having the baby!

***
United Nations Chapel - March 19, 1977

Arthur Ashe had just gotten married that morning, and now it was my turn. Rabbi Roy Rosenberg was waiting patiently, as were Ramsey and Georgia Clark, my best man Kenny Jackson, J.J. and his wife, and thirty or forty other friends and family. I was waiting, too, on the outside steps of the U.N. Chapel, my teeth chattering, watching the crisp, cold wind snap the flags briskly on the poles across the street. They were the only things moving as I looked up and down the deserted street for Gail and her childhood friend Marla, who was the Maid of Honor. The show was to start at five o'clock, and here it was twenty after! My friend Vinny came out a few times to cheer me up.

"You think she wised up and flew the coop?" I smiled.

"Naw, they both probably stopped to turn a quick trick before the final sacrifice! Stop fucking worrying, huh?" Vinny offered.

"Hey, you think maybe they had an accident--" I began, but Vinny just laughed and went back inside.

Just than Gail and Marla came tear-assing around the corner, gasping like fish out of water. Gail wore her beige gown and little hat.

"This is my first baby," I thought to myself, my eyes welling with tears of pride at the glow of love and happiness in her face.

"I--I'm sorry, Joe, but I had a hard time finding a parking spot," she said, trying to control her breathing.

"You ready, honey?" I asked, looking into those soulful eyes.

"I'm ready, Sully!" she smiled radiantly.

"Do you like my gown?"

"I love it--I love you. Let's go!"

Everything went nicely. It was a quiet, dignified affair. I even managed to break the glass the first time I stepped on it. The reception was much livelier, with about two hundred and fifty quests. We were like one big, happy family. I often wonder where they all have gone...

The music played, the food was devoured, and the wine flowed freely during those hours that seem like an eternity ago. When I danced with my mother-in-law (whom has passed on and that I miss to this day), she asked me if I was happy with her daughter.

"How could I not be when she's so much like her mother," I answered.

She beamed proudly and whispered, "L'Chaim."

Gail and I spent a few days in a deep, bubbly, heart-shaped tub in some cottage at Penn Hills in the Pocono's. We were planning to spend our honeymoon in Europe, England, Ireland and Scotland later that summer.

J.J. and I finally caught up with Billy "The Butcher" Mahoney the day after the 4th of July, in the "Starburst Saloon" on 10th Avenue, between 50th and 51st Streets. Seems he was living in some high-rise across the streets with his girl for about two years.

Mahoney got the handle "The Butcher", not from the fact that he had learned to be a meat cutter during a short stint in Attica Prison in the 1960's, but more so for the state-of-the-art manner in which he applied those newly learned talents upon his numerous victims. It was common knowledge that he enjoyed his "work" and approached it with the gusto of a ghoul. It is supposed that it was he whom Jimmy C. studied under, and learned the art of dismembering the unfortunate. "Pickling pricks" or keeping some bum's head in a freezer for months on end to "goof on" when things were slow was a good indication of their psychopathic mindset. But then, some might say that that's like the pot calling the kettle black, I understand.

Taking out "The Butcher" was like an instant replay of the Devore job over on Lexington Avenue, and many others: the same modus operandi down to the minutest of details. It amazed me how guys living the lives they did, with so many skeletons in their closets, would fall so easily into these death traps, exposing themselves like sitting ducks.

J.J. was worried about Mahoney, but to me he was just another guy whose skull would shatter upon the impact of a .38 hollow nose slug like everybody else's--always serving to make me more aware of my own vulnerability and mortality. The qualifying difference between myself and this breed of predator, the difference that served as my saving grace, was that I was not greedy and had no hunger for power in any sense. My demons were personal ones whom I was well on my way to exorcising in this unconventional manner.

As I sat, once again unnoticed, at the far end of the bar studying Mahoney, I felt both a sense of empathy and anger because in him I saw so much of myself. I wondered how many more times I would have to kill myself before the demons were appeased.

As I began to walk towards "The Butcher" and the door, he said the most eerie thing.

"Had a great day yesterday. Can't say let's do it again next year, 'cause any day someone might walk through the door and blow my brains out, right?" he guffawed.

"That's right, buddy, " I whispered silently, seeing the short dark hairs on the back of his neck as I pointed the short snub-nosed barrel above his right ear and squeezed off. I watched the bright red fruit of my labor paint the bar's side wall, as the roar of the gun seemed to thunder its approval.

Most men seem to freeze in such moments of horror. The exception will react instinctively, as did one of "The Butcher's" boys.

"What da fuck?" a squat, barrel-chested gorilla snorted lowering his head to charge.

I cocked the gun, still backing towards the door.

"Take just one step and you'll join your friend." I commanded quietly, but the words resounded thunderously in the bars deadly stillness. Backing out onto the sidewalk, I looked both ways casually then began my home-run trot towards 11th Avenue.

The questions never changed, as once again I slid into the passenger's seat breathless. "You got him? He's gone?"

"Yeah, he's gone, J.J. He's gone." Each time with a great deal less enthusiasm than had the wide-eyed knave who began this descent into hell.

Once again, that night, a short blip on the radio identified the assailant as a Hispanic of medium build and complexion, with an Afro!

***

European Honeymoon - 1977

Gail and I left Kennedy Airport on British Airways the following day, on our long anticipated honeymoon. We arrived at Heathrow Airport on one of those Jack-the-Ripper London evenings, damp, foggy and not especially conducive to a tourist's idea of a pleasant welcome. Secondly, the joint Gail had booked us in looked like some fleabag dive on the Bowery, with fucking bums in dirty dresses and turbans running all over the place.

"What the fuck is this?" I asked Gail, looking around our room. It was no bigger than a prison cell, plaster falling from a hole in the ceiling from which leaked a steady drip of rusty water onto what once might have been described as a double bed.

"Jeez, Joe, this *was* a nice place fifteen years ago." Gail had traveled here as a student.

"We *paid* for this shit? Who are those fucking people running around? Sneaky looking bastards! We could have gotten murdered in New York in our sleep free of charge..."

"Joe, I--I'm sorry," Gail whispered, tears welling in her eyes. "W-we could look for another place."

I felt like a heel. She had wanted our arrival to be special, too.

"Hey, it ain't your fault. You didn't bomb this joint--but who are these people?"

Gail was smiling now, too. "I guess they're from Calcutta or Bombay, huh? Let's move the mattress on the floor and turn it over."

We were both whispering conspiratorially now, pausing every time we heard a footstep in the hallway outside.

"Looks like this mattress could move and turn over by itself if we ordered it to. It must be full of lice! Don't get me wrong, I've slept in a lot worse places, but never paid for it!" I teased her.

It was a long, rough night, and when "Tonto" woke us up in the morning for "room-service" he handed us a greasy, crumpled cardboard menu that said "Continental Breakfast" on top. When he simply said, "Order, sir?" we knew there wasn't anything safe for human consumption to be had. We shook our heads in the universal negative. As Tonto was leaving I asked Gail if his robe was gray or just dirty.

"I think a little of both," she laughed. My Archie Bunker mannerism was contagious.

We'd decided that if this joint were any indication of London, we would pick up the rental car and depart forthwith for Edinburgh Scotland. With the exception of enjoying the stage show "Godspell" in Picadilly Circus, the filth and human vermin in the area made "Times Square" look cleaner than an operating room for open-heart surgery and only hastened our departure.

On the way to Scotland, we stopped off in Willie Shakespeare's hometown "Stratford upon the Avon." We stayed in a beautiful hotel overlooking the Avon River, directly across from the Royal Shakespeare Theater, where we saw a great rendition of King Henry V. We both enjoyed the show immensely, and as the sun came down, enjoyed an hour of serenity on the footbridge of the Avon, watching the sailboats and graceful long-necked swans maneuver their way along the placid river.

Shakespeare's house was itself a surprise to all who entered it, especially in view that everything within (table, chairs, bed, writing table, etc.) was built for an eight year old, or a midget. However, no one present could doubt the size of the man's mind, soul, or singular genius.

We left that quaint, clean little town the following morning and drove straight through to Edinburgh, a nice, old, conservative city, the highlight of which is a huge, imposing castle fortress sitting high on a mountain top. Nestled high above on the mountain, one could easily understand how perilous it must have been to attack centuries earlier.

We boarded a plane at Gatwick and flew to Dublin, staying at the Hotel Hibernia while we caroused the city's sights, including a few friendly pubs, though drinking warm Guinness Beer wasn't something I could develop a taste for.

When we boarded a train for Belfast, I don't think that Gail or myself was ready for the security, slums and schizophrenia that we found gripped most of the city, with the exception of small enclaves in the Protestant sector, where we stayed in a Bed & Breakfast for the night due to the fact that most of the bigger hotels had been bombed out. It blew my mind-- British commandos with bomb-sniffing canines hiding in doorways! We had to take a Protestant taxi to get to a checkpoint that separated the

Protestant and Catholic sectors, having to pass ourselves and our luggage through a metal-detecting machine before getting a Catholic taxi to our destination on the other side.

Distant relatives, whom I had never seen, lived in the infamous Falls Road area, a notorious I.R.A. stronghold. As Gail and I exited the taxi we couldn't help but to compare it to the South Bronx, or even East Berlin as it must have appeared after the Second World War. We could feel the unseen eyes upon us, but as spoiled Americans never having been touched by *real* oppression or war, we were totally ignorant to the deep paranoia of a suffering people. All street names have been removed from display to make it more difficult for their would-be jailers or assassins to find them.

A few young men in their late teens eyed us suspiciously, but not with the disrespect or bad intentions one could expect in New York's more downtrodden neighborhoods. Even under the worst conditions, these people managed to retain their sense of morality and fair play, which, myself being a descendant of this land, made me feel a sense of pride and kinship.

"Hey, buddy," I called in a friendly manner, leaving Gail about ten yards back as I approached one of the young men standing out in the street talking.

"Doesn't anybody want to be found around here?" I joked as I stepped in front of them. They looked at me silently.

"I'm looking for the Wilson's," I said, offering the address I had written down. The older kid glanced at it briefly, and then smiled.

"You from New York? Boston?"

"New York. The name's Sullivan!" I said proudly.

"Ahh, Sullivan," he nodded.

"I know where they live, follow me," he quipped, leading Gail and I through a maze of alleyways and inter-connecting houses that seemed to have no end.

The people we met were to prove typical of all the people we met in Ireland. They were warm, friendly and generous to the point of dismay, sharing the little they had with us while feeling uncomfortable whenever we returned their generosity. We stayed with Tony and Anne and their three kids for five days on the "Black Mountain," outside Belfast, where the original Gaels were supposed to have lived when they first migrated from Constantinople and Highlands of Europe. They had a sparse summer cabin there.

I spent most of the days helping a neighbor take in hay and helping to repair an irrigation ditch that led from further up the mountain. In the evenings we'd sit around talking and enjoying the antics of the children, a lost pleasure in most American families.

It was hard saying good-bye, especially knowing the uncertainty of their future. But they are a strong people with a fatalistic sense of humor, who have grinned and bore a thousand years of oppression and remain undaunted by the tyrants of a dying mongrel empire. "Slainte," my friends.

Since I have never learned to drive a standard, which are the only rentals available in Europe, or so it seemed, Gail was the designated chauffeur as we drove through the towns (I'd have gotten us killed) and I drove only on the highways when Gail would change the gears as I tried to manipulate the peddles, all the way across Ireland, to the beautiful towns of Galway. We stayed in a B & B overlooking the Bay of the same name, a name so often referred to in Irish songs. Seeing Ireland was a dream I never thought would become a reality. Yet here I was, how lucky I felt to have a dream come true!

I finally learned why Ireland is called "The Land of the Midnight Sun" when I awoke after twelve o'clock one night. Upon seeing the sun as bright as it would be at high noon, I thought the world was coming to an end. Gail simply laughed at the frantic joy I took in this seeming miracle of childlike discovery.

Up until that point Gail and I had only *thought* we'd seen Ireland. Until, for thirty bucks a piece, a small Cessna plane flew us about fifty miles off the coast to the Irish "Isles of Aran." There we beheld an ambience that took us back five hundred years in time to a land of solitude, where in more recent times literary greats the likes of Yeats and Lady Gregory would escape to do some of their best writing.

We landed on the Island of Inishman, a top a small mountain where a field of knee-high green grass acted as a landing strip. That by itself had Gail and I grinning in awe as we jumped down from the doorway of the plane wondering where we go from here. The pilot laughed and pointed to a narrow walking path that twisted its way down the small mountain to the fishing village below where, to our dismay, we found that all the natural inhabitants spoke Gaelic, a dying language. Winding our way down with the cows and occasional goats that shared our path, we gaped in silent wonder at the stone houses and their straw thatched roofs that must have dated back to the 16th and 17th centuries.

We waved excitedly to the leather-faced people with calloused hands, whose woolen clothes bespoke a poorness of peasants that I had only read about. They were a people who subsisted on what they could glean from a too often cruel sea, and the pittance the handful of life's ignorant travelers brought their way. My instincts told me that the majority of these people would rather do without the few extra dollars than have the serenity of their placid lives disturbed.

"My God!" I thought. The sheer ignorant innocence of their human decency blew my mind. There were no TV's or radios--couldn't understand the English language if they had them. What would be their reaction if I could relay the life in my progressive society, where drugs, muggers, pimps, prostitutes and the racial hatreds of fellow human beings runs rampant, faggots and child molesters are idolized like Greek Gods. And where the media and "silver screen" people make billions while destroying the "oppressive society" they live in, and which I am a product of. A willing participant in aiding this once-great country's downfall with my own brand of domestic terrorism! Something, I'm sure we will all live to regret when total chaos and anarchy rule supreme, as it sadly shall. Have these people ever locked their doors in fear of their neighbor robbing and killing them, or raping their wife, daughter and wheelchair-bound mothers? Do they greet each other on the street with, "What's happening, motherfucker?" Is this gentle salutation a word they even comprehend, no less incorporate into their language?

I have come too far to change, good people. But God, how I wish the world could be more like you. It is dying --I am dying. How lucky you are not to be participants, or witnesses to its ungodly degradation.

**

September 18, 1977

We knew the baby could decide to make his debut two weeks before or two weeks after the due date, so we had everything ready and parked just inside the door: suitcase, extra gowns, robe, etc. I thought I was mentally prepared for the first addition to our family, until Gail called from the bathroom one morning,

"J-J-Joe! I--I think my water broke!"

She could not have known, nor could I, that those simple words were to change our lives. I thought I was ready, but I was self-centered and immature, too much so to realize I was being blessed with God's greatest earthly gift.

"W-what? Y-you're sure?"

I didn't know whether to shit or go blind when zero hour struck. In spite of all the classes I attended, such knowledge simply vanished and total helplessness set in.

"Uh, are you a-all right? What should we do?"

"I'm f-fine, Sully. Just call Dr. DiIorio and let him know my water's broken, and should we go to the hospital," she said calmly. She had never cried, whined or complained one time throughout her pregnancy, as I was told most women do. Instead she was climbing mountains in Scotland while six months pregnant, and worked, traveling by train most days back and forth from Manhattan. She only stayed home nine days before going into the hospital. On the other hand, if I came down with the slightest cold I'd expect the whole world to stop and cater to me. I only remained outwardly calm because she never lost her composure--my little trooper!

"Let's roll, honey. He says it's time!" I felt completely breathless.

"I **know** i-it's time!" Gail laughed nervously as I helped her on with her coat. "We got everything, Joe?" she smiled, never looking more beautiful, save for the day we were married.

"Yeah, honey, but don't worry. Whatever you'll need I can always bring later. C'mon, let me help you to the car."

I made real good time from our home in Cypress Hills to Long Island Jewish Hospital. When we arrived at the hospital a prep team was ready and took her to a labor room, where I was allowed to root and encourage her in labor--push, push, breathe, etc., until I was blue in the face myself. Though all that crap sounded great in theory during the child-bearing classes we had attended, she wasn't dilating. After going through a hell you couldn't pay me enough to endure, Dr. DiIorio, a nice guy as well as an extremely competent Gynecologist, suggested he do a cesarean section. Gail was worried about how I'd feel about a scar--women! She wanted a bikini cut! All I knew is that I was getting scared for her. I wanted her pain to end and for everything to be all right.

"Everything's going to be all right, honey." I whispered, kissing her on her sweat-glistening forehead.

"I'll see you in a little while, okay?"

"D-did I do a-alright, Joe? Were you proud of me, not screaming and embarrassing y-you?" I thought I'd cry right there.

"Yeah, baby, I'm proud of you. But I'd have screamed my ass off!" I grinned. Sitting atop a growing mountain of cigarette butts, my ulcer killing me, I was checking my watch for what seemed the thousandth time when my friends Kenny, and moments later Rocky, walked into the waiting room area. They helped make the wait bearable with their acid tongues and cynical senses of humor, but most of all by giving assurances that things would turn out fine. My first and foremost concern was for

Gail. I could always have other children; I couldn't have another Gail.

I looked at the long list of numbers of people Gail wanted me to call just as soon as she delivered the baby. I had complained that she had everybody but the kosher butcher on that fucking list! But watching the elevator for the doctor, I knew how thrilled I would be to make all those calls a hundred times over. I actually did call more people than were on Gail's list, immediately after Dr. DiIorio came off the elevator giving me both thumbs up.

"Gail's fine and resting. You can see her in a little while. The baby's fine."

"Thanks, Doc. Thanks a lot!" I felt my eyes misting as I ran for the phone.

"Hey," he called after me, "it's a boy!"

People claim that all newborns are indistinguishable--not true! When I looked through the glass at the dozen or so babies lined up and wrapped in their temporary swaddling clothes, my eyes were drawn to my son as if he had called to me. Hot tears of love, and shame at the thought of how undeserving I'd become, almost overwhelmed me. I looked around quickly, embarrassed by my lack of composure.

"I don't know what I'm going to do, little guy. I know I've got to change. But I'm still honored to meet you, Ramsey Kenneth Sullivan."

"Would you like to see your child?" a nurse asked sweetly, coming out of the door. The baskets hadn't been tagged yet, just the wrists."

"Uh, is t-that Sullivan over there?" I pointed.

"Why, yes, it is! But how did you know?" she looked truly amazed.

I turned to the side. "Look at the profile," I teased her.

"Couldn't you have spotted the Sullivan look?" I joked. But it really was much more, a strange experience.

Gail was sedated and sleeping lightly when I walked into the room. I kissed Gail on the lips and she opened her eyes. She looked drawn and tired, but smiled happily.

"The baby is beautiful, honey. How are you feeling?" I asked.

"Just tired, a-and a little sore. He's really beautiful, Joe!" she beamed happily.

"Yeah, and so is his mother."

A few months later we moved from our little apartment under the El on Crescent Street in Brooklyn, where we had shared many happy moments together, to a house in Richmond Hill, New York. We bought the house. My mother-in-law moved in with us, occupying the upstairs apartment. Having my mother-in-law living with us was a blessing to us all, and especially to my sons Ramsey and Kelly, who adored their grandmother and learned so much from her while my wife worked days. They were both crushed when she died a few years back. Her death created a vacuum that we all felt, particularly Gail, who was everything a daughter could be to one's mom in her Golden Years.

After the baby came into our lives, I was no longer the center of Gail's life--or so I thought. Being immature and not understanding what a family unit was all about, I became a "loose cannon." Being too tense and wired up mentally, I was not ready for a family. I did not have the patience to listen to the baby screaming and waking me at all hours of the morning, but was pretty good most of the time and really did enjoy my son when I allowed myself to relax and do so.

It was during the early part of 1977 when I first went into a disco called "Kisses," on Queens Boulevard near the 59th Street Bridge. And who was at the door but two "bouncers" in tuxedos: Billy Sharkey, a heavy weight boxer; and an old friend of mine named Stevie C., who became my other half in our "Butch & Sundance" team. We used to work out on the weights together in Auburn Prison with Paddy Penna, another old friend.

Stevie and I became like two peas in a pod. Besides Stevie and my childhood friend of forty years Rocky "The Jockey" Hanan and his wife Sandra, I did not get close to too many people. Very few of my friends, with the exception of Kenny Jackson and Allie Cirillo, knew the insanity I was so deeply involved in. It was either to Rocky's or Stevie's house I'd run to when I needed to talk, or simply unwind and feel comfortable.

This was around the time, mid-1977, when J.J. and I had been trying to keep track of Lilo's (Carmine Galante) movements in and out of the can. Having tracked him to a high-rise apartment he lived in on 33rd Street between 3rd and Lexington, I had spent months watching him from a bagel-nosh on the corner of 33rd and 3rd Avenue. I had to be extremely careful not to be "made" by the Feds, who dressed as Con-Edison men and set up shop in a manhole directly across the street. They had even set up a yellow canvas screen around the sewer with peepholes in it. How subtle can one get? With the exception of his daughter, Tina, a foxy lady tougher than most guys, and the bodyguards who picked him up each morning, he never had any visitors. But now he had another visitor. Me!

He suddenly emerged through the glass doors and walked up towards Lexington at a fast pace.

"C'mon, J.J., that's him!" I pointed.

Nobody who had seen a picture of Lilo, the fedora with the rim rolled up, cigar sticking out of his arrogant, pugnacious face, could forget that distinctive look.

Our car had been parked at a meter on 3rd Avenue. We ran to it and made a quick turn at 34th leading towards Lexington. J.J. was silent as I removed a .22 automatic, silencer already attached, from beneath the floor mat. I pumped the action, sliding one round into the chamber, and put the safety on. As we turned left onto Lexington heading downtown, I told J.J. to pull over and double park right on the corner of 34th and Lexington. He wasn't in sight but he couldn't have gotten farther than this, I explained to J.J. I told him that if I got out of the car, to just back down 33rd and park on the other side of 3rd Avenue, on the same street.

I had my piece in a folded newspaper in my left hand when I spotted Lilo stepping out of a candy store about twenty yards away. I got out and walked around the back end of the car. "Piece of cake!" I thought, looking in both directions as I stepped onto the curb. His back was to me.

"Joe," J.J. called. I froze like I'd been shot, then turned around slowly to see him motioning me back, which I had no option but to do as he must have seen something I hadn't.

"What is it?" I said, sliding back into the car.

"It--it don't look right," he said, looking around nervously.

I was flabbergasted.

"That's it? It don't look right?" I said, turning my head to see if I still had a shot. Lilo was gone.

"God Damn!" I banged my fist on the dashboard.

"God Damn! We had him J.J.! We had the cocksucker!"

I was fucking sick. J.J. had blinked. We didn't have words, but it was the first time I had felt anger at him, and disappointment in him. I dropped him off and went home. I didn't call him for a week and told Gail I was out if he called.

It was around this time, that I started hitting the disco "Kisses" heavily and partying. I wasn't so much involved with the broads, as snorting cocaine and drinking scotch by the barrel to try and mellow out enough to go home and sleep for eighteen hours at a clip. I even went as far as telling Gail that I got a part-time job as a bouncer at the disco so I could go there whenever I wanted to. The cocaine was passed out freely there and whenever I wanted to "get away from it all," I went there. My nerves were shot and my mind was totally fucked up.

Stevie and I, along with another partner named Marco, started sticking up payrolls, jewelry guys from the Diamond District, and anyone we felt worthwhile.

Later that year, I got a second shot at Lilo. A brisk September afternoon found me standing by a bank of phones on the corner of 59th and Broadway. J.J. was checking in with "Fish," which he did every couple of hours when I was in the city with him. Vincent "The Fish" Cafaro, a future resident in the Federal Witness Program, relayed all messages of significance to J.J. I could see the excitement in J.J.'s body language--unrecognizable to those who didn't know him.

"Fish says Roy Cohen just hung up with the 'fat guy'. Lilo will be at his office in about twenty minutes. He said Lilo never stays for more than ten to thirty minutes."

We knew that Lilo was client of Cohen's. The "fat guy," aside from being his friend of three decades or better, also gave him a million a year retainer just to be there for him, whenever. "Whenever" being only twice in the fat guy's life. When he finally did need Cohen during the Commission Trials, Roy had already died. J.J. had told me back then that he had AIDS and wasn't expected to live much longer. The strange thing, especially for "wise-guys," was that I never heard anybody castigate Cohen for his homosexuality. He was simply "one of the guys," and a genius to boot.

J.J. told me that the fat guy was "reaching out" to Roy for help, and obviously he had finally capitulated --which in itself was no great surprise, as to know Lilo was to fear and despise Lilo. This was a common consensus amongst workers on both sides of the law.

"How the fuck are we going to get the 68th and Park in time?" J.J. looked frantic.

"It's fucking rush hour, just look at that shit!" He pointed to the graveyard of bumper-to-bumper traffic crawling like a snail around Columbus Circle.

"Did you ask if I could hit him inside the office?"

"N-no, I didn't think to ask."

"Shit! Get on the phone and find out! I can run through the park and get there in eight to ten minutes. To blast him on Park Avenue during rush hour ain't my cup of tea."

J.J. was shaking his head "no" at me where I stood ten yards away at a Sabrett hot-dog stand, drinking a ginger ale.

"What did Fish have to say, J.J.? Obviously nothing good, huh?"

"That was the 'fat guy'--he said Roy freaked out when he suggested taking Lilo out inside his office, etc."

"That's it?" I asked, a bit cynically.

"No," J.J. grinned, "he wants to know what's the problem hitting him outside?"

"Problem? He wants to know what's the 'problem' with whacking a guy on Park Avenue during rush hour?! I got no problem with that at all, J.J. I realize I'm dispensable, but call the 'fat guy' again and tell him I'll beat the guy to death with a baseball bat in the middle of Park Avenue if he gives me Cohen's retainer for the next year!" I spat out.

"Take it easy, Joe. No big deal, we'll just pass on it. We were late getting there."

"This shit's wearing thin, J.J. I gotta find a better way. If it weren't for you, I'd be long gone," I said tiredly. He looked into my eyes and nodded with understanding.

Cocaine running all around my brain, I was really fucked up, short tempered and paranoid. But it seemed that the more guilt I felt about the way I was living--deceiving Gail and my son--the more I looked to escape through snorting cocaine and drinking alcohol. Especially on those days, those short periods when I would straighten out for a while and be clear-headed, enjoying the time we spent together like a family, like a human being. In spite of Gail's beseeching me to seek help and go into a program, I insisted I didn't have a real problem. Actually I had much, much, more than a cocaine problem. Cocaine was just a symptom resulting from a more serious underlying condition.

If J.J. ever saw the change in me from the guy he knew so well the first two and one-half years, he never mentioned it. But then, I made it a point never to be high when going to see him in the city, but would still find myself needing a "couple" of drinks during the days when we were together just to take the hyper edge off the affects the cocaine had on my nervous system, having me wired like a pit bull.

***

Merry Christmas! - December 1977

J.J. told me that the I.L.A., the International Longshoreman's Association, was throwing a big gala Christmas party in a Hilton Hotel suite in Manhattan the last week of December. He said he was bringing his wife and thought Gail might enjoy going, too. I thought it was a great idea, but should have known that he had other motives for looking forward to such droll festivities.

"Johnny 'The Greek' Plakos will be there." He grinned like a Cheshire contemplating the canary. But he did arouse my interest.

"Plakos! You're kidding? What's bringing him out of the woodwork, he become senile?" I asked curiously.

Plakos was the last of Mickey Spillane's lieutenants, who we had been beating the bushes for, along with Spillane himself, for two years!

"Scotto," he replied grimly.

"Tony Scotto?" I didn't know much about him except that he was a power on the docks in Brooklyn and a capo in Castellano's Gambino Crime Family. Other than that, the word was he was a candy ass; soft and born with the proverbial silver spoon in his mouth just like "Big Paulie" himself. More of the new breed of tough guys!

I was also told by J.J. that he was being groomed for the national I.L.A. presidency. He was squeaky clean, campaigned at Jimmy Carter's side in Brooklyn, and would have gotten the job going away but he took a bust shortly after his run-in with The Greek and went away to the "can," his image besmirched. Maybe when he dies Cardinal O'Connor will deliver as stirring an eulogy as he gave for Teddy Gleason at St. Pat's a short while back.

"So, what's the beef between Scotto and The Greek? And what's our position here?"

"Well, number one, Joe, I want you to get a good look at The Greek. We've learned where he lives and a little about his movement. Secondly, Big Paulie reached out to the 'fat guy' and asked for his help in seeing that Scotto gets out of the Hilton alive. Once he's back in this car, it ain't our problem no more."

"Scotto's coming alone, knowing The Greek's gonna show up?" I was amazed.

"No, he'll have two or three bodies with him. But that's all they are. The 'fat guy' wants you there, or at least in the vicinity, when Scotto leaves."

"Is Greek crazy enough to move on Scotto in the Hilton, even outside for that matter?"

"Naw, he's crazy but not stupid. It's his way of intimidating Scotto. Seems he's been trying to extort him. Bring something small but keep a real low profile. There will probably be as many agents as there are union officials and wiseguys."

Gail and I took a private elevator up to the Hilton suite. Upon entering, we were both impressed by the size and grandeur of the joint, although we wondered why anybody would want to live in a place the size of Yankee Stadium. We didn't particularly enjoy ourselves because we saw immediately it was a very impersonal affair, with guys huddled around the ballroom and bar in groups of four and five while the wives who had accompanied them sat on couches spread around their area, sipping their drinks, looking stupid and wondering how they got there.

"Some party, huh?" I said apologetically, sitting next to Gail.

"Listen, I got to see somebody. As soon as I do we'll get out of this overrated castle, okay?"

"Don't worry about me, Sully. I'm fine. Do what you have to do."

She had a good idea of my business with J.J., although not the specifics. She knew J.J. had a motive or reason every time he called the house or invited the wives somewhere. In this instance the wives were a good front to make us appear more as union business agents or officials, to those who didn't know better.

When Greek rolled in, anybody with a sense of danger could feel the atmosphere change. The stage was set, I thought grinning. I'm right in my element now!

I moved to the bar, keeping my distance. He was a short, mean looking bastard pushing close to sixty years of age, had iron-gray hair and a noticeable limp. Greek never took his overcoat off, and had the balls to carry a wrapped up paper bag under his left arm, which I knew he had a pistol in. I admired his chutzpah. Who was going to ask him, "May I check your bag, sir?" His countenance alone defied such a question.

When Scotto walked in with three "pinky-rings" ("Pinky-rings" being a term used then for Italian men as bodyguards.) trailing behind him and spotted Greek, his olive complexion went as white as the underbelly of a flounder. The Greek gave him a frightening, contemptuous look that spoke a thousand words. "I'd kill them and you, too, if I was of the mind to," his eyes seemed to bespeak. Other than the icy stares, though, there were no problems, and none that I could sense building.

J.J. came over to me about fifteen minutes later and whispered, "He'll (Scotto) be leaving in about fifteen minutes, Joe." That was my cue to go down and check out the lobby area and street. After doing just that, I stayed outside the door bullshitting with the doorman, smoking a cigarette until Scotto came out with his retinue of useless clowns, not even glancing my way in passing an arm's length away. I breathed a sigh of relief as they piled mindlessly into their pretty limo and sped away.

I nodded to J.J. as I came off the elevator and stopped by the bar to have one more look at The Greek, keeping my distance while I burned his face indelibly into my mind.

"You got a good look?" J.J. asked.

"Couldn't forget him if I wanted to. Let's get out of here."

The Greek was living in an apartment building on 33rd Street between 9th and 10th Avenues. The building had double-glass security doors where the doorman stood, in between buzzing people in and out--very secure! Greek exited every weekday morning at 6:15, give or take five minutes. He usually waited on the sidewalk in front of the doors, till in three or four minutes a black Lincoln Town Car turned up off 10th Avenue and picked him up.

Other than an occasional man or woman walking the streets in those early morning hours for their dog's daily constitutional, the street was deserted and barely turning light. J.J. and I had taken turns watching his movements through the mini opera glasses from where we were usually parked for those fifteen minutes, on the corner of 9th Avenue. How I would move a hundred yards down the streets without arousing his suspicion was our main problem. He was smart and dangerous, and wouldn't hesitate to pull his piece out on whoever he felt was out of place and approaching him. No doubt there was a hole in the paper bag where the trigger guard was located.

We'd seen all that was possible to see, but were still stumped on the approach. J.J. told me to go home and give it some thought for a few days, as he would himself. This was during one of my spells where I was staying away from the places where cocaine tempted me. I stayed at home where I belonged, taking my son Ramsey sleigh riding in the park, jogging with Duke (Gail's dog), and spending enjoyable evenings before a fireplace with Gail and Ramsey. Life was at its best always when I lived it simplest.

One day while I was jogging with Duke along a freshly plowed road leading through Forest Park in Queens, New York a thought hit me in the head like a lighting bolt.

"Damn!" I shouted, causing Duke to jump and look at me as if to ask, "You okay, buddy?" I laughed and ran to a bank of phones on Woodhaven Boulevard and Jamaica Avenue.

"J.J.? Yeah, I found a way! It's beautiful and so simple it eluded us. Yeah, see you in the morning for coffee," meaning I'd meet him at our regular spot, a restaurant on Broadway and 63rd Street.

We were on our second cup of java after some eggs over-light, home fries, the works, when J.J. erupted with impatience. "Okay, what's the deal?"

"What's our main problem?" I lowered my voice.

"The approach, getting close without alerting him," he played along with me.

"Why can't we?" I questioned.

"Well, first, you got to walk a hundred yards down 33rd from 9th Avenue. If you were to approach from 10th Avenue you'd have your back to his men when you made your move, if they were to turn the corner at that moment. And last but not least, there ain't nobody on the fucking block at that hour but a few people walking dogs."

"That's it, buddy!" I smiled.

"What are you talking about?"

"A dog! I got to walk my dog. Actually, Gail's dog. She'd kill me if anything were to happen to him, but tomorrow morning at 6:15 me and Duke are going for a walk down 33rd Street."

"Son of a bitch! Yeah! Son of a bitch," he laughed.

"Listen," I continued, "right next to those glass doors, about fifteen yards going towards 10th, is an alley way that leads straight through to 32nd Street where you'll be waiting with the motor running. If the car with his bodyguards turns the corner before I'm close enough for a shot, I'll just pass and we try again the following day, nothing lost. But as you know, it's rare Greek ain't standing there at least three or four minutes before his ride shows up."

"Yeah, but that bag right under his arm? This prick is dangerous, Joe don't sleep on him because of his age," J. J. warned.

"Listen, I'm not sleeping on him. You should know me better by now. But if Duke and I do our thing convincingly, he should never get a chance to touch that bag. And Duke and I have been hanging out together for a long time," I grinned at his reservations.

"Does Gail know you're bringing Duke into the city?" J.J. laughed at the thought.

"Are you kidding? She'd kill me. I'm just taking him for a light morning jog. If I didn't feel good about the chances, I'd look for another dog to use."

"What will you wear?" This guy's got a memory like an elephant. He saw you at the Hilton too, you know?"

"But I'll be Hispanic, remember? And I'll also have a sweat suit with a hood, which makes sense because it's cold and may snow again. The big front pocket will be cut inside. So with one hand on the leash, and my right in the front pocket on the .38 tucked in my pants beneath the sweatshirt, and all hunched over in the cold, it will be a natural look. Know what I mean?"

"Yeah, I like it," J.J. whispered. "But don't look his way, Joe, not till you're ready to commit yourself. He'll know if your eyes meet. He's that dangerous, " J.J. cautioned me seriously.

"I'll remember, J.J. Thanks."

***

Duke Makes His Debut - January 1978

"Should be any second now," J.J. said, looking at me in the rear-view mirror as I was trying to calm Duke down for the championship fight. He was a little jittery in the strange surroundings.

"Just a little walk, buddy," I whispered to Duke, rubbing his head and neck the way he liked.

"A hundred yards and we'll buy you a diamond-studded collar--get you laid. How about a nice, big steak? You name it, you're the star of the show, Duke!"

Gail had always said Duke was almost human in his intelligence, so when he gave me a look that said, "Who you bullshitting?" I was not surprised.

"He just stepped out--go!" J.J. hissed through clenched teeth. I followed Duke out of the car into the ankle-deep slush.

"Shit!" I muttered. I switched the leash to my left hand and slid my right into the pocket of the sweatshirt, my hand clasping the rubber grip I had put on the snub-nose, and began the agonizingly slow walk down 33rd Street. After about forty yards of patiently allowing Duke to sniff every steaming turd and yellow piss stain in the slushy snow along the curb, Greek came into sight of my peripheral vision. He stood like a cigar store Indian with his ever-present paper bag clutched beneath his arm like a security blanket. There wasn't a soul on the street.

"C'mon, buddy, I'm freezing!" I yelled at Duke loud enough to be heard by The Greek.

"You gonna shit or what?" I said, hoping Greek would become bored with my presence, accepting my right to be there.

"No car yet. Just a little further, ain't got much time left," my mind warned. Thirty yards now, just get a little closer--of all times Duke chose now and began to drop into a squat to take a shit!

"Jesus Christ!" I cursed, giving his leash a short, violent tug to bring him out of his crouch, hoping Greek did not pick up on this strange behavior.

"C'mon, buddy," I almost whined when Duke looked at me indignantly, "ten yards now!"

My motor started humming, "No car--move now!" my mind commanded and I obeyed, dropping smoothly into a crouch, not wanting to panic Duke and have him leap away on me. Both his leash and pistol cradled in my left hand, Greek sensed it, spun and moved backwards toward the glass doors, eyes like a deer caught in a car's headlights. He **knew** it was too late but still reached across his body for the bag in desperation. The old buck was too slow.

"BOOM!" the snub-nose roared its final objection, breaking the morning silence, echoing back to me from the city's high, cavernous walls, which bore witness as the hollow-point slug sent the wild old buck sliding along the plate-glass doors. The doorman peered from his fishbowl inside, eyes bulging in stark terror, watching in fascination as Greek collapsed in a broken heap, his legs folded uselessly beneath him. The brown paper bag was lying next to his outstretched hand.

Simultaneous to the shot, Duke had leaped four feet off the ground, wrenching his head off the collar. I had no time for a coup de grace.

"No--oh shit! Duke!" I yelled as he took off toward 10th Avenue in pure fright.

"Duke!!!" I screamed, running for the alleyway. He had stopped and spun to look back at me.

"Duke!" I yelled one last time before ducking into the alley, "let's go home. Let's go home, boy. Let's go home!" I shouted, hoping he would follow, not wanting to be left behind in this strange place.

I would have bet on him against any greyhound that morning as I watched him blow by me in the alley.

"Yeah, good boy!" I screamed, laughing hysterically as J.J. threw open the back door upon our blazing approach to the finish line.

"Yeah, Duke, in the car. In the car!" I cried out, diving in behind him and hugging his trembling body after pulling the door closed.

"You get him?" J. J. asked, never one for sentimentality.

"Yeah, we got him. Didn't we, Duke? God damn, J.J., he leaped four feet into the air when the shot went off, and was all the way to 10th Avenue before coming back to me. I was more worried about what I would tell Gail if I lost him than getting busted!"

When Duke and I had calmed down I answered J.J.'s stream of questions. "Damn, J.J., hard to say, but with a hollow-point mid-chest, third button down, I don't see how he could handle that. And the way his legs collapsed under him like he was just K.O.'d with a crushing left hook, I'd say he's dead, or beyond help getting to him quick enough. Damn! With Duke I didn't have time for another shot."

"Don't worry about it," he nodded "The legs. When the legs fold like that it's a good sign."

J.J. called me at home about three hours later.

"Say, remember that guy with the chest problem? Well, he checked into a hospital but they couldn't do nothing for him. Left town a few hours ago! Give me a call in a few days."

***

A Bad Can of Tuna - May 13, 1978

I was in the bathroom brushing my teeth and Gail had the "Mr. Coffee" machine on when the phone rang. It was an early, lazy spring morning.

"Hi, J.J.!" Gail's voice drifted to me.

"I'm fine. How's Margaret, the family? Yes, he's here. Hold on."

"Joe, it's J.J." she called, and was pouring some java as I picked up the phone.

"Hi, how are you feeling?" J.J. chirped happily.

"You coming into the city today?" Often on a Saturday afternoon when things were quiet, which wasn't often, I'd shoot into the city, park on the West Side and walk leisurely with J.J. over to the East Side, and have lunch, a few burgers and beers, in P.J. Clarke's on 3rd and 55th Street. It was nice atmosphere to unwind in, and casually rehash our state of affairs.

"Naw, J.J., not unless it's necessary! I was just getting ready to take Ram for a ride on the bike, do a little shopping with Gail, make a few phone calls, ya know."

"No, relax, there's nothing pressing. I just wanted to tell you an old friend of ours caught a bad can of tuna." J.J. always talked in riddles on the phone, and for good reason.

Tuna? A bad can? Ptomaine, lead poisoning? I couldn't help but laugh, finally catching the drift.

"All right, so who was it?"

"Remember the guy who I told you ran to Teddy while we were in Florida?" He meant Spillane.

"You're kidding! Where did it come from?"

"The fat guy said it was the 'Young Lions'." That's how we referred to the conglomeration of Hell's Kitchen's young Irish renegades and misfits, called the "Westies" and whom Big Paulie was insightful enough to recruit as his ace in the hole to protect his interests on the West Side of Manhattan. This, of course, conflicted with those of the fat guy and the Genovese Family, and his "Jaws" downtown. Now, with the old Irish crew virtually decimated and a non-factor any longer, the fat guy was turning his eyes on the Westies, one particular Westie, Jimmy C. I knew him well, having spent time together with him in Auburn

Prison, breaking bread and enjoying his quiet intelligence and sense of humor. He was deadly and possessed good common sense of organized thought. His "pest control" expert and so-called ex-Green Beret Mickey Featherstone, now a member of the fed's free housing program for converts, I was much less impressed with. Whenever this jungle fighter had to do hard time he'd run straight to the prison psychiatrist (especially in a dangerous joint like Riker's Island, where animals ran amok and unchecked) claiming flashbacks, seeing little yellow Viet Cong charging him as he fought off the hordes heroically-hand-to-hand, knife clenched in his bared teeth, of course. In reality, however, his heart pumped pure Kool-Aid and the only Viet Cong he was seeing were black and brown, little wild-assed ghetto fighters from the South Bronx, Brooklyn, and Manhattan. The little prick would shoot some unsuspecting victim in the back of the head--no big thing-- but at 140 pounds soaking wet, he wasn't ready for any *real* hand-to-hand combat. So he got on the jet fuel line for his cup of Thorazine twice a day, and subsequently was sent to the P.C. Unit (Protective Custody), or "Playboy Club," as guys referred to that specially protected area for guys who were either stool pigeons or for strange reasons suffered these sudden nervous breakdowns as soon as they heard that steel prison gate clang shut behind them. Some had no problem checking their hearts in along with their tough guy images.

In essence, I never thought of the "Indian" (Featherstone) as a serious threat, as long as I didn't fall asleep and could see him coming.

The fat guy had a personal beef with Jimmy C., feeling he was the one who snatched his long-time friend and moneyman Ruby Stein, and had decapitated him to avoid paying a sixty grand debt. The fat guy was really irate when Ruby washed up on Rockaway Beach, minus his top-piece!

I didn't particularly like the idea of going after guys I once broke bread with them, but this was war! I also didn't relish the thought of being reduced to a piece of meat in some tenement bathtub on the West Side, listening to these psychopaths giggling as they stripped down and climbed in with their cutlery to dissect me.

"What da fuck is wrong wit deese kids today? Dey got no morals? Dey got no respect? Jesus Christ! It ain't enough to kill a bum, you got to chop him up!" J.J. once mimicked the fat guy's shock at his friend's less than regal passing.

I was also close with Jackie C., Jimmy's brother, from Clinton Prison. But we were all big boys now, and had chosen our own fates. I knew if push came to shove, I could only give them the same shot I knew that they'd give me --none!

Jimmy and Mickey had been keeping a low profile on the West Side after Devore and Mahoney had gone down. They hadn't known where it was coming from no less whom. We heard Jimmy was living in Jersey somewhere but didn't know where Featherstone was. The last time I had seen Mickey was a few months after I came out of the joint in January 1976. I had seen him in the Plaka Bar and Restaurant, where I had went to see a friend named Bill Comas. Comas later blew his own brains out in the Hotel Opera next door, when his time came to testify against Coonan on a murder case. Hell of a way to change ones mind!

Featherstone was with Jackie C. that evening (I was still working with Offender Aid and Restoration with my friend Kenny Jackson at the time). Between the junk and booze, they were both so high they could barely walk straight and yet were about to stick up a card game upstairs from the Plaka Bar and Restaurant. I bid them all a quick adieu and departed.

"Out went the old lions and in came the new ones--this shit don't never end, huh, J.J.?" I asked.

**
Our Friends' Place

I had met with Jon Voight and director Hal Ashby a few times in Manhattan. Jon had visited me in my home in Queens, showing an interest in doing my life's story. It was to be built around my escape from Attica in 1971. It had been in the negotiation stages, with Ramsey Clark handling my interests, and the parole office had even authorized my travel to California when it became necessary to do so. As luck would have it the Writer's Guild went on strike so my life story was put on hold. During this time, I wasn't quite myself, living on a fine line. Al Cirillo and my other friends would talk to me and tell me to wait the strike out, but my impatience won out. I never got that story done, but Jon was in my corner. Jon is not only a great actor, but a wonderful, deeply spiritual human being and a man I call my friend to this day.

It was during Jon Voight's visit to our home in Richmond Hill, N.Y. that I, along with my friend Marco Tedesco, escorted Jon, and his good friend and director Hal Ashby over to John Gotti's "Bergen Fish and Hunt Club" on 101st Avenue in Ozone Park. As Jon had expressed interest, for the sake of reality in an up-coming movie, of seeing first hand just how one of these neighborhood social clubs functioned. The sport's betting, card games, make-up of the characters, etc. This was in the summer of 1978. Before all the hullabaloo and later allegations as to whether John

Gotti was the Godfather, or the world's best dressed plumber. To me, he was just a great guy, and as special a kind of man as one could meet behind prison walls. He's one of the few people I've ever felt an instant affinity toward. The fact that Gail and I had bought a home in Richmond Hill, just six blocks from the social club, made it easy for me to stop in now and then to say hello to John and a few other guys, like his brother Genie and Angelo Ruggiero who I also liked a great deal. When I asked John if he would mind my bringing Jon Voight to visit the club when he came to Queens, he graciously gave his blessings without the slightest hesitation, and his brother Genie and Quack-Quack (Angelo) went out of their way to lay out a real nice spread from a neighborhood Italian deli. Jon himself has a great sense of humor, so about twelve of us spent a pleasant afternoon telling war stores and listening to Angelo Ruggerio's endless repertoire of jokes. Hence, the reason from the Moniker "Quack-Quack"-- he never stopped talking. Jon and Hal Ashby were made to feel right at home.

"You know," he mused upon leaving. "I liked all those guys!"

"So do I, Jon. That's why I brought you here."

It was also around that time that I had an interview with Robert Dinero. I spent a few very enjoyable hours rapping with him while Cis Corman and John Hancock waited patiently. I did a cold reading with him for a part in an upcoming movie called "Weeds," which I understood was later done by Nick Nolte. It was a goof for me, but I enjoyed his company. He was a knock-around guy from Mulberry Street whom I felt completely at ease with, and who I felt I could just as well have met in a prison yard except for that fickle finger of fate, which seemed to call the shots in timing and the direction a man takes at a given moment in time.

***

Miami, Florida - 1978

"Damn!" I shouted, slamming the kitchen phone back into its cradle.

"What is it, Joe?" Gail called from the bedroom where we had been unpacking, separating the clothes for the wash and the things I would bring to the dry cleaner. We had only been home for about three hours after our vacation and were completely exhausted.

"J.J. needs me in Florida. I got reservations waiting for me at Kennedy on Eastern," I checked my watch, "in about three hours."

"Do you have to go?" Gail moaned, knowing it was useless.

"You know you can't keep on like this with the baby and all. He needs a father, a-and I need a husband," she said quietly, but with deep concern in her voice.

"Yeah, I have to go, honey," I mumbled, walking into the bedroom to throw a few things together in an overnight bag. The thought "*have* to go" or "*want* to go" haunted me all the way to Kennedy Airport.

I had not been able to keep Gail in the dark forever. She had seen the guns in the different places I kept them, and had seen who my friends were at different holiday parties and functions we attended now and then. She also knew the make-up and afro I kept atop her dresser on a dummy's head were not for some school play I was auditioning for, although I had started taking acting classes a few nights a week at the "Herman Bergdorf School for Acting" on Bank Street in the Village.

One night, while I was sneaking into the bedroom and quietly undressing in the dark, trying not to wake her, I was frozen in my movement.

"Is it that bad, Joe?" Gail whispered sleepily as I was about to slide into bed.

"Is it so bad y-you can't w-walk away from it all?"

I just stood there for what seemed an eternity, searching for her face in the darkness, numbed by her spoken thoughts, the same thoughts that had become my own as of lately. It had nothing to do with my physical fear, but more so with the senselessness of my actions, particularly in view of our child and the great possibility I would die or go to prison for life, leaving her to fend for herself with our baby.

"Yeah, honey," my voice trembled breathlessly, "it's bad, worse than bad. I don't know who, or what, the fuck I am anymore. I'm going purely on instinct, and this other guy inside me wears a face I've never seen before. It's an ugly one I don't like at all."

"A-are you afraid to stop? That they won't let you walk away?" her voice trembled breathlessly.

"No--no, honey," I laughed sadly, "that crap's only in the movies. It's not them. It's not even J.J. I would have his blessings, whatever I decided to do. I've more than paid my dues. It's me Gail! It's me!! I don't know *how* to walk away. It's like I have a hand to play out, where either something will happen to stop me, or whatever it is inside that drives me, will somehow feel sated and die."

"M-my God, Joe!" she cried softly.

"I can only hope you will last a few more years--long enough to outlive this. I--I've never wanted anything from you! No money, no fancy clothes, jewelry, or cars, just a husband and friend to grow old with, and to watch our children grow," she cried as I held her in the darkness that hid the salty tears that slid over my own cheeks, and stung my parched lips.

Stepping off the plane and walking towards the arrivals area was like a trek through Dante's Inferno. Heat, I don't mind, but there wasn't a breath of anything resembling oxygen or a hint of breeze in the air anywhere.

"How do you guys manage to look so fresh and cool?" I laughed, shaking hands with both J.J. and Dougie, an old friend of his from New York now living in Florida.

The drive to Hallandale was virtually in silence, other than small talk about the Yankee's chances of winning the pennant, etc.

J.J. had secured a nice little utility apartment for us at some small motel-like complex owned and run by a retired wiseguy from Brooklyn. Our rooms were clean, air-conditioned, and had a spacious lawn running down to a dock that overlooked Biscayne Bay. Dougie and J.J. joined the lone man sitting at a poolside table in the shade of a candy-striped beach umbrella, sipping tall iced lemonade. Not being one to ask questions (actually preferring to work on a "need to know" basis) I went about my business, which at that moment was to get into the pool as quickly as possible. J.J. would tell me all I needed to know in due time, so I enjoyed myself in the water, that was just a tad cooler than luke-warm, until J.J.'s co-conspirators departed.

"So what's up, buddy?" I grinned, flopping onto a chair in the umbrella's shade and reaching for a cold drink in the ice chest.

"The Hoffa shit again!" J.J. lowered his voice, looking in all directions.

"He's dead," I quipped, "So what's the problem?"

"Yeah, he's dead. And the fat guy and Tony Pro, who just left with Dougie, want to make sure he stays that way!" he replied.

"So do you," I thought, but said, "Is this about that O'Brien guy who you were telling me about in P.J. Clarke's a few months before I went Ireland with Gail?"

I mused while sipping the throat-soothing iced tea. It was obvious that this Chuckie O'Brien had been instrumental in setting up his pseudo-father (Jimmy Hoffa) to get "whacked" in Detroit on the orders of Funzi (then boss of the Genovese Crime Family) at the request of Tony Pro, a powerful Genovese captain based in Jersey and a "business agent" in the Teamsters. Tony Pro hated Hoffa's guts, and the feelings were mutual. Anybody knowing of the falling-out they had while in federal prison together, knew this.

J.J. told me, after about six to eight Michelob's, that Jimmy's "adopted son," Chuckie Boy, had met his father at some diner and drove him to a wise-guy junkyard in Detroit. The meeting was supposed to be a sit-down with Tony Pro, where their differences would be ironed-out. It was to be mediated by an old friend of Jimmy's called Jack. He was another wiseguy connected to the Genovese Family in New York. Jimmy had gotten assurance from both Funzi, and the fat guy, that everything would be all right, and that Tony Pro wouldn't mind if Jimmy's son, Chuckie, escorted him to the sit-down, nor would he mind Jimmy's old friend Jack acted as a neutral mediator between them. And why should Tony Pro have objected? Never in Jimmy's wildest dreams could he have imagined that his "son", to whom he had given everything, would accept an offer he couldn't refuse (thirty pieces of silver) that would last him a lifetime or, as the alternative option, a slow death. Jack, on the other hand, did not have to be bought because he *was* family, and family came first and negated any temporary friendship of convenience.

And so J.J. had told me, unaware of how much the alcohol had loosened his tongue (a rare occurrence for him), and I didn't attempt to stop him. I, like millions of others, was curious about what had actually happened to this national figure.

"Never expected a thing," J.J. had gone on.

"He pulled up to the joint and came into the office, leaving Judas (Chuckie) sitting behind the wheel of the car. He was actually relieved because he was getting a chance to bury an old bone. He had that winning smile in place when he stepped into the office, seeing both Tony Pro and Jack smiling also, but only for the length of heartbeat before a volley of shots from silenced automatics were fired into his head at close range by the two assassins who lie in wait behind the door. Chuckie O'Brien got out of the car and walked away just as soon as the door had closed behind his father forever. Tony Pro and Jack exited stealthily moments later and went their separate ways. Under the cover of darkness, J.J. and Sally Bugs had no fear of discovery as they worked quickly to dismantle the car, before placing the body in it and moving it into the crusher."

I had been listening to J.J. 's slurred voice with one ear while listening to Rocky Graziano and Jake LaMotta tell their "war stories" to some young admirers. They held court at a corner table in P.J. Clarke's almost religiously.

"So you're telling me Hoffa's a recycled bumper on some new model car in the Motor City, huh?" I laughed.

"Yeah," J.J. slurred, a momentary glint of recognition appearing in his eyes to what he had been saying. I prudently never brought up the conversation again.

"P.J. Clarke's? O'Brien?" his eyes squinted in concentration.

"I mentioned this to you before?" his face one of concern I did not like.

"Not really, J.J." I said offhandedly, taking a big gulp of iced tea.

"Ahh, that tastes good! All you mentioned was the possibility that we might have to see this guy in the future as the fat guy was concerned about him, just as you always seem to prime me beforehand," I smiled at him, and the tension in his face drained away.

"Oh, oh yeah. Well, maybe we'll only need to talk to him. Tony and I will meet him for lunch at Charlie Brown's tomorrow. He'll feel safe with the big lunch-hour crowd. I got a 'quiet one' for you, and if this piece of shit doesn't come up with the right answers in reference to what we *heard* he was thinking, about talking to certain people. I'll give you the nod and you can hit him in the shithouse where he belongs! He drinks like a fish and pisses like a clam, so you'll have a half a dozen good opportunities if necessary. There's Valet parking, but the guy who owns the joint will leave his car out back by the office entrance, keys behind the visor."

"Why bother, J.J.?" I asked.

"Why bother what?" he looked confused.

"All these amenities when there's so much doubt about the guy?"

"I agree with you, Joe, but it ain't my call." he spat out bitterly. "I guess the Bug's enough in one year." (By the "Bug" I took it for granted that J.J. meant Sal Brigoglio, Tony Pro's man and his cohort in the Hoffa assassination, whom it was learned by the fat guy and "jaws" downtown was talking to the Feds, trying to get out from under a drug case they had him cold on.)

That evening I jogged a few miles and took a cool shower before taking a ride with J.J. to look the joint over and get my bearings before returning to the apartment to get some sleep.

J.J. went to the "Jockey Club," a plush point in Hallandale, to see an old friend, Teddy Gleason. Gleason was once long-time national president and power behind the I.L.A. (International Longshoreman's Association) when the docks were the DOCKS, on the West Side of New York. Up until then, he was living a life of luxurious leisure in his retirement. Gleason told J.J. that Mickey Spillane had been down to see him about a week ago, beseeching him for old-time's sake to intercede for him to the fat guy, as he was in hiding and running; scared since the sudden demise of his two lieutenants, Devore and Mahoney. He felt the noose tightening, but we had been unable to find the hole he had crawled into, in spite of our scouring the West and East Sides six to ten hours a day, seven days a week.

***
Charlie Brown's - Hallandale, Florida

I was sitting at the bar listening to soft piped-in music and surveying the casually dressed lunch crowd in the dining room area. A piece of celery from my Bloody Mary (which I thought appropriate for the occasion) was jutting out of my mouth when J.J. and Tony Pro walked in like they owned the joint. They did own the owner! With Chuckie O'Brien bringing up the rear, their eyes darting to and fro like a trapped rabbit, following them to the near corner table where J.J. and I would have no problem making eye contact in the bar's mirror.

Chuckie Boy was a squat, sloppy-looking prick of medium height. His face resembled that of a prizefighter- a losing one! He sat before Tony and J.J. like some chubby wimp, nodding his head like it were on a rubber band when Tony was speaking, and raising his hands in prayer-like supplication when pleading his case. J.J. just started at him, his frosty glare freezing Chuckie Boy's anal canal.

Three times Chuckie got up to take a pee-pee, having consumed a dozen Heinekens in less than half an hour. Each time J.J. gave me a barely perceptive negative nod, while he and Tony went into a huddle deciding Judas' fate between pit stops.

"Tough way to live," I thought.

The only time I saw Chuckie smile was when J.J. and Tony rose from the table, leaving him sitting there with the tab, which was cheap, considering. About thirty seconds later, he scurried out the door, his step much more bouncy and with a zest that had been absent upon entering the bar.

Personally, I felt affronted by the reprieve, because of all the guys who gotten their craniums ventilated, Chuckie Boy, Judas, was by far the most deserving candidate. But who was it that had told me, "Life is a bitch"?

I paused, looking at the stranger in the mirror above the bar looking back at me as I stood, threw a bill over the bar and walked out into the glaring sun. A gray Lincoln Town Car stood at the curb with J.J. behind the wheel and Tony Pro watching my approach from the passenger's side, turning to me with a big grin as I settled in the back.

"Slow day, huh kid!"

"I don't mind," I returned his smile.

"I'm over worked anyway and needed a breather."

At this, Tony and J.J. both cracked up with laughter, relieving the tension we all had been feeling.

***

Mickey Featherstone/The Indian - June 1978

"We found the Indian!"

J.J. smiled as I slid into the booth and picked up the dog-eared menu. It was a needless but comforting ritual as I always ordered eggs over-light, home fries, rye toast, and a big cup of java religiously. The Theater Bar and Restaurant was our regular morning haunt, situated directly under the Empire Hotel on Broadway and 63rd. I always used the entrance on 63rd facing Lincoln Center, cutting across the hotel's lobby, which had an entrance to the restaurant, just to avoid a possible unpleasant surprise. It was convenient as J.J. lived right around the corner and I had no problem finding a parking spot.

"No shit!" I grinned, sipping my coffee. His ingenuity at finding prospective victims never failed to amaze me--might take a month, a year, but like the Canadian Royal Mounted Police, J.J. always gets his man!

"Don't tell me," I spoke through a mouthful of eggs, "he's been right under our noses all along?"

"Right! As a matter of fact, he's only a few blocks from here on 56th, between 10th and 11th. Lives with his wife Sissy and a couple of young kids. I got the address. Here, 520...13th or 14th floor."

"No doorman? We can walk right in?"

"Yeah," he laughed, "if you'd like to. The fat guy was telling me yesterday that some poor clown walked right in there a few months back. Seems Jimmy, Mickey and a third guy were lying on the guy. Beat him half to death with black-jacks, and as they were dragging the bum across the living room to throw him out the window or off the terrace, Mickey's wife was following behind with a bath towel screaming, 'You've ruined my rugs!' while mopping up the blood."

"God damn!" and we both started laughing picturing that ghastly scene. "That joint's like the Black Flag Roach Motel, huh? They can get in but they can't get out! So what do you think, J.J., we take him on the streets?"

"It ain't that simple, Joe. I had nothing better to do, so I've been sitting across the street the past few days. It's a big complex, like a project with five different exits. And it's obvious he uses them all, unless he's down with the flu. I never saw him!"

"We'll think of something. But didn't you tell me it was more important to hit Jimmy C., as without the head, the body (his loose-knit crew) will fall?"

"Yeah, I'd prefer it that way. But a bird in the hand is worth two in the bush--something like that," J.J. laughed.

"Well," he continued, "at least we know where the Indian wig-wam is. Let's sit on him for awhile and just watch."

For the next two weeks we did just that, changing cars every few days and splitting up so we could observe at least three of the five exits.

"Nothing! Nada! You sure the little fuck lives in this joint? It's all blacks and Hispanics, and they look at me like I'm J. Edgar Hoover or something!" I said derisively.

J.J. became heated himself. "If the fat guy says he's there, you can take it to the bank!"

"All right, all right! But ain't it possible there are other Featherstones in this city?"

"Yeah, but the cops questioned *our* Featherstone about that guy flying without a license from his building. Know that I mean?"

"Yeah, I forgot that," I grinned apologetically.

"Let's both take a break for a week or so, we both need it. I'll give you a call."

A few days later I was flying down a one-way street on Fountain Avenue in Brooklyn, when out of nowhere came some dust-head from a side street, clipping me in front of the passenger's side with such force that my upper plate hit the windshield and my shoe laces came undone almost totaling me along with the car. Not caring to jump on the "A" train everyday to Columbus Circle, I spent the next month at home. I'd go bicycling with my son attached to a bucket seat in back of me. We went everywhere and had a ball. We even took a trek to Rockaway beach, almost thirteen miles away. Coming back I thought I'd have a massive coronary, as the little guy in the bucket seat kept yelling, "Faster! Faster!"

But even then, as I rode along the long stretch that was a government protected bird sanctuary and radar base near Howard Beach, I couldn't get the Indian off my mind. It was then that I decided to take the unauthorized initiative to push the issue and go see him. "Why not?" I thought. I never had any beef with him, or any of the Westies for that matter. I had seen him a few years back in the Plaka Bar on Broadway. All right! But what can I say to get him and Jimmy to come and see me together?

"Hi, Sandy! Is Rocky home?"

"Is Rocky home? He's always home! You want to rent him for a day?" she laughed.

Rocky and Sandra's house was like my second home and, along with the home of my friend Stevie and his wife Maria, was the place I would run to when I felt the pressure building and didn't want to put it on Gail. Gail could sense the pressure, knowing my moods so well. When she would see me begin to wander around the house like a caged tiger she'd say, "Why don't you go see Rocky or Stevie?" She knew they were the only guys I felt liked me just for me, and that I didn't have to be on stage with. And this was true, as it allowed me a period to get back in touch with myself and not with the monster I began perceiving myself to be. They asked for nothing and gave everything. Although they had little in the material sense, they had heart and love and never closed their door in my face, not even in my darkest and most dangerous hours--when all was unraveling at the end.

"Rocky the Jockey," people called him. He was a great rider but couldn't deal with being a "butt-boy" for arrogant owners and pompous trainers, just to get the good horses to ride. I'd known and grown up with Rocky when I had first moved to the Woodhaven section of Queens from "Irish town" in Rockaway Beach in 1946. I was eight years old then, and Rocky was still riding a tricycle. We went to St. Elizabeth's School together, and though I was closer to his older brother, Blackie, he was a friend to my younger brother Jerry. He was always special in my eyes and I always defended him against his brother, Blackie's arrogant ways and taunts.

As it turned out years later, Rocky was a diamond in the rough. His pseudo-tough guy older brother, Blackie was simply glass. He was a cosmetic showpiece through and through. Being in and out of reform schools and prison from the age of fourteen until about thirty-seven years old, I didn't see Rocky again until I got out of Dannemora Prison in 1975. It was then that I met his wife Sandra, a sweetheart, and their children. We've been like two peas in a pod ever since. Rocky and Sandra are a volatile Irish-Italian duo; witty, acid-tongued and never boring.

"Listen, Rock," I asked, wiping the reaming sauce from the plate of another of Sandy's gourmet meals.

"I need a ride to the city. My car's in the garage and I've got to see someone real bad."

"Damn, Joe, I wish I could help you, but my trunks already full!" he laughed morbidly.

"C'mon, Rock, this is serious. Do you mind, Sandra?"

"What do I mind?" she shrugged her shoulders at the kitchen sink.

"Just make sure you stop at an insurance office and get him covered, some of that double-indemnity, you know!"

"See what I got to put up with from this guinea bitch!" Rocky snickered.

"Yeah, right. The Irish prick's always complaining but never leaves!" she returned.

Rocky knew me like a brother--the good, bad, and ugly--so I ran it all down for him and he became all business.

"I'll take you, Joe, but I don't like it. You sure you don't want me to stay with you?" he asked, and he meant it, even though he was a working, family man.

"No, Rock. I appreciate your thoughts, but I'll be all right."

I had Rocky park on 56th Street on the East Side of 10th Avenue.

"Listen, Rock," I said, looking at this stern, worried countenance, "I want you to give me forty-five minutes," we checked our watches, "if I'm not back in that time I want you to go home, you hear?"

"I ain't leaving without you!" he answered stubbornly.

"Hey! C'mon, I'm just telling you this because it might take longer. I may get into some extended conversation and--"

"Bullshit!" he spat out.

"Whatever, bullshit or not, please do as I ask, Rock," I pleaded.

"All right, Joe, but watch that cocksucker! Don't give him your back, you hear me?"

"You know he can't get Mrs. Sullivan's boy," I smiled with more bravado than I felt, and reached through the window to squeeze his shoulder before turning and sprinting across 10th Avenue, dodging the traffic.

"I'm fucking crazy!" I thought as the elevator softly hummed its way up to the 13th floor. "I should have at least told J.J. I was coming here, just in case this thing backfires. But too late for that now, " I said to myself as the doors hissed open and I stepped out into a dim-lit hallway, the multi-cultural smells of a United Nations soup kitchen assailing my nostrils, making me gag momentarily. "Must be rat stew or some other delicacy. Probably chinks, they love cats, rats and assorted domestic animals," I thought to myself and laughed.

I pressed the button and listened to it buzz within. I heard shuffling feet and whispers. I patted my left forearm for assurance that the .25

automatic beneath my sport jacket, secured in place with a sleeve-style Ace bandage, was not slipping.

"Who is it?" a voice demanded nastily.

Stepping back from the doorway to give the occupant a better view, I smiled my best smile, "Mickey, is that you? It's me, Sully. Joe Sullivan." I listened breathlessly as a bar-type firelock was pushed aside, chain lock removed, and the door unlatched.

"Hey, Sully! Good to see you!" Mickey smiled, pumping my hand as I stared in shock at the skinny, disheveled, longhaired apparition that stood before me. He still had that innocent, boyish look and my heart momentarily went out to him.

"B-but what are you doing here? How'd you find me?" he asked in surprise rather than suspicion.

"It's a very long story, Mick, " I said, passing through a dark foyer.

My eyes were darting everywhere, my mind was alert and humming like a General Electric plant. As I stepped into the living room, electricity expending, my old friend from Clinton Prison stepped forward from where he stood by a window, a big smile on his cunning face.

"Sully, how the hell are you?"

I was surprised to see another old friend there, Bill Comas. I thought Mickey stayed by himself most of the time. After the glad-handing we all sat down, me on the couch facing them. After a quick but reasonable explanation of how I had been canvassing the West Side for days in search of him, and how I luckily had stumbled upon some non-descript in a bar on 9th Avenue who just happened to know him, I got down to brass tacks.

"Listen, Mickey, you know me, so no sense me trying to bullshit about why I came to see you." I paused, gathering my thoughts while he sat there glassy-eyed but attentive. Bill Comas just looked on in friendly confusion.

"I know you and Jimmy have joined forces with Castellano in Brooklyn and I want to hook up with you guys--simple as that."

"Jeez, Sully, I don't know," he said, running his fingers through his long hair. I could have taken them both out right then.

"I-I'd have to talk to Jimmy."

"I understand, Mickey, but listen," Now I was on dangerous ground.

I had to take a chance, even shock them if necessary to bring him and Jimmy to see me. I knew there was no love lost between them and Spillane & Company- deceased!

"You call Jimmy when you get a chance and tell him I said we got to stop killing each other for these treacherous guineas." Mickey had never wanted an alliance with them.

"We don't need *them* to take what we want on the West Side, " I whispered as Mickey and Comas sat quietly at attention. Now I got brazen.

"Who do you think whacked Devore, Mahoney, and the Greek?" I questioned, watching their mouths drop open, the instant recognition of their own imminent danger surfacing in their eyes, which I made a quick point to dispel.

"Take it easy!" I smiled.

"I got no beef with you guys, never have. But I want you and Jimmy to understand that there's more happening out there than meets the eye. We're all on the guinea hit parade. It's just a matter of time and convenience. Just look at Spillane and his crew. Your personal feelings aside, do you expect a better deal from them when your usefulness has expired? They don't want nobody around them they feel is a threat, especially a bunch of Irish loose cannons. Think about it?"

"Jesus Christ," he whispered as if awakening from a bad dream.

I stood to leave.

"Tell Jimmy all I've said, Mick, and that I'd like to talk to him, along with you and Jackie. Would the Plaka Bar be all right, say, Thursday at noon?"

"Damn!" he shook his head looking confused.

"I -I'll call Jimmy, Sully. You take it easy, huh."

"Yeah, you too, Mick. I hope you can convince him how important this is to all of us."

I didn't breath freely until I stepped out the front doors and onto the street again, feeling the warm summer breeze on my face and sucking in a lung full of delicious, polluted New York City air.

"Nice day to be alive," I laughed.

Poor Rock was pacing beside the car like an expectant father, and broke into a big grin when he spotted me.

"How did it go?" he asked, starting the car.

"I'm here, ain't I? That's good for starters. Actually, I won't know for a few days. Mickey went for it, but whether Jimmy will is a horse of a different color."

Two days later I got a call from J.J., telling me to meet him in the plaza by the fountain in the Lincoln Center complex where, on nice days, we'd sit and sip white wine and the little wrought iron tables from the outdoor bar. J.J. sounded all right on the phone but as soon as I walked up, he exploded in a quiet manner I had never seen before.

"Are you fucking crazy!" he snarled.

"Take it easy. What are you talkin--"

"Don't play games, Joe, this ain't a game! You KNOW what I'm talking about," he barely suppressed shouting.

"All right! All right!" I felt guilt turning into anger at having blown it somehow. " I had to do something before, one day, we found ourselves on the receiving end."

"Jesus," he said, shaking his head as he sat on the fountain's edge to calm down.

"What happened, J.J.?" I asked weakly.

"You went there, right?" he stated simply.

"Yeah, I went there."

"You mention my name, or the fat guy's?"

"No," I said softly, realizing I'd made a serious mistake. And so I ran down the whole scenario to J.J., explaining how I was just trying to set them up.

"Okay, what's done is done, we can't change that. But you must have scared the shit out of Jimmy because as soon as Mickey called him he ran straight to Big Paulie, telling him what went down. And Paulie went to see the fat guy." J.J. relayed their conversation.

"'What the fuck is going on?' Castellano says. 'Who is this guy Sullivan, he wit you? Jimmy says he's the one been whacking all those guys!' Paulie protested."

"Never heard of da bum! But you know how those Irish guys are," the fat guy said to Big Paulie, tapping his temple with his finger, "they're all fucking crazy! You sure he isn't one of those Westies of yours?" the fat guy asked him suspiciously.

"This turned the tables, making Big Paulie think just how tenuous his hold was over the loose-knit crew of madmen." J.J. was speaking in a voice more serious than I had ever remembered hearing before.

"I'm sorry, J.J., I was going to handle this by myself. I should have talked to you first."

"It's all right, nothing lost but your anonymity. But that edge is everything in this game. You're no longer the 'phantom' I've tried to keep you. Remember that," he said with great concern.

"You know, I've never thought of it like that."

"I know," J.J. said softly, looking like he had aged ten years.

"Go home and stay in Queens for a while. Let them think you were just running your mouth. Give it time, Joe, it will die out like everything does."

I stayed out of the city for a while. J.J. would call every week to see how I was doing.

"You sure you're all right?" he would ask. And of course my standard answer was, "Feel great, buddy, just taking it easy out here in the suburbs."

And that couldn't have been more of an understatement. I was bored to death, especially with Gail working all day. I also started seeing Stevie's wife's younger sister at this time, which was all part of my self-destructive roller coaster ride down the tubes. Theresa was an attractive raven-haired girl about twenty-three at the time, and no more deserved my deceiving her than Gail deserved my destroying our life together. After all, she had given me her heart, a beautiful son, and everything a man could ask for or want in life. But I didn't have a high opinion of myself, and didn't feel that I was deserving of anything decent and normal to begin with. I knew I was well on my way to losing it all- forever.

Theresa and I were hot and heavy, and started hitting the clubs, which of course meant more cocaine and drinking. But I always made sure to pick Gail up in the evenings at Queens Boulevard Subway Station. In my ever-growing sense of guilt and drug-induced paranoia, I took more pleasure in seeing her each evening than ever before. She was my rock, my life support. On those hot and humid summer evenings, before going home we'd always stop at an air-conditioned ice cream parlor in Forest Hills and cool off with a black and white ice cream soda. It was a ritual we both remember fondly, but one with which I eternally associate my daily deceit and self-destructive lies.

After telling me of the hectic routine at her advertising firm, the conversation would always drift back to me somehow.

"So how was your day, Sully, bored yet?" she'd smile lovingly. And I'd always repeat the same lies by rote, offhandedly telling her how I'd slept until noon--probably why I hadn't heard the phone ring when she'd called. Or how I'd gone up to Forest Park and jogged, came home, showered- blah, blah, blah! The lies never failed to make me feel a little sicker at heart each time I repeated them. Gail didn't suspect my running around because she had total trust and faith in me, which only made matters worse in my mind.

Gail is far too intelligent not to have had a good understanding of my problems, having tried getting me to see a shrink and enter a drug program for my obvious addiction to nose-candy. She was still unaware of my cheating on her because of her absolute trust in me, or perhaps she simply disallowed her mind to acknowledge the possibility.

"You don't look good, Joe. You're losing so much weight I can see it in your face. Your whole personality is changing. You don't want to go anywhere or even answer the phone. You're paranoid every time you hear the doorbell ring, and short-tempered with Ram, and me. You don't even realize it. You've got to do something, Joe!" Gail pleaded, not lecturing but simply trying to give me a picture of myself.

"I--I'm all right," I lied, looking at the pale, ghost-like image in the mirror beyond the soda fountain, which my self-hatred assured me was a fitting one--death! The inner darkness of my soul was so obvious now, even in the light of day. The cocaine habit, along with my ever-increasing homicide habit, had taken their toll on me, mind and body and soul.

"Joe, let's go away, at least for a few weeks. We b-both need to get away." I knew it was solely for my sake she was speaking.

"Y-you know you've always wanted to see Italy, the south of France, Monte Carlo," her eyes implored. "I--I've NEVER told you what to do, Joe, but I'm not stupid! I know what you do with J.J."

"Gail, don't..." I shook my head.

"B-but you know *why* I've never said anything, Joe?" she went on shakily.

"Because as horrible as that is, at least I knew you were safe with J.J., because he's cunning and he's in control of himself. That is his WHOLE life and he can live with it, but you're out of control, running around snorting cocaine and God knows what else. And why? Because underneath that hard exterior it is not your life! For twenty-five years you have been on-stage in those God forsaken prisons playing whatever part was necessary to survive, and you've brought that stage home with you!"

I just sat there staring at Gail, numbed by truths I was aware of but found impossible to change.

"My God, Joe, what have they done to you? You're like a fucking chameleon! I watch you change before my eyes, adapting according to every place you go, adjusting to every person you meet. You're afraid to offend anybody for fear they may say or do something that insults your sick prison credo, because you know no solution short of killing them! I've watched you when you were short-changed in restaurants, and charged for work a mechanic did not do on your car, but you'd only smile weakly and shrug it off when I told you to confront them with it. And now I know why, Joe. It's because in that insane world you've lived in all your life there was no middle ground, no room for compromise of 'rules,'" she sobbed openly, "in those warehouses of walking dead men. I'm afraid, Joe. For you, for me, for Ramsey, and for my hope of a life together with you. Stop hating, Joe, stop the killing! Get off the stage and stop killing yourself."

"Organized crime?" she laughed harshly through her tears.

"You're not tough guys, Joe, you're cowards! Afraid to face real work and the harsh self-sacrifice a real man must make for his family. And the greatest sacrifice a good man makes, Joe, is when he relegates his ego and vanity second to the wife and children he professes to love, so that he will never be separated from them, leaving them to fend for themselves in this world. No, Joe, you don't *only* kill each other. That's a lie you make yourselves believe! You kill the very reason to live for hundreds of wives and thousands of innocent children who need their husbands and fathers--just as Ram and I need you."

"Gail, I--I'm sorry..." I gasped, feeling a hot, burning sensation in my chest, as If I'd been stabbed with a knife. The truth cuts so surely and deeply.

"I wish it were forever," I thought aloud, dreamily.

"W-What, Joe?" she looked at me, composing herself.

"I wish we could go away somewhere, just leave everything and go," I whispered.

"Joe, that's not the answer. It's you! It doesn't matter *where* we run to, because wherever you go in life you have to take yourself with you," she shook her head sadly.

"You're right, h-honey," I acknowledged wearily, "but let's go to Europe, at least for starters, huh?" I smiled.

With Mom taking care of our son, Ramsey, we finally took off from Kennedy Airport on Air France for what we laughingly refer to as our "second European tour." We naturally both felt guilt at leaving Ramsey behind, but we understood that at two years old he wasn't ready for extensive traveling. We agreed, however, that we owed him a trip to Disney World when we returned home.

Gail was the ideal prototype for the American image in foreign countries: Her courteous manner, outgoing warmth and friendliness, and respect for cultural differences in people, foods and day to day lifestyles. I was Archie Bunker, the ugly American. Although I didn't voice my complaints outwardly to the people in their native countries, I'd blame Gail for everything I didn't like in the different parts of the world we went.

"What is this crap?" I'd whine over a meal I had found distasteful, or because we had to pay extra for ice water with our meals in European countries.

The crime I became most indignant about, however, was not being able to get a good cup of coffee. Gail solved this problem by carrying a thermos wherever we went, filling up at a McDonalds' franchise that would see me through the day.

It didn't take me long to realize how spoiled rotten the majority of Americans are, myself included. How we take a thousand different little luxuries and conveniences for granted as if they were our birthright, and look down our noses, unconsciously, at those who are not so fortunate and are unable both financially and technologically to live up to the standards we know in America. It was in the Western European countries that we traveled.

"What," I always asked Gail, "must the Eastern Europe and third world countries be like?"

She'd simply smile and accuse me of being a spoiled brat when I'd tell her that there were more conveniences in a prison cell in America than a lot of people around the world ever know in their so-called freedom. I was learning something after all!

Upon landing at Orly Airport outside of Paris, my senses were immediately assailed by the smelly, garbage-strewn, corridors of the airport.

"The garbage men on strike here or what? Look at this fucking cesspool! I could have went to Times Square or Picadilly Circus in London if I wanted this!"

"Please, Joe, DON'T start, huh?" Gail snapped angrily. Once she looked around, however, she had second thoughts herself. The scene must have brought to mind the grime-coated Indian snake charmers we'd run into in London a few years back.

"It *is* terrible!" she grinned weakly, crinkling her nose.

"But don't you want to see the Eiffel Tower, and--"

"Fuck the Eiffel Tower! I see the Empire State Building everyday and, besides, I had an erector set when I was a kid! Let's head south to the sun and sand on the Mediterranean, huh?"

"Good idea, Sully!" she laughed, pinching her nose at the Bowery odors that seemed to have followed us across the ocean.

"Ah, the French Riviera," I moaned while toweling my hair and running a comb through it, looking at Gail where she lie topless on a Rattan Beach mat, her body oiled and glistening, already getting a nice color after only three days there.

"This is much more in tune with my good taste," I laughed.

"Yeah, Sully," she retorted sarcastically, eyeing me while I ogled all the jet-set type broads prancing topless along the water's edge. Their breasts were of all sizes, shapes and colors, and quivered and danced gloriously on their rib cages as they strutted their goods before the male species at large.

I must admit that for the first few days my eye balls were in a constant state of protrusion, as was my uncontrollable lower extremity, until the floor-show became commonplace.

On our last night in Cannes, before driving to Monte Carlo, we put on our Sunday best and dined in the International Hotel and Casino. Though we enjoyed the hotel and casino immensely, we knew we were out of our league with those high rollers from all over the world. Nevertheless, I was dressed in conservative good taste and enjoyed myself, fooling people, while Gail gave me that look, "You're on stage again, huh, Sully?"

Meanwhile, back in our cut-off dungarees, T-shirts and sandals, a loaf of French bread, cheese and fruit stocked in our rental car, we reluctantly left paradise, but not without lasting memories, and drove along the Coastal Mediterranean Highway.

We entered Italy at San Remo, and began to take in the historic, though admittedly less erotic, sights.

We bought two matching hand-blown lamps in Venice, while our gondola waited in the less than romantic, murky canal outside the shop's door. I imagined that the canal was non-polluted when Marco Polo departed on his voyage to China, centuries before this once-beautiful island and gateway to the Orient began its slow decent into the sea, which even the rats must have sensed as they scurried around in panic as freely as the pedestrians.

After leaving Venice, we then traveled to the town of Pisa where I almost made history, becoming the first American to take a dive from the third landing of the "Leaning Tower." I had staggered sideways and, with a little help from its renowned angle and a bit too much vino, almost toppled over the waist-high balustrade. Gail's quick reflexive actions, however, saved the day. In no mood to be making history, I meekly retreated to the grass below, and slept off the grapes while Gail continued on her ascent of the tower.

Two days later, and grape-free, I stood in awe of the beauty that is Florence. The architectural make-up of the city equaled the works for the great masters we viewed: Michelangelo, Da Vinci, etc. The Statue of

David alone was worth the trip.

After two weeks of sight-seeing, living out of suitcases, and quick snacks at sidewalk cafes, where we'd stop to write our postcards and where Gail would search for little gifts of memorabilia to bring home to family and friends, we finally came to the decision to spend the last five days of the journey in Lake Como. It was the Valhalla of my dreams. Gail's boss, and our family Rabbi in so many ways (he kept Gail working while I was on the run and didn't complain when she went to all the trials), recommended it to us for sheer peace of mind, solitude and delight.

Lake Como was about thirty miles from the bustling, industrialized city of Milano. When we got there we couldn't help but feel as excited as teenagers, sitting in the plaza sipping espresso, awed by the beauty of this quaint town that looked out over Como Lake, dwarfed by the snow-capped peaks of the Swiss-Italian Alps that seemed to loom only a stones-throw away.

"I'd love to live out the rest of my life right here," I whispered to Gail, momentarily oblivious to the murderous rat race I had left behind.

"Anything is possible, Joe, if you'll just give yourself a chance, and give Jon (Voight) the time to get you out to California to work on the movie. Jon's a special kind of guy and would help you find your way. Then there's Deniro, who you told me you felt comfortable with and liked. What better people could you have in your corner? It won't be much longer now, and I know if you can just last until then, this insanity will end. It's why you're in conflict with yourself now."

"Hey!" I laughed.

"You gonna bill me for this session now or later?"

"Sully," she said, looking sad and forlorn, "I just hope you're around for me to bill you later."

"C'mon, we had a great time, didn't we? We'll have to come back in a few years, maybe with Ramsey." Gail simply stared at me as if I were some ancient ruin she was taking a picture of, to be remembered in some distant time.

***

Ol' Blue Eyes — July 13, 1979

"Joe!" Gail called, shaking me awake. "JJ 's on the phone."

"You told him I was home?"

My voice *was* accusing. Things had grown tense between Gail and me as I had been staying out for days at a time on cocaine and alcohol binges, coming home only when I was at the point of physical exhaustion. Unconsciously, I was trying to end my relationship with Stevie's sister-in-law and also with J.J., by staying away from them. But, because I was too concerned about hurting their feelings by being up front with my own, I continued to destroy Gail, myself, and our family in the process. Then I'd look at J.J. and see how old and frail he was becoming. I'd remember how he was the only one who had helped me when I was on the run after escaping from Attica. Since I'd been with him, he had become like a father or big brother to me. We had survived a lot of dangerous situations together, and I'd always go out of my way to keep him out of the line of fire.

"He needs me," I thought. But my priorities were ass-backwards. Gail and my son needed me, too. I guess I needed to feel as if I belonged somewhere, regardless of how negative that "somewhere" might be. Yet, I knew I belonged at home.

"How are you, J.J.?" I said wearily.

"I'm fine, where have you been?"

"I haven't heard from you in weeks!" he sounded worried.

"Ah, I'm all right. J-just tired, I guess." I wanted to say, "I'm tired of it all," but again I failed to say what was really on my mind.

"Can you come in tomorrow? I'm having lunch with the fat guy, and he told me to bring you with me." I could almost hear him smile over the phone. He knew what my reaction would be.

"He wants to see me?" I said, caught completely off guard.

I had been with the fat guy; working for him, for four years and never once had met the man.

"W-what for?" I asked with a hint of suspicion that made J.J. laugh. "Nothings wrong, Joe." I guess his curiosity has gotten the best of him because he kept on saying, 'bring the kid, make sure you bring the kid.'" J.J. laughed, but I knew him too well. I knew something big must be going down for the fat guy to want to see me personally.

"How should I dress?" I asked stupidly.

"Suit and tie, nothing fancy. We ain't going to a funeral. Pick me up by the building at ten o'clock."

"Sure, J.J." I said hanging up the phone suddenly feeling rejuvenated and alive again and feeling the need to run and exercise to clear my head.

Gail stood in the bedroom doorway shaking her head in pitying amazement as I tied up my jogging shoes, probably wondering "who is he now?" I didn't know myself anymore.

When J.J. and I walked into the restaurant on 60th street and 2nd Avenue the following morning, the fat guy (Anthony "Fat Tony" Salerno, boss of the Genovese Family) was already seated at a table smoking a cigar. He was a short, heavy-set elderly man in his late sixties, whose eyes were hard and penetrating, and were the only thing that set him apart from any other old man. Next to him sat a diminutive little man with an ancient, cadaverous face and wearing a dark beret. With a deep raspy voice he said, "How ya doing kid?"

J.J. introduced him as Funzi. (Frank "Funzi" Tieri, former boss and elder statesman of the Genovese Family) He was once a boss with the Genovese family but now, in the golden years of his life, reduced to the status of a roving ambassador; as the fat guy took over the reins and ran the day to day operations of the Family with the aid of Jaws, his under boss downtown, and Fish, his Captain. To my amazement, nothing of substance was spoken of. I became even more aware of just how much I did work on a "need to know" basis and how tenuous my position was. We talked baseball, when Funzi was not reminiscing, in an often-senile manner, about the old days with Luciano, Lansky, Frank Costello etc. Otherwise, we simply shared a nice quiet lunch with two grandfatherly gentlemen. Upon parting, the fat guy simply shook my hand saying, "Keep up the good work kid," and waddled out with what appeared to be a great deal of effort.

"Alright, J.J.," I said after ordering another cup of coffee for us both, "what the hell was that all about?"

J.J. leaned halfway across the table, "OL Blue Eyes," he whispered conspiratorially.

"Ol Blue Eyes? Ol Blue Eye--" my mouth fell open in total surprise. "Y-you don't mean...damn!" I laughed, shaking my head.

"Ain't nobody safe?"

"Yeah, that's why the fat guy wanted to get a good look at you first hand. This hit ain't sanctioned, it's a long-time personal beef. And the fact that there's been whispers that Frank's considering talking before some sub-committee about that Westchester Premiere Theater crap hasn't endeared him any further in the fat guy's eyes. He says if Frank wants to make a clean break once and for all with any ties to this life that is well and fine. But he ain't going out like that!"

"So why me?" something stunk here.

"As I said, this ain't sanctioned. So the fat guy can't use a made member or anybody connected to the Family. This is very dangerous, Joe. It's like killing a king? If there's even a whisper where it came from, we're both dead and so's the fat guy. Do you understand what I'm saying," J.J. asked in deadly earnest.

"Yeah, J.J. I understand. But what's the reason for keeping me alive afterward, even without a whisper, when I've become such a liability?" I grinned nastily. J.J. looked offended.

"It don't work like that, Joe. But one word and we'd never survive it," he repeated. We went outside for a walk up 2nd Avenue to finish our conversation.

"Does it bother you--I mean, who it is?" J.J. asked.

"No, Maybe it would have when I first started with you four years ago, if he'd been my first. B-but now he's just another guy. Does that sound crazy to you?"

"No", J.J. said softly, his eyes clouding over, no doubt recalling a much longer history than my own.

"It's beyond being personal, Joe, or for that matter about personalities. It's 'us' and 'them'. Frank's become 'them', simple as that." J.J.'s words made me wonder forebodingly, when "I" would become "them".

"Could you make him if you walked into a joint without having *seen* him before? We may not have time for that."

His question brought to vision the thousands of photos I'd seen of Sinatra since I was a kid: young, old, with hair and without.

"Yeah, I wouldn't have a problem with that."

"Well, here's the deal. He'll be in the city about the first week of September, for a quiet sit-down with the fat guy at 'The Sign of the Dove,' a classy restaurant and bar on 60th and 3rd Avenue. He should arrive between eight and eight-thirty in the evening, escorted by some legitimate stiff that owes the fat guy big time, but he goes too, know what I mean?" I simply nodded.

"Since you have two targets, what do you want to use?" J.J. asked.

"Well, I got a little sawed-off double barrel. Ain't no missing with that. And since I'll be close up, ain't no chance of either surviving. Two blasts should do it. But, I'll want a 9mm for backup in case things get hairy."

"You got it. We'll have time to see what the restaurant and traffic looks like around that time of evening, and also find a spot for me to set-up and wait. Your best move would be to walk out right behind them and hit them before they move in any direction."

"That's what I figured on doing."

For ten days I'd been running and doing calisthenics and test-firing both the double barrel and 9mm. I was cleaning them until they were squeaky clean. I was all yeasted up and ready to go. So naturally, I was totally crushed when on the big day, and after standing at the bar in "The

Sign of the Dove" for two hours, Ol Blue Eyes had taken ill and wouldn't make it.

"So much for our rendition of 'My Way', huh?" I smiled sickly at J.J., I could see that he was just as psychologically exhausted as I was.

**

The King Gets A Pass - June 1980

By mid-June of 1980 my cocaine habit was out of hand, though you couldn't tell me that. Gail had screamed, pleaded, and tried to wake me up to that reality on many occasions. Furthermore, the past few months, I had been getting the "silent treatment" which she knew infuriated me to no end. A gram of coke had become a mere one and one for me and when I reached the point of exhaustion after a two or three day binge, I'd need a Quaalude or a few valiums for a chaser if I had any designs on a nights sleep.

On those nights, I managed to find my way home. However the welcome mat to our bedroom was turned facedown and I was exiled to crash on the living room couch. Duke, Gail's dog and my former buddy and jogging partner, took up residence on my side of the bed. So much for a dog being a *man's* best friend. The treacherous bastard had become her co-conspirator and even *he* was giving me the cold shoulder. The coke had me so fucked up I started catching delusions on Duke for my sad state of affairs and started booting him around whenever Gail left for work in the mornings. Though not without a great deal of guilt and subsequent apologies in the form of special treats and bones. I wanted so desperately to reach out to Gail, to ease her pain as much as my own. I could see now deeply I had hurt her. It was all so obvious in her once bright, but now lackluster eyes, the slump of her shoulders and her absolute refusal to look my way. I knew I was killing whatever love and respect she once had for me. Such observations were only in my few remaining lucid moments. As no sooner did she leave the house, I'd be dipping in my plastic sandwich bag for breakfast. A hefty one and one, a half quart of orange juice and the world was a beautiful place. Only when I shaved did I have to look in the mirror and face the emaciated asshole glaring back at me in a most frightening manner: A semi-human apparition with tombstones for eyes.

Of late, even J.J. had begun to question me about my weight loss and lack of appetite, suggesting I see a doctor.

"I'm fine John, just fine." I assured him as we sat at a table in P.J. Clarke's, our usual haunt, to meet and talk in the late afternoons after the lunch hour crowd had thinned out. And, with the exception of Rocky

Graziano and Jake LaMotta at their regular corner table exchanging war stories and stirring the air with phantom left hooks and right hands from yester-year, the front room was empty with the exception of a few guys at the bar.

J.J. was impeccably dressed, as always; slacks, sport jacket and open-neck silk shirt, while I sat there slovenly in dungarees, windbreaker and applejack cocked jauntily on my head.

"Hey, take it easy, I'm just concerned about you, ok?" he said softly.

I hadn't realized I'd sounded so agitated or raised my voice.

"I'm sorry buddy," I said barely able to keep the hamburger down and took another sip from the frosted mug of Michelob.

It was a beautiful mid-June summer day, and the beer went down easy. "So, what's the deal? You sounded like you had something on your mind when you called last night?" I grinned my "who now?" smile at him.

"It's Frank again." He said quickly.

"Frank? Who's Fra--- oh shit! Not again!" I whispered as it dawned upon me who he meant.

"I thought that was history J.J.?"

"As did I, Joe. But it's obvious the fat guy is still worried about him with the hearings still going on and the feds looking to indict 'the Dome" and possibly fat Tony himself now that Funzy Tieri is dead."

"Who's the Dome? Never heard of him?"

"He's with us, Joe, a Capo with fat Tony, a few guy's were convicted last year of defrauding Westchester premiere investors by skimming the receipts for a Sinatra concert. Now it seems the feds are looking to indict Louis Pacella on some criminal conspiracy type shit. He's been in the can for contempt over a year now:"

"What's this got to do with Sinatra?" I asked, truly bewildered by all this machiavellian intrigue.

"Fat Tony feels he's shaky and has possibly been talking indirectly via secret meetings with prosecutors to the New York Federal Grand Jury. Hence, this possible up-coming indictment on Louie 'The Dome' Pacella and God knows where else it will lead, or to who else, including Tony."

"It's that bad, J.J.? He knows so much he could bring the whole house down?" I asked stupidly.

"You kidding? This fucking wannabe has been rubbing elbows with all the heavy weights since 1947. He was Luciano's mule in Havana when Lucky was in exile and got passed on to Frank Costello, Vito Genovese, Frank Tieri, and now fat Tony Salerino. He declared himself with the

Genovese family decades ago and now he's the fat guy's headache and basically that's the whole fuck'n deal, you got it?" J.J. grinned over the brim of his glass at my obvious confusion and consternation.

"Not really, J.J. How about all these other guy's he's suppose to have been in bed with over the years, such as Giancanna in Chicago or Carlo Gambino? Don't those family's inherit this responsibility also?"

"Not at all, Joe," J.J. shook his head definitely.

"Whatever any of those family's did with or for him was only at the sanction and blessing of the Genovese family to whom he was committed. So, as the saying goes, 'the buck stops here'."

"So, is this it," I smiled tiredly, "or just another dry run?"

"Could go either way, Joe. The fat guy doesn't want to have to whack this clown no more than you or I; the grief, too dangerous, too much fallout. As I told you last year, it's like killing a king. We'd get just as much heat if we whacked the Pope or the president. Believe me, nobody needs this, but if Frank can't convince Tony he'll ride off into the sunset quietly, he's dead meat, you with me?"

"You need to ask after five years together? What do you want me to do?"

"'Well, today's Friday," he said reaching in his pocket and peeling off eight one hundred dollar bills off a thick roll.

"What I need is for you to check into a hotel or motel and stay on call for me. Frank will be attending a wedding reception at the Westchester Country Club tomorrow evening and will be brought down to the Social Club to see Tony."

"The one on 117th street and 1st Avenue?" I interrupted, as we had used it before.

"That's it, perfect spot if we got to take him out. We'll set up the same way we did for the last guy, ok?"

"No problem. What time you want me to call? What should I bring?"

"Nothing heavy, he's an old man. Ya still got the .22 automatic with the silencer?"

"Yeah, and I also have the Browning 9mm you gave me last month. It's still clean!" I laughed good-naturedly.

"With you, one never knows," he smiled.

"Well, give me a call at eight tomorrow night. I should know the deal by then."

Friday evening I had Theresa rent a room at the Golden Gate motel in Sheepshead Bay (a wise guy hide-away) where everybody took their girlfriends to get laid on the weekends. Theresa was a beautiful girl and at twenty-six years of age had a long-legged slamming body set off by thick shoulder length black hair and an olive complexion. And though not a rocket -scientist by any stretch of the imagination, she was earthly and street-wise. She also had a closed-mouth; covering things she had witnessed (aside from family business) which were many. Had I not loved my wife Gail so deeply and adored my son Ramsey (though it was hard to tell by my actions), Theresa and I might have hooked up permanently. My good friends and stick-up partners were Theresa's brother-in-laws, married to her sisters Marie and Toni. Both Stevie Catalanotte and Joey Martin were always telling me,

"Stay away from Terry. She's a fuck'n nut!"

But, in the mid 70's with the Disco's jumping and cocaine flowing freely we were all wild and crazy in our own manner. While it would be so easy to lay the blame for my philandering ways on her doorstep, I cannot do that. Theresa might not have been good *for* me but she was good *to* me.

Before even going to the room that Friday evening, we drove to the "Shanty," a clam joint on Emmons Avenue in Sheepshead Bay, where we sat looking toward the water, an old wooden footbridge leading to Manhattan Beach on the far side. The baked clams were delicious, and ironically the walls were covered with a collage of prints depicting Ol' Blue Eyes himself in different poses and settings. On the way over, I had ran the deal down to her. Not for whom I was doing this or with who, but just the simple fact that he might be history in a short while and things could get real hairy for me should certain people decide I had suddenly become expendable.

"How can you kill that nice old man?" she whispered and I looked up from my clams to catch her still gazing at the photos.

"It bothers you?" I asked.

"Why shouldn't it? He don't bother nobody!"

"Depends on where you're sitting, Theresa. Some people see it differently."

"B-but he's a great singer.... a-an-icon." she protested weakly.

"That's the Italian in you, Theresa. Sure he's a great singer, but suppose he was a great Italian plumber or electrician, would you feel the same emotions?" I grinned.

"Fuck you.....you Irish bastard." she laughed.

"Good idea!" I grinned rising from the table.

"Let's go back to the motel, take a quick dip in the pool out back then see if we can't overcome this coke in my system, what do ya say?"

"Impossible," she said in a derisive voice.

"Nothing is impossible my dear you just have to work diligently. What the fuck! If J.C. could raise Lazarus from the dead, surely you are capable of performing a minor miracle such as this, huh?"

"You really are a piece of work, you know that don't you? But hell, let's go see what we can do," she laughed, "anything's possible."

We checked out of the Golden Gate around twelve the following day and stopped by the apartment on Avenue "X", where she lived with her mother, to get a change of clothes and pick up the tools I would need. Before heading into the city, we stopped at "Joe's" on Avenue "U" and McDonald Avenue and devoured a huge platter of soup da mussels and a side order of rice balls, the best clam joint in the five boroughs.

About 4 o'clock that afternoon, Theresa checked into the Skyline Motor Inn on 10th Avenue and 50th street, while I waited in the car. When she came out I drove into the under-ground garage and we took the elevator up to our room on the second floor where I wasted no time calling J.J. at his apartment on Columbus Circle just a half dozen blocks away. J.J. didn't want to talk but simply said he was on his way out to see Jilly, in his joint. (Jilly's Bar: a club in mid-town owned by Jilly Rizzo, long time friend and half-assed body-guard for Sinatra. More importantly a long time affiliate of the Genovese crime family) and that I should call back at eight that evening.

"Perfect spot you picked," he said before hanging up.

I was in a dead sleep when the phone rang at eight.

"Yeah?" I answered, glancing at Theresa who sat scrunched against the headboard of the bed. She had been watching T.V. but now her eyes looked big as saucers as she watched me like a man on death row hoping for a stay of execution.

"It's on." J.J. said almost casually, though I could detect the strain of tension in those two words.

"Pick me up in front of Lincoln Center at nine. I'll fill you in on the way uptown, you all right?"

"Yeah J.J., I'm all set. See you later."

"Well, what's going on?" Theresa asked nervously pacing in front of the bed as I walked to the bathroom to throw cold-water on my face and toot a one and one for a wake-up.

"What's going on?" I called from the bathroom.

"It's show time!"

"Show time?" she damn near shrieked.

"What are you, fucking crazy? What am I suppose to do here? When will you be back?"

"Theresa," I said softly, but firmly.

"Relax, I don't need you like this. What are you suppose to do? Absolutely nothing, but wait here. And, if you can't do that, you can take a cab home now."

"W...when will you be back?" her voice trembled, but she was bringing herself under control.

"Take it easy, huh?" I said putting my hands on her shoulders looking into her eyes.

"Everything will be fine. I should be back by twelve at the latest. If I'm not back by two, grab a cab and go home, okay?" I hugged her, patting her on the back.

"Just like that, huh?" she laughed nervously.

"Yeah Baby, just like that. Hey, you ain't gonna wish me to 'break a leg' or something?" I said putting on my windbreaker and apple-jack while heading for the door.

"Yeah," she sighed, "break a leg, ya Irish asshole, but just get back by twelve."

I took the elevator down to the garage and walked to the right far corner where I had parked in the shadows and out of line of the security camera. I quickly grabbed the legitimate dealer plates from under the back seat and slapped them over my front and rear license plates. I pulled the trunk open and took both pieces out, tucking the 9mm inside my belt at the small of my back and slid the .22 automatic in the front of my waist pocketing the silencer. As I rolled out of the garage and up the ramp onto 10th Avenue, I could feel the adrenaline kicking in. I was ready for a bear and from whatever direction it chose to come my way. J.J. had his game face on, and was dressed casually; dress slacks, Bally shoes, and a pale yellow sport shirt beneath a dark windbreaker. As he slid into the passenger seat he told me to hook a right up to 72nd street and cut through Central Park where we'd take 3rd Avenue uptown to East Harlem. I drove carefully as I always did when we were loaded for bear, not wanting to run a light or get pulled over for some minor violation. I kept my silence, glancing occasionally at J.J. as he sat stiffly erect in the passenger seat, his washed-out steely blue eyes staring off into space as he gathered his thoughts.

"It's a quarter to nine," J.J. barely whispered as I turned up 3rd Avenue. "Jilly Rizzo will be bringing Frank from the wedding reception in Westchester to Rao's, on 116th Street and pleasant Avenue. They'll have a few drinks and at that point one of Tony's guys, probably Fish, will whisper in his ear that the Fat guy wants to see Frank alone and that Jilly should wait outside in the car."

"Does this Jilly know what's going down, J.J.?"

"No, all he knows is he has orders to bring Frank for this 'sit-down.'"

"And, if Frank goes down?" I asked.

"In that case Jilly goes down too. I'll go outside and tell Jilly that Tony wants to see him for a moment. But, Tony will already have left via the side entrance on 114th Street, and Jilly will precede me through the second door, and when he does you clip him, you got it?"

"No problem. Do we set up the same as before?" We had used the social club located on 1st Avenue between 114th and 115th streets, a few times before.

"Yeah." J.J. said, as I parked the car just off 1st Avenue and 117th street. As we walked the few blocks down 1st Avenue, I was relieved to see it was pretty well deserted with the exception of a dozen or so Puerto Rican kids hanging out smoking joints, drinking beer and listening to some salsa shit on a boom box. The club itself was actually a dingy, morbid fuck'n place. J.J. and I laughingly referred to it as the "Black Flag Roach Motel," whose T.V. advertisement was, "they get in, but they don't get out." It was located on the ground floor of an equally squalid tenement building that permeated the eternal smell of Rice and Beans emanating from the apartments above.

The storefront size window was either painted black or had fifty years of cockroach shit on it, either way no passers-by could see inside. Though in any event the front room held nothing but empty soda cans, assorted garbage, used tires, etc. As we passed through both the first and second doors, they locked behind us which, in itself, made a sound of finality that never failed to send a shiver up my spine. As I followed J.J. through the second door to the inner sanctum, the first thing I saw was "Fat Tony" sitting at the huge round green-felt card table which took up most of the 30x30 square foot room, sipping a cup of espresso, and holding the chewed up butt of a long-dead cigar in his right hand. Directly behind Tony, to his right, was a small bar with a big silver espresso machine atop it with the only other decorative piece being a 30-year-old refrigerator parked against the right hand wall. It was parked in front of a dark narrow passageway which ran about thirty feet and harbored a side-door that you could only find by feel, but would first have to know of its existence.

"John." Tony nodded.

"Good to see ya kid!" he growled in that deep raspy voice but not without an appreciative grin.

"We ain't got much time, just got a ring on my cell telling me they just left and should arrive in about five minutes. Hopefully I can put the fear of God into this arrogant cock-sucker:"

"Damn, Tony," I couldn't resist the pun, "the fuck'n guy may have a massive coronary before he gets through the second door! I get goose-bumps just walking in here, and I ain't no virgin to this shit." I smiled as both Tony and J.J. cracked up with laughter.

"That's the whole idea, kid." he grinned devilishly.

"Now, here's what I want you to do." he said.

I took up position crouched behind the refrigerator at the entrance of the passage-way pulling down the black stocking I had rolled up under the brim of my apple-jack, surgical gloves on and .22 automatic in hand with the silencer attached and safety off as Tony had suggested. J.J. was directly across the four-foot wide passageway in a door less bathroom that featured a shit-bowl and sink and was comparable to that on a Greyhound bus. Just as Tony poured two espressos and set them on the table I heard the outer street door click clearly behind whoever had entered. Then a mumbled curse as he stumbled in the darkness. "T…Tony, y…y…you in there?" Came a trembling falsetto voice.

Tony waited about 10 seconds before answering.

"Yeah Frank, come on in," said the spider to the fly, I thought, suppressing a chuckle as I looked across at J.J. who was also getting a kick out of this.

Looking through the opening between the refrigerator and wall, I was taken back by the old, bald-headed, and frightened looking figure that entered the room. Only the "eyes" were familiar to me.

"Jesus Christ, T-Tony," his voice trembled with false bravado.

"Couldn't you find a place with a little more ambience." he said and set Tony off.

"You want ambience, you cock sucker?" Tony screamed slamming his right hand on the table.

"I'll give you ambience in a pine box, ya rat bastard! Now sit the fuck down and enjoy the espresso."

"T-Tony, what's wrong?" Frank stammered damn near in tears.

"I'd never hurt you or the family. I.. ….."

"Where were ya last year when I called ya to the Sign of the Dove?" his voice became soft and deadly.

"You could have had your fuck'n ambience there."

"I-I sent word Tony, I was sick, I just couldn't make it...."

"You couldn't make it, huh?" Tony hissed leaning across the table on his forearms like a barely restrained Pitt-Bull.

"Let me tell ya something, ya little pimp...I'm not MoMo in Chicago or any of those other cock suckers you're used to dealing with. I don't want your rubber-holes or comp at those whorehouses in Vegas! The next time I send for ya, I don't give a fuck if they have to medi-vac ya, ya come, ya come. Just like ya run when them federal prosecutors call ya for those back room meetings and closed door hearings. And, if next time ya don't come, I'll personally chop ya fuck'n head off...."

"Tony... I...."

"Don't Tony me, Frank. We got three or four guy's in the can and my guy 'The Dome,' facing criminal charges over that Westchester shit and I ain't going to let him go down because you can't stand up," he snarled.

"I've said nothing, Tony, nothing, I swear it!"

"Is that right?" asked Tony in a whisper.

"How I hear it is, ya broke down and cried like a bitch in one of those hearings last year?"

Frank was ghostly white and aging by the second as the realization of his immediate dilemma seeped in.

"I...." his shoulders sagged in resignation, "I lost control of my emotions Tony, they started talking about Dolly, my mother, her death was all too fresh in my mind, I..."

"I believe ya, Frank, and ya always had my sympathy. But, you have ta understand my position and we've got-ta reach an understanding before we leave this room, ya get the drift, Frank?" Tony asked kindly.

"I understand, Tony." Frank barely whispered slumped in the chair, the sweat glistening on his baldhead and running in rivulets down his craggy face.

"How long ya been on the family tit, Frank?" "

"Ha...I don't understand?"

"You know? Lucky.... Frank....Vito....Funzy, it's got to be thirty-thirty-five years now, huh? We've always been there to pick your sorry ass up, Frank. You've always wanted to be a tough-guy and we legitimized that image also. But, that was our mistake..." Tony sighed heavily leaning back in his chair, hands folded on his big belly as he stared at Frank.

"Do you know what a real tough-guy is, Frank?" he asked softly.

"No. Don't try to tell me..." he held up his hand silencing Frank.

"I'll tell you. It ain't about them Bensonhurst Disco-Ducks you see running around preening and posturing with a neck full of loud gold-chains and a mouth to match 'em. Dem bum's are a dime a dozen and can't stand the thought of doing a year when it comes time to stand up. When a tough-guy shits in his pants, he sits in it alone Frank, no whining, no crying, no finger pointing, and above all, no regrets! Because, he knew the deal, when he sat down and asked to be dealt in. Do you believe in the code of Omerta, Frank?"

Upon those words I stepped from behind the refrigerator in the semi-darkness of the hallway and ratcheted a slug into the chamber that was deafening in the eerie silence of the room, and simply stood there like the grim reaper. The gun was down at my side as if simply awaiting his answer, which we were.

Frank's horror was instantaneous as he pushed back in his chair and jumped up his hands out imploringly, the tears coursing down his worn and weary face.

"I--I'd never hurt you Tony! I'd never hurt anybody."

A long 20 seconds passed as Tony watched Frank squirm impassively. "Do ya want to see your 65th birthday, Frank?"

"Y--yes," he sobbed.

"Please Tony, please! You've got to believe I'd never hurt you! I'd go to the can for a year, a hundred years before I'd do that!" he cried, his eyes locked on the ghastly apparition I must have presented.

"You're looking at the wrong guy, Frank. He can't save ya. Again I ask, do you believe in our code of Omerta?"

"Yes, Yes, I always have." he gagged, falling to his knees in supplication, a broken man.

I stepped back into the dark hallway as Tony motioned me away behind his back. He spent the next ten minutes comforting Frank, and putting cold rags on his face and eyes, trying to make him presentable to leave.

"I believe you, Frank. I believe you, and I'm going give ya a pass. But, I want you to walk away from all involved in this life and live quietly, ya understand? Be a nice guy, do good things, people love ya. Ya did a nice thing here tonight." Tony smiled patting his back as he led him to the door.

"Huh?" Frank mumbled in a stupor of fear. "W--what was that?"

"Ya saved your friend's life, Frank."

The implication finally dawned upon him.

"My--my friend? Y--you mean, Jilly? Oh, thank God." he whispered.

"God ain't got a fuck'n thing to do with it, Frank. Thank me," he grinned.

"Thank you, Tony. Thank you," he whined with reverence, as he slipped out the inner door of hell and ran to freedom.

After a few beers in Emily's Pub on the west side, I dropped J.J. off at his apartment and headed back to the Skyline motel. But, not before stopping at a pay phone.

"Gail? You and Ram all right?" I asked in a thick emotional voice laden with guilt. Although she wasn't talking to me at the moment she could always sense my distress signals.

"Joe? Where are you? When will you be home?"

"I love you Gail," I managed to croak. "I'll be home in the morning."

When I walked into the motel room Theresa jumped off the bed and hugged me.

"God, I'm so relieved you're all right. Uh, how about, you-know-who?" she looked in my eyes.

"He's just fine, Theresa."

"Oh thank God," she whispered in relief.

"No, thank Tony!" I laughed.

"Huh? What are ya talking about?" she said, looking at me as if I were crazy.

"Nothing, Theresa. Just a bad joke, just a bad joke. Let's go to sleep, huh?"

***

A Big Banana To Peel - April 17, 1980

I had been sailing along pretty good for months after the near-encounter with Ol' Blue Eyes. I was trying to limit my addictions to weekends by keeping myself occupied with my son Ramsey during the days Gail worked--much to his joy and more so to my own. We had a pretty busy summer schedule. When I wasn't taking him for rides in a little red wagon we had bought him for Christmas, we were going on little safaris though Forest Park; climbing hills and exploring the different narrow paths, that led us through the woods for hours on end. When we would finally re-enter civilization, the day was not complete until we went to the candy store and bought a cold Yoo-Hoo soda and a fistful of big, salty pretzels, which we'd carry with us across Forest Park Drive to the base of the monument of the "The Unknown Solider." We would bask happily in the sun, sipping our chocolate Yoo-Hoo and munching on our pretzels, talking about our latest trip into the jungle. We simply enjoyed our time together. He loved the park, but my son's favorite trips were those that we'd take on my bike to

Rockaway Beach thirteen miles away, with him directing me and the traffic from the basket seat behind me. I was "Popeye," and his personal chauffeur. The trips to Rockaway Beach were also my favorite, as I've never had a greater time or laughed harder than I did when watching him tumble in the big waves where I'd throw him time and again, snatching him up quickly and hugging him to me as he choked and spit out seaweed, and looked up at me for approval of his latest feat, his eyes full of love and trusting admiration. And why shouldn't there have been? I was "Popeye" and would always be there for him.

It was times such as these that I would often suddenly become overwhelmed with emotion and fear because of the precarious position I had put my family in. All I could do, though, was hold his wet, warm little body to my own and tell him--or myself, "Popeye's a little messed up right now, Champ."

The words would choke out of me as he wrapped his arms around my neck for the trip back to the boardwalk, where our bike was parked, "but he's going to be all right, we're all going to be all right." That was just another broken promise.

Late one evening in April 1980, I was half in the tank from too many Bud Lights, and was trying to keep my eyes open in the bottom half of the ninth inning, with the Yanks coming up in a tie game, when the phone crashed through my stupor.

"Yeah, who is it?" I asked, my voice nasty and suggesting that the caller better have a good reason for dialing this number at such an ungodly hour.

"J.J.?" I was surprised. He never called after eleven.

"You still up? Get some sleep! You got to meet me by my building by eight, we got a big banana to peel." His voice was tense.

"Should I bring anything?" I suggested, not knowing who or what the problem was.

"No, no, everything will be here. But be sure to give yourself plenty of time, I don't want you getting caught in traffic. This is too important, okay?"

"Don't worry, J.J., I'll be there," I promised.

I caught the light coming off the ramp of the 59th Street Bridge and headed cross-town to the West Side. I had made good time in Queens.

J.J. was standing at the curb in front of his building when I pulled up, and by the look on his face when he slid in, I knew there was some serious shit about to go down.

"Where to, buddy? What's up?" I said lightly, attempting to ease the tension in him.

He was wearing a floppy sun-hat and shades, with a light windbreaker and dungarees. I was dressed basically the same, minus the sunglasses and with a pair of jogging shoes while he was wearing some fancy loafers.

"The produce store on First Avenue. Fish said he'd meet us there. This is a big one. Remember Angelo Bruno in Philly?"

"Yeah, he got whacked last year, right?"

"Right. He was killed on orders from his own friend and consigliere, Anthony Carpozo, AKA Tony Bananas."

"Sounds like something to eat," I laughed, but J.J. wasn't in a laughing mood.

"We're gonna eat him all right! Angelo Bruno was boss in Philly for twenty-five years, and a close friend of the fat guy. Tony Bananas whacked Bruno without sanction from the Commission and has taken over in Philly for the past year. But Philly's always answered to New York. He's finally realized his hold is a very tentative one, and that he's got to fall in line. So he reached out to the fat guy, who told him to come in and sit down. No sense having a war when this could be ironed out. Just Tony Bananas and the fat guy are supposed to sit down this morning in the social club across First Avenue from the produce store." J.J. answered

I pulled into a parking spot across the street from a junior high on 114th and 11th Avenue. We were a block away from the social club and store, in an area that was basically a Spanish Barrio.

Fish was pacing the back room nervously when we walked in, sweating profusely though it was cool spring day.

"What time will they be here?" J.J. was all business.

"Should be about 10:30. I just got a call from the fat guy, told me they were on their way and that Tony Bananas' driver would continue downtown to have lunch with Jaws," he grinned.

"Jaws all set down there?"

"Yeah, J.J., no problem. You wanna take a look downstairs?"

J.J. nodded and we all walked outside. Fish looked nervously in both directions before leading us around the corner by a little candy store where the fat guy would sit outside on summer days holding court for the steady trickle of visitors who came to pay homage, ask favors, etc. But court was in recess this morning.

The steel cellar door in the sidewalk creaked eerily on its rusty hinges as Fish pulled it upward, revealing a dark, narrow cobwebbed stairway leading down into the cellar.

"The light's at the bottom of the stairs on the right wall," Fish said. I reflexively started down with Fish behind me, and instantly regretted it. I felt a shiver run up my spine--shit! Was this charade really meant for me? Had I outlived my usefulness and become a liability? It was too late if I had made a mistake!

Spitting cobwebs out of my mouth, I ran my hand up the crumbling cement wall and hit the switch. I immediately spotted two open freezers to my left with meat-hooks on the wall, and spun around, only to see J.J. with a wide grin on his face, knowing what had been going through my mind-cocksucker!

"In there," Fish pointed to a freezer on the left, lit only by a single dim light bulb dangling from an extension cord that hung from the ceiling.

J.J. went to a huge wooden rain barrel and opened up a heavy-duty garbage bag inside.

"Take your pick, Joe. It's your show."

"You say this guy, Bananas, is real big, J.J.?"

"Big? He's a fucking gorilla! Belongs in a zoo, right Fish?"

"Uh, oh yeah. He's a monster!" Fish suddenly shuddered.

I settled on a .45 caliber Mac-11 with a lightweight 18-inch silencer, the first I had ever seen on an automatic weapon. When I slapped in a clip and squeezed a short burst into some sacks of potatoes, I was pleasantly surprised by the soft, dull thumping sound the weapon emitted. Putting in a new clip and clicking the safety on, I placed it in a long cardboard box along with the .22 automatic and silencer that J.J. had picked for back up.

"Bring the box across to the club," J.J. ordered Fish.

"People are used to seeing you come and go, but we're out of place here."

"You're right," Fish nodded.

"Follow me over in about five minutes."

"Damn, J.J.!" I exclaimed upon entering the social club.

"This joint's like a Black Flag Roach Motel!" We both laughed and shuddered when I heard the two doors click locked behind me.

"You get in but don't get out, huh?"

"That's the idea--a fucking death trap!" J.J. laughed.

It was all of that, I mused. Between the first door leading into the club off First Avenue and the second door, there was a small, semi-dark room filled with empty beer and soda cases, a few bicycles and other assorted crap. When I stepped through the second door, the first thing that caught my eye was a huge, circular card table that took up a great portion of the middle of the room. Along the wall to my right, stood a refrigerator. In the corner to the left, along the rear wall was a small bar with a cappuccino machine atop it. Stepping past the refrigerator, I noticed a small bathroom to my left. A dark, narrow passageway led to the rear of the building where I spotted a crease of sunlight filtering in under the door.

"Where's this lead to, J.J.?"

"Right out onto 115th Street," he whispered into my ear.

"Where do you want to set up?"

"Well, once he's through that second door he's in for keeps." I said, removing all but two folding chairs from the card table, and arranging those two on opposite sides, facing each other. I wanted it to look official, to give his first impression a sense of legitimacy--just him and the fat guy.

"Fish, when you usher him in, relax him. Offer him coffee; tell him to take his jacket off. I'll be squatting right here behind the fridge," I said, taking up my position and telling J.J. to go in the bathroom directly across form where I squatted.

"Let's give this a dry run, Fish. Go outside and wait a minute before you come back in, and don't make anymore noise than you normally would." With J.J. across from where I squatted with the Mac-11 and silencer in my right hand pointed upward, I told J.J. I had a clear view of both doors between the fridge and the wall but I'd be blind once he reached the table.

"Listen, if he sits down, Fish will have a chance to walk out before the shit hits the fan. If Bananas decides to inspect the premises, I'll hit him with the whole clip as soon as he steps into view, so stay down on one knee. If he sits, I'll peep out, holding my left hand, and I'll drop it only when I'm ready to move, okay?" I explained.

I could see the strain on J.J.'s face; he wasn't getting any younger. In the past I had always kept him out of these kinds of situations.

"Hey, it ain't necessary for you to be here, J.J.," I smiled, having no doubt he was hell on wheels in his time.

"This is fine. This is perfect, don't worry," he grinned as we heard Fish come through both doors perfectly clear.

"S-say, g-give me a chance to get out the front door before you open fire, will ya?" Fish muttered shakily.

"Don't worry. How much time you figure we got?" I asked as we all checked our watches.

"Figure on twenty minutes, maybe less. You guys want some coffee?" he said, relieved when both J.J. and me nodded negatively. He couldn't get away from us fast enough.

"So that's a capo, huh?"

"A sign of the times, Joe." J.J. responded.

"And where's the fat guy?"

"On his horse ranch upstate!" J.J. laughed.

"And the driver, Tony Bananas' man, he really expects to have lunch with Jaws downtown?"

"He won't see Jaws, no more than Tony Bananas will see the fat guy. They are lunch," J.J. said lazily, his back to the doorjamb leading to the bathroom, facing me where I sat behind the fridge, the piece cradled straight up between my knees. Should be any minute now! I looked over to J.J., and he seemed to be aging before my eyes.

"How have you done it all these years, J.J.?" I have never felt closer to him than at that moment. He was like my surrogate father, and I think he realized it.

"I'm so tired, J.J. Not physically, just so weary inside. You're the only reason I'm here. Four years...seems like a lifetime."

"I know," he stared thoughtfully, "but you'll be on your way to California soon. You've paid your dues and have all our blessings. You know that, don't you?" he smiled sincerely. "A fucking movie star, huh?" he teased.

"Naw!" I felt embarrassed. "I just want to get away, do something decent, meaningful. I'm dying inside, J.J. How long we been together, three, four years? Remember how I thought this was all a big game, how excited I'd get? It was never the killing that I liked, J.J., it was always the challenge, the hunt. But I realize now that this life is a never-ending senseless war, where today's friends are tomorrow's enemies- targets! When I can sit here like I'm waiting to give this guy a telegram or slice of pizza when he walks in, then something's wrong. I--"

Click. The door! Showtime!

We both came to one knee simultaneously, easing the safeties off on our weapons.

Peering between the back of the fridge and the wall, my fucking eyeball almost popped out of my head when the inner door opened and the "beast" stepped in, with Fish right behind him. "Tough Tony Galento" was the first image that came to mind, the raging three hundred pound bull who had fought Joe Louis for the heavyweight championship. This animal was his clone facially, from the thinning hair and meaty lips to the brutal look. And bodily, in the sense that he was as wide as he was tall, about 5' 10" and between 280 pounds and three bills! He had on a tan sports jacket and a white, open-necked shirt, from which a thick profusion of black hair spilled over his collar.

Fish could have won an Oscar. J.J. and I smiled our approval of his performance.

"God, it's hot in here!" Fish complained. The beast just grunted his agreement.

"C'mon, sit down, take your jacket off. The fat guy will be right over. Whadda ya want? Danish? Coffee?"

"Yeah, Danish," the guttural voice rasped.

"Make the coffee black."

"You got it," Fish said amiably. "Be right back."

As the inner door closed I nodded to J.J., raising my left hand as I peeped around the front of the refrigerator. Tony Bananas had already removed his jacket and was placing it over the back of the chair, facing me as I dropped my hand and stepped out quietly. About fifteen feet stood between us.

"Hey, Tony," I called softly. Without hesitation he reacted, recognizing that he was a dead man. He growled deep in his chest like a bull moose, lowered his head, and charged instinctively. I stood my ground and hit him with a ten round burst high in the chest, watching his shirt shred as he went reeling back against the wall. I took two quick steps forward and fired a second burst as he roared in pain, and had begun another attempt to charge. This blast put him at the back of the wall, and I watched as his eyes rolled back in his head and he slid slowly along the wall to his left, leaving a bright red smear as he went. I hit him with the rest of the thirty round clip as he crumpled in the corner in a broken heap, his legs twisted oddly beneath him, his chin on his chest, wheezing out his final death song.

"Kill him!" J.J. hissed, popping two shots at him over my shoulder.

"Jeez, give the guy a few seconds to die, huh?" I whispered in awe. I had never seen a guy die tougher than this, and was thankful I had chosen the weapon I did. Any less firepower and *we'd* have been lunch!

As planned, we left our weapons right there for the clean-up crew, and walked through the dark hallway and out into the spring sunshine. "What a beautiful day to be among the living," I thought as Fish came jogging around the corner, breathing heavily.

"Just called the fat guy. Everything went fine downtown. Everything all right here?" he asked J.J.

"Yeah, your guys got some mess to clean up, and a lot of plastering and painting to do."

"No problem--no problem," said the capo, in full control.

J.J. told me a few days later that Fish was whining to the fat guy, "The fucking kid almost killed me! I wasn't two steps outside the door when half a dozen slugs came through the window. The kid's crazy!"

"He ain't crazy, you're slow," the fat guy had simply replied with his deadpan look.

***

Kelly R. Sullivan – 11 February 1981

I was snorting greater amounts of cocaine than ever. A gram was good for a one-and-one, and for chasers, just to sleep; I'd need a half-quart of booze and a few Valium.

Stevie, and his brother-in-law Joey M., were just as fucked up on heroin as Marco and I were on the nose-candy. We were sticking up everyone and anything. "The Four Blind Mice" we had become.

Gail was pregnant again, and bigger than when she gave birth to our son, Ramsey. We had been arguing, of course, over my ways and cocaine habit that made me ill tempered and very hard to live with. I knew deep in my heart that Gail was right, but cocaine leaves no room for common sense, love, understanding, or anything else. I used whatever excuse I could find as a selfish opportunity to move some of my clothes out of the house and stay away. I could do my thing unchecked and uncensored. I used to sit in Stevie's house night after night, when I wasn't home but was living with his sister-in-law at her mother's apartment in Brooklyn, speaking in a maudlin manner about where all this insanity was leading us. Maria, Stevie's wife, a sweetheart of a woman but never one to bite her tongue, would simply look at us and say time and again, "You're all fucking crazy. Do you know that?" And whenever I'd speak of Gail being pregnant and expecting any day, she'd just look at me and say, "Joe, I love my sister Terry, but I also happen to like and respect Gail. You know where you belong, so don't get me involved in this!"

Stevie would just look at me, throw up his hands and smile as if to say, "I'm out of this!"

Even Theresa's mother, who was as close with her daughter as a mother can be, while knowing I cared about Theresa and treated her well, knew I loved my wife and son and could never leave them. On occasion, she'd look at me wistfully when I was in my quiet moods and say, "Joe, you're a grown man, you have to make your own decisions, ones that are right and that you can live with." Otherwise, she was very sensitive and respectful of other people's personal affairs and did not voice her opinion one way or another.

I knew where I belonged but I also knew Theresa wasn't going to let go so easily after all these months. The cocaine made it easier to deal with the situation I didn't know how to walk away from, because I don't like to hurt people and yet I knew my place was with my wife because it was her that I loved. Doing cocaine let me stay in limbo. I didn't have to hurt anyone but myself, I thought. Yet, in the end, I hurt everyone.

One day I was sitting at the kitchen table at Stevie's and called home to see how Gail was feeling, the guilt and thoughts of her and Ram never ceased to follow me. Gail's mom, whom I loved like the mother I never really had, answered the phone an in a very cool voice told me that Gail was in Booth Memorial Hospital in Queens, waiting to give birth to our second child.

"Oh no! Oh, Gail!" my heart cried out as I hung up the phone. I was completely disorientated.

"I-It's Gail, she's in the hospital. I got to go," I mumbled almost incoherently, while Stevie and Maria nodded their affirmation of support.

"Why am I hurting so many decent people? Where did it all start? Why am I so selfish and so devious?" I thought, lowering my eyes from theirs and rushing out the door.

Minutes later I was making my way through the drifts of snow on the Belt-Parkway leading to Queens, and Booth Memorial.

I left my car in the back of a diner across the street and raced through the hospital doors and up the steps to the maternity floor, gasping for breath in the doorway just as they wheeled Gail into the hallway on the way to the delivery room. I felt like a little boy approaching the gurney she lie on, and could not contain pent-up feelings when she looked up at me in happiness, her big, brown eyes filled with love--after all the heartache I had caused her. "I'm sorry, Gail. I'm s-sorry, honey. Are you okay?" I slobbered, tasting the salt of my tears unashamedly.

"I'm glad y-you're here, Joe," she smiled through her pain.

"I--I'll be right outside the door, honey. I'm not going anywhere."

After what seemed no longer than two minutes but could have been hours, one of the delivery room nurses poked her head out the door.

"Mr. Sullivan, if you'd like to watch your wife give birth, it would be all right if you stood just inside the door here. Would you like that?" her eyes glimmered mischievously above her mask.

"I, uh, s-sure!" I stuttered and smiled weakly.

I stepped inside the slightly opened door and saw Gail, her head turned towards me, a look upon her face that needed no words to tell me where I belonged.

Dr. Immerman bent over her to perform a second c-section, and I almost fainted. What seemed like only moments later, he lifted my second son from her belly and held the wrinkled bundle of pink flesh up for my inspection. All I could manage was to stand there and gaze in open-mouthed awe at the result of the age-old miracle I had just witnessed.

The nurse stopped the gurney momentarily in front of me, in the process of taking Gail to a room she shared with another women who had given birth the day before.

"Another boy, Sully. Do you mind?" she smiled tiredly.

I felt so sick of my even sicker make-believe life.

"I love you, Gail. Whatever else, I love you." Her eyes told me that she knew I spoke the truth. And I knew that her greatest hurt was that she couldn't help me, but could only stand by and watch me killing myself, while she brought our second son into the world.

Gail came home from the hospital a few days after giving birth to our newborn son, but Kelly had to remain an extra three days to be treated for a touch of jaundice. The doctor told me that this was a common ailment in newborns, but for some reason I still felt responsible. So while Gail rested and regained her strength, I'd go to the hospital in the evenings. I'd sit in an old fashioned rocking chair the nurses were so nice to provide. I'd sit with Kelly for a few hours, rocking back and forth while I informed him of my sad state of affairs, and how his big brother, Ramsey, now four years old, was anxiously awaiting his homecoming.

It was in those quiet hours of solitude that I felt and sensed a terrible finality about my own future, though I had already made up my mind that I was going to stop seeing Stevie's sister-in-law, Theresa. J.J. already knew that I needed to get away from it all.

I stayed close to the house for almost two months, taking advantage of the winter snow by going sleigh riding with Ramsey on the little hills and slopes in Forest Park, only three blocks away from the house in Richmond Hill. I was feeling human again, both mentally and physically. I didn't miss the cocaine, alcohol, or the insanity that gave birth to these vices--crutches really that served to enforce my belief that everything I was doing in my life was just fine and allowed me to accept my distorted priorities.

***

The Hammer Fell

Then the final hammer fell at a time when my weak and tender psyche was striving to make a comeback. I feel, in hindsight, it was the most significant factor in finally leading me to do some terrible and foolish things, things that I knew in my heart would hasten my downfall and allow me to escape the problems and responsibilities I did not know how to handle. Putting myself in a position where I was forced to go "on the run" somehow was a more comforting thought than facing my personal life. I was not forthright and honest enough with myself, my wife, or Theresa, to deal with it in a sensible and civil manner, as hard as that may have been. But then, I've never had a medium where problem solving was concerned. I had spent all my life in prison, where options were extremely limited. Actually, there were always only two: you either kill the problem or you run away from it. I chose the latter for the first time.

Theresa was a beautiful girl and a good woman in her own right, and was undeserving of my classical method of solving problems. Although I never seem to mean harm (the story of my life), I played with her heart, her hopes and her dreams as I've done with so many people who have placed faith and trust in me. Theresa was young, twenty-three, while I was forty-two years old. She was a dark, lithesome beauty who did wonders for my vanity and ego. And unlike my wife, she never questioned my actions or the direction my life was taking, she was just along for the ride. With my increasing coke habit, I thought I could have my cake and eat it too! After all, she was part of my "coke life," nothing more. I was the exception to life's ridiculous protocol- it didn't apply to me. It never does, or it never appears to, until my sins are staring me in the face, as happened one spring morning late in April.

I was lying in bed around 9:30 one morning, trying to decide whether to simply roll over and catch a few more hours of sleep or go see the movie "Popeye" with Ramsey. It was playing in Forest Hills. Popeye won, and I got up and made a quick cup of coffee, after yelling upstairs to Gail's mother to get Ramsey ready. Then the phone rang.

"Joe?" It was Theresa. The blood surged to my temples.

"I thought I told you never to call here!" I could barely control my anger.

"W-well, I haven't seen or heard from you in weeks," she said nastily. "What was I supposed to do?"

"All right. What is it you called about?" Ramsey had come running into the kitchen all excited, and hung onto my leg.

"Well, I just wanted to tell you I'm pregnant," she said matter-of-factly. My whole world seemed to come crashing down on me.

"A-are you still there, Joe?"

"Yeah, I'm still here," I gagged.

"Well, are you happy about it?" I couldn't believe my ears. Was I that good of an actor? She had been unable to conceive before, so I thought she was barren.

"Oh, uh, yeah. That's great! I'm thrilled!" I said, still concerned about hurting people's feelings.

"Listen, I got to run right now. I'll see you tonight, okay?"

"All right. You're not angry, are you?" she whispered.

"N-No. Why should I be? Take care," I said, hanging up the phone in complete daze, until Ramsey brought me back to reality.

"Popeye! Popeye!" he was yelling excitedly.

For the following three or four weeks I continued my "I'm delighted" charade, until I couldn't stand it any longer and told Theresa as much one evening when I was especially depressed and she couldn't help but sense it.

"What's wrong, Joe? You having second thoughts about this?" She asked.

"This don't make any sense," I stated flatly.

"What doesn't make any sense?" she bristled.

"You...a baby. You can't even take care of yourself! What are you going to do with a baby? I have my wife and sons. I'm not going to leave them, you knew that from the start, Theresa, so what's the purpose? Besides, I don't even know if the kid is mine."

"You Son of a Bitch!" Theresa screamed.

"You asking me to have an abortion?"

"Yeah, I got enough problems," I said softly, "I don't need more."

"You don't w-want the baby?" her voice quavered.

"No, I'm sorry. Didn't you tell me you took your girlfriend to a clinic on Long Island a few months back when she had her abortion, how simple it was and how she was out of there in an hour. What did you say it cost, twenty-five hundred? I'll get the money, okay?"

"No!" she answered angrily. "I want this baby for myself! I don't need you to take care of it."

"All right, but just remember what you said. It's *your* baby!"

Time and again I wanted to go to Gail and tell her everything, to ask for her forgiveness and guidance as to what I should do. Even if she had a solution to this mess, I knew I had to take control, for this was my mess. But each time I planned to do so, I couldn't bear the thought of the scene, the anger, the tears and harsh words. Above all, I dreaded the thought of her face staring aghast at me, in shock at my betrayal of her absolute trust in me. I would rather have died than to face that. In a sense, that's exactly what I did, pursuing the course I did simply to avoid such a confrontation. It would be comical if it weren't so sadly true. Here I stood in mortal fear (love) of a hundred-and-twenty pound woman's anger and recriminations after having spent twenty-five years in prison, and the last four years killing killers without any concern about my life or well-being. But then, while it's always been easy for me to maim or kill someone I perceived as an enemy, I have always been defenseless against those that I love or simply take a liking to. I couldn't bear to hurt these people, even with words, for fear of losing their respect, love, or friendship.

In my torment and need for soul cleansing, I committed an unspeakable crime by exposing my wife to danger, where I had her accompanying me as a final witness to my self-sacrifice. At that specific time, I didn't feel I was endangering her as the past six years had, in my mind, made killing a state of the art endeavor, as common as eating a ham and cheese sandwich. I never thought of the killing as murder, but as the war that it was, there were no shrinking violets. I can't recall exactly when the evil seed settled into the murky soil of my mind, but most likely it was a few weeks before Gail and I had first entertained the thoughts of going to St. Anthony's Festival in Little Italy in early June. I'd imagine that what ignited my thoughts was knowing that I'd be in such close proximity to an old cell-mate of mine from the Tombs (Manhattan House of Detention) who had owed me money for over a year, and who continued to duck my many phone calls.

So on that warm summer night in June, unbeknownst to Gail, before we left the house for the drive to the city, I tucked a .22 automatic beneath my belt at the small of my back and dropped the silencer into the pocket of my sport jacket, and did a little cocaine. It was a beautiful summer evening, and I recall the salty smell of the polluted water as the Caddy rolled smoothly across the Brooklyn Bridge. I was always aware of the tall ominous federal detention building to my right every time I came down off-ramp on the Manhattan side.

"Hey, hon, why don't we stop in and see Brian--have a few drinks before we go to the feast. I haven't seen him for awhile." I looked at Gail.

"Sure, why not," she smiled.

"It's only 6:30 now," Gail said, looking at her watch as I hooked a left towards the West Side Highway, and thought of how I'd met Brian Molese almost ten years before.

After my escape from Attica, I had been captured and housed in the famous, rat-infested shit-hole called "The Tombs," where I would await going to court on a possession of weapons charge before being sent back upstate. Brian was a dark-haired, square-chinned, good-looking, jet-set type of guy, whose M.O. was that of a swindler and con man. We shared the same cell for about three months, and got pretty close. He and his wife Alice, who he was wrongly accused and convicted of killing, had stood up for me when I married the sister of a friend of mine. I had only known her for a few months when I was A.W.O.L. from Attica Prison, and, as fate would have it, I left her about three weeks after I was released from Dannemora Prison in November of 1975.

Brian had hidden the fact that he was gay very well in prison, but his lifestyle alone quickly revealed the secret when I met him again in 1979. He was a decent guy, though, and his personal life was his personal life-- whose appendage he enjoyed playing with, or vice versa, was not a priority concern to me. What bothered me about the loan was not the money, but his complete lack of respect in not even giving me the simple courtesy of a return call saying, "I ain't got it, Sully," or "See you when I do." But all that aside, with all my recent problems, he simply became my subconsciously designated victim. I somehow thought "taking care of him" would be the cure to all my problems. I was about to level the playing field!

Gail was perplexed when I pulled into a parking spot a block off the West Side Highway, on 12th Street.

"Why are we parking so far away, Joe?" she asked.

"Finding a spot on 6th Avenue is impossible this time of the evening. Besides, it's a nice night for a walk. It's only six blocks away, not miles!" I laughed; telling myself I'd just have those few drinks and leave after all. How could I think of such a thing with Gail present?

On the corner of 6th Avenue and 10th Street, I gave Gail Brian's number. "Tell him we're going to the feast, and since we're in the neighborhood we thought we'd stop by for a few minutes."

"W-why don't you call him, Joe, is something wrong?"

"Naw, he owes me a few bucks and has been ducking me, with you along he'll feel I won't raise the subject," I said lightly. (I wanted Gail to make the call as I wanted to do a few more snorts of nose candy in the men's room while she was on the phone.)

"There's not going to be any problems?" she eyed me cautiously.

"Problems?" I hadn't thought of it that way.

"No, there ain't gonna be no problems." I wasn't really lying because I wasn't sure myself how I would act when I saw him.

After a moment on the phone Gail nodded to me.

"He sounded pleased I called, and said to ring the bell in the lobby and he'd buzz us in."

Brian lived in an old but well-kept and expensive four-story apartment building on 10th Street, right off the corner of 6th Avenue. It was a very busy area, especially on a warm summer evening, and was obviously a stronghold for those of the gay persuasion.

When the door buzzed. we had to walk up two flights and to the left, where his apartment was situated facing 10th Street. Waiting to greet us at the door was one of Brian's butt-boys, performing the social amenities and leading Gail and I to the inner sanctum. Brian was seated at a desk in the living room, sipping cognac and shuffling through some papers, which he graciously set aside to entertain us while his friend Chris made us drinks and fluttered about the apartment, managing to look very industrious. The only time he sat still was to tell Gail bout the fabulous trip to Europe that he and Brian had just returned from.

As Chris continued to ramble on I whispered to Gail, "Pick up the glasses and take them to the kitchen. Stay there till I call you."

"Joe, what are you going to--"

"Please, just do as I ask. I want to speak to Brian privately for a minute," I assured her and simultaneously excused myself to go to the bathroom, where I screwed the silencer onto the automatic before returning to the living room.

After a few minutes of small talk, Chris excused himself to use the bathroom. I took advantage of this momentary distraction to remove my piece, and was holding it, with the safety off, between my right leg and the arm of the couch where I sat, with Brian at the desk to my right. We were all alone.

"So, you're broke, huh?" I hissed softly. His eyes flew open in realization, the charade was over and the wolf was in the lair!

"Uh, I--can explain--" he began to protest.

"Why didn't you answer my calls?" I smiled nastily.

"Joe, I was meaning to, I really was. I--"

"Don't bother! Did you have a nice time in Europe? Spend a lot of money on your girlfriend in there?" I nodded toward the bathroom.

Sensing that my script was nearing its end and the curtain was about to fall, he hunched forward to rise from his desk.

"N-no, don't..." he whispered, rising to his feet and throwing his hands in front of his mug as the first slug coughed an apologetic whisper and caught him above the right eyebrow, causing him to collapse like a rag doll. Getting up from the couch from where I had fired, I walked around the desk and leaned over, serving him with the coup de grace behind the right ear. That shot also could not have been heard above the music, neither in the kitchen nor bathroom down the hallway from which butt-boy returned seconds later. He had no more time but to gasp at the sight of Brian upon entering the room, when two more burps erupted and the hostess dropped, only feet from his lover, with barely a sound on the plush wall-to-wall carpeting.

An eerie silence seemed to fill the room as I stood there listening for sounds beyond those of glasses tinkling and water running in the kitchen sink, and the mellow classical music that lent an air of dignity to an otherwise sordid affair. When I walked into the kitchen, gun hanging in my hand and pointed at the floor, Gail looked into my eyes and turned deathly pale.

"Joe, what have you done?"

"Everything's fine," I tried to smile, "just wipe off everything you might have touched in here. I'll take care of everything else. I--"

"Oh, my God, no!" she began just as a bone-chilling scream filled the entire apartment.

Spinning around, I could only watch in sick dismay as the two former corpses darted across the hallway and out the front door in what had to be Olympian record time. I couldn't believe my eyes, but when I looked down at the gun in my hand, one I had not test fired upon receiving it, I could understand how dead men could get up and run as they had. The entire cap on the tube of the silencer had been blown off, probably on the last shot, with the first three shots splintering and simply delivering shrapnel from the cap because it was improperly aligned with the barrel of the automatic itself.

"Oh, Joe. Oh my God, Joe!" Gail's body shook convulsively as I put my hat on her head, pulling it down to her ears.

"Just hold on and stay behind me," I spoke urgently as we ran out into the hallway, almost slipping in the trail of blood as we descended the stairs and ran out the door onto 10th Street, where Brian lay in the middle of the street, surrounded by a growing crowd of people. He was wounded, but not hurt badly enough to prevent his pigeon-like instincts from causing him to point his finger at us from where he lie and shriek, "There they are!" like a little bitch.

I whispered to Gail while pointing the gun at the crowd to hold them at bay, "Stay to my inside against the wall, and when we turn the corner onto 6th Avenue be ready to run."

For someone I could rarely get to jog or exercise in all our years together, when we turned the corner and I yelled, "Hit it!" and took her hand. She ran step for step with me like an All Pro corner back in the NFL. She ran her ass off that night, and was still trying to catch her breath when we arrived home in Queens a half-hour later.

As I packed a few suitcases, Gail sat at the kitchen table still in shock.

"W-what are you doing, Joe? Where are you going?" she cried softly.

"It's all over, Gail. I got to go now," I said half in relief and half in guilty resignation.

As I looked around the house I had been so comfortable in, as if seeing it for the first and last time, looking in on my sons sleeping in their bedroom, tears began to sting my eyes in the knowledge I had betrayed and deserted them, in much the same manner I had been deserted, or felt I had been, as a boy. But this was the only way I could escape, wasn't it?

Before I kissed Gail good-bye, I told her to call Ramsey Clark and let him know everything that happened, as she was totally innocent of any crime other than being married to me.

"Please, Joe, don't run away. They're not dead. Talk to Ramsey-- it can only get worse for you," she pleaded.

"I'm sorry, Gail," I said, sickened at the thought of how many times I'd said that in my life.

"I'll get in contact with you when I can," I said, and ran, as I had run away from everyone and everything all my life.

After a few days at the houses of my friends Rocky and Stevie I moved in with Theresa on Avenue X in Brooklyn, as there was yet no connection made between us there.

I went on a few scores with Stevie and Marco, or Stevie and Joey Martin, who was married to Theresa's sister, Toni. I became close with Toni and Joey both, and was deeply hurt when shortly after I was captured Joey was found in the Gravesend section of Brooklyn with nine slugs in his back and head.

Around mid-August 1981, having heard that a special task force of federal agents and city detectives was formed to bring me down, I hastened my departure from the five boroughs. I headed southwest by car and arrived in Phoenix, Arizona about five days later, after a careful and exhausting drive. I stayed with an old friend from Attica named Tony, who had married and moved out there a few years prior to my arrival. Tony had recently been laid off his job, so we basically camped out by his sister's swimming pool, a few blocks away in a quiet suburban neighborhood. That is, when we weren't coaching a woman's softball team that his sister played on, which was taken very seriously out there. It was a nice, slow graveyard type of life, not so bad at all if one doesn't mind living in a 117-degree oven a good portion of the year, and making a daily pilgrimage to the nearest mall to interact with other homo sapiens. Above all else, I missed my wife and sons, and the simple life I took for granted but could never know again.

I knew that if I were to survive I'd need money and a passport to leave the country. I'd also need a completely new identity, which meant a driver's license, birth certificate, social security card, etc. I knew I wasn't going to get any of the things I needed there in Death Valley. I had to go home to the jungle that I knew best. Though the question of whether I was simply the proverbial moth returning to the flame did cross my mind, but it was quickly ignored.

So I packed my few possessions in the trunk of my car and said my good-byes, but not without first reassuring Tony that I would give him a call if something decent came up for us to move on, as he was looking for some quick cash to bankroll a load of smoke out West. It was often as "dry" as the climate.

Though the drive coming to Phoenix had been tiring, it was a novelty, highlighted by a sense of safety as the miles between myself and New York had grown. My return trip, however, was one of apprehension and uncertainty, which only grew stronger when the New York skyline finally became visible through the swirling snow. The familiar sights of the city did nothing to alleviate the cold knot of fear that had been building in my stomach.

My greatest hurt, loss and sense of rock-bottom desolation, outside of the pain I had caused my own family, came when I arranged a meeting with J.J. at Amy's Pub on 9th Avenue between 55th and 56th Streets. I don't know what I expected or had a right to expect, but after more than four years of what I had thought of as a father/son kind of relationship, I felt that if the time came when the whole world closed doors in my face, J.J. would always be there for me just as I had always been there for him. During our years together I had made J.J.'s enemies my own, and never failed to rise from the stool when the bell rang in the 15th round, despite my own personal problems. In the very least, I thought that he would be there to give my family the support that I wouldn't be able to provide while I was being hunted. J.J. was among the great defenders of those often abstract words-honor, loyalty, principle, blah, blah, blah! Moreover, I felt it would be of little consequence for the fat guy to open his coffers and part with a few bucks, being on the "Fortune 500" list of organized crime like he was. As it turned out, however, my judgments would prove to be in error.

The J.J. who walked into Amy's Pub was not the J.J. I thought I knew, loved, and shared so much in common with. The way he walked, the way he looked around nervously, the smile that appeared on his lips but never reached his eyes, made me wonder if it was he, rather than myself, who was being hunted so desperately. His every action told me that he didn't want to be there, and couldn't get away fast enough. The entire scene made me feel like crying, so great was my disappointment, so wrong was my judgment.

I had never asked, no less begged for anything, though, and I wouldn't start now. J.J. knew my needs. I wasn't supposed to have to ask. He had been funneling a grand a month to me, two-fifty a week--a welfare check! This same pitiful dole Gail received from him for about two years, until they saw that I "stood up" and was no longer a threat to them.

"Jeez, how are you, Joe?" J.J. mouthed emptily, glancing quickly toward the door as he sat down.

"Relax," I smiled, feeling as if I'd just met him.

"You gonna have a beer?"

"Uh, Yeah, I'll have a quick one. I haven't got much time..." for four years he wanted every day, every moment of *my* time!

"You're in a hurry, huh, J.J.?" I managed a sickly smile.

"Uh, yeah, I got to see the fat guy. Have you been getting the money?" he said magnanimously.

"Money? Oh, you mean the thousand dollars each month? Yeah, I've been getting that, J.J. Thanks." I felt like a fucking beggar, and would have killed anybody else who dared subject me to this gut-searing sense of humiliation and betrayal. But I couldn't hurt J.J., couldn't even rant and rave that they owed me this small pittance. I loved and respected him that much. I practiced those words of chivalry that they only paid lip service to. Was the camaraderie all a lie acted out simply to deceive the young and foolish, until their usefulness expired and they were rewarded with a ride in a trunk, or a ride to the penitentiary? It was a bitter disappointment to find that he was not the kindred spirit that I had always been looking for, and thought I had found in him.

"I need money, J.J., a passport and I.D. papers. I want to leave the country." His eyes clouded over in an attempt to camouflage the lie he was about to tell me.

"Yeah, all right. I'll try to reach out. Give me a little time. Uh, maybe it's best you don't use my number. I think I got people watching me," he mumbled, never looking me in the eyes.

And now it was I who couldn't wait for him to leave.

"You sure you're all right?" he said, getting up to leave. I felt like puking!

"Yeah, buddy, I'm just fine. You better get going, huh?"

I smiled, knowing there was no reason to continue this charade, and no need for good-byes.

As I watched him turn and walk away, I felt as if someone were tearing my heart out and could hear the warning that Gail had given me years before, when she saw how much trust I placed in J.J.

"He's not like you, Joe. You're living in a world that no longer exists."

Only now, as I watched him crossing 9th Avenue through the front window, did I fully understand and my soul shuddered deep within.

"I could never have walked away form you, J.J., no matter how bad things got. I destroyed myself and my family in the process of showing you that."

***
Back to Brooklyn - November 1981

"Joe! Hi, how are you? Where are you?" Maria's genuine friendliness served as a soothing balm for my wounded spirit, bringing me back to life.

"In Manhattan." I laughed at her elation.

"How are you? Is Steve there? How's Theresa doing?"

"Theresa's just came home from the hospital, Joe. She gave birth to a baby girl two days ago." So much was happening so fast.

"Was somebody there with her?" No woman should be alone at such a time in her life.

"Of course," she laughed.

"My mother, sisters, we were all there for her. She came home this afternoon."

"Stevie and I were just going to my mother's house to see Theresa, she just came home from the hospital."

"Would it be all right if I went there too."

"Sure, I think Theresa would like that. She'll really be surprised to see you. I'll call my mother and let her know you're coming."

"Good! Tell Stevie I'll see him there."

Theresa's mother was always a lady. She made me feel as if I had never left the house.

Stevie was the first one I saw when I walked into the house. Theresa was asleep in the bedroom. After my experience with J.J. only a few hours before, Stevie made me regain my faith in what friends are supposed to be all about. He welcomed me unashamedly, hugging me with tears filling his eyes, "I missed you, buddy, and I'm glad you're all right. But you got to be crazy coming back to New York."

"I need money and papers, Stevie. I got to get out of Dodge."

"Why don't you see your friend in the city, they owe you big time."

"I just came from there, buddy." he looked at me in astonishment when he caught the drift.

"Those guinea cocksuckers! I don't believe it!" he rasped.

"Hey, is that anyway to talk about your peasans?" I laughed.

"Peasans? Treacherous bastards! Why do you think I never fucked with them, Joe?" he shook his head disgustedly.

"Well, maybe they feel they don't owe me nothing since the shooting in the Village wasn't job related, huh?"

"Are you nuts? You're talking like they're affiliated with Blue Cross or something!"

"Well...it's over. I just wish I'd have grown up four years ago-- I'm a slow learner. I just hope they take care of Gail and the boys, as J.J. promised at the beginning." Stevie laughed cynically at that naive thought.

"You should have blown his brains out!" he snarled.

"He was never fair with you, never gave you the money you deserved! You were cheap labor, Joe. He knew you respected him and used that for his own benefits. Gail knew that too, everyone knew it but you!"

"Maybe you're right. But right now I want to say hello to Theresa."

When I entered the room, Theresa had her back to me and was arranging some clothes.

"How are you feeling, Midnight?"

Midnight was a name I had always called her, in reference to her long raven hair, dark eyes, and olive complexion.

When she spun around her eyes went wide with surprise, and then she smiled, shaking her head in disbelief.

"I--I'm all right. How are you? What are you doing here?"

"I don't know --like a bad penny, I guess. You mind that I came?"

"No, I'm glad you came. Have you seen the baby? It's a girl," she said.

I thought about how a decent human being she basically was. She deserved to have someone she could call her own.

I felt like a fraud when she gave me the baby and placed her in my arms. "You poor, poor little girl. What a great start you have in life," I mouthed silently to the closed-eyed, unsuspecting infant.

About two weeks later I was at Stevie and Maria's house watching TV and playing with their daughter Jill, who was only about two years old, when the phone rang and Stevie answered it, giving me a troubled look as he listened.

"That was Theresa. Some F.B.I. agent and a couple of local detectives just left the apartment on Avenue X. She said to tell you they know about your relationship with her. She said she's bringing the baby to her sister Marion's house and will meet you in the lounge of the Golden Gate Motel about ten tonight."

"Whose phone did she use?" My mind was working overtime.

"No problem--public phone. Listen, you can stay here," he offered, knowing it was only a matter of time before they followed up on my connection to all the family.

"No, it's no good, Stevie. I couldn't do that anyway," I said, nodding toward Maria and Jill in the kitchen.

"Whatever you do, keep in touch with me, okay?"

"I won't call," I nodded.

"I'll have Theresa come by. We'll stay in touch that way."

Theresa insisted on staying with me. She was never short on heart and loyalty, and was instrumental in finding us an apartment in a decent building on Cropsey Avenue in Brooklyn; a stone's throw from the Belt Parkway. Our entire furnishings consisted of a mattress, linens, blankets, a kitchen set, and full refrigerator. Though the furnishings were few, the place was clean. Not much else was needed at the moment. We didn't expect, and didn't care to receive, any surprise visitors.

We got along well under those very adverse conditions. She would go out to her mother's during the day, visit the baby at her sister's, do some shopping, and then drive around Brooklyn for fifteen minutes or so, making sure she wasn't being tailed before returning to the apartment. Like Count Dracula, I only ventured out after dark. Theresa and I would slip out a side entrance in our sweat suits and hoods, and jog over a nearby overpass above the Belt Parkway all the way to the Verrazano Bridge on a walking path that ran along the sea wall. We'd walk back, cooling off before stopping in a Roy Roger's for our ritual hot chocolate, and then return to the apartment. On nights when it was snowing too heavily, we'd take in a movie, with Theresa purchasing our tickets before we went in so I could avoid standing on line, possibly being recognized.

Around the second week of December, our funds were close to nil. Although we were assured of a roof over our heads for the next two months, I had to do something. I gave my friend Tony DiMasse in Phoenix a call, and was told by his wife that he had just flown to New York a few days before. She expected he'd be up in Utica, New York, visiting his brother for the next couple of weeks, though I imagined he had other things on his mind.

I told Theresa to go to her mother's for a while, and that I'd be back in week or so. I left that evening during rush hour, when traffic was heaviest leaving the city. I needed all the camouflage I could get.

I was fairly familiar with the city of Utica, having stayed there for a few months during my escape from Attica. So after arriving on the outskirts of the city and giving Tony's brother a call, I had no trouble finding the bar he directed me to on Mohawk Street, where he said Tony had gone that evening. It was a knockdown, drag-out type of neighborhood joint that catered to hard rockers and pot heads in their mid-twenties and early thirties. I immediately sensed that they didn't care for strangers when I walked through the door and all activity ceased as if E.F. Hutton had spoken.

I was contemplating doing an about-face and exiting the premises when Tony's voice pierced the deadly silence.

"Sully, you old fucking bastard! I don't believe it!"

His words indicated a familiarity that soothed the souls of the two-dozen potential assassins who already had me buried, or at least hospitalized, in their minds. And thankfully so, as I may have had to put myself at great risk, being on the lam as I was, in disappointing their blood lust.

"Hey!" I laughed as he hugged me, half in the tank.

"What is this, a Ku Klux Klan meeting? Looks like a den of thieves," I whispered, looking around me.

"It is!" Tony laughed. "Only problem is, there ain't nothing in this town worth robbing!" he complained.

"Yes there is," I offered, smiling at him.

"What are you talking about?" Tony's ears perked up.

"Banks! When's the last time there was a bank robbery in this town, Tony?"

"Never!" His eyes lit up, catching my drift.

"I've lived here all my life and never heard of one. They're ripe, huh?"

"Yeah, there's a few real sweet ones I was looking at during my escape from Attica, like that old Oneida Savings Bank in the Chicago Mall. Easy to control as it ain't no bigger than your living room. Low counters, cameras, but you can beat that with a stocking mask and gloves, which I no longer have a need for. In and out, two minutes. You scoop and I'll cover. What do you think, Tony?"

"What do you think it's worth, Sully?" he was all business now.

"Well, since this is virgin territory, unlike New York City, they probably ain't afraid to put money in the drawer. Say, thirty to fifty grand, with the possibility of catching some bags being readied for delivery if we catch them early in the morning. Enough to bankroll a load of smoke for you, and keep my rent paid."

"Can you get a car?" I smiled.

"No problem. You got guns?" Tony laughed.

"No problem," I laughed in return.

"How about it, you with me?"

"Fuck it! I ain't going home broke. Let's do it."

"All right. We'll look the joint over in the morning, specifically where we'll switch cars en route to the thruway and the Syracuse Airport, where we'll check into a motel and whack up the money. You'll jump on a plane to Phoenix and I'll drive on to Rochester. But remember, Tony, two minutes is our max in there. I'll keep the count, and when I yell 'out' don't fuck around, okay? I know this type of shit ain't your thing, Tony, so let me make the calls on this one. All right, buddy?"

"Hey," he laughed, "You don't see me arguing, do you?"

"No," I smiled fondly at him. "But I don't want to have to call your wife, or tell my son that I got his godfather killed. I know you think all the cops in this town are Mickey Mouse yokels, but until we're in that motel in Syracuse I want you to think of them as if they were elite Special Forces troops."

"I'll do my job, Sully," Tony said sober-faced.

"I have no doubt of that, Tony. Just a wake-up call we both need. This is real cowboy type shit, nothing to get exotic about. So we'll just keep it simple."

"Everybody freeze!" I barked, stepping inside the bank door three steps behind Tony, leveling the sawed-off pump shotgun from my hip as I watched Tony leap the counter with his left hand, his right clutching a snub-nosed .38. Once the tellers were on the floor, he immediately tucked the pistol into his belt and removed a pillow case form his back pocket.

"Put your hands down at your sides!" I yelled to a few people who had instinctively raised them in the air, which would alert passersby outside. "Move it! Move it!"

"One minute!" I barked for Tony's sake, my eyes darting back and forth looking for any sudden movement.

"Thirty seconds, buddy!" I yelled, but then quickly changed my call to "Out! Out! Let's go!"

From the corner of my eye I caught a flash of the outer door opening. When I turned, all I saw was the back of some guy who must have taken one step in and, by the manner of the people standing as rigid as mannequins, sized up the situation immediately.

"Everybody on the floor! Now!" I screamed as Tony vaulted the counter, heading toward me, bag in hand and eyes wide behind his ski mask.

"Keep your gun down against your leg, but watch yourself going out," I told him quickly, and then waited bout five seconds before following him out of the bank, pulling the shotgun beneath my long leather coat, where I controlled it through a cut-out right pocket.

Tony was almost to the car about sixty feet away when I stopped outside the bank into the mall area, where ten or fifteen people were pointing fingers at me from a safe distance. I ignored them but was vigilant for that chance off duty cop or responding patrol car. Nothing!

"So far so good," I thought, feeling the blowing snow flakes sting my face and melt as I walked briskly toward the open passenger's door.

"Just drive to the exit normally, Tony. As soon as we hook a right remove your mask and put your foot on the tank."

We sped about eight blocks to where my Caddy was parked; making two turns in the process. We saw no trails.

It was smooth sailing to the Syracuse airport area about 45 miles away. Once there, I sent Tony for a few six packs of Heineken while I put the pillowcase of money into one of my suitcases in the trunk of my car, and then checked into a motel with it. As soon as I hit the room I lay down and closed my eyes until I had collected my thoughts and was breathing normally again.

"Oh, yeah! Oh, yeah! I love it!" Tony yelled with boyish exuberance when he barged in. His enthusiasm quickly infected me.

"Damn, that shit was easy! We should do it at least once a week!"

"My heart couldn't take it, Tony!" I laughed, tipping the bottle for a healthy swig as Tony dumped the pillowcase on one of the two beds.

"Damn, don't look like much, Joe. There was still another teller's cage."

"We're safe, Tony. That's worth more than whatever was left," I said tiredly. I made a call booking a flight to Phoenix for Tony, which would be leaving in about two hours.

"Shit," Tony muttered, "counting this fucking money is harder than robbing the joint! Thirty-eight thousand and change, not bad for a few minutes work. You got something to put this in?" he said, separating the two piles.

"Yeah, I got a leather shoulder bag I bought in Florence, Italy, when Gail and I went on vacation a few years ago, and I have an overnight bag you can take right on the plane with you."

After dividing up the money we both knocked off a few bottles of Heineken and were feeling real mellow and relaxed.

"Why don't you come back out to Arizona? You can stay with me. You'll be safer there."

"No, Tony, I'm going to leave completely, all I need is some I.D. and a new passport now. I can't use the old one. You ready to go? The taxi should be here any minute now."

"Jeez, Sully..." he was choked up.

"Just what I need, you getting all emotional and sloppy. Get the fuck out of here!" I said laughing, but a little blurry-eyed myself.

"Thanks, Sully," he said simply.

"No, thank you, Tony. I didn't have anybody else."

As I was seeing Tony off, little did I know that had I returned to Phoenix with him I'd have been in his house when the F.B.I. surrounded it two days later on a tip from the "friend" he had gotten the car from. Instead I was in the town of Webster, near Rochester, New York, staying with my friend G.I. Joe (so called for the tour he took in Vietnam). He had a nice little trailer in some fancy trailer park, so I stayed with him and relaxed for a few days.

G.I.'s trailer was ideally situated in a far corner of the trailer park, free from the view of any rubber-neckers witnessing my movements coming and going. Gail and I had spent a week or so at the trailer the summer before, after a two week vacation with our boys in a cottage on Lake Ontario, which my old friend from Attica, Tommy Taylor, had rented and invited four or five close friends and family. It was a carnival atmosphere spent predominately outdoors beneath a huge green and white striped tent that looked like something from out of Ringling Brothers. The barbecue was going eighteen hours a day while young suckling pigs sizzled in their own fats, revolving slowly on a spit over the pits we had dug. The beer and wine flowed freely, and was replenished often over the two-week period as dozens of former friends stopped by for a day with their wives or girlfriends. The show went on beneath the Big Top even on rainy days, which were few. During the late evenings we'd sit by a bonfire enjoying the cool, gentle breeze that blew if off Lake Ontario, drinking and reminiscing about the old times in the joint, making them sound like the good times they never were--to the boredom of our wives, who had heard the war stories a thousand times before and would roll their eyes back in mock agony at the thought of suffering through the same stale tales yet again.

It was during this memorable event that I met Tom Taylor's partner, Tom Torpe. Torpe was another huge Irish guy like Taylor himself, who played pulling guard on our football team during the late 1960's. He cleared the way for me on our jail house version of Vince Lombardi's Green Bay power-sweep, all dressed in our Buffalo Bills donated equipment and helmets. Both Toms stood about six-foot-four and weighed well over 270 pounds. Torpe was gentleman and I liked him, though I only saw him on a few occasions.

I also met a guy during our stay at the Lake Ontario camp that I *thought* was an imposing figure (as I imagine he did himself) until he checked into the federal witness protection program after the incident I am about to relate.

Louie DiGiulo was his name, pretending was his game. He was a big, good-looking Lou Ferrigno look-alike, who resembled the Hulk in that he had muscles on his muscles. It was not his size, however, but his gentle way with my kids and his quiet mannerism that impressed me most. He was supposedly a strong-arm guy and main gopher for Tommy Taylor, who they all referred to as "Eagle-One" due to his penetrating eyes and the glistening dome that he kept closely shaved and highly buffed.

I had gotten real close with Taylor during our football days in Attica through 1967-68, but didn't see him again until 1980. So naturally when he had related to me how he and Torpe had been blown up in a car by remote control, while acting as bodyguards for an opposing boss of an entrenched Rochester mob faction, I was concerned for his welfare. For the past three to four years he and Torpe had been moving independently, running card games, a few porno shops and peep shows.

While Louie wasn't exactly a mental giant, which became obvious the first time he would open his mouth, Taylor told me he was a genuine tough guy and loyal to the core. So, in turn, I accorded him the same respect that I gave Taylor. He was a friend of a friend.

The Hulk came to the trailer with some cocaine, which was common in his circle. As we snorted, he began telling me how he was in debt to some Rochester "capo" for twenty-six grand, and how he sensed that the guy was getting ready to "move on" him because he could not come up with the money. I couldn't help but feel concerned about his problem, especially in the condition we were in. Wasn't he one of the guys, a friend? I became even more interested when he went on to tell me how this capo, John "Johnny Flowers" Fiorino, was one of the guys who okayed the hit on Taylor and Torpe, along with their boss who didn't survive the blast.

"Have you told Taylor about this, Louie?"

"N-no," he whispered, looking at me like I was crazy for even asking.

"The Eagle don't know I've been gambling in their joints. He'd kill me if he knew." He didn't mean that literally.

"I can't tell him, Sully. He's bailed me out of shit like this once before, and went crazy that time," he mumbled, hanging his head like a whipped cur.

"What are you gonna do, Louie?" That wasn't the reason why he came to see me.

"What do you *want* to do?"

"Jeez, Sully, I--I don't know."

"You wanna whack him, right?" I laughed.

"Well, y-yeah, but it ain't exactly my thing. Sure, I've broken guys up and all that, but t-this is something else."

"All right," I laughed, thinking what a sucker I was.

"Can you get this Johnny Flowers to meet you somewhere?"

"I--I'm not sure, Sully."

"Will he come if you tell him Taylor and Torpe said they needed to see him about something urgent, and would meet him at six tomorrow, say, in the Blue Gardenia Restaurant, that wiseguy joint? He'd feel safe going there, wouldn't he?"

"Yeah," Louie smiled happily, "but how do I tell the Eagle and Torpey without telling them my problem?"

"You don't tell them anything, Louie, just say I need to see them there at six tomorrow, because this Johnny Flowers may call to see if they show up before he comes."

"I--I'm not sure I follow you," he looked confused. "What will the Eagle and Torpe think when he walks in?"

"He ain't going to reach the door, don't worry," I said, peeling off a few bills, courtesy of the Oneida Savings Bank.

"Meantime, tell Taylor to get me a room in that motel by his house, okay? You got any bread?"

"I ain't got shit, Sully." Gamblers rarely do.

"Here's a few bucks. Pick me up at the motel tomorrow morning, okay?"

"Yeah, sure. Thanks, Sully. I appreciate this."

The following morning, Louie pulled up in front of the motel at ten sharp, driving an old beat up looking Ford that belonged to his girl. I had him take me to the mall where the Blue Gardenia Restaurant was located, on Empire Boulevard in Irondequoit, a suburb of Rochester. It was a real country type area, and not a place I'd relish getting stranded under duress. Aside from the mall itself, the entire surrounding area consisted of private homes. The sole exception being a small neighborhood bar about three blocks down from the mall on Empire Boulevard itself was a main thoroughfare that led into the N.Y. State Thruway.

I showed Louie where we would be parking, midway between the Blue Gardenia and the exit from the mall. It was beginning to snow lightly when Louie and I followed the same route we would take after the hit--two miles up Empire to the Thruway, and another two exits to the motel where I was staying. I explained how I wanted him to coast slowly out of the parking lot that evening with the lights off, but to flick them on before we actually rolled onto Empire Boulevard.

"No problem, Sully, don't worry," he assured me with bravado.

"I know what I got to do."

When Louie met me at the motel that evening, we did a little nose candy that he had brought with him. I handed him the keys to my beige colored Cadillac, which at night appeared as if it were white. My worldly possessions were all packed into the trunk, with the exception of my leather shoulder bag that contained bank money, a few handguns, identification papers, etc. I had tossed that casually on the back seat. I felt completely comfortable and didn't foresee any problems.

The snow was coming down hard now and was swirling in the strong wind. I felt that this was a plus because it would reduce visibility.

When we pulled into our designated spot in the parking lot of the mall, it was 5:45 in the evening. Taylor's dark blue Thunderbird was already there, parked about thirty feet from the restaurant too.

"Good, they're here.'" I said, looking at Louie in the dim interior of the car. He looked kind of green around the gills, just sitting there like a catatonic staring straight ahead.

"You all right, Louie?" I said, adjusting the pump sawed off shotgun between my legs while I took the .38 Cobra from my overcoat pocket and tucked it in beneath my belt. I was wearing jeans that were pulled down over boots that came to just below my knees, a light wind breaker over an equally light bullet-proof vest, and an ankle-length goose down coat that would prove to be instrumental in saving my life. Atop my head I had a fancy Western-type fedora with a wide brim. In one of the deep side pockets of my goose down I had about three grand. And in my left boot I had a razor-sharp bowing knife in a leather sheath.

"You sure you can make his car right away in this weather, Louie? I don't want him reaching the door, you got to let me know as soon as he pulls in,"

I asserted.

"I'll know it," he replied in a sickly voice. Just then it struck me that he was almost paralyzed with fear.

"Is that it?" I pointed to a brown Lincoln Town Car that had just turned in.

"Is that him?" I snapped.

"Y-yeah, th-that's him," Louie's voice trembled.

"Hey, be cool. Just relax, okay?" I tried to soothe him as the brown Lincoln glided into an empty spot about twenty feet from Taylor's car.

"I've got to move now if I'm to catch him before he reaches the door. Be right back, Louie," I called over my shoulder as I opened the door and slid out, holding the shotgun down along my right leg.

I broke into a trot upon seeing Johnny Flowers exit his car quickly and walk briskly toward the restaurant. Just as he was stepping onto the mall sidewalk, I raised the weapon to my shoulder—

"Fiorino!" I yelled, firing and feeling the jolt almost in unison with the deafening roar that numbed my eardrums. I closed the distance between us in a dead run.

The first blast, I saw, had ridden high when he spun around, catching him in the right shoulder area and knocking him down. He was clawing desperately at an ankle holster for his .38 snub-nose when I arrived. I fired a second load of double-0 buck that sent his near-headless body tumbling across the sidewalk before coming to a stop near the doorway of the Blue Gardenia. Turning immediately, I trotted back to the car.

No sooner than I had jumped into the car, barely getting the door closed, Louie panicked and floored the gas pedal, sending us careening out of the exit sideways, having spun out of control on the sloppy, snow covered ground. He managed to straighten the car out just as I screamed, "You coward cocksucker!"

I reached under the steering column to pull the stem for the headlights, but it was already too late. I heard the siren first, and when I looked into the rear-view mirror saw the revolving red light atop a sheriff's cruiser closing the distance between us. I doubted that he had heard the shot or was aware of the body in the mall parking lot he just passed, but what he did see was a car sliding sideways out onto the highway without any lights on, which in his mind must have translated, "drunken driver." I couldn't stand a frisk or even having my license ran through a computer, regardless of what he may have thought.

"Move it! Head for the Thruway!" I shouted in Louie's ear while sliding two more shells into the shotgun.

The light about forty yards ahead on Empire Boulevard had just turned yellow and would be red against us any second.

"Hit the horn and hold it! Let them know we ain't stopping!" I screamed. Louie's hands were frozen to the wheel as we shot across the intersection. We almost made it but were clipped on the right rear fender, sending us into a spin and off an embankment to our right, where we settled in a shallow ditch, the rear end of the Caddy pointed straight up into the air.

Neither of us was hurt. Louie barely had time to blubber, "W-what do we do now?" before I tossed him the .38 from my belt. He fumbled with it like it was a hot potato.

"It's Showtime, buddy!" I yelled, pushing open the passenger's door and diving out into the snow, keeping myself between my car and the cruiser, which had just pulled up about forty feet behind us.

"Go at them, Louie! We'll go at them from both sides. Hit it!" I screamed, psyching myself as I came around the Caddy and charged up the slippery embankment--firing, falling, firing again and again, watching the windshield and revolving red light above the cruiser, disintegrate, until I was crouched before the nose of the cruiser, peering above the hood into the shattered windshield. Complete silence. A quiet that made me spin around looking for Louie.

He was on the ground back by the car. I thought he had been wounded as I ran toward him, thinking about getting the moneybag out of my car.

"You all right, Louie?" I asked, bending over to help him.

"Where's your piece?" I shouted.

"I--I fell, twisted my ankle," he moaned pitifully. I knew he had tossed the gun and was running away when he slipped and fell.

"Freeze!" the deputy sheriff screamed, and then emptied his revolver at me from about thirty feet away as I spun to face him. Other than the feeling of a hard punch in the chest, I felt nothing when I suddenly found myself on my back in the snow, feet pointing up at the Big Dipper. My mind couldn't decide whether this wasn't more comical than embarrassing before I bounced back upon to my feet, like the Joe Palooka punching bag I had as a kid and couldn't keep down.

"Yeah!" I screamed at the deputy in this out-of-body experience, as I caught him re-loading and pulled the trigger. I heard only the sound of-- what? Nothing, but my own ragged breathing.

I immediately spun around and ran, seeing Louie going over a ten foot high wooden fence about twenty yards away, which I ran to and leaped myself, barely managing to grasp the top and get one arm over. Louie was rising to his feet and our eyes met.

"Help me, Louie," I gasped in exhaustion, watching him turn and run as I slipped and fell.

"Halt!" The deputy screamed, as I darted along and around the corner of the fence, just ahead of a few hurried shots. I found myself on a tree-lined suburban street in the middle of nowhere! Without rhyme or reason, I spotted Louie's tracks and began to jog along in them through the deep snow.

A distant part of my mind was aware of the converging wail of sirens; another part was screaming its urgent warning.

"You got to get off the street, Sully. Now! A garage? A cellar window?" My eyes darted about frantically. I couldn't believe that the people in these houses weren't alerted by the shots and looking out their windows. The snow must have acted as a curtain, deadening the sound of the gunfire. Or the shooting sounded like a car backfiring.

Still running, just about on my last leg, my eyes caught sight of a freshly shoveled sidewalk. Without a second thought, I instinctively jumped about six feet from Louie's tracks onto the lightly covered pavement. Spotting a deep drift of snow blown up against a tightly knitted row of shrub bushes that ran along the front of the house, with barely a two-foot distance between the house and line of two-foot high shrubs. I walked up to the stoop quickly, pretending to ring the bell as I casually checked the windows of the surrounding houses. Kneeling down, I lowered myself head-first over the side of the stoop, burrowing down and under, using the side of the stoop itself to drive the entire length of my body beneath the surface of the deep snow drifts that had accumulated on and behind the shrub bushes. With both hands holding the collar of my goose down over my head and my elbows tucked under me, I squirmed and slithered, fighting for the extra inches till I felt sure my feet were also out of sight.

My first surprise was that I could breathe, if only in shallow gasps. For fifteen minutes I laid in my surprisingly warm tomb of snow, waiting for the man hunters to come.

I heard the muffled barks of the dogs before I heard the voices of the men. They seemed like they were coming from far away, but I knew they were but a few feet away, maybe looking beneath the shrubs right now. The snow had been blowing heavily for the past fifteen minutes, so I was certain that my footsteps on the lightly glazed walk and stoop had long been covered. What had my heart in my throat was the thought that some keen mind and eye would think to look behind these shrubs, and see that one spot of churned-up snow I had disappeared through. What saved me, I know, was that the men were understandably looking for the remains of tracks. If there weren't any on the road or lawns outside of Louie's, they'd never think that anybody could possibly leap the thirty feet from the road to the houses. They also wouldn't think to take into consideration the possibility that one Good Samaritan may have shoveled his stoop and walkway. And as for the dogs, they could not pick up my scent beneath the new snow.

Another posse passed through about an hour later. I had to keep flexing my arms and legs because they were losing circulation. It was becoming cold, but nothing I couldn't bear in my goose down sleeping bag. After the second pass I became braver, and poked a small hole up through the snow with my fingertips, getting my first real breath of air in what? An hour? Two? "I'm going to have to come up out of here soon," I thought to myself. They'll probably wait until daylight and then go over the area with a fine-toothed comb. But where do I go, and how, without exposing my presence or bringing attention to myself?

Coming up out of the safety of the cold womb, I felt like the Abominable Snowman. My body was stiff as a board as I pressed my back against the house, into the deep shadows beneath a large bay window. I worked some warmth back into my limbs as I brushed as much of the snow from my coat and legs of my pants as was possible in the constricted area.

My senses came fully alert when a door opened a few houses away and three young men stepped out, laughing and saying good-bye to their host. It was obvious that they had been drinking.

"Take care, John, Charlie, Bobby. See you guys tomorrow." The door of the house closed as they stepped off the stoop and started down the walk.

"Now or never," I whispered to myself, stepping out and jogging down the sidewalk after them.

"Hey, fellas!" I waved my arm in a friendly manner as they turned and awaited my approach. From the looks of them they were all feeling pretty good. Nice kids, just out for a beer party with friends.

"Hi," I said, smiling a bit sheepishly.

"I hate to bother you guys, but I was supposed to meet a friend in a bar on Empire Boulevard. Could you possibly tell me if I'm even close?" I laughed good-naturedly.

"Sure! I know the place you must mean. Only one around," said the bigger of the young men. They all looked like athletes.

"C'mon, we're headed that way ourselves."

"Jeez, thanks, fellas," I grinned and fell in step with them as they headed directly toward Empire Boulevard.

I saw the tavern out of the corner of my eye, and a sheriff's car with its red light swirling lazily just ahead of us.

"Hi, guys," the tall deputy greeted us as we approached him.

"There's been a shooting in the mall a few hours back," he pointed with a gloved hand.

"Wouldn't have happened to see anything unusual in your travels, would you?" he asked in a friendly manner, looking at none of us in particular.

"Why, no, officer," we all looked at each other and parroted in chorus.

"Good thing these kids' brains are half-pickled in alcohol," I mused to myself while giving thanks.

"That's the place over there," the big kid pointed when we were still only about ten steps past the deputy sheriff. A chill ran up my spine wondering if he heard, recognizing that I was a stranger to these guys.

"Thanks a lot, fellas." I returned softly, and trudged through the deep drifts across Empire Boulevard, barely a hundred yards from the wild scene of just a few hours before, to the brightly lit bar that stood out in the surrounding darkness like a beacon in some God-forsaken wilderness.

I noticed an unusual number of parked cars in the area around this small, insignificant little bar, but didn't give it another thought until I opened the door and stepped inside.

I immediately felt like Daniel in the lions' den, feeling my heart accelerate and my sphincter muscle twitch spasmodically. Every fucking pinky-ring and would-be wise guy in Rochester had converged on this little shit-hole in the boondocks. Some Frank Nitti type was snarling into a phone on my left, "The rat cocksuckers just whacked Johnny Boy!" Another candy store gangster was preening and posturing at the crowded bar for a few heavily made-up, red-neck gun molls who looked at this asshole in admiration, cigar sticking out of the side of his face.

"On my mudder's grave, dey will pay for dis shit!" Blah, blah, blah, he went on. I thought he must be auditioning for "Godfather Part X" or something.

I quickly scanned the crowded bar for any familiar faces from the joint, but these guys were harmless wannabees, not the type to risk their gold chains, dirt bikes and ski mobiles. I kept the bewildered look of some local yokel on my face and made my way through the chaos toward an elderly couple I had spotted sitting nonplused at the end of the bar.

"My God!" I smiled in mock-horror, sliding up to them. "What's going on here?"

"Aw, nothing really. Seems one of these clowns killed another clown down the road a piece at the mall," the old man guffawed, and his wife nodded in agreement.

"Just another public service rendered," she laughed, raising her stein of beer in a gesture of salute.

"What will it be?" The beet-face bartender quipped as he hustled about, looking like he was about six heartbeats away from a massive coronary. Business had never been so good.

"Give me a double Dewar's on-the-rocks," I ordered.

"Hey, Rocco, change the channel--check the ten o'clock news. Let's see if they got anybody yet."

I ceased breathing as the local anchorman ran down the shooting at the Blue Gardenia, stating how one low-level local hood name Louis DiGiulio was in custody, a huge, mug-shot of the Hulk flashing in the background. The newscaster went on to say that a second man, believed to be the shooter, had somehow vanished during the ensuing chase, and is being sought by authorities.

"DiGiulio? That piece of shit!" one guy snarled. I couldn't help but smile and nod my agreement.

"The hit must have come from Taylor and Torpe," another piped in.

"I've got to get out of here real soon," I thought to myself. Finally a phone was available and I wasted no time jumping on it.

"Bobby? Yeah, it's me." I laughed.

"Where am I? Unfortunately, in some bar on Empire Boulevard surrounded by Philistines. What? Yeah, it was me. You've been watching it on TV? Great. Now come and get me the fuck out of here before it's my face you're watching, or this posse of frustrated Don Corleones either takes me out to the nearest tree or turns me over to the proper authorities! You find that funny, huh?" I said, having to laugh myself.

"But hurry, okay, Bobby? Pull up in the back so I can get in the trunk unnoticed. One more thing, work the bar before you come near me, as I'm sure you know half these birds. Hurry, my friend, hurry!"

Bobby Comfort was one of the guys on the big Hotel Pierre heist in New York City years back. He was a close friend of mine since the 1960's, so I never doubted that he'd come for me. He was as brazen as the prison day is long and a real sweetheart of a guy, but when he walked in that bar and saw just how precarious my position had been, he went absolutely pale.

When he finally finished his handshaking and politicking, he moved up to the bar beside me. He nodded his head when I whispered that I'd be walking out in about thirty seconds, and that he should wait a few minutes before following. All he said in a barely audible voice when I settled up with the bartender and turned to leave was, "The trunk's open." And of course, I climbed into it as soon as I reached it out back, and settled down comfortably on the half-dozen blankets Bobby had spread out for me.

I heard footsteps approach and held my breath.

"You called a cab, sir?" Bobby laughed.

"Where do you want to go, Sully?" he said in a more serious tone.

"Buffalo Airport, Bobby. Hey, thanks for coming."

"You ever doubt I would?" he laughed.

"No--never," I said tiredly as he pressed down on the trunk door, the latches snapping closed with a dull click. And that was the last sound I heard until we reached the airport, having succumbed to a peaceful sleep after having run on nothing but fear and adrenalin for the past six hours.

I managed to catch the late flight leaving that night to Newark Airport. Upon arriving in New Jersey, I took a cab to the apartment on Cropsey Avenue in Brooklyn.

I had lost everything during the fucking nightmare in Rochester, I thought groggily, half asleep in the rear of the cab as it sped through the Brooklyn Battery Tunnel, the clicking sound of the meter grating my senses like some ominous countdown. Money, car, guns, clothes, even the little bit of I.D. I had managed to scrape together over the past seven months--all lost! And for what? For who?

I didn't reach the apartment until two that morning, but was asleep five minutes after I shed my clothes and crawled into bed. The following morning, I was pleasantly surprised to see Theresa staring at me.

"I heard what happened upstate. I was hoping you'd be here. You Okay?"

"I'll feel better in a moment. Come over here."

"Oh, Joe! I was so worried!" She whispered. crawling up on the bed next to me and pressing her lips against mine, dropping her hand and giving me a gentle squeeze.

"Ain't nothing wrong with this!" she laughed.

"Oh, Yeah!" I moaned mindlessly as she moved over me, emitting little sounds of pleasure until we both were caught up in convulsions of mutual pleasure.

"Feel better, baby?" she whispered, her face buried between my neck and shoulder as I tried to control my ragged breathing.

"Yeah. That's a hell of a cure for depression," I laughed.

"Hey, is that coffee I smell?"

"Yep," she chirped.

"Just thought I'd give you a breakfast snack first. How's bacon and egg's sound?"

"Great, I'm starving! But I need a shower first."

"I know. I couldn't help but notice." She tossed a smile at me over her shoulder as her saucy, quivering buttocks turned the corner and disappeared.

"Joe, I've got some bad news. Stevie was shot. I--"

"What?" I yelled, jumping out of the bed and running into the kitchen.

"What did you say?" I stared unbelievingly.

"Calm down, will you?" she answered; calmly dropping strips of bacon into a sizzling pan.

"He's all right. But the cops are looking for him also now." she shook her head.

"I only know what Maria told my sister, Toni. "

"And what's that?" I asked, sitting at the kitchen table in my birthday suit while she went about her task and gave me bits and parts of the story as she heard it.

It appeared that Stevie had got a tip (a set up) from some police informant he thought was a friend, about the routine of some diamond dealer, a Hasidic Jew, and since it was a "one shot deal" and I wasn't around at the time, he grabbed some non-descript to make the move with him. It was to go down at the dealer's private house in Brooklyn Heights, where the dealer worked. To make a long story short, the dealer was also in on the set up, giving Stevie a bag of "glass." When Stevie and the kid were on their way out to the car, about eight vested, shotgun wielding, task-force detectives piled out the back of a nearby van, lined up like a firing squad, and started blasting in the same breath that they screamed the order for Stevie and the kid to freeze. The kid with Stevie dove to the ground surrendering, but Stevie made it to the car somehow. While he was screeching away, head down over the wheel, he caught a couple shotgun pellets in the back through the rear window.

"So where is he now, Midnight?"

"Some dump in Staten Island, near the water. You want toast?"

"No, this is good," I mumbled through a mouthful of eggs.

"How long's he been there?"

"Almost three days. Nobody wants to go near him, Joe." I knew the feeling all too well.

"Damn! I don't even have a car, and can't drive that stick shift you got."

"So, I'll go with you. What's the big deal?"

"What's the big deal, you ask? What have you got, a fucking death wish?" I asked angrily.

"You shouldn't even be here with me!"

"Yeah?" she tossed at me in a shitty, cynical tone.

"Well, where would you be if I weren't? Where would you have lived on and off these past seven months? You can't walk into a motel in the five boroughs. You couldn't have rented this apartment. You can't even go out to go fucking shopping! Be serious!" she snapped at me.

"I'm sorry, you're right. But you still shouldn't be here." I said feebly.

"Joe, if I didn't want to be here I wouldn't be here. So let's forget all that, okay?"

"Okay," I smiled. "We'll take a ride in a little while."

Staten Island looked like another planet to me, as I had never had reason to cross the Verrazano Bridge before. Theresa took a left coming off the bridge, and five minutes later I thought I was on a tour of the Everglades. We wound our way down dusty roads with reed-filled swamps to either side of us, and where a little community of shanty-looking bungalows ran along the water's front.

"That should be the house over there," Theresa pointed, double-checking the address on the paper in her hand.

"Damn!" I laughed aloud, gaping at the waist-high weeds surrounding the house, whose roof was buckled like the back of an old packhorse. The front screen door hung off its lower hinge like it had a hangover.

"Whoever lives here must parachute in. There ain't even a path!"

"Maybe there's a back entrance," Theresa laughed.

"We'll go around the back."

Sure enough, a dirt road barely wider than the car itself ran through the weeds, into an open area behind the house that was a virtual junk-yard of car parts, used tires, empty bottles and other unidentifiable debris.

"What a pig sty!" Theresa said, wrinkling her nose in disgust as she pulled up beside a stoop-less wooden porch. I thought I saw a shade move, but the windows were too filthy to see through clearly. Stevie couldn't have found a more secluded spot to hide, though it was a sure death trap if he was discovered--only one way in and one way out.

When we both jumped up onto the back porch, Stevie poked his head out the barely-opened door, his eyes darting about wildly like a trapped animal. In spite of the seriousness of the situation, both Theresa and I couldn't help but laugh at the sight of him. His face, which was always thin, was now hollow and gaunt. And in contrast to his three-day growth of black facial hair, the Howdy-Doody dye job somebody did on his hair was absolutely ridiculous. A glaring mop of orange hair jutted out at all angles!

"Jeez, Stevie, I'd never have known you!" I said tongue-in-cheek. Theresa giggled.

"Not bad, huh?" he grinned, raising a hand self-consciously to the disaster above. I could see the tension leaving his face, taking comfort in the presence of friends.

Stevie put his finger to his lips indicating silence, as he led us into a cesspool unfit for hogs.

"The old broad is an alcoholic and is sleeping one off. She gave me the dye job and took the pellets out of my back," he whispered, lifting his shirt and turning around.

"She used to be a nurse."

"At least she did something right," I said dryly, eyeing the angry though clean-looking wounds.

"They don't appear to be infected, Stevie. But you'd have been dead and stinking if those pellets had hit you in the head."

After I told him of my own recent near-death experience, I think he felt better, being able to laugh at my detailed and dramatic version. We mutually agreed that our own private Butch and Sundance show had come to a close. His wife Maria was a near basket case over this latest development. He told me that with the help of a close relative and his life long friends Joey C. and Flip, he was going to leave the state with his wife and two-year-old daughter, Jill.

"Let's get out of here." I felt the shack closing in on me.

"Where to, Stevie?"

"Take me to Joey's in Brooklyn, Mill Basin. I'll meet Maria there."

"Why don't we go with them?" Theresa asked me. Though Stevie and I looked at each other momentarily, no words were needed. We both knew that even if such a course were feasible, it was not possible because as good as Theresa had been to me, Gail and my sons were, and still remain, ingrained in my very soul. Stevie knew this. Were such not a reality, my course would have been different.

It was at such times as this that I brooded about J.J. and the fat guy, and how they could have made things so easy for me to start a new life with my family. If J.J. was the kind of man I thought him to be I would have made a good salary on my "no-show" job and money for each hit I did. This was not the case. Gail had to work to help keep up the household and I had free time on my hands. When I needed him for "papers" for my family, so we could all leave the country, he turned his back on me. And here I thought he'd do the right thing. What a fool I was and what a bigger fool I had become. Yet, when I had the chance to blow him away, I couldn't because I actually looked up to him. Loyalty is a rare commodity as I found out. I was lucky to find that loyalty in Gail and perhaps that's why we are still together. My loyalties were misplaced, but I see that now, perhaps a little too late.

After dropping Stevie off at Joey's in Mill Basin, I somehow felt as if the final door of this insane melodrama had closed behind me, and a deep sense of apathy washed over me. All I could think of was seeing Gail and the boys, somehow, before the bottom fell out completely.

"You all right, Joe?" Theresa asked, looking at me from the corner of her eye as she negotiated the rush-hour traffic on the Belt running out to Eastern Long Island, where her sister Toni had invited us to dinner.

"Yeah, I'm fine."

"Just Dandy," I thought, drifting off with my eyes closed and head resting a top the seat of the small Volkswagen. Tomorrow is Saturday, I mused dreamily, listening to the hypnotic clicking sound of the windshield wipers fighting off the big flakes of fresh snow that had just begun to fall. I'll go over to Rocky's and have Gail meet me there with they boys. Not a good idea, but just this once.

"Joe," My body jumped. "We're almost there. You want to pick up a cake or something? There's a bakery in the mall over there."

"Good idea." As a rule, I avoided stores or any public place whenever possible, but I needed to walk and stretch a little I felt reasonably safe so far out on Long Island.

"Joe, I don't think it's a good idea--" Theresa started to say when I got out of the car with her.

"Don't worry!" I laughed, cutting her off.

"They run TV cables this far out in the boondocks?" Theresa just looked at me, still shaking her head as we entered the bakery. We were immediately embraced by the warmth and assailed by the fresh oven baked smells that permeated the entire store. These things alone were

worth the risk, as was the pleasant, rosy-cheeked young girl behind the
counter, who turned to wait on me.

"May I help..." her voice started, and then ended in a squeaky
whisper, "y-you, sir?" Her pretty blue eyes were as big as saucers, causing
my antennas to vibrate.

"Something wrong, Miss?" I smiled.

"Oh, n-no!" She stammered.

"Sorry if I was staring, but you remind me of someone." she recovered
nicely.

"That's all right, " I laughed.

"Let me have that delicious strawberry short-cake." I pointed toward
the display case at the end of the counter, where Theresa had just ordered
a few loaves of freshly baked rye bread that were being cut by another
young girl that she was exchanging small talk with.

"Did you know the young girl who waited on you?" I asked as we
walked toward the car.

"Yes. I have been in here a few times before."

"How about the other girl?" I countered.

"No, she's new. I-- did she recognize you?"

"I don't know," I said uneasily.

"Probably just getting paranoid. She thought I looked like someone
she knew." Theresa stopped looking back at the bakery.

"We can leave. We don't have to go to Toni's," she suggested.

"No, we're already here. I need to see Joey anyway. I'm probably
imagining things."

Joey and Toni had a beautiful ranch-style home on a quiet tree-lined
street that featured a spacious backyard, enclosed by an eight-foot-high
redwood picket fence. It was great seeing them both again. As Toni was
preparing a roast with the trimmings, we all shared a bottle of white
wine. The atmosphere was cordial and relaxed, if not a jubilant one.

After an hour, Joey and I withdrew to the den and began discussing
the possibility of a few good moves we could make that would put us
both over the top. Knowing of my debacle in Rochester, he had just
given me a snub-nosed .38 and an AR-15 automatic rifle, which he was
showing me the general rudiments of, when his head snapped toward the
front window behind me.

"They're here," he hissed. I didn't know whether to shit or go blind
as I spun toward the window, looking out onto the dark, snow-covered
street. The whole neighborhood looked as serene as a painting on a
Christmas card.

"I don't see anything," I whispered to Joey.

"Toni, Theresa!?" he called out.

"Four guys, maybe five, packed in a Corolla passed the first time about ten minutes ago. I wasn't sure and didn't want to panic you--they're bulls, Joe."

Toni and Theresa appeared in the doorway, looking confused.

"What's wrong, Joey?" Toni asked wide-eyed.

"Cops are here," Joey said calmly.

"Don't open the door right away, give us about two minutes." He said, throwing on a light jacket with me following his lead.

"I'm taking him out the cellar window and through the backyards. I'm parked around the corner."

"A car just pulled up!" Theresa exclaimed excitedly.

"They're getting out--they g-got vests on!"

"Oh, God," Toni moaned. I stared at her numbly.

"Can I get a rain-check on that roast?" I smiled weakly.

My fate was in Joey's hands. Whatever problems he might have had with drugs, he always had the balls of a lion. Tonight, however, he was showing me a new dimension with his cool, analytical thinking under extreme pressure.

"Let's go, Sully. Give me the .38 and take the AR-15."

We flew down the cellar steps, and Joey began removing a winter storm window, which was no bigger than a gun-port. I doubted it was large enough to squeeze through. A heavy pounding on the front door upstairs filtered down to the cellar clearly.

Joey had the window out and was sliding through when the banging became more insistent--and came with the order of authority.

"F.B.I., open up!"

The last thing I heard before passing the automatic weapon up to Joey and wiggling through the window myself was Toni's voice.

"All right, all right! Hold on a second!"

I was lying in a foot of snow --it was Rochester all over again--as I waited for Joey to secure the window that hung from a short chain. Joey had modified the weapon I held, so it could function as originally intended when manufactured: either single shots, burst of three rounds, or rapid fire. I eased the selector button to the latter as I lay in a prone position, trying to cover both ends of the house. There would have been no contest that night, as now the rabbit had the gun, or at the very least, the firepower. But it was the last thing I wanted or needed.

Joey waved his arm and I followed him on my belly like a commando to the farthest end of the yard, where between the spaced slats of the fence we saw two agents standing in the light of the open car doors, tightening the cinches on huge bulletproof vests that gave them the appearance of baseball umpires. The guys had to be computer or forensic experts, because they certainly had no sense of danger.

Joey cupped his hand to my ear.

"I'll go over first, then pass me the guns. But don't make a sound." he whispered, handing me his .38.

I couldn't help but grin after we had scaled the fence and I padded along behind him. He could see like a cat in the dark, and moved with the quiet stealth of a fucking Apache.

"I'm glad you ain't tracking me," I whispered hoarsely as he paused to get his bearings, and laughed softly. He was actually enjoying this shit!

I never got to thank Joey properly, but I told Toni after his death.

"A lot of guys would have shown me to the window and pointed out into the darkness, but I don't know of anybody else who would have led the way for me, as it was not his business. He didn't have to risk dying in his own backyard."

"He really liked you, Joe, and that was enough for him. He felt that you were both very much alike in that respect." Unfortunately, more so for him, we were.

When we reached Queens, Joey grabbed a car for me by a paper and cigarette stand on Cross Bay Boulevard, near the Belt Parkway. Some unsuspecting motorist had left his car running with the keys in the ignition while he dashed into the store to make a quick purchase, and ended up looking for a taxi when he returned. I quickly exchanged the plates with another parked car on a nearby dark street. I was back in business.

Theresa came into the apartment about eleven o'clock that night, telling me how the Feds had questioned Toni and her, calling them liars when they denied flatly that I'd ever been there. The Feds never mentioned the bakery, protecting their source. But the young girl in the bakery needed no protection from me. She wasn't a "rat" of my world. She was a decent, legitimate human being doing what was right. The only one I could blame for my latest close encounter was myself.

"That's all they said?" I asked Theresa.

"N-no, Joe. They were very nice and polite. One guy reminded me of you, and I told him so, at which he smiled. But he wasn't smiling when he told me when--not if, *when* -- I saw you again, to tell you that they are going to kill you," Theresa's voice quivered.

"My kind of guys!" I grinned, trying to relax her.

"They meant it, Joe."

"No shit, Dick Tracy!" I said in exasperation.

"You're just realizing this is not a game? Why do you think I've been telling you to go home? If you're in the way when they catch up with me, you're history. I'm going to see Gail and the boys tomorrow," I said softly.

"You are fucking crazy! You know that, don't you?"

"You never let me forget it!" I joked.

"You sure you don't want to jog first?" I asked as she undressed and headed for the shower.

"Go fuck yourself!" she snapped back angrily.

When Rocky called Gail and invited her over to his house the following day, she understood his message. When she pulled up in front of his house, with Ramsey jumping up and down on the front seat at the sight of me, it was obvious in her voice and gaunt, drawn features how heavy a toll my actions had taken on her both physically and mentally.

"I--I'm afraid for the b-boys, Joe. If you get in the car..." she pleaded with her eyes through the rolled down window.

"Maybe I was followed."

"Daddy, Daddy!" Ramsey yelled excitedly.

"Hi ya, Champ!" I choked, staring forlornly at him and his little one-year-old brother double strapped in a car seat in the back, who also smiled at me, caught up in the excitement of his brother.

"Da!" he managed to make the association.

"Yeah, lil' guy!" I smiled through misty eyes.

"I understand, Gail, I'll move away from the car. There'll be no problem, you know this."

"How are you, Joe?" Her heart was in her eyes.

"I'm all right, but you look like hell," I teased gently.

"Joe..." her voice broke and her body shook uncontrollably, all the pent-up fears and emotions bursting through the dam she had erected.

"I love y-you, Joe, but I'd rather see them k-kill you. Can y-you understand me?"

"Yeah, honey," I said, wiping her eyes and cheeks with my handkerchief through the window.

"I really do."

I wanted to add that I didn't know whether I was brave enough or unselfish enough to do so, to end everybody's suffering--including my own.

When Gail calmed down and felt reasonably assured that we were safe, I got into the car and we drove to Ally Pond Park. I walked through the snowdrifts with Kelly on my shoulders and Ramsey holding tightly to my free hand, looking confused. He wanted to know when we were going sleigh riding in Forest Park like we used to. I looked into Gail's eyes. "Maybe someday soon," I lied. We all needed hope, didn't we, something to believe in and hang on to?

After a few hours the sky became dark and overcast, and the snow began to fall heavily. So we called it a day and went to a McDonald's, spending our last supper together in the car in a far corner of the parking lot. I couldn't eat, but spent those last moments together drinking in their images, feeling very much like Judas Iscariot in that I had robbed them of a normal life.

I had Gail drop me a few blocks from Rocky's house, where my stolen car was parked. Gail and I were both too spent for any emotional farewells, so I just hugged the kids quickly and kissed her without dramatics.

"Just take care, Joe," she said strongly.

"You know I'll always take good care of our boys. I-if somehow things work out, you know where to find me. I'll always be here for you, Joe." All I could do was just swallow the lump in my throat and walk away.

Throughout the first few weeks of February 1982, I stayed close to the apartment, occasionally going out to see a few friends and to jog in the evenings. Toni's husband Joey, who I had been counting on, waiting for him to clean up his act long enough to accompany me back upstate for a few bank withdrawals, only appeared to be getting worse with his heroin addiction, to the point where all he wanted to do was sit around and nod all day.

***
Rochester - The Betrayal

I decided I'd go upstate for a few days and check out the possibilities of doing a few of the smaller banks on my own. After a short argument with Theresa, I caved in and allowed her to go with me. We left on the early evening of February 20th, 1982, arriving in Utica late that night.

We stayed in a Howard Johnson's just off the Thruway exit. Theresa would always register under a bogus name, while I'd lie on the back seat of the car until she came out and drove around to the unit, where I'd get out and enter the room only after getting the "all clear" sign.

After looking at one particular bank the following morning, and a few more in the outlying Syracuse area that afternoon, I told Theresa I'd like to take a quick trip to Rochester to see my friend Tom Taylor. Almost four months had passed since the incident, and I felt I owed him an explanation. Besides this, I wanted to find out how the Hulk, Louie DiGiulio, was doing.

"That's all over, Joe. Why are you pushing your luck? Let's go back to Brooklyn, I don't like this, it's crazy!" she yelled.

"Relax, will you? This is the last place they'd expect me to show up. Just in and out, okay?"

"Only if you promise we'll leave as soon as you see your friend," she insisted stubbornly.

"You got it," I said. And I meant it, having begun to question my own impulsiveness.

When we arrived in Rochester about six o'clock that evening, February 21st, I directed Theresa to the area and cul de sac Taylor lived on, and we parked in a dark spot across the street from his house. I told Theresa which bell to ring and watched her from the darkness of the car. I was surprised when she began to walk back, as I had distinctively seen a curtain move in a window to the left of the door.

"Nobody's home, Joe," she said, looking a little spooked.

"Somebody's home. I saw movement in the window."

I showed Theresa the way to the Dennonville Inn in Webster, a rural community a short distance away. I knew the area well, as only a hundred yards down the road was the trailer park I had stayed in with my friend G.I. Joe a few months back.

We went through the same routine in registering, and as soon as I got in the room I called an old friend named Liam, who was also close with Taylor from our days in Attica. He wasn't home, but his wife gave me the number of the Golden Nugget where she said he tended bar for Taylor a few nights a week, besides his regular job. That is, when he wasn't singing and playing his guitar in different predominantly Irish bars in the area, where he'd sing his Irish ballads and fight songs. Liam was born in Ireland and still had strong feeling for, and affiliations with, the I.R.A. He was always a straight up kind of guy, without any tough guy pretenses. I trusted him, something that had not changed until this day.

"Damn! How are you, Sully? Where are you?" he gasped when I told him.

"Yeah, I'm in Webster, that restaurant and bar Graziano's. Remember it?"

"Jesus Christ," he breathed in his lilting Irish.

"I don't believe it!"

"Listen, Liam. Where's the Eagle? I want to talk to him."

"Jeez, I don't know, Sully. He must be home."

"All right. Do me a favor, huh? Call him and tell him where I am, and to meet me in the parking lot of Graziano's in an hour, say, eight o'clock, okay?"

"All right, Sully. I'll call and tell him."

At about five minutes to eight I cruised into the fairly crowded parking lot, backed into a far corner and waited with the lights off, but with the motor and heater running as the weather was bitter cold. I was looking for Taylor's car, so when Liam stepped out of another that had pulled in, I was taken by surprise, and jumped out.

"Liam!" I called. He froze on his way to the front door and then started toward me at a brisk pace.

"Jeez, Sully. Good to see you," he said breathlessly.

"You too, buddy. Get in the car before you freeze your ass off!"

Once he was settled, I asked him what he was doing here. His eyes bugged out at the sight of the AR-15 laying on the floor and seat between us.

"Uh, the Eagle told me to tell you he's being followed, Joe, and can't make it." Liam stuttered and I noticed that he was perspiring, in spite of the sub-zero temperature.

"Where did you call him from, Liam?" I asked offhandedly.

"At home," he answered nervously.

"At home, huh? How come you're sweating like that?"

"Too much drinking, Sully. Out of shape, too." he laughed.

"Listen, Liam. I've been ducking the Feds, SWAT teams, and some Brooklyn task force for the past ten months. I'm certain if he has a tail he knows how to lose it. I'm in room six at the Dennonville Inn. You know the joint. Go back and tell Tom I want to see him at twelve o'clock tonight, okay, Liam?"

"S-sure, Sully, I'll tell him. Good to see you."

"You too, Liam. Thanks for coming."

Theresa was smoking and pacing the floor when I let myself in the room. "Did you see him?" her voice asked hopefully.

"No," I shook my head, throwing my hat, coat and gloves onto a wing chair by the door.

"My friend Liam told me Taylor said he was being watched closely and couldn't come. He was home when you knocked on the door, Theresa. I told our mutual friend, Liam, to tell him to meet me here at twelve."

"You told him where we were?" she stared.

"Joe, wake up! Something's wrong here! Let's leave," she pleaded.

"All right, but I want to wait till twelve and see if he shows."

"Oh my God, I don't believe this!" She turned and threw herself facedown on one of the twin beds. I laid down myself on the other one--lights out, AR-15 cradled across my chest as I listened to the ticking of the clock on the night table, watching its luminous hands move ever so slowly.

I had fallen asleep when Theresa's piercing whisper brought me out of the bed and to the window in one bound.

"Joe, a car just pulled up," she warned.

I moved the drape aside and could barely control my anger when I saw Liam approaching the door. I yanked it open just as he raised his hand to knock, staring at him for what must have appeared a lifetime to him, before motioning him inside. I didn't say a word, but just simply stood there waiting for him to talk. Liam looked very uncomfortable at the position he had been placed in.

"Listen, Sully," Liam threw up his hands as if to say, "Hey I'm just a messenger!" And it had its affect on me.

"Taylor told me to tell you that he really couldn't make it, but that he'd be here in the morning with Torpe to take you to some resort where you can lay low."

"How low?" I grinned, looking at Theresa.

"Uh, uh, he told me to give you this." He held out his hand, giving me three one hundred dollar bills and a small packet of what I imagined was cocaine.

"What's this for, Liam? You saw him?"

"Y-yeah. He told me to give you the message, and t-that," he indicated with his hand.

"What time did he say he'd be coming, Liam?"

"Uh, he didn't. Just said in the morning." He smiled nervously at me and nodded in a friendly manner at Theresa, who stared at him as if he were some insect.

"All right, Liam. Listen, when you go back to Tom, tell him he could always sneak out early in the morning--pretend like he's going to pick up a newspaper, donuts or something. A resort, huh?" I laughed reflexively. "Take care of yourself, Liam and try to lose some weight before you catch a heart attack!"

"I will," he laughed feebly, and scurried out the door.

When I turned around Theresa was already throwing things into her suitcase.

"Hey, what are you doing? You don't want to go to a resort?"

"Yeah, right!" Theresa sneered.

"Plot seven, row eleven! Is that what they call the cemeteries up around these parts? Resorts? I want to leave tonight, Joe. Now!" She pleaded.

"We'll leave, Theresa." I shook my head, feeling suddenly depressed. "I just want to lie down for a few hours before we go."

"All right, Joe," she sighed, unable to hide her disappointment. She curled up beside me on the bed, still fully clothed.

What brought us out of a deep sleep simultaneously and in a panicked state of mind, I never figured out. It was already light when I jumped out of bed and ran to the window with the AR-15 clutched in my right hand. Nothing! Nothing moving at all. The snow had stopped and there was a fresh three-inch white blanket covering the ground. Not a footprint, tire track-- nothing. It was ten o'clock, so we had been in a coma-like sleep for almost eight hours.

"Theresa, go out and start the car, and put the suitcase in the trunk. Look around as best you can without being obvious."

I watched the windows of the units in my vision the horseshoe shaped compound, but my view toward the front was severely restricted.

When Theresa ran into the room she was shivering--not from the cold.

"It looks all right, Joe, but it's so quiet. I didn't see a single person."

"I'm sorry, Theresa. I should have listened to you. You ready?" I grinned sickly, sticking the automatic weapon in a pillowcase that only came up to the trigger housing, and had to be held in place with my left hand.

Following Theresa out the door, I took a deep breath of crisp clean air, marveling at what I thought a beautiful, calm, sunny morning.

The stolen car was a four-door Ford. Feeling secure, I opened the rear door and placed the weapon on the floor of the car. As I straightened up and glanced over the roof of the car at Theresa, her contorted face and mouth that was wide open in a frozen scream told me it was over. She finally got my name out of her mouth in a keening wail, "Joe!" At that moment I heard the screeching of tires and the dull thud of feet pounding through the snow, the clack! Clack! Clack! of steel against steel as numerous guns pumped rounds into their chambers. They were running out of motel units, obviously vacated while we slept.

Their guttural screams, "Don't move, Sullivan, F.B.I.!" were anti-climatic.

"Don't move at all, Theresa," I whispered to her urgently as I raised one hand slowly, then the other, placing them on the roof of the car. Looking into her eyes, I saw my own sense of betrayal reflected in hers.

I heard nothing the Feds were yelling as they grabbed me. I was totally lethargic and removed, as if this were happening to somebody else. The constant thought that pierced my heart like a bullet was an instant replay. A trip to a "resort" would have been acceptable. I could respect that! But not like this. Never like this!

And so I once again became the proverbial "bone," with so many different agencies wanting to take credit for the work of a single coward.

The only time I was capable of any semblance of feeling was when I was in a cell in some federal building and they brought Theresa in, after what I imagined to be a few hours of threats and intimidation. Her hair was disheveled and her eyes were red rimmed and swollen from crying. She really looked pathetic.

"Joe, what should I do?" she blubbered, and I thought it was comical from where I sat in a cage weighted down with enough chains to sink a battleship. She thought this was bad? Had I moved or even farted loudly, they'd still be scooping bloody chunks of our remains from the crimson snow.

"Call your mother, Theresa, " I said softly as she sniffed, making me feel terrible for not demanding that she go home months ago.

"Call Toni and Joey, they'll know what to do. You've done nothing and know nothing about me, but you need a lawyer. A few days of questioning and you'll go home, so stay strong and don't worry about hurting me. Cooperate with them as best you can okay? You'll be all right."

A few days later I was transferred from the Monroe County Jail in Rochester to the Public Safety Building in Syracuse, and held in total isolation, with a twenty-four hour visual watch. I was to be tried for the Utica bank robbery first, despite the fact that many more serious charges were pending. The purpose of this ploy being that if I was convicted of the bank robbery, I would become a federal prisoner, and regardless of whatever state conviction followed, I would be eligible for their federal horror house in Marion, Illinois. As it were, they needn't have worried about a lack of proper retribution, as the State of New York picked up the slack by keeping me locked down 23 hours a day for ten of the first thirteen years.

In spite of the federal government's rigorous effort to convict me, I was found "not guilty" of the bank robbery charges. This was due to an even greater effort by two men who were viewed as perhaps the most competent trial lawyers in upstate New York, Joseph E. Fahey and Emil

Rossi. I came to admire and respect both of these men from a human standpoint as well as a legal one. It was only on the recommendation of Ramsey Clark that I was fortunate enough to secure them as my attorneys, as he felt it was imperative in those early stages that I had people representing me whose sense of dignity and integrity equaled their legal prowess.

***
I thought I was your "Bonnie"

Seeing my wife and Ramsey Clark in the federal building in Syracuse has been the single most painful vision of my life, and I have been unable to expel it from my mind to this day. The look of disappointment and dismay on Ramsey's face was enough to bear, but the sight of my wife standing silently behind him, beyond the reaches of my cage, with tears streaming unchecked down her cheeks, was by far the darkest moment of the ten months of trials I would have to endure. And she stood by my side throughout the entire ordeal.

Tentatively, she took a step toward the cell and whispered,

"I--I thought *I* was your Bonnie?"

She was speaking in reference to a "Bonnie and Clyde" type snapshot Theresa and I had posed for at a fair and that was later found upon a search of our Brooklyn apartment and plastered on the front page of the New York Post, with a huge caption that read: "Mad Dog Seized!" Gail was not speaking of her being my "Bonnie" in any gun-moll sense of the word, for her background and innate sense of human decency is beyond reproach. She was speaking as my woman, friend, sole confidant, and as the mother of our sons.

The sight of Gail standing there in her own lonely world of betrayal and devastation hurt far worse than all the sentences that I was to receive combined. I was looking at the end of the dream I had always desired, and for some reason had been blessed with. Now, having failed to appreciate, respect, nourish, and cherish the living reality, I was witnessing the dream's demise. The demise of the dreams that were not only my own, but all those that belonged to Gail, also.

***
A Change Of Voice

To this point I have told Joe's story in his voice however his voice was silenced when he lost his right to life outside of prison walls forever. He is currently serving a sentence of 75 years to life. Joe will die in prison. We have become one voice now. When things were going on in our house, we all spoke to Joe to figure it out as a family. Joe became very much involved with family happenings. Our family knows everything that he has done, and understands him as I do. We love a good man that has done some very bad things. I realize this might be difficult to comprehend, though anyone that comes into contact with Joe and gets to know him cannot help but like and respect him. One day, when I introduced myself to someone from New York State saying I was Mrs. Joseph Sullivan whose husband is an inmate in New York State, he knew Joe right away, and said he was one of the most respected inmates on both sides of the fence.

An investigator for Rudolph Giuliani put it well when he told Joe, "I've met a lot of bad good guys in my line of work and a few good bad guys-- you're a good bad guy, and it's a shame it had to come to this."

Gail W. Sullivan, M.Ed. is the wife of Joseph "Mad Dog" Sullivan and is the mother of their two sons. She is a teacher and has written for Fortune News. She lives in Orange County, New York.